THE EARLY CHRISTIAN CENTURIES
──◆──

For Val

THE EARLY CHRISTIAN CENTURIES

Philip Rousseau

An imprint of **Pearson Education**

London · New York · Toronto · Sydney · Tokyo · Singapore · Hong Kong · Cape Town
New Delhi · Madrid · Paris · Amsterdam · Munich · Milan · Stockholm

Pearson Education Limited

Head Office:
Edinburgh Gate
Harlow CM20 2JE
Tel: +44 (0)1279 623623
Fax: +44 (0)1279 431059

London Office:
128 Long Acre
London WC2E 9AN
Tel: +44 (0)20 7447 2000
Fax: +44 (0)20 7240 5771
Website: www.history-minds.com

First published in Great Britain in 2002

© Pearson Education Limited 2002

The right of Philip Rousseau to be identified as Author
of this Work has been asserted by him in accordance
with the Copyright, Designs and Patents Act 1988.

ISBN 0 582 25653 4

British Library Cataloguing in Publication Data
A CIP catalogue record for this book can be obtained from the British Library

Library of Congress Cataloging in Publication Data
A CIP catalog record for this book can be obtained from the Library of Congress

All rights reserved; no part of this publication may be reproduced, stored
in a retrieval system, or transmitted in any form or by any means, electronic,
mechanical, photocopying, recording, or otherwise without either the prior
written permission of the Publishers or a licence permitting restricted copying
in the United Kingdom issued by the Copyright Licensing Agency Ltd,
90 Tottenham Court Road, London W1P 0LP. This book may not be lent,
resold, hired out or otherwise disposed of by way of trade in any form
of binding or cover other than that in which it is published, without the
prior consent of the Publishers.

10 9 8 7 6 5 4 3 2 1

Typeset in 11.5/14pt Garamond by Graphicraft Limited, Hong Kong
Printed and bound in Malaysia

The Publishers' policy is to use paper manufactured from sustainable forests.

CONTENTS

	Preface	vi
1	Giving a shape to early Christian history	1
2	Paul and the Jewish past: an apostle and his world	23
3	Jesus of Nazareth: portraits of a saviour	47
4	Individual virtue and its social setting	84
5	Churches as learning communities	124
6	Heroes and survivors: Christians engage with the world	153
7	The Christian empire, a contested experiment: Constantine and his successors	187
8	A crisis of authority	237
9	An ancient legacy and its post-Roman future	280
	Epilogue: the price of success	313
	Further bibliographical notes and acknowledgements	320
	Index	323

PREFACE

In writing this account of early Christianity, I had in mind the reader who was curious to know where the first Christians sprang from, and why they thought and behaved in the way they did; the reader who was also prepared to devote the reflective attention necessary in order to discover the answer. I myself wanted to uncover both the subjective and the objective elements of early Christian experience: what it meant to be a human being, and how the world about one might be interpreted. I also wanted to consider the effect of such reflections on the ways in which Christians organized their lives.

It is impossible, however, to please everyone, when presenting a book of this scope. Sceptics may consider me too generous, too tolerant of ignorance, prejudice and cruelty. Firm believers may find me too hesitant, too quick to dismiss the honourable ambitions of churchmen and the telling arguments of those with a vested interest in one doctrinal view. Theologians often want more theology, social scientists more circumstance. In the end, perhaps, one pleases oneself – in this sense, that I wanted to know not only what inspired and formed those first Christians but also what I should therefore think of them, my spiritual ancestors. I wanted, as I explain in my first chapter, to identify the *shape* of early Christianity. I was prepared to believe that, if I myself had found the inquiry interesting and important and was able to demonstrate why, then others would find it so as well. There is, perhaps, a historical methodology lodged in such an assumption; and I make no apology for attempting to share both my puzzlement and my enthusiasm.

Much of the work published on this topic has been, I believe, too preoccupied with the development of doctrine and church order. What people believe, and how they arrange their relationships accordingly, are undoubtedly matters of significance; but the temptation has been to separate those elements from other forces in people's lives, thus suggesting that both doctrine and church order were carried forward exclusively by principles intrinsic to themselves. The result is often a mere succession of parties and arguments, or else a focus on themes – literary, for example, or philosophical. I have tried here to maintain a sense of momentum within Christian society; and I have given prominence to those concerns that instilled an urgency into individual lives, dictated a certain pattern of relationships among believers,

Preface

and passed comment on their attitudes to the bewilderingly varied society around them.

It is always difficult to know when to end a book of this sort. Not every solution to the problem has been a happy one. I am particularly averse to ending at a moment of apparently doctrinal significance, such as the Council of Chalcedon in 451. It seems more natural to end with clear challenges to the hegemony of the Roman world – challenges represented by both the establishment of settler kingdoms in the West during the fifth and sixth centuries and the rise of Islam in the East during the seventh. Those events carry us into a world where Latin and Greek Christians had become increasingly distinct, and where a large sector of the Church found itself permanently under Muslim domination. In other ways, however, there are no endings. One of the themes of this book is the notion of constant and inconclusive interplay – particularly the interplay between Christians and Jews, and (among believers themselves) between spiritual intimacy and ruthless cruelty. The sixth and seventh centuries did not bring such tensions to a close.

The debts incurred in writing a broad survey are always great. Many of them are acknowledged in my various bibliographies. My own generation has been dominated by the syntheses of Henry Chadwick and W.H.C. Frend, who have both written works that I am in no position to usurp and that I have every reason to honour. I thank most warmly my former colleagues at the University of Auckland, an institution that I have always found both wise and generous in its support of research and travel. I acknowledge in my dedication my particular indebtedness, over more than twenty years, to my colleague Valerie Flint. A substantial proportion of my secondary reading was completed when I was a Visiting Scholar at Wolfson College, Oxford and a Bye Fellow at Robinson College, Cambridge, and I am most grateful to both bodies for their kindness and support. I have now found new friends and mentors at the Catholic University of America, particularly, in their help with this book, William E. Klingshirn and Robin Darling Young. Large portions of the manuscript were read by Paula Fredriksen, Morna Hooker, Judith Lieu and Rebecca Lyman, whose advice was always of great value, although I did not always succeed in keeping up to their mark. Pauline Allen and Robert Markus read the whole work with great attention more than once, and I cannot overestimate the authority and precision of their judgements. Professor D.F. Wright of the University of Edinburgh also saved me from a blunder or two. None of those invaluable guides should be blamed, however, for my errors and predilections. I also count myself lucky to have worked in a generation of late Roman historians characterized pre-eminently by their

Preface

enthusiasm, learning and kindness; and, as on previous occasions, I happily single out the inspiration and support provided by Peter Brown. Finally, I owe a great debt to my family, especially to my wife Thérèse, a shrewd and tolerant critic, and my chief source of unstinting encouragement.

Philip Rousseau
Catholic University of America
July 2001

Chapter 1

GIVING A SHAPE TO EARLY CHRISTIAN HISTORY

Food, sex and death: these have remained the fundamental components of human experience. About food and sex – about hunger and lust, greed and desire – Christianity, like any major religion, has always had a good deal to say. Fasting and virginity, for example, the welcoming of abnegation and discontinuity, were, from the beginning, vivid symptoms of Christian commitment. But historical inquiry soon uncovers deeper reflections on material things in general and the body in particular; on the value and destiny of the visible world and of the human beings within it. For that reason, Christianity has always been more than a prescriptive programme, focused on wayward passion. When first defining its characteristic notion of a world larger than life, it seems to have focused in a special way on death.

Jesus of Nazareth, in the eyes of his followers, redefined death and, by extension, sacrifice and loss, making them the gateway to a state more significant and worthwhile. 'Anyone who wishes to save his soul', he is supposed to have said, 'will lose it, but anyone who loses his soul for my sake and for the sake of the Gospel will save it'; and 'unless the grain-seed falls into the earth and dies, it remains alone; but if it dies, it yields an abundant harvest'. That sentiment was not unique to Jesus; but he seems to have endowed it with a particular intensity, suggesting that his followers could transfer themselves, perhaps very quickly, into the 'kingdom of God', which transcended and rendered obsolete the common experience of human inadequacy and curtailment. Subsequent Christian reflection saw in his life the major symbol, indeed the chief instrument, of that 'victory': swift submission to a cruel death, followed by a resurrection to be shared with those who committed themselves to his teaching and self-sacrifice.

The history of Christianity is rooted in that one conviction. What set its adherents apart was their sense that one should lose all to gain all. Their development was shaped by the twin convictions that personal worth, on the one hand, mocked by the imperfections of individual capacity and fortune, was subject to overriding forces of evil, while, on the other hand, a victory was assured, for oneself and for humanity, both in time and in eternity. Death and resurrection, suffering and triumph: those were the persistent poles between which belief and community worked to achieve their destiny. The exalted confidence that flowed from that belief and infused that community coloured both the notion of individual liberty and the understanding of who Jesus of Nazareth was; a confidence that the human had been captured and transformed by the divine. It also alleviated isolation and impotence and encouraged internal discipline and outward expansion.

Religion is a personal and, for that reason, partly inaccessible experience. The motive power of the Christian religion – that is to say, the faith of its devotees – was the fruit of individual commitment. But the exhilaration of personal faith can be hard to sustain. Early Christians soon came to appreciate a necessary irony in their lives. While admiring abnegation and almost courting death as keys to a promised transformation, they continued to nourish their bodies and invest in their biological future. Their understanding of transience and decay encouraged the belief that one could penetrate at once the curtain of materiality between earth and heaven, between the human and the divine; but they found themselves also drawn along a more horizontal axis, constituted by reproduction and governed by inheritance. The paradox gave rise to a certain poignancy, a sense of suffering and release, or, to use the Christian terminology, of sin and redemption. It imparted a historical shape to what might otherwise have been a merely psychological experience. As it became obvious that both individual weakness and the hostility of the surrounding society would persist, strategies were demanded, extended over time, whereby to foster and protect the creed and courage of the community.

So, the history of early Christianity became part of a broader story – the history of the Roman world and of its immediate neighbours. Although the grander dramas of the time are not enough to explain the new religion's emergence, expansion and success, Christians found themselves figures in a larger landscape, forced to acknowledge their relations with the Jews from whose culture they sprang, and with the Greeks and Romans whose culture they appropriated and transformed. Partly for that reason, they created only slowly a united 'church', committed to a single corpus of ideas and a single system of administration and government. It is fruitless to seek, in those early centuries, either a stable acceptance of supposed 'orthodoxy' (of which more below) or a principled espousal of diverse belief. Christianity was, nevertheless, a social phenomenon, with characteristic patterns of worship, authority and mutual obligation. Above all, it underwent change. It was not launched in its full panoply at Pentecost but altered and developed its organization, refined and reformulated its ideas, and adjusted its sense of destiny. Those five features, therefore, governed the early Christian centuries: personal commitment, dialogue with those of other faiths, diversity of doctrine and practice, increasingly strong social forms, and a capacity for growth.

In this opening chapter, I want to offer readers a clue as to how they might envisage that development. Almost everyone will think of the reign of Constantine (306–337) – the reign of the first Christian emperor – as marking a fundamental divide in the history of early Christianity. His policies undoubtedly invited Christians to embark upon new experiments in self-definition; but they also fostered disillusionment and crisis, as the Roman Empire faced less predictable opportunities and demands. I explore those later features in Chapters 7, 8 and 9. The founding elements of the new religion are provided for us, however, in the teachings of Jesus and Paul, and in the interpretations placed upon them by their immediate followers. I examine those in Chapters 2 and 3. The remaining three chapters, 4, 5 and 6, are more thematic in character, dealing with structure, culture and engagement. The fabric of Christian life at once predated and outlasted the brilliance of Constantine's achievement: it created circumstances he took advantage of, but it also survived his failure. Hence, we uncover what I have called here the 'shape' of early Christianity. How, we ask, were Christian communities formed, first on a small scale and then across the Roman world? How did they formulate and bequeath their ideas and the documents that preserved them? How did they relate to the surrounding Roman society and with what confidence and success?

THE ROOTS OF CHRISTIAN COMMITMENT

One of the most enduring images of the early Christian community is of a small band of men and women who, with remarkable swiftness, converted the Roman world. Their own literature emphasized the miraculous scale of their achievement – the gospel story of the tiny mustard seed that grows into a great tree; the terrified group of disciples, who, at Pentecost, as described in the *Acts of the Apostles*, acquired the inner courage to broadcast their belief to crowds of pilgrims in Jerusalem. Reflection may modify the simplicity of the account; but the impression is retained of heroic and inexorable drama.

This book is designed to alter that impression. Christians did not form, even in their first decades, an embattled cell, pitted against an irreligious world. Some sections of the New Testament were eager to suggest that they did – the *Gospel of John* in particular – but the Mediterranean world of the first century was not irreligious. Christians were obliged to prove themselves initially against their fellow Jews, who were heirs to a religious tradition both ancient and rich. As they expanded their missionary efforts, they met at every stage profound and equally well-established systems of philosophical and theological speculation and a widespread and enthusiastic participation in a range of cults.

To become a Christian, therefore, was to make a choice, to declare a preference in the face of variety. What inspired any particular group to make the choices that they did? There is no reason to suppose that the first Christians were fundamentally different from us. Human nature has not changed that much in two thousand years. Men and women felt then, as they do now, a need for nourishment, affection and a sense of personal significance. Their lives, as I say, were governed like ours by hunger, desire and the fear of death. They no doubt appealed to religion more than we do in the face of such demands: for religious faith was a deeply embedded feature of the Roman world. Not that religion is merely a matter of assuaging or rationalizing one's longings and anxieties. A religious person supposes that those emotions, along with much else, are part of a plan, intended and perhaps controlled by some divinity. They are to be used, or tamed or overridden in the interests of a lasting, transcendent perfection or destiny. Nevertheless, the religious response is a response to experience and is coloured by the wish to provide a wider context for a fragile, short and turbulent life. Here, then, is a major theme, expressed in the phrase from chapter 21 of *Revelation*, 'a new heaven and a new earth': a new way of understanding the nature and destiny of the cosmos and the nature and destiny of human society. One's few decades of individual joy and effort, taken up into the shared sweep of human history, were to be cast in a new light, defined from the viewpoint of a higher being.

A sense of our common humanity should not obscure, however, the differences effected over time. The modern believer, in particular, can too readily suppose that his or her convictions, often expressed in seemingly analogous terminology, are subject to the same inspiration as those of their 'forerunners in faith'. The spectacle of a religious system at once familiar and distant can also provoke powerful emotions and fierce loyalties, and the devout can misjudge their ancestry as easily as the sceptical can disdain it. Great shifts of experience and attitude separate the modern world from that of the Romans. Our view of nature, of humanity's place within it, of its composition and patterns of endurance, is vastly different from that of men and women in those earlier times. Their religious instincts were prompted and governed in ways that rightly seem strange. That is not to say that the early Christians were childlike precursors of modern faith, or prisoners of ignorance unworthy of attention in a scientific age. They were neither naive nor insincere. They were capable of logical thought and were genuinely curious about the nature of the physical world. Their remoteness, however, in both temperament and time, invites us to ask what was specific to their religiosity. As we imagine ourselves in circumstances only partially comparable to ours, we are challenged to unravel on its own terms the logic of first-century belief.

THE 'BIG PICTURE'

The challenge demands, inevitably, a search for a general trend. Traces of the 'ordinary Christian' are, in the earliest centuries, virtually non-existent. Even the trend has to be deduced, more often than not, from a small number of documents written by an unrepresentative élite. Historians take refuge from those two difficulties by placing early Christianity in a wide context. They try to create the richest possible impression of 'Mediterranean religion', in order to catch in their net the maximum amount of information that will give substance to Christian experience. That means looking, first, at the history of the Jews, from the end of their Babylonian captivity in the sixth and fifth centuries BC to their subsequent engagement with the Hellenistic world. The conquests of Alexander are also part of the story, integrating disparate states and cultures in Egypt, Asia Minor and the Levant, and reaching deep into Persia, thus creating a world where Greek ideas and practices could be widely dispersed and where 'oriental' culture could be absorbed in return. Then came the Romans, extending their influence across the Alps to touch Britain, Spain and the peoples of the Rhine, and pressing deep into the Hellenistic world, first by military adventure and colonization and then by a startling assertion of imperial power. Finally, the Roman Empire itself had to grapple with fresh confidence in Persia from the early third century onwards, pressures on the Danube and the Rhine during the fourth and fifth, and the swift expansion of Islam in the early seventh. The Mediterranean world was constantly subject to geopolitical shift and stress, which tumbled whole populations from one cultural setting to another.

We are not dealing merely with a history of armies on the march – of conquerors like Pompey, Caesar and Augustus in the century before Jesus and Paul, or Alaric and Attila in the fifth century, or Chosroes and Abu Bakr in the seventh. Even the dignity of emperors and the greed of governors, the mundane pressures of tax and law, fail to provide us with the full picture. Romans were witnessing at that time a loosening of their heritage. Their culture and religion faced a backwash from the eastern societies they had conquered, inducing doubt about their own traditions. Behind the placid façade of citizenship and imperial cult, behind the fence of forts and colonies, were layers upon layers of cultural identity – familial, civic and provincial; linguistic, ethnic and religious; aristocrats, artisans, soldiers, peasants and slaves. If we call to mind the colourful, turbulent, pompous and cruel pageant of British India in the nineteenth century – with its array of languages, cults and petty rulers; its transport, administration and civil service; its regiments both native and metropolitan – and if we picture it flung across the map of Europe and the Middle East from Scotland to northern Iraq and down towards the African desert and along the Nile, we may gain some understanding of what it meant to be 'Roman'.

That diversity generated great tension. There was wealth to be gained and oppression to be rid of. There was a sense of loss in the face of universal power, especially among the urban élites of the East. Material improvement did not always bring higher status to the less eminent. The range of cults and philosophies encouraged a fragmented response to idealism and anxiety, fostering antagonism but isolating the enthusiast. The grand events and stunning achievements of the period could, at a personal level, instil a sense of loneliness, helplessness and insecurity. Doubts could arise about the purpose and scope of individual lives and about the stability and destiny of the visible world.

There lay the new religion's chance. It has often been argued that Christians were blessed by the steady achievements of the Empire from the time of Augustus through to the third century. However, the providence of the *pax Augusta* was imagined largely in retrospect, when Christianity was beginning to enjoy a *pax Constantiniana* and to see itself as heir to a new kind of progress in the Roman world. (I explore both the definition and the loss of that inheritance in my closing chapters.) In earlier centuries, each Christian community was intimately affected by challenges and opportunities within the surrounding society. Belief was neither the cause nor the effect of that exchange – neither a source of disruption and anxiety nor a result of weakness in the traditional ethos. Christians were not destructive antibodies, thriving on the decline of religions they rejected. If we separate them from the broader tensions of the Roman world, they become scarcely intelligible. Neither the significance nor the definition of those communities was exhausted by their inner qualities. That is not to deny the specificity of Christianity's message and appeal. Christians sought greater theological precision and spiritual refinement and were soon recognized by others as distinctive in their ideas and practices. Yet they also shared many convictions with their contemporaries – a belief in souls, immortality and heaven, for example; in angels and demons; and in the possibility that divinity could display itself in human form.

CHRISTIANS, JEWS AND PAGANS

Christians began their venture as a Jewish sect, following other Jews into the communities of the Diaspora (especially after the destruction of the Temple and the dashing of rebellious hopes in 69–70). There they developed characteristics that helped to distance them from their Jewish siblings; but the process was slow. The conflicts described in the *Acts of the Apostles* between Peter (the disciple of Jesus), James (Jesus's 'brother') and Paul (the 'apostle to the gentiles') bear witness to both the pain and the affinity involved. At stake, then and for many decades, were the authentic definitions of Jewish history and expectation, of Jewish identity, morality and cult. The Christians who responded to Paul and helped him in his ventures did not renounce immediately, as we shall see, their Jewishness. Indeed, there remained for centuries scattered pockets of Christian believers who continued to think of themselves and conduct themselves as Jews. Nor, finally, did expansion represent the abandonment of Jerusalem or of Christians less engaged with the Greek-speaking world. The traditions represented by James and his immediate fellows were maintained or developed within the ancient heartland of the movement.

Because of those enduring relations, almost every aspect of Jewish history is relevant to an understanding of the daughter faith. Christian views on spirituality and creation, on the authority of Scripture, on priesthood and sacrifice, on humanity's heritage and destiny under a single God, all remained stamped with a Jewish character, in spite of a developing rhetoric of distinctiveness and hatred. Take, as a first example, the issue of relations with 'outsiders'. This is a huge topic, covered in several of the chapters that follow. The depiction of Jesus depended to some extent on the Hellenization of the Jewish Messiah (Chapters 2 and 3). Paul and his imitators planted little 'churches' over a wide area – communities that were rooted in both Jewish and Roman society and culture, and that affected in turn the environment within which they had emerged (Chapters 2 and 4). In time, those communities co-opted the philosophy, ethics and literature of the ancient world (Chapter 5) and successfully confronted the authority and ambition of the empire (Chapter 6).

Speaking more generally, the interaction of Christianity with its Jewish matrix had a direct impact on its relations with the wider world; but it did not become less Jewish simply by becoming more Greek or more Roman. Roman conquest, especially under Pompey in 63 BC, had exacerbated an already existing confrontation between those Jews who were ready to embrace an alien culture and those inspired by the Maccabees' reaffirmation of the Mosaic covenant in the revolt of 168 BC. Christians inherited that tension and only gradually adopted the notion of a covenant with God that could be fulfilled in a non-Jewish world. While Roman observers regarded them as equally suspect minorities, Christians and Jews continued in their own eyes to be rivals. Their mutual resentment sprang from a fear of being confused – in the eyes of potential converts as much as of civil authorities. Christians strove to invite and retain the loyalty of those who found Judaism attractive – because of its antiquity, its moderation, the beauty and dignity of its worship, and its special brand of social coherence. Jews, for their part, were equal to the contest. 'Godfearers' were widespread and numerous in the cities of the Roman world – gentiles attracted to the Jewish faith, generous to its institutions and active in its ceremonies. Each religion was ready to detect and respond to the disturbance of Roman confidence that I referred to above.

Many men and women had begun to search at that time for a larger worldview. An inclination to monotheism or to syncretism – either a belief in a single god or a willingness to subsume local deities under the names of gods of more universal appeal – had been evident in some places for centuries. Both inclinations were attractive to those with philosophical interests, and acceptance of monotheism could encourage adhesion to Judaism as well as to Christianity. If Christianity was to make a convincing bid as the religion of the future, it had to be specific in its answers to the questions that other people were asking. Its dialogue with Judaism, increasingly audible to onlookers, was a means to that end. A single God, an ancient and revered literature, models of virtue, a programme of salvation and an assurance of spiritual and everlasting destiny – such values seemed acceptable to a growing number of people. Argument was focused on the form that such beliefs should take. The pluralism, curiosity and inventiveness of Roman society, the constant opportunity it afforded for discussion, were factors essential to the success of any single view. Christianity did not immediately overthrow the traditional beliefs of the empire but attempted first to voice more convincingly (at Judaism's expense) the desires and fears endemic among religious people generally.

To take a second example, many Christian arguments about authority in the early centuries echoed similar arguments in the Jewish community. That community had already recognized a certain rivalry – although not an exclusive division – between two spheres of leadership, the temple priesthood and the interpretation of the Law. The task of interpretation, closely associated with the Pharisees, was inherited by the great rabbis of the Diaspora. The priestly cult of sacrifice, however, suffered from the destruction of the Temple in 70. Jewish leadership thereafter depended less on family connections among a de facto aristocracy and more on the quality and effect of religious instruction. The rabbis were men of learning and their pedigree depended on their discipleship of older masters. It is, of course, a Christian canard to suggest that they restricted themselves to petty regulation. The overwhelming emphasis in the Mishnah is on moral discipline and the interpretation of scripture upon which that depended. The dispossessed Jews retained their devotion to the Temple, which they now thought of as the temple of the heart. They sought a pathway to inner purity, which was the new analogue of ritual observance. A comparable contrast between priest and scholar was carried over into Christianity. Bishops, heirs to the sacrificial culture of the Temple, did not relinquish the right to interpret Scripture; but their facility was challenged by those with an independent mastery of the text. And here another set of distinctions came into play: that between the prophetic and the institutional. The first depended on personal qualities and often appealed to the direct inspiration of God, establishing a species of vertical relationship. The second was more horizontal in character, dependent on formation within a temporal tradition and on the exercise of authority within an ordered system. What we have to recognize (as in the case of the Jews) is that those two qualities were found in both cultic and charismatic leaders. Christian bishops were 'prophetic' in their claim to be chosen and inspired by God's Spirit. Their establishment in office by the 'laying on of hands', symbolizing the approval of their predecessors, was also a way of imparting that Spirit, even though suitability for office could depend equally on worthy parentage and formation within a clerical élite. Those marked by a more rabbinic legacy may have based their teaching on openness to the voice of God, but they also valued the discipline and skill of the interpreter, laboriously acquired from a long line of masters. Both types of leader strove to exercise those skills in homilies and exegesis, in public oratory and private counsel. Finally, the prophetic tradition long admired by many Jews was associated with ascetic practice. The simplicity of John the Baptist's dress and diet, for example – his camel-hair tunic and his locusts and wild honey – became an influential Christian icon, and encouraged bishops no less than more independent teachers to be abstemious.

Christianity did not merely 'break away', therefore, from the older religion. If its own theology – of Jesus and salvation especially – was to retain any logic, it could not jettison the Jewish faith as something obsolete. Joint heirs to the biblical tradition, Synagogue and Church (to speak in abstract terms) competed in their interpretations of the Jewish past (and neither party was single-minded in its assertions). Memories had to be either assuaged or built upon. What we too tidily refer to as the 'pagan world' was simply the arena within which the two religions achieved their adjusted view of destiny. Christians laid an increasingly exclusive claim to the Jewish past – that is, to the promises of God enshrined in the Jewish Scriptures – with crucial consequences (described more fully in Chapters 3, 4 and 5). The Jews, both in Palestine and in the Diaspora, continued to explore their own new paths of self-definition; but Christianity gained increasing advantage, first in terms of numerical expansion and then by access to political power. The failure of the Zealot campaigns and of Jewish revolts in 66, 115 and 132 had encouraged a certain reticence among Jews but fostered in turn a greater confidence among Christians. Yet the strident, venomous oratory with which they continued to attack their old rivals betrays their sense of enduring threat. As late as the sixth century, well after the conversion of Constantine, Jews were still developing a confident and public identity, enshrined eventually in the Babylonian Talmud, to replace the culture of the Second Temple period. The legal codes of Theodosius II and Justinian I and the sermons and conciliar decrees of Frankish Gaul suggest a fear among Christians that their victory might still be reversed. Indeed, several forms of reversal were partly realized. They did not, however, depend entirely on armed bigotry or the weight of the law, nor did the weakening of the Christian empire surrender it into the destructive hands of barbarians. A persuasive quality at least helped its claim to be a universal religion. Those faithful to an older heritage found its forcefulness increasingly hard to match.

THE ILLUSION OF COHERENCE: 'HERETICS' AND 'GNOSTICS'

Christianity's ability to articulate convincing answers to current questions, within the broad setting of Mediterranean society and its religious traditions, should not encourage us to assume, however, that its answers immediately formed either a coherent body of doctrine or a single community of believers. Indeed, historians argue as to whether there were any typical Christian answers to the questions of the day – a typical religious vocabulary, a typical social setting or a typical moral programme. Belief takes social forms, and it may seem reasonable to suppose that a Christian view of the self and of the world, of earth and heaven, would have been defined and acted upon in a unified way. The nature of the surviving evidence, however, makes that difficult to prove – which is scarcely surprising. Two long-established and influential lines of argument have had a particularly misleading effect on the historical 'shaping' of the Christian past and have both failed to gain unreserved acceptance. The first operates under the banner of 'orthodoxy', the second under the banner of 'gnosticism'.

An appeal to orthodoxy as an explanation of development rests on the notion that a single set of Christian beliefs was accepted from the outset and successfully defended thereafter. The 'Tübingen School' of church historians, emerging in the 1840s, proposed the contrasting thesis that conflict of opinion was the most prominent feature – perhaps the formative force – in early Christian history. Adolf Harnack, among others of his generation (at the turn of the twentieth century), modified the Tübingen view but continued to defend an emphasis on development – a development governed by faith, morality and mission. Scholars influenced by Harnack suggested that different communities expressed in different ways both their own beliefs and their relations with those who did not share them. They thought in terms of proclamation and conversion, rather than of reticence and hostility. In 1934, Walter Bauer proposed that what were thought of as the heresies of the first Christian centuries were not deliberate repudiations of a primal orthodoxy but reflected simply a variety of theological opinion, inevitable in the early phases of reflection. Orthodoxy, he argued, was a later achievement, a reaction against developments already in place. Right opinion (which is what the word orthodoxy means) could not be taken as the sole explanation of its own success. It had been forced to demonize alternative positions and depended on privileged and powerful support. It may not have been, in any case, as successful or as widespread as the survival of its documents suggest.

A more detailed examination of orthodoxy – of its rationale and development – occupies much of Chapter 4. I argue there that practical considerations – prayer, discipline and virtuous conduct – counted for more than doctrine in forging the unity of Christians, first at the local level and then more broadly. As one might expect, the scholarly attempt to dismantle the orthodox paradigm did not meet with universal approval. It offered a double satisfaction to some, since it made dispute and change theologically less threatening, and permitted a federal rather than a hierarchical image of the first Christian communities. Others continued to insist, however, that doctrinal unity was consciously recognized, valued and defended from the earliest days. That difference of opinion had a paradoxical result. Some scholars began to make diversity itself into an alternative monolith, labelled heterodoxy – as if to suggest that early Christians, even as they tolerated a range of tastes in theology and discipline, were drawn together by an overriding antagonism to an orthodox view. Notable thinkers of the second and third centuries appeared to encourage that opinion – Irenaeus of Lyon, for example, leader of that church from *c.* 178. They often branded their opponents with a single epithet, 'gnostic'. There were, certainly, patterns of belief and behaviour among many early Christians – patterns both coherent and popular – that were antagonistic towards various styles of authority, intensely spiritual in their emphasis, bizarre or eccentric in their interpretation of Scripture, dismissive of marriage and estranged from the body and from the material world generally. It would be rash to suppose, however, that such attitudes underpinned a single community or an endemic theology that could then be labelled 'gnostic'. Gnosticism represented a cast of mind rather than an independent sect or religion – a cast of mind neither wholly separable from Christianity nor dominant within it. Some scholars, nevertheless, began to find gnosticizing Christians everywhere, and took them to represent a norm, against which orthodox authorities mounted a fruitless attack. Others countered the thesis by depicting the gnostic viewpoint as wholly foreign to Christianity, and therefore doomed to extinction.

Recent debate has been able to escape that impasse, chiefly because historians have been forced to face the misleading character of the term 'gnostic'. I explore more fully some of the issues involved, first in relation to the writing of gospels (in Chapter 3), then in relation to senses of order and historical development (in Chapter 4), and finally in relation to Christian interpretations of the Jewish Scriptures (in Chapter 5). I want to present here a more general picture. For a long time, historians placed considerable faith in the writings of the gnostics' self-declared opponents – Irenaeus of Lyon (already mentioned), the 'apologist' and martyr Justin (executed *c.* 165), Tertullian (Irenaeus's north African contemporary) and the third-century Roman presbyter Hippolytus (to name the most obvious). (I discuss their views at greater length in Chapter 4.) It was difficult to do otherwise. Direct access to alternative opinions was limited to the so-called *Pistis Sophia*, the *Books of Jeu*, the *Odes of Solomon*, and extracts from the *Apocryphal Acts of the Apostles* – all of them Christian texts, which encouraged the tendency to set up 'gnosticism' as a species of heresy, a perversion of true Christianity; a view that coincided comfortably with the judgements of men like Irenaeus. But towards the end of 1945, the historian's view was transformed by the discovery of a series of papyrus documents, in a sealed jar, in the Nag Hammadi district of Upper Egypt, near the village of al-Qasr. Through a murky series of deals, sales and revelations, covering the best part of a decade, an extraordinary story began to emerge. The collection consists of thirteen codices – books with bound leaves, like the ones we use today. They were in various states of repair and contained the whole or part of some fifty separate tractates written in Coptic in the late third or fourth centuries, based on earlier sources (many of them second-century), of which they were for the most part translations. Here, it seemed, was a wonderful corroboration, although also a correction and expansion, of what was known of gnostic thought. The weird mythologies and often extensive treatises indicated also long development, broad coherence, ingenuity and inventiveness, and wide dissemination of a rich theological tradition. The dry Egyptian climate, so scholars argued, had accidentally preserved what the physically more hostile environments of Gaul, Italy, Asia Minor and the East had also undoubtedly once contained.

With the exception of the 'Dead Sea Scrolls' (associated with the Jewish community at Qumran), no discovery has had so great an impact on the modern understanding of early Christian practice and belief. However cautious the distinctions that experts feel obliged to make, everyone agrees that the Nag Hammadi collection displays a remarkable range of beliefs. More important, most of them claimed to be Christian and, with one or two exceptions, they make no sense outside a Christian context. However much a man like Irenaeus might have wished to present them as alien to his own faith – some of the Nag Hammadi material can be linked with the circles he criticized – the authors of the tractates were debating with those whom they regarded as fellow believers. The gnostic emphasis, where the use of the term can be justified, was no exotic parasite. Opponents attacked gnostics as perverters of Paul and the gospels, but they wilfully obscured what they obviously had in common with their foes. They may not have liked the gnostic answers, but their own positions were based on the same inquiries and appealed to the same authorities.

The special interest in Genesis that one finds in much of the Nag Hammadi material was an aspect of its Christian character. Like those later thought of as orthodox, the authors modified and in some instances supplanted Jewish traditions of exegesis and spirituality. Some Jews in the past had already been outraged by those too attached to 'wisdom', in the sense of esoteric knowledge (which is what the Greek word *gnōsis* can imply). They saw them as mounting an eccentric, novel and dangerous challenge, fostered by political dissolution and the impact of Hellenistic culture. They regarded the gnostic interpretation of Scripture as at odds with an appropriate loyalty to ancient social forms, cultic practice and moral principle. Among Christians, one finds the same theological tendencies and the same reactions. Paul, as we shall see, took up his cudgel, as a Jew and specifically as a Pharisee, against a familiar foe. His Christianity was designed among other things to thwart those who threatened, in his eyes, the true meaning of what it meant to be a Jew (a major theme in Chapter 2). From Paul's time forward, therefore, Christian literature argued for and against a gnostic view and in causes that Jews would have recognized.

The Nag Hammadi discovery does not make any more convincing, however, the notion that gnostics constituted a homogeneous majority among Christians. The range of beliefs that the codices reflect is too carelessly given a single designation. Their special brand of pessimism, their suspicion of the body and of the physical world, runs counter to a tendency no less evident among Christians at large – an eventual affirmation of this world's value and an eventual willingness to be integrated within the social and political structures of the Roman Empire. What we can say is that the gnostic spirituality, if such we may call it, the gnostic exegesis, the gnostic understanding of community, were neither isolated nor exclusive. *Gnōsis,* knowledge, has been too often taken to imply an élitist belief in special and continuing revelation, granted only to a few. Those attacked as gnostic heretics never in fact used the adjective *gnōstikos,* and they recognized that *gnōsis* could be an arrogant and destructive force as well as a worthy acquisition. Their central concern was to rescue the spirit both from the weight of the body and from the weakness and ignorance of the soul, allowing it to return to its true setting in the divine sphere. That explains their special interest in the biblical account of creation. No less than their opponents, they wanted to understand why humanity's links with its maker were so distant and obscure and how intimacy with God could be permanently restored. They wanted to identify and interpret authentic sources of revelation. They explained the painful experience of distance from God by suggesting that the visible world, the world of souls and bodies, was the work of a 'demiurge', a subordinate being, who could be malevolent towards human beings and often ignorant of God's true purposes. They equated this demiurge with the God of the Jews. Human beings were created spirits, trapped in a darkened and often vicious world. Yet the spiritual essence of their humanity predated the creation of Adam. It could not be suppressed by Adam's inadequacy but marked out, even in the stages of its estrangement from God, a pathway by which it might return to his presence and favour. It was a long time before such a view could be marginalized. It emerged, no less than any other, from the common seedbed of Christian experience and contributed to central debates for many centuries.

CHRISTIANITY AS A SOCIAL PHENOMENON

In spite of diversity in doctrine, early Christians soon acquired a cohesion in social structure, certainly at a local level. The variety and obscurity of gnostic solutions to puzzlement and anxiety made all the more clear the principles of unity that were slowly gaining ground more widely; the principle above all that one could combine a sense of God's enduring presence with the historical continuity of the community of believers. It was a principle that set its face against disembodiment. Slowly and with difficulty, a majority of Christians employed the vocabulary of sign, mystery, image and sacrament. Such terms made history, visible circumstance and human association the instruments whereby a transcendent God could be made permanently present in the material world. They served to rescue, in the name of religion, what many at the time (including most gnostics) were willing to dismiss – the body and the material drama of food, sex, pain and death that enclosed it. Relations between God and his creation remained a puzzle, but Christianity's complex and rich ceremonial, especially in the centuries after Constantine, sealed its firm commitment to the visible. Marble and mosaic, the sounds and scents of ceremony, the music, the processions, the awesome gestures and incantations, all transported the faithful to a heavenly world that those physical elements were designed to represent. Believers were prepared, in the same cause, to heal the sick and feed the poor; to imitate the human and practical sympathy of Jesus their founder.

In order to sustain both their patterns of worship and their concern for the well-being of their members, Christian communities required leadership and order. Our understanding of that development will depend on more than observing the emergence of bishops, priests and deacons, and on listing their juridical credentials or institutional tasks. They were not the only ones to lay successful claim to leadership. Here, too, diversity was evident, explained in part by the competing traditions (which I outlined above) inherited from the Jewish past. Bishops never enjoyed a monopoly of power. They differed among themselves in their style of command, just as they differed from the ascetics and exegetes who sometimes challenged their authority. They also had to contend with the rivalry and criticism of lay men and women, who were often supported by independent wealth and status.

That last point serves to remind us that Christian communities were inevitably linked with the society around them. It is impossible to suppose that they led, before Constantine, a private existence. We need to assess Christian social behaviour in relation to existing expectations and tensions within the public sphere. The distinction between private and public was carefully drawn in ancient society. The poles of cultured life (in contrast to that of peasants and slaves) were the *oikos* and the *polis*, the home and the city. Definitions depended on such distinctions – between family and community, kinship and politics, child and adult, female and male. Because, however, males dominated every sector, the father was at once the root of kinship, the master of the household and the arbiter of authority in the state. He was the source of knowledge, sharing with women the task of forming the young – or rather, supplanting by his ordered instruction the warmer influence of the nursery. Religious distinctions ran along comparable lines. Civic cults attracted the loyalty of a whole city and symbolized its antiquity and special character. Domestic cults were especially associated with ancestral spirits and the commemoration of the dead. As I shall suggest in Chapter 6, several features of early Christian experience – martyrdom, for example, or literary debate with those of other faiths – inevitably placed leadership in a civic as well as in a domestic sphere. Early Christians most often worshipped in their homes and – in the eyes of the pagan Celsus, for example (d. probably in the 180s) – acquired as a consequence a reputation for secrecy; but they were no more hidden from the public eye than other mystery cults, burial societies or banqueting clubs, many of whose members held public office and gained public esteem.

Christians were placed, in other words, in a world of carefully defined and rigorously defended roles and spheres of influence and authority. They did not choose one sphere to the exclusion of others. Like all free citizens, they were subject to the scrutiny of their fellows. There was, nevertheless, a certain tone of subversion in their social vocabulary. They used consistently and generally, for example, kinship terminology – father and mother, brother and sister. They described their 'church' as a household and as a bride or mother. At the same time, it was a city, and its members citizens. Christians also used the vocabulary of instruction, of teachers and disciples (a tendency I explore in Chapter 5). Traditional believers would have found that vocabulary entirely intelligible. Such habits of speech had persisted and would persist for centuries. Shifting circumstances imparted different meanings, certainly. 'Fellow citizens of the saints and members of God's household' – the phraseology of the *Letter to the Ephesians* – did not carry the same implication as 'the heavenly city' or 'the city of God' in the works of Augustine, more than three hundreds years later. Yet there was clearly continuity between the two sets of ideas, and a species of judgement upon current social expectations. By blurring or crossing thresholds originally confirmed in terms of family and public life, Christians were able (shockingly, as some thought) to call into question the presumed purpose of marriage, the proper setting for cultural formation, the justification for power, the permanence of the state and the qualities of authentic leadership.

RELIGIOUS CHANGE

History is essentially dynamic; specifically, a study of change. Chronologies have to be established and developments have to be explained. However, given the fact that we know so little about ordinary Christians in the earliest centuries and that we have to deduce broad developments from élite literature, we are forced to base our suppositions about religious ideals on the institutional structures that were designed to support them. By the time more detailed evidence becomes available, in the third century, the factors that had first aided Christianity's growth had already achieved their effect. In attempting to suggest what those factors might have been, historians have often relied on models of change borrowed from the analysis of other times and places; but one has to be sure that one is assessing what were genuinely the operative factors in the period one is dealing with. The title, for example, of Harnack's famous work *Mission und Ausbreitung des Christentums, The Mission and Expansion of Christianity*, implies not only that Christianity expanded but also that it did so under the impulse of a sense of mission. A missionary urge is certainly discernible in the early period. Sociological theory supports the view that the heightened self-consciousness of a schismatic and beleaguered coterie (which, in relation to much of Jewish culture, Christianity undoubtedly was) would have demanded enthusiastic proselytism, if it were not to collapse inward under the weight of its perceived rejection by the world. That is not to suggest that the whole of Christian history can be described primarily as a relentless appropriation of alien territory. Even when blessed later by toleration, Christians still formed scattered pockets remarkably different from one another. And the expansion thesis has several strands, each beguiling but all problematical. Christians did not invent the anxious self and then gradually invade the psyches of those around them. They did not start Jewish and progressively become less so. There was no primitive egalitarianism that was forced to succumb to the growing assertiveness of bishops. The new religion did not begin in households and then slowly envelop cities. All those opinions have been expressed; but the change we are talking about cannot be described in such terms.

One of the reasons why the evidence for early Christianity is thin and limited overwhelmingly to an élite and enclosed view is that few noticed its arrival and growth. Its early records have survived in relative abundance only because later Christians found them significant. It is commonly suggested that it was not until Eusebius of Caesarea wrote his *Ecclesiastical History*, immediately before and during the reign of Constantine, that the Christian past was ordered in a recognizably coherent form. Neither the Christians of the first two centuries nor those who brushed against them socially had any such notion of progress and destiny. Wisdom after the event was essential to the later image. The canon of early Christian literature was not invented by fourth-century theologians; but their use of that literature reflected their current preoccupations as much as it did the preoccupations of the first believers. Yet that skill, that constant reappropriation of its own past, was a major instrument in Christianity's historical development. Each generation of believers placed its own interpretation on the legacy of the faith. Texts were read repeatedly, and each reading created further layers of meaning, which transformed or disguised the opinions of the dead and carried the living into new situations. One cannot suggest that, within their different settings, readers had complete power over the substance of the past; but a church was a reading community (I describe the notion in Chapter 5) and overlaid its experience of change with a consistent but shifting appeal to original beliefs and social forms.

What does that do to our own traditional sense of period in the early Christian era? At intervals during the intermittent reinvention of the past, Christians enjoyed moments of calculated reflection, which then had their own influence on subsequent practice. Those gathered-up moments of thought allow historians to mark off significant phases in Christianity's growth. In the early years of the second century, therefore, we think of believers as starting to identify more precisely what distanced them from the Jews. Towards the end of the same century, decisive choices were made in theology – in relation to gnostic and other suspect formulations on the one hand, in relation to the agreed significance of the Jewish Scriptures on the other. Both sets of choices helped to create a distinctively Christian religious culture. Styles of leadership became firmly established, although they remained diverse. The conversion of Constantine in the early fourth century allowed at least one interpretation of Christianity to gain a greater hold over the public life of the Empire. Finally, in the fifth and sixth centuries, it was forced to engage with barbarian society and to face the fading of its dream of unity. Those phases correspond in some ways to traditional divisions of early Christian history – the apostolic age; the age of the apologists and martyrs; the heyday of Clement, Origen and Tertullian; the so-called conversion of the Roman Empire; and the separation between East and West, Greek and Latin, imperial and barbarian worlds. Any number of modern books are divided along those lines. Such neatly paired contrasts were, however, the result of reflection. They point to historical pauses for breath, when Christians readjusted the significance they attached to the past. Such readjustments were made in relation to less clearly articulated issues – fundamental desires and fears, the definition of the self, the aspirations of the spirit, the recognition of authority and the destiny of the physical and social worlds. Once entertained, however, and worked out in prescriptive, pedagogical and textual forms, the very history they appeared to encapsulate impelled Christian society forward, in directions often unforeseen.

I hope I have created a general sense of how we ourselves should gather up our impressions of the period. The rhythm of events must be made to sound in a modern ear within some overriding structure. The titles of the chapters that follow should convey what I have in mind: the impact of two great figures, Jesus of Nazareth and Paul of Tarsus; a struggle for identity, involving a new understanding of the Jewish heritage, a strong moral and liturgical impulse towards social cohesion, a wish to learn and to impart learning, and a painful engagement with the Roman world; then an exciting and in many ways disastrous flirtation with political power; and finally the hesitant welcome of a new world, coloured and sustained by the preservation of much that was old. For us, this is all wisdom after the event. In order to understand historically what started the process, what first fired the Christian imagination, we have to unmask the layers of reading that have contributed to the history of the institution we are studying. Much of what survives in our libraries reflects what later Christians agreed upon as the past to which they could appeal, the past on which they were prepared to base their convictions. They rejected and thereby obscured as much as they accepted. They attempted to set aside much that can now help us to envisage more accurately the earliest communities. The gospels, the *Acts of the Apostles*, and the letters that bound together the first Christian communities contain a wealth of imagery that coloured eventually all Christian belief and practice; but they also contain, even if in a less immediately accessible form, original experience. Can we peel away the subsequent layers of reflection and look directly at the earliest believers? Let us turn to see.

Further reading

In English, two books have long dominated a general interpretation of the topic: Henry Chadwick, *The Early Church*, reprinted many times since 1967 by Penguin Books, and W.H.C. Frend, *The Early Church* (1965) (London: SCM Press, 1982). The latter's *The Rise of Christianity* (Philadelphia, PA: Fortress Press, 1984) gives a fuller account; and his *The Archaeology of Early Christianity: a History* (London: Chapman, 1996) presents an arresting tale of discovery. A crucial contribution has also been made by Peter Brown, both in his general survey, *The World of Late Antiquity* (London: Thames & Hudson, 1971) and in his more particular study, *The Body and Society: Men, Women, and Sexual Renunciation in Early Christianity* (New York, NY: Columbia University Press, 1988); and see his collected papers in *Society and the Holy in Late Antiquity* (Berkeley, CA: University of California Press, 1982; paperback 1989). Very useful is the collection of essays in Ian Hazlett (ed.), *Early Christianity: Origins and Evolution to AD 600* (London: SPCK, 1991).

Among an enormous number of general studies, I have found the following stimulating at various stages of my work: Robert Doran, *Birth of a Worldview: Early Christianity in its Jewish and Pagan Context* (Boulder, CO: Westview Press, 1995), Howard Clark Kee, *Christianity: a Social and Cultural History* (New York, NY: Macmillan, 1991), Ramsay MacMullen, *Christianizing the Roman Empire, AD 100–400* (New Haven, CT and London: Yale University Press, 1984), Robert Markus, *Christianity in the Roman World* (London: Thames & Hudson, 1974), Graydon F. Snyder, *Ante pacem: Archaeological Evidence of Church Life before Constantine* (Macon, GA: Mercer University Press, 1985) and Gedaliahu G. Stroumsa, *Barbarian Philosophy: the Religious Revolution of Early Christianity* (Tübingen: Mohr Siebeck, 1999).

Turning more specifically to relations between Christianity and the Roman world, one may begin by consulting the following: Mary Beard, J. North and S. Price, *Religions of Rome*, 2 vols (Cambridge: Cambridge University Press, 1998), J. Davies, *Death, Burial, and Rebirth in the Religions of Antiquity* (London and New York, NY: Routledge, 1999), Garth Fowden, *Empire to Commonwealth: Consequences of Monotheism in Late Antiquity* (Princeton, NJ: Princeton University Press, 1993), Robert M. Grant, *Gods and the One God* (Philadelphia, PA: Westminster Press, 1986), Martin Henig and Anthony King (eds), *Pagan Gods and Shrines of the Roman Empire* (Oxford: Oxford University Committee for Archaeology, 1986), Robin Lane Fox, *Pagans and Christians* (Harmondsworth: Penguin Books, 1986), David Potter, *Prophets and Emperors: Human and Divine Authority from Augustus to Theodosius* (Cambridge, MA: Harvard University Press, 1994), Frans Theuws and Janet L. Nelson (eds), *Rituals of Power: from Late Antiquity to the Early Middle Ages* (Leiden and Boston, MA: Brill, 2000), Frank R. Trombley, *Hellenic Religion and Christianization, c. 370–529*, 2 vols (Leiden: Brill, 1994) and Robert L. Wilken, *The Christians as the Romans Saw Them* (New Haven, CT and London: Yale University Press, 1984).

Relations between Christians and Jews have now become an essential topic in the study of the period, and I make no apology for presenting a lengthy list, drawn from among a huge range of other works: Peder Borgen, *Early Christianity and Hellenistic Judaism* (Edinburgh: T. & T. Clark, 1996), Shaye J.D. Cohen, *The Beginnings of Jewishness: Boundaries, Varieties, Uncertainties* (Berkeley, CA: University of California Press, 1999), Douglas R. Edwards, *Religion and Power: Pagans, Jews, and Christians in the Greek East* (Oxford: Oxford University Press, 1996), Mark J. Edwards, Martin Goodman, Simon Price and Chris Rowland (eds), *Apologetics in the Roman Empire: Pagans, Jews, and Christians* (Oxford: Oxford University Press, 1999), Erich S. Gruen, *Heritage and Hellenism: the Reinvention of Jewish Tradition* (Berkeley, CA: University of California Press, 1998), Judith Lieu, John North and Tessa Rajak (eds), *The Jews among Pagans and Christians in the Roman Empire* (London and New York, NY: Routledge, 1992), Lee I. Levine, *Judaism and Hellenism in Antiquity: Conflict or Confluence?* (Seattle, WA: University of Washington Press, 1998) together with his earlier *The Rabbinic Class of Roman Palestine in Late Antiquity* (Jerusalem and New York, NY: Yad Izhak Ben-Zvi & Jewish Theological Seminary of America, 1989), L.V. Rutgers, *The Hidden Heritage of Diaspora Judaism: Essays on Jewish Cultural Identity in the Roman World* (Leuven: Peeters, 1997), two older but splendid books by Alan F. Segal, *Rebecca's Children: Judaism and Christianity in the Roman World* (Cambridge, MA: Harvard University Press, 1986) and *The*

Other Judaisms of Late Antiquity (Atlanta, GA: Scholars Press, 1987) and the extremely useful Hershel Shanks (ed.), *Christianity and Rabbinic Judaism: a Parallel History of their Origins and Early Development* (Washington, DC: Biblical Archaeology Society, 1992; London: SPCK, 1993).

On gnosticism, see Robert McQueen Grant, *Gnosticism and Early Christianity* (New York, NY: Harper & Row, 1966), Hans Jonas, *The Gnostic Religion: the Message of the Alien God and the Beginnings of Christianity*, 2nd edn revised (London and New York, NY: Routledge, 1992) and Kurt Rudolph, *Gnosis: the Nature and History of Gnosticism* (1977, revised 1980), translated and edited by R. McL. Wilson with P.W. Coxon and K.H. Kuhn (Edinburgh: T. & T. Clark, 1984).

Still worth reading is the classic study by Franz Cumont, *The Oriental Religions in Roman Paganism* (1906), translated by Grant Showerman (Chicago, IL: Open Court Publishing Company, 1911). Two other older works that I mentioned in the chapter are Adolf von Harnack, *The Mission and Expansion of Christianity in the First Three Centuries*, translated and edited by James Moffatt, 2 vols (New York, NY: 1908; reprinted Gloucester: Smith, 1961) and Walter Bauer, *Orthodoxy and Heresy in Earliest Christianity* (1934), translated under the direction of Robert A. Kraft and Gerhard Krodel (Philadelphia, PA: Fortress Press, 1971); to which one should add the classic by Arthur Darby Nock, *Conversion: the Old and the New in Religion from Alexander the Great to Augustine of Hippo* (London: Oxford University Press, 1933).

Where to begin?
Hershel Shanks (ed.), ***Christianity and Rabbinic Judaism.***

Chapter 2

PAUL AND THE JEWISH PAST: AN APOSTLE AND HIS WORLD

The voice of Christianity is carried to us first in the writings of Paul of Tarsus – a Jew, a Roman citizen and an artisan, but also a scholar and moralist, raised in the tradition of the Pharisees. It is an ancient voice, therefore, springing from centuries of Jewish tradition; but it is also a voice of liberty – a liberty in some sense inherited; a liberty to be shared with living believers; and a liberty promised to future generations. If we listen with an objective ear to this outpouring of exhilarated conviction – intense, grand, complex, seeking ever greater clarity and coherence – we shall gain some sense of what Paul's words might have implied for his limited but eager audience. He assured them of a personal release – from sin, from weakness of temperament and from the errors of their past – but also a release from forces outside themselves – from oppression, from social failure or insignificance, and from malignant powers within the cosmos. Liberty had been bought for them by Jesus – a man, but also an intimate and powerful emissary of God; humiliated by execution, but raised to a new life as the 'Christ', the 'anointed' Lord of the universe.

This Christian voice was not Paul's alone. His letters, and the texts that can be associated with them, disclose a scattering of small communities across the eastern Mediterranean world, each expressing in religious terms the hopes and limits of human experience but achieving at the same time a remarkable coherence of belief. Paul did not 'invent' Christianity. By the time he came upon the scene, the new sect was well enough established first to attract his persecution and then to supervise his repentance. His own message, however, and his ideal of community provide a particularly rich impression of the cosmos and of the human person within it – of origins, destiny and social relations. His views were not unchallenged. He did not monopolize in his own time, let alone later, the definition of what it was to be a Christian. His unusual vigour and inventiveness, on the other hand, brought him honour among an increasing number of believers, so that he eventually came to exert, through the preservation and interpretation of his words, an influence far beyond the scale of his immediate endeavours. To read Paul, therefore, is to learn how a church might first be formed and, at the same time, how fragile and contested its formation might be.

CONTEXT

The account of Paul's career in the *Acts of the Apostles* is vivid but unreliable. It brings archaeology to life and helps one to picture the world in which he worked – the weariness and danger of travel by land and sea; the loud and thronging streets and porticoes of the Roman Mediterranean; the public enthusiasm, even hysteria, of its religion; the congested bustle of its workshops and markets; the intimacy of its cool interiors, its banquets and its attentive devotees. But the author had his own agenda. (Let us call him 'Luke', although his connection with the writer of Luke's gospel is not beyond dispute.) Where he contradicts the authentic letters of Paul, the letters should be given greater weight. *Acts* is not fiction – it had to ring true to have persuasive force – but, with Paul's death decades past, there was room for interpretative adjustment as well as confusion and forgetfulness. The work is governed by literary conventions, a cultivated amalgam of skill and imagination. It claims its place as a traditional 'history', with long and polished speeches that reveal the character and ideology of its author as much as of its subjects. It is also novelistic, filled with wonders, adventures, perils and escapes.

Paul based his personal authority on his calling by Jesus. *Acts*, written later, links that assurance with Paul's famous vision on the road to Damascus. The text goes on to present a broad canvas, emphasizing Paul's enduring respect for the synagogue. As he journeys from city to city, he visits the Jewish community first; only in response to its rejection does he turn to the gentiles instead. This version of events is clearly tendentious, but we need not dismiss it entirely. Even though he did not make much of it in his own writings, Paul undoubtedly benefited from the initial convenience of having an audience ready-made among the Jewish communities of the Hellenistic world. The availability of such well-established groups is crucial to an understanding of Christian success. Although Christianity transformed the lives of many first-century Jews, the matrix provided by the synagogue-communities does much to explain the social confidence of the Pauline churches. The first converts were bedded already in family, religious and economic associations that provided a secure springboard for subsequent expansion.

Paul had relatively little to say about those who first nurtured him in his new religious loyalty. If we accept his own account in *Galatians*, that was probably because he spent several years adjusting to his change of view – longer than *Acts* would like us to believe. *Acts*, ignoring his earlier reflections, quickly homes in on Barnabas, a Cypriot Jew, who had joined the Jerusalem church in its early days and had championed Paul, naturally suspect as a former persecutor. After spending a year or more in Antioch, the pair set out for Cyprus – the beginning of what *Acts* presents as 'missionary journeys' – and then travelled through southern Turkey from Perga to Derbe and back again. *Acts* emphasizes 'signs and wonders' and antagonism between Jews and gentiles under the impact of their preaching. It sets the stage, in other words, for conflict and its resolution.

The admission of gentiles into the Christian community had certainly caused misgivings. Peter, another hero of *Acts*, had at some stage acknowledged a need to move beyond the world of the Jews. A vision of foods rejected by the Law but 'cleansed' by God (as *Acts* puts it) had led him to accept a greater openness. In connection with disputes of that sort, although obscurely related to Peter's change of heart, an assembly was held in Jerusalem. James, seemingly more prominent at that time than Peter, crafted a compromise. He did not demand circumcision for gentile Christians but did require of them some of the dietary restrictions practised by Jews. There is no reason to suppose that the gathering did not take place, and Luke's account suggests that Christians in Jerusalem were still confidently claiming control over teaching undertaken elsewhere. Whether they had Paul and Barnabas immediately in mind is less certain (in spite of the chronology that *Acts* adopts). The Christians at Antioch had, in any case, gone rather further; but Paul may have felt himself vindicated by a series of reluctant shifts of attitude in Jerusalem. He certainly continued to reach out to the gentiles on a grand scale. His own account of his relations with the Jerusalem church, at the beginning of *Galatians* (which may or may not refer to James's 'council', as described in *Acts*), shows no signs of doubt or defeat: 'They saw that I had been entrusted with the gospel of the uncircumcised, just as Peter had been entrusted with the gospel of the circumcised'. 'Entrusted' was the key word, a token of independence. 'The good news proclaimed by me', he wrote, 'is not to be measured by human standards. It did not come to me from human hands, nor was I taught it: it came through a revelation of Jesus Christ.'

The meaning he attached to that 'revelation', and the resulting changes in his self-awareness as a Jew, explain almost everything that followed in Paul's career. But the rupture with the past has to be assessed with care: neither *Acts* nor Paul provides the whole picture. Well-educated in his faith and strict in his observance – 'zealous', as he put it in *Galatians*, 'for the traditions of my fathers' – Paul cannot be divorced from his Jewish context. He was part of the history of Judaism in the Roman world. His 'Jewishness', like that of his Christian successors, was not an old error surmounted but a quality open to development. Moreover, no less as Jew than as Christian, Paul was one among many. Judaism was not a monolithic creed. 'Advanced in Judaism beyond many of my own age', Paul was a Pharisee. He had been reared in a tradition emphatic in its moral stance but also adaptable and open to spiritual and even mystical experience. It was a tradition that Paul did not so much reject as submit to fresh definition, fresh exegesis and a fresh sense of moral rigour. Not all his fellow Jews would have accepted even his Pharisaism, let alone his sectarian novelties; but he believed that he had begun to make better sense of the Jewish past he valued.

MISSION

The two witnesses to Paul's achievements – his letters and *Acts* – are not impossible to reconcile, or at least to make sense of as disclosing the same person. Thirteen surviving letters appear to be 'Pauline', but only seven can be attributed with certainty to Paul himself: the others, 'deutero-Pauline', reflected later order and practice. Some scholars place *1 Thessalonians* first among Paul's 'genuine' letters, as written in Corinth in the early 50s; others are prepared to open the collection with *Galatians*. *1* and *2 Corinthians* were written in Ephesus, probably in the middle of the decade. Some would argue that *Galatians* was written when Paul went to Greece a second time. *Romans* certainly was, and should probably be placed later than *Galatians*, whatever the latter's date. *Philippians*, and perhaps *Philemon*, probably date from Paul's final years in Rome. About *Colossians*, *Ephesians* and *2 Thessalonians* there is more debate. *Colossians* could be by Paul – otherwise, *Ephesians* would hardly have imitated it so carefully (for Ephesians, even though close to representing Paul's views, was almost certainly written by an associate). *2 Thessalonians* seems to reflect a subsequent stage of Christian thought, although it can be linked convincingly to *1 Thessalonians* on other grounds. The letters to Timothy and Titus are later.

The letters introduce us to an 'apostle' – a man with an urgent message to impart. They are a sharp reminder of the conceptual inventiveness one could expect to find among the urban enthusiasts of the age. They reveal also a missionary network of itinerant helpers, who bound together a growing commonwealth of local churches. These wanderers were not intent merely on religion. Fortunately placed in centres of trade and communication like Thessalonica, Philippi and Corinth, they took advantage of the chances for mobility so much a feature of the age. They represent, even so, only a narrow segment of the early Christian world. We need to remember where Paul did not go – not to the West beyond Rome, not to North Africa, not to Egypt and Mesopotamia. Even in the inland parts of Asia Minor, his impact was less than secure. His claim to be an apostle and his tireless travel are only part of the early Christian story.

The world of this letter-writing missionary is at least hinted at in *Acts*, although we cannot be sure that Paul followed the reported routes exactly, or at the times suggested. I present here a summary of the account, not because it will bear the scrutiny of the professional historian, but because it offers useful incidental detail and constructs a view of Paul that would influence later Christians in their readings of his letters. After the assembly at Jerusalem, Paul supposedly sets out once more, accompanied by a new assistant (Silas) and a convert (Timothy, from Lystra). After a swing through central Turkey down to the coast at Troy, they are said to have crossed to Greece and to have visited Philippi, Thessalonica and Beroea. While Silas and Timothy linger in the north, Paul proceeds to Athens (where *Acts* has him addressing the Areopagus). The 'missionaries' are reunited in Corinth, where they meet new patrons – Aquila, a Jew from northern Turkey and a tent-maker like Paul, and his wife Priscilla (called Prisca in Paul's letters). *Acts* suggests that at Corinth Paul began to react more defiantly against his fellow Jews – a view not supported in his letters to that community. Luke wished to emphasize that Paul embraced ever more wholeheartedly his sense of mission to the gentiles. He is portrayed as staying in the city for nearly two years, beginning to write as well as preach. With Aquila and his wife, he then crosses to Ephesus on the Turkish coast and proceeds by sea to Caesarea and Antioch.

He does not rest long. After vague allusions to central Turkey, the text brings us back to Ephesus. We are introduced at this point to the Jew Apollos – 'an eloquent man, forceful in his knowledge of scripture'. Originally from Alexandria, Apollos had been preaching in Ephesus; but Priscilla and Aquila feel that he needs more detailed instruction. He leaves for Corinth, moving along that crucial axis of the early Christian world from the great centre of Hellenistic and Jewish philosophy in Egypt to the growing communities of the Pauline mission. Paul himself remains in Ephesus for over two years. *Acts* continues to harp on his conflict with non-Christian Jews. He works hard to bring an originally small Christian community to a fuller understanding of his message. His stay culminates in a riot over presumed threats to the cult of Artemis, which may say something about his success in converting non-Jews; but he has to leave and never returns. After a few months' breather in Greece (which, on other grounds, would seem to have included visits to Philippi and Corinth as well as the composition of *Romans* and (possibly) *Galatians*, he goes back to Troy and then slowly by sea to Caesarea.

Whatever the accuracy of that famous narrative, Paul's impact on his fledgling communities was likely to have been at once dramatic and consoling. A tight bond was forged between apostle and church. His letters are marked by prayerful affection. Distance did not threaten intimacy. Paul's written words offered symbolic proof of what they purported to establish. 'You are our letter', he assured the Corinthians, 'written not with ink but with the Spirit of the living God.' The declaration was no mere formality. 'When you are gathered', he told them, 'my spirit is present.' His arrival in person may have been 'weak' in its effect but his letters carried 'weight and strength'. Such a 'presence' in the imagination of his audience contributed much to the cohesion he achieved among them. Alongside the 'power' of God, letters sent and received had a crucial role to play in the formation of the churches. We need to know now whether Luke's account did full justice to the patterns of thought that those letters reveal.

A COSMIC DRAMA

The historian needs to understand those patterns of thought. Not only are Paul's letters remarkable for their insight into human weakness and idealism and for their subtle and broad-ranging acknowledgement of philosophical and religious traditions: his abstract reflections were wholly interwoven with his view of the world and the religious community. His religious language cannot be taken as a mere front for social concerns, but it was to some degree a sociological language as well. He was adept at presenting vignettes of belief, which brought together a range of concepts, the essential building-blocks of his thought. Scattered throughout his letters, they allude to a cosmic momentum, arching across time from the creation of Adam to the final judgement and drawing individual believers into a greater history. The thesis endured among his successors, in the grand phrases of *Colossians* and *Ephesians*. 'In [Christ] all things were created . . . he is before all things and all things in him are set firm together.' The crucified Jesus, in *Colossians*, had 'stripped the principal rulers and powers', and now, having become their 'head', 'the first-born from the dead', he was also 'the head of the body, the church'. 'Body' was more than a political analogy. Christians were not mere members of an institution but, 'buried with [Christ] in baptism' and 'raised with him', they were able to share in God's 'fullness', the long foreseen completion of his plan for humanity. Individual Christians were swept up into a cosmic tableau; were, as *Ephesians* put it, already enthroned in the 'heavenly places'.

Paul's own thought became more complex as he grew more confident. He described the Corinthians (in his second letter to the city) as masters of life and death, of the present and of the future. 'One', he wrote, 'has died for the sake of all', which meant that 'all have died'; and Jesus (the 'one') had accepted that death, 'so that the living might live no longer for themselves but for him who dies and rises on their behalf'. So individual life and death were interwoven with the paradoxical destiny of Jesus, crucified but risen. The delivered Christian was not transferred simply from one state to another but relinquished self for a new relationship with both the Saviour and the saved – became, as Paul put it, a 'new creation'. According to *Romans*, one was destined 'to share the form of the image of [God's] Son' – a destiny impervious to cosmic threat and realized through baptism, the transition from death to 'newness of life': for baptism, as *Galatians* emphasized, brought deliverance by 'clothing' believers in the dead and risen Jesus. They did not need to reach literal, cosmic heights. 'The word', as Paul put it in *Romans* again (echoing *Deuteronomy*), 'is near you, on your lips and in your heart.' 'As long as you acknowledge with your lips the Lord Jesus and believe in your heart that God raised him from the dead, you will be saved.'

But Paul did not leave the 'historical' Jesus behind. He knew that Jesus was 'born of woman', 'born from the seed of David according to the flesh'. He did not obscure the cruel reality of Jesus's death, 'delivered up', in the words of *Romans*, 'for our transgressions and raised for our justification'. 'I do not wish to become boastful', Paul assured the Galatians, 'unless it be in the cross of our Lord Jesus Christ, through which the world has been crucified to me and I to the world.' The statement was, at one level, symbolic and interior, but it would have been meaningless had the suffering not been real. Similarly, his image of the Christ's humility in *Philippians* – 'he did not think of equality with God as something to be held onto, but emptied himself' – depended for its force precisely on the historical realism of the passage – 'acquiring the likeness of humanity', 'obedient to death, death on a cross'. The later advice tendered to the churches at Colossae and Ephesus was to comparable effect. They must 'put to death what is earthly' and be 'brought near in the blood of Christ'. 'The fullness of the deity dwells [in Jesus] bodily'; and, while God wished on the grand scale to 'reconcile everything to himself', he did so 'through the blood of [Jesus's] cross'.

The Jesus who died and was risen had been part of the creator's plan from the beginning. Paul's letters to Corinth and Rome develop the theme. Jesus represented a 'mystery' that predated time, the 'hidden wisdom of God', made manifest at the appropriate moment. Paul and his associates were 'stewards' of such mysteries. A curtain had been drawn aside: 'All of us, with faces unveiled, gazing upon the glory of the Lord, are changed into his likeness'. 'Mystery' had a technical sense. 'From the time of the world's forming, [God's] invisible qualities have been visible to our understanding in the things that have been made.' As for the worshippers of idols, 'knowing God, they did not honour him as God . . . and their senseless hearts were darkened'. To become like God, to share 'the form of the image of his Son', heralded characteristic preoccupations: foreknowledge, predestination, calling, justification and glory. At the end of time, God would 'cast light on what is hidden in darkness and reveal the wishes of [our] hearts'.

KNOWLEDGE, POWER AND SPIRIT

Within this account of cosmic purpose and fulfilment, the unveiling of God's power remained fundamental. Paul was extrapolating the central component of his calling by God. He had brought his message to the Christian communities 'in power and in the Holy Spirit'. He wanted his converts not only to experience but also to understand that power and to express it appropriately among themselves. For that reason, he retained a cautious regard for 'knowledge' and 'utterance' (*gnōsis* and *logos*). He thus set in train a tradition reflected in *Colossians* and *Ephesians*, where a link between understanding and the cosmic drama is consistently affirmed. At the same time, he did not wish Christians to confuse this knowledge with mere *sophia*, 'the wisdom of the flesh' – thus anticipating the dangerously different ways in which gnostics developed such notions. He championed instead, in *1 Corinthians*, the 'folly' and 'weakness' of the world, 'the base' and 'the contemptible'. In order to retain substance and dignity for his own perception, he appealed to the 'power' of God's 'Spirit'. Only the Spirit 'understands what lies at the heart of

God', and Christians received that Spirit, 'so that we can recognize the ways in which we have been graced by God'. Paul himself imparted 'the teaching of the Spirit', and thus 'we possess the mind of Christ'. The intervention of the Spirit gave vital intimacy to the individual's relationship with God's cosmic purpose and to the association of Jesus and believer. The Christian was God's temple, the Spirit's dwelling-place. Within the human heart, the Spirit was set as a 'seal', 'the guarantee of our inheritance', ensuring glory on 'the day of redemption'.

Emphasis on the Spirit and on genuine understanding allowed Paul to set in place antitheses and paradoxes that became the hallmarks of his discourse. He contrasted the 'unspiritual' (literally the 'psychic') with the 'spiritual' (the terms *psychikos* and *pneumatikos* were to have a long future): the first is trapped by 'folly', by an inability to 'understand'; the second 'assesses all things but can himself be assessed by no one'. Paul was the minister of a 'new covenant' – not 'of the written sort' but 'of the Spirit': 'What is written kills but the Spirit brings to life'. In *Romans* he set 'the law of the Spirit of life' against 'the law of sin and death', distinguishing 'Spirit' from 'flesh', the mortal from the resurrected life. The Galatians were 'mindless' precisely because they could not appreciate the difference.

THE DAY OF THE LORD

Essential to the Pauline drama was the notion of fulfilment. From the beginning of his mission, Paul spoke of a 'coming', of 'a day of anger', as he put it in *Romans*, 'when God's just decree is revealed'. He was prepared to share with the Corinthians the view that 'the end of the ages' had arrived, in the sense that resurrection was already guaranteed; but Jesus was an *aparchē*, a sacrificial firstling among those who had 'fallen asleep'. Resurrection was an extended reality. Paul wished to temper the Corinthians' excitement, evoking (as in his cosmic scenario) time, change and fulfilment. 'You know what time it is' he wrote in *Romans*; 'you know that the hour has already come for you to wake from sleep. Our salvation is nearer now than when we [first] believed. The night is advanced, daylight draws close.' We detect, therefore, a readiness to wait, which is also present in *2 Thessalonians*, making it less alien to Paul's thought than some have asserted. Jesus was to be 'revealed from heaven with the angels of his power in burning fire, bringing vengeance upon those who do not know God and who do not submit to the good news of Jesus our Lord'. However, the day was still distant. 'We ask you, brothers . . . not to be hastily disturbed in your minds, or frightened by a movement of the spirit, by a statement, or by a letter apparently from us suggesting that the day of the Lord is imminent.' Other horrors had to precede it: a 'revolt' by 'the man of lawlessness', 'the son of destruction... presenting himself in the guise of God'. In these passages, Paul (if it was Paul) came closest to the apocalyptic tradition in Jewish literature. Yet the particular quality of the expectancy, the declared readiness to wait in the belief that the rebel was as yet 'held in check', would allow a Christian community to attach longer-term significance to contemporary events and to place itself within a historical framework.

Subsequent reflections on Paul's ideas, in *Colossians* and *Ephesians*, presented a grander but less terrifying scene. Christians could watch, against the backdrop of time, a victory already achieved. God's wrath was deflected away from the redeemed and visited upon the 'powers' of the world, the 'cosmic elements', whose virulence, effectively punished by God, was a familiar theme in Jewish apocalyptic. In *Galatians*, they appear anew. Christians without a Jewish past had been 'enslaved' by them. The world's false wisdom was their work, but baptism destroyed their dominion, offering a passage from death to life. The 'mystery' of earlier letters, 'the abundant variety of God's wisdom', was now, in *Ephesians*, flung in the face of those dark forces. All Christians shared in the task: 'Our struggle is not against blood and flesh but against the principal rulers, against the powers, against the world masters of this darkness, against the spirits of wickedness in the heavens.' They knew that victory was assured. They should be 'watchful' and proclaim boldly 'the mystery of the good news'. For all the scale of the conflict, there was an air of calm. Christians had been carried beyond a tense and fearful expectation. They understood fully both their history and their circumstance.

FROM LAW TO GOSPEL

A series of anecdotes in the closing chapters of *Acts*, not echoed in the letters, opens with the description of a final visit by Paul to Jerusalem. Luke produces a finely crafted speech (which was, he says, delivered by Paul in Hebrew), in which the apostle outlines his spiritual path, from study under the Pharisee Gamaliel through his vision outside Damascus to his eventual call to the gentiles. Arraigned subsequently before the Sanhedrin, he cleverly sets Pharisee against Sadducee, appealing to Pharisaic belief in spirit and resurrection. Transported to Caesarea, he continues to present himself in Jewish terms: 'I worship the God of our fathers, believing everything laid down by the Law or written in the prophets, having a hope in God which these themselves [his accusers] accept, that there will be a resurrection of both the just and the unjust.' Nowhere in the early texts is Paul's enduring Jewishness more clearly presented. Faced subsequently with a new governor, he appeals to the emperor; and in another speech, delivered in the presence of King Agrippa, he speaks again as a Pharisee, claiming 'hope in the promise made by God to our fathers' (namely, resurrection from the dead), 'saying nothing but what the prophets and Moses said would come to pass – that the Christ [i.e. the Messiah] must suffer and that, by being the first to rise from the dead, he would proclaim light both to the people and to the gentiles'.

Those concluding vignettes in *Acts* represent one Christian response to the issues that Paul addressed. The words as they survive are Luke's and serve the purpose of his work. Can we take them as an accurate account of Paul's own views? It seems, with reservations, safe to do so. The central elements of the speeches – belief in 'the promise made by God to our fathers' and in a Messiah destined to suffer, die and rise again – inform also the letters. The proclamation of a promise, its fulfilment in history and its realization in the person of Jesus reflected the Jewish character of Paul's cosmic drama. The same is true of his formula in *Philippians*, where God rewards filial obedience to the point of death.

There had been a degree of trauma in Paul's religious development, but the adjustment it demanded had been far from negative in effect. To make persuasive his claim that the God of the Covenant was to be a God for all, Paul used the texts on which his Jewish identity had been based. His occasionally harsh tone, his espousal of a 'new covenant', his belief that a veil still darkened Jewish eyes, did not prevent him from acknowledging the harmony demanded. 'To those who are called, both Jews and Greeks, Christ [is] the power of God' or, as he put it in *Romans*, 'there is no distinction between Jew and Greek'.

The Jews had been 'entrusted with the oracles [the *logia*] of God' and salvation based on faith would be granted 'to the Jew first'. The fulfilment of God's expectations depended on their characteristic fidelity. Those of them now turning to a Christian interpretation of the past could continue to claim their rights, grafted as 'natural branches' onto the tree of faith. Jesus, in that context, was 'a minister of circumcision', because he proved God's veracity by 'confirming the patriarchs' promises'. The gentile Christian's dispensation from circumcision, on the other hand, did not mean that he could not 'naturally put the Law into practice'. To talk about the 'hidden Jew' (as Paul does in *Romans*) and about 'circumcision of the heart' was to remain firmly within a Jewish tradition. Those whom we now think of as 'Christians' – gentiles who had begun to think of themselves as, so to speak, Jews with a difference, but still Jews – naturally claimed the same legacy. The arch of time, the tilt from purpose to fulfilment, retained its Jewish colour. 'The promise made to Abraham and his descendants – inheritance of the world – was not brought about through the Law but through the righteousness of faith', and gentile Christians were able to share that 'faith of Abraham, who is the father of all of us'. Faith, therefore, counted for more than observance. To respond to God's promises with faith was to 'affirm the Law' rather than 'rob it of effect'. Only the inclusion of the gentiles in the economy of God's promises could make plausible the hope that they might 'inherit the world'.

Paul felt obliged to claim, on the other hand, that the affirmation of that gentile right was justified in part by a failure on the part of Judaism. Nowhere has the complexity of his argument had so devastating a future effect. Several assertions competed in his mind. First, the Jewish Law had failed because it had not been observed. Second, observance was in any case fruitless. Third, nevertheless, even a gentile informed by the Spirit could fulfil the Law. His attention shifted from the rights and wrongs of observance to the reality of sin. Sin's nature and effect might have been less obvious, had it not been for the declarations of the Law. But sin, for Paul, was not simply a distortion in human history: it was a terrifying and active force that threatened each human being at every level. He was less concerned to judge the Jewish past than to judge the weakness of human nature. Observance of a law that was 'spiritual' proved unavoidably frustrating. A radical distinction was involved: 'I delight in the law of God in my inmost humanity, but I see another law in my body's limbs fighting against the law of my mind and making me captive to the law of sin within those limbs.' From this captivity the Messiah, dying and rising, had liberated Christians – not that they might sin with impunity but that they might escape from the necessity of sinning. They could live now 'not according to flesh ... but according to spirit'.

The quality of that release and the gentile claim upon Abraham's inheritance are treated with particular clarity in *Galatians*. God's original covenant recorded in *Genesis* had mentioned, according to Paul, an 'heir' in the singular, whom Paul identified with the Christ. Through association with the Christ, all believers could become, as the Jews had always been, God's sons. The period governed by the Jewish Law had been clouded, however, by bondage to 'elemental spirits', whereas God had been concerned with a longer arch of time, reaching back beyond Moses. As part of his argument, Paul used the stories of Ishmael the son of Hagar and Isaac the son of Sarah, both of them Abraham's children, 'one by a slave and one by a free woman'.

Hagar represented 'the enslaved Jerusalem of the present day'; Isaac's heritage devolved upon Christian Jews and gentiles alike, making them 'the Israel of God', destined to achieve fulfilment in 'the free Jerusalem above'.

The combination of freedom and transcendence was to have a long Christian future. More immediately, in *Colossians* and *Ephesians*, the reconciliation of Jew and gentile was fused with the reconciliation between humanity and God. In spite of a continuing link between ritual preoccupation and 'cosmic elements', the Jewishness of the Christian community was in other ways unstintingly maintained. Gentile Christians, before their conversion, had been 'separated from the community of Israel' and were 'strangers to the covenants of promise'. Now the Christ 'has made us both one and has dismantled the wall that divided us'. And when the Ephesians were further assured that they were 'no longer strangers and transients but... members of the household of God', the new society was portrayed in terms familiar to the Jewish tradition – 'a holy temple', where converts might 'share in spirit the abode of God'.

Paul's emphasis seems at times antagonistic and obscure, but careful attention to his words can redeem the tragedies of subsequent misinterpretation. His passionate defence of his own insight and his recognition of weakness, both in himself and in the Jewish past, created a purifying fire, in which God's ancient promises and the triumph of the risen Christ combined to resolve the painful tension between flesh and spirit, bondage and freedom, estrangement and inheritance, presenting an account of human history that reached without break from creation to the final day of glory.

SHAPING THE COMMUNITY

Paul identified Christian commitment with a repudiation of idols – a repudiation traditional among the Jews and demanded now of gentiles. Yet his forceful rhetoric disguises the difficulty involved. Christians did not immediately develop a distinctive public profile in Mediterranean society. Their experience of conversion invited them to define themselves against an unbelieving city and an unbelieving empire, but they shared many of the values of that unacceptable world and even more its habits of thought and behaviour. As they moved within the Greco-Roman culture of the cities, their non-Christian contemporaries need not have found their religious practices entirely strange. Distinctiveness depended more on a profile developed domestically, away from the public eye. Baptism, taking the place of circumcision as a marker between believers and the world, formed more than a cleansing threshold. It constituted the essence of the new community and represented its enduring character and orientation. It bound Christians once for all in a new and continuous relationship with the cosmic Christ. Formerly 'enslaved', they 'now knew God'. It bound them also to one another, with the Spirit as their companion and guide.

Paul and his associates had to respond to existing social opportunities and limitations. A beguiling tool of recent historical analysis has been the notion of 'status inconsistency', focused on a moderately wealthy and mobile artisan class within Greco-Roman urban society. Here were people with some economic power, based on manufacture and trade, who did not fit into the traditional and rigid social orders of the Roman and Hellenistic world. A combination of ambition and frustration could have made Paul's notions of liberty, spiritual possession and the expectation of a new age attractive to persons excluded in that way. Some leaders in the earliest churches seem to have been precisely enterprising opportunists poorly rewarded by current social canons. Men and women of the 'middling sort' were prominent among Paul's converts. Aquila (in *Acts*) was a tentmaker; Gaius (in *1 Corinthians* and *Romans*) had a house big enough to hold all the gathered believers of his city; Erastus was a 'city treasurer', Crispus 'the ruler of the synagogue'; Chloe's 'people' (again in *1 Corinthians*) may have been relatively prosperous freedmen. While Paul could deplore their snobbery – he criticized the church at Corinth for reinforcing, within its worship, divisions of wealth and civic dignity – those were the types upon whom he depended for support.

That enduring social and economic containment within a city setting would have made it hard for Christians to adopt a way of life visibly at odds with the tenor of life around them. Even while attempting to influence others, Paul ('all things to all men') was diplomatic and adaptable in his address to the unbelieving world. He showed an early aversion to mixing with 'unbelievers' and referred later to 'a bent and perverted generation', in the midst of which Christians would 'illumine the world'. But he demanded obedience to 'those in authority', which included paying taxes and observing the traditional ranks of society. He also wished Christians – those in Thessalonica, for example – to present an attractive face to 'outsiders', even while they cultivated their own 'holiness'. If *Colossians* was Paul's work, one can read in the same light the letter's distrust of harsh asceticism, although there is again some hesitancy to the writer's forcefulness, which would have enabled believers to reach beyond the accepted social boundaries between Roman and non-Roman, slave and free. A church could combine, therefore, a relative degree of public acceptability with the private intensity of a community of converts. With a skill destined to become endemic, Christians were quick to distance themselves from one another when necessary. Those who falsely bore the name of 'brother' aroused great misgivings. Faced with a situation like that in Corinth, Paul could be driven to say, 'Is it for me to judge outsiders? Are you not to judge those inside [the church]?' The pattern of missionary endeavour may have served to exacerbate the problem. Based on the conversion of disparate urban households, it lent itself to divisions within a single city – the seed of later strife.

The images of incorporation used by Paul tell us much about the specific cohesion of the Christian group. As we might expect from a reading of the gospels, 'kingdom' makes an occasional appearance. It is not allowed, however, to form a literal contrast with the Roman state. God had rescued Christians from 'domination by darkness' and transferred them 'to the kingdom of the Son', but the implied polity is either identified with the powerful action of the Spirit or postponed for fulfilment 'in heaven'. More common and more characteristic is the image of the body. Paul brought it into play within the Corinthian setting, where divisions were rife and spiritual gifts in competition. His deepest convictions were fused in these passages, which are focused on spirit, baptism, liberty and the Jews. 'Just as the body, being one, has many limbs . . . so also the Christ. For in one Spirit we were all baptized into one body – whether Jews or Greeks, whether slaves or free – and we were all given one Spirit to drink.' He then extended the image to his understanding of eucharistic unity: 'The bread that we break, is it not fellowship in the body of the Christ? That is, there is one bread, and we, though many, are one body, for we all partake of the one bread.' The references to both baptism and eucharist link the 'body' of the Christian community firmly with the Christ. To become a 'new creation' was to enter into a new set of relationships; to be, with all the baptized, 'in Christ'. Once set in place, the imagery was assured of a future. The strong corporate phrases already noted in *Ephesians* spring straight from the baptismal and eucharistic teaching in *1 Corinthians*: 'Now in Christ Jesus you who were once far away have been brought close in the blood of the Christ'; and *Colossians* and *Ephesians* link the body imagery to the cosmic progress of believer and church, destined under Christ their 'head' to grow 'to full manhood – a maturity measured against the fulness [the *plērōma*] of the Christ'.

The tenor of those passages makes clear the abstract force of the imagery. The world of social experience is more immediately conveyed by the vocabulary of kinship and household. It was a 'son' that God had sent into the world, enlivening in new ways the already paternal relationship between creator and creatures. The familiar terms of the Jewish tradition continued to command respect. The Jews were naturally the ones who should have been enjoying 'sonship', but Abraham was 'the father of all of us', so that gentile Christians inherited yet another of God's ancient promises – 'I shall be a father to you and you shall be to me sons and daughters'. Access to the Spirit included 'the spirit of sonship'. Similarly with household, 'the household of faith': Christians (at least in Ephesians) were to grow into 'a holy temple', 'built into it', to 'share in spirit the abode of God' and become 'fellow citizens of the saints and members of the household of God'. On a more human level, Paul, both a father and a mother to his churches, exalted 'the name of brother' from the beginning. A Roman household was not limited to blood kin: so a broader use of kinship language was a natural adjunct to domestic imagery. Formulae such as 'the church in their house' became habitual in the closing sections of letters. In Acts, at Philippi and Ephesus, whole households undergo conversion and then offer hospitality to Paul.

In the ostensibly 'political' vocabulary of 'kingdom' and 'community', antagonism towards the state was avoided in literal terms. 'Domestic' vocabulary, on the other hand, implied considerable subversion of social expectations – a further comment on the possible relief of 'status inconsistency'. For example, the distinction between slavery and freedom – a rigid social marker within any household – came to represent for Paul the distinction between Jew and Christian, which disposed him to modify the pressure of literal enslavement among his converts. 'A slave called in the Lord is a freedman of the Lord. Similarly, a free man called is a slave of Christ.' Philemon was to regard his slave Onesimus 'as ... more than a slave, as a beloved brother'. Only later did some Pauline churches (at Colossae and Ephesus) modify that generous optimism by reinstating more rigid traditions.

Even more striking is the effect on marriage and on the status of women generally. Paul has acquired a reputation for misogyny. He reflected, certainly, the prejudices of his time but his willingness to challenge them is equally significant (and of course we cannot blame him directly for sentiments in *Colossians*, *Ephesians*, and the letters to Timothy). The several women mentioned in his correspondence were, like the men, of moderate wealth and standing. They were subject not to Jewish convention (which was not, in the Diaspora communities, unduly restrictive) so much as to the conflicting social and legal attitudes that governed women's lives in Hellenistic and Roman culture. That may have helped to confirm them in their new Christian roles, alongside their male colleagues. They were clearly essential to the success of Paul's mission. Those, according to *Acts*, gathered for prayer on the riverbank at Philippi (including Lydia, the 'seller of purple goods') must have been typical of the female devotees that Paul and his companions were able to attract. His earliest comments are moderate: 'For this is the will of God . . . that each of you should know how to take a wife for himself in holiness and honour, not in the passion of lust like the peoples who do not know God.' If *Galatians* is an early document, then even more fundamental will have been his conviction that distinctions between male and female had been transcended by baptism 'in Christ'. In *1 Corinthians* he appears to go further: 'I say to those unmarried and to those widowed, it is good for them, if they remain [single] as I do.' The honour thus allowed to women outside the married state reinforced the distance between Christians and the 'heathen' world. But the recommendation was made 'because of the imminent necessity', since 'the time is shortened'. Misunderstanding was rife at Corinth about the time's ending and its implication, and Paul was anxious to warn the community that, while a new liberty was being granted them, they should not allow their hope (or their fear) to encourage a disparagement of marriage or an exaltation of men above women. 'It is not the woman who governs her body, but the man. Similarly, it is not the man who governs his body, but the woman.' Balance was to be maintained.

The new status gained by the unmarried and the widowed may have been short-lived, waning with the temporal expectations that justified it; but a memory of their spiritual rights was thus embedded in what would become the canon of scripture. And we should not be too hasty about the waning. *Colossians* and *Ephesians* require precise interpretation. In the first, while wives are 'governed' by their husbands (literally, 'placed under'), husbands must not be 'sharp' but must 'love' their wives. The same pairing is employed in relation to fathers and children (children must 'obey', but fathers must not 'provoke') and to slaves and masters (slaves must 'obey', but masters must act 'with even-handed justice'). Wives may seem to be aligned, therefore, with children and slaves, but clear obligations are laid upon husbands, fathers and masters. The prescriptions follow recommendations of forbearance, forgiveness, love and peace. *Ephesians* makes similar points, perhaps more obviously in the context envisaged by *1 Corinthians* – 'redeeming the time, because the days are evil' – but also under the general rubric, 'subject to one another, in fear of Christ'. Once again, wives are 'governed', husbands 'love'. But the picture has been complicated by the writer's associated reference to Christ's relationship with the church, conceived as a marriage and bringing into play the notions of headship, of the body and of the unity between them. That is why 'husbands should love their wives as their own bodies' – meaning 'as if' they were their own bodies, rather than merely 'in the way that' they love their own bodies. The passage unfolds, as it says, 'a great mystery', but it intertwines what Paul had kept separate.

BEHAVIOUR AND WORSHIP

Most of our evidence about the shared life of the first Pauline communities concerns either morality or prayer. An agreed code of conduct depended on harmony, and Paul's insistence may reflect how frequently harmony was threatened. The security of a church's social boundaries had to be based on mutual affection and measured self-discipline. Paul wished from the outset, especially in relation to Corinth, to impose coherence on what might otherwise have been a confusing, even divisive range of interests and spiritual talents. Many texts comment upon the affection Christians were supposed to show each other, as in Paul's hymn to love in *1 Corinthians* and his more generally tender sense of identity with his churches. He exhorted them with equal force to comfort and to forgive. He hoped that the Thessalonians 'grasped ... how [they] ought to conduct themselves', and he urged the Corinthians to take note of his own conduct – of his 'ways in Christ, as I teach everywhere in every church'. His earliest spiritual counsel focused overwhelmingly on that imperative. The immense wrench of conversion imposed quite enough demands, while fuelling fidelity. Nevertheless, there were other 'traditions', imparted 'either by word or by letter'; and recipients (as in Thessalonica) were urged to become 'imitators of us and of the Lord'. They should show forbearance, cultivate self-sufficiency and guarantee their generosity by manual labour. Such demands were to be sustained by the Spirit's gifts – faith, utterance, knowledge, earnestness and love. Taking his cue (in *Romans*) from what he saw as the essence of the Jewish Law – namely, *Deuteronomy*'s 'obedience of the heart' – Paul offered an equally straightforward prescription: 'If you acknowledge aloud the Lord Jesus and believe in your heart that God raised him from the dead, you will be saved.' That candid interior surrender remained the enduring touchstone of spiritual achievement, allowing Christians to prophesy, teach and exhort, while showing liberality and cheerfulness, courage in the face of opposition and kinship with their fellows.

The 'more excellent way' recommended to the church in Corinth was designed to identify the Spirit's most important gifts and maintain at the heart of Christian endeavour a sober assessment of human talent and destiny. Whatever else modern Christians may think of his cast of mind, they can be grateful that Paul's churches did not explode with ecstatic fervour or ossify under the pressure of a bitter rigorism. The passage of time, however, demanded a more precise evaluation of humane ideals and temperament. As the writer of *Colossians* put it, 'idolizing one's own willpower, cultivating inner abasement, placing ruthless demands upon one's body – these are worthless in the face of the insatiable flesh'. The theme in Matthew's gospel – 'What passes out of the mouth comes from the heart, and this defiles a man' – reached beyond any simplistic view of 'flesh' and, in the Jewish terms essential to the teaching of the Pharisees, appealed to the value of an inner purity. A secure understanding of this subjective landscape depended on more than heroic energy. In the letters to Timothy, a subtle definition of 'conscience' and 'sincerity' informed the larger values of faith and love, carrying Christians forward along the path from exhilaration to dogged discipline.

Early Christians formed more than a body of worshippers, more than a cult in a limited sense. But any religious community will reveal its hopes in its prayer, and the drama of salvation lent itself naturally to liturgical expression. The worship of early Christians symbolized their view of God's purpose for both the cosmos and the individual. It also defined for them, and helped them to act out, their relations with one another and with the world around them. A Christian's whole life was an act of worship. He or she became a 'living sacrifice'.

We have no clear description of baptismal practice in the Pauline period, and it would be dangerous to read back the customs we discover in later documents like the *Didachē* or the *Apostolic Tradition*. It is sensible to assume, however, that immersion was frequent, as Christian art and later architectural practices suggest, and that a change of clothing was given symbolic importance. Paul combined what *Acts* can appear to treat separately – ritual washing and the gift of the Spirit. Many formulae in the Pauline corpus seem to be primitive prayers or allusions to rites and gestures – burial with Christ, 'putting on' the new man, crying out with the Spirit, 'Abba! Father!'

About the eucharist, we know more. Its celebration was the most visible expression of Christianity's character. Although there is no evidence for direct imitation of synagogue practice, the Greek word for church, *ekklēsia* (more properly 'assembly'), owed more to Jewish models than to civic institutions. The associated notion of 'gathering' sprang directly from a conviction that Christians, like the Jews before them, had been 'called', 'gathered' or 'chosen' by God. The celebration of the eucharist reinforced that new sense of covenant. *Acts*, in a vignette of early worship, suggests that the rites (consistently referred to as the 'breaking of bread') were performed once a week, probably on Sunday. The discussions associated with the reception and distribution of Paul's letters imply familiarity with the Jewish scriptures, and reading and interpretation of those texts soon came to form part of the celebration. Later, in *Colossians* and *Ephesians*, we find reference to 'psalms, hymns, and spiritual songs' – probably original Christian compositions, several of which are included in the Pauline corpus. About the sacramental meal itself, Paul was informed by oral tradition and personal experience. The formulae quoted in *1 Corinthians* are reproduced in the gospels: bread and wine were blessed, then eaten, with explicit reference to words of Jesus, connecting the ritual with his death and expected 'coming'. Christians acquired their specific identity by 'fellowship in the body [and] in the blood of the Christ'.

A famous and striking ritual was speaking with tongues. Such a 'gift' was not necessarily spontaneous or unpredictable. Everything should be done, Paul wrote to the Corinthians, 'with elegance and order', which suggests a degree of control. He laid down complex guidelines and assumed that interpretation would follow prophecy, bearing witness to its rational content. The 'building up' of the whole community was the paramount consideration, 'so that everyone may learn and everyone may be encouraged'.

LEADERSHIP AND AUTHORITY

A certain intensity, both social and religious, coupled with the spiritual inspiration of both leaders and adherents, did most to hold the early communities together. Paul himself was a special case – an apostle who had 'seen Jesus our Lord', had been chosen 'by the will of God' – but the vocation of apostle was intrinsic to the first burst of missionary zeal that led to the founding of the Pauline communities. Apostles were 'ambassadors' and 'messengers'. When they spoke, it was as if God were present. Their seizure by the divinity flowed into the communities they addressed. 'Signs, marvels, and acts of power' were the marks of the true apostle. Paul presented himself as a preacher, certainly; but 'the kingdom of God', he wrote to the Corinthians, 'rests not in words but in power', 'not in the persuasive words of wisdom but in the manifest proofs of the Spirit'.

The contrast was governed by Paul's attitude to 'folly'. Trust in God's power was linked with a vocation to face persecution and to suffer as Jesus had suffered. It was in misfortune that strength would be most reliably revealed: 'My power is made perfect in weakness.' Here was another model calculated to subvert contemporary expectations. Humility was to be the guarantee of leadership – Paul was the 'servant' and 'slave' of Jesus. Experience had reinforced that understanding of his destiny. His words of farewell to the Christian elders of Ephesus, reported in *Acts*, anticipate suffering or death in Jerusalem, the culmination of earlier persecutions; and later tradition about his martyrdom colours with tragic irony the novelistic story of his final voyage to Rome. His characteristic interpretation of death and resurrection played its part. The victory effected by baptism was not a reward but a gift. It underpinned all that a Christian achieved, curtailing aimlessness, overriding frailty and ushering in a genuinely human fulfilment. The natural leader, therefore, would be visibly affected by that transition 'in Christ' from death to life, and would be capable of making others understand and desire it.

Paul was aided by his enemies, those who did not regard him as an apostle: *2 Corinthians* hints at rivals, preaching 'a different Gospel'. An independent courage, such as he is said to have displayed later as a martyr, may have helped him to circumvent their influence. We have portraits of some competitors. Apollos at Corinth is the most obvious, imposing and eloquent; a Christian sophist. (The account in *1 Corinthians* is corroborated in *Acts*.) Paul, on his side, may have been as divisive and partisan as his opponent. Apollos was infuriatingly handy with words, 'the debater of the age'. Paul no doubt betrayed at Corinth the distaste he expressed in *Romans* for 'mere quibbling in argument', for intellectual curiosity as a value in itself. *Colossians* and *Ephesians* also deplored 'engaging address', any 'philosophy and hollow fraud' that was based on 'human tradition'. Those practised in such arts were indifferent to the community's peril, allowing it to be 'tossed on the waves by teachers, tugged here and there by their every squall, encompassed by men's trickery, by the villainy of their crafty misdirection'.

So, a church could not be an intellectual coterie, and Christian communities did not merely ape the power structures of the society around them. Respect was achieved within an extended community, a collection of households, not just among immediate disciples or admirers. The urban artisans, the small-scale traders, the petty officials among Paul's followers were patrons, ready to provide buildings and even respectability, but not necessarily spiritual leaders. In deciding who might be, the model of Paul's own apostleship would have carried immense weight. Forceful and articulate conviction, free from naive enthusiasm and arrogant intellect, had been his recommendation. His letters, symptoms of mobility and broad concern, added further to an idiosyncratic persuasiveness inseparable from successful mission. The competition he faced in Corinth shows us what a church looked for in its mentors – a convincing path to knowledge and power; a knowledge that reached beyond learning and a power that reached beyond status.

We have to measure Paul's self-image by comparison with the account in *Acts*. His early experience under Barnabas at Antioch may have introduced him to principles of seniority already current within the Christian community. The new sect, as it moved away from its Jewish matrix, was distinguishing slowly between its own style of leadership and the traditional structures of the older faith. The believers (who included 'prophets and teachers') were inspired with foresight as they worshipped; they fasted and prayed, then 'laid their hands' on the pair. When Paul made his second visit to Jerusalem, he sought out (according to *Galatians*) 'those of visible standing', the 'pillars' of the church, namely James, Peter and John. The 'visible standing' seems little more than carefully earned respect. So also in his own letters, leadership was already functioning in the churches he addressed: he did not inaugurate everything. Among the Thessalonians, there were 'those who toil among you and are placed over you in the Lord and admonish you'. The language evokes talent more than rank. The community had already identified necessary tasks and Paul simply fostered collaboration. Similarly in Corinth, he imposed order on a hierarchy of labourers – apostles, prophets, teachers, 'the wielders of [miraculous] power', healers, helpers, administrators and '[those who speak] various sorts of tongues'.

More precise reference to office occurs only in later texts. The bishops, deacons, and widows of the deutero-Pauline letters operated within communities that in Paul's time had yet to be formed. The concept of 'ministry', *diakonia*, does appear in *Acts*, specifically in connection with the material support of widows. 'Hellenes' were supposedly jealous of 'Hebrews', whose older women were (according to the 'Hellenes') unfairly favoured. Peter and his associates, according to Luke, decided as a consequence to devote themselves 'to prayer and to the ministry [*diakonia*] of the word', while others were to 'serve [*diakonein*] at table'. The description has been coloured by later practice. Rather than representing an early instance of the diaconal order, those special 'servers' probably constituted a gesture towards Greek-speaking Jews. The situation in Ephesus, as reported in *Acts*, suggests that the vaguely depicted 'elders' were already being thought of in the terminology of the future: 'The Holy Spirit', so Paul is reported as saying, 'has set you up as guardians [*episkopoi*] to feed the church of the Lord.' *Philippians* addresses in an apparently comparable way the 'saints . . . with the bishops and deacons [again, *episkopoi* and *diakonoi*]'. Paul's colleague Timothy was singled out in this same letter as a stranger to self-interest and deserving of honour, which may help to explain why the 'letters to Timothy' were addressed as they were – letters in which the vocabulary of leadership was so considerably expanded. However, Paul's authority was being claimed for practices current only after his death. The allusions in *Philippians* and *Acts* suggest at the most that words like 'bishop' and 'deacon' were available for later embellishment.

Paul, wrestling with the cosmos and with his own soul, built into Christian discourse refined judgements that helped his successors to make simpler responses with less reflective skill. Their world of sober inheritance and carefully transmitted discipline will demand separate attention in due course. Paul set in place, meanwhile, a paradigm of 'church' and a corpus of ideas that gradually gained the loyalty of many Christians. Paramount were his understanding of the historical continuum within which Christians thought themselves placed and the terminology he applied to the inner life of the religious individual. His understanding of Jesus was, in that context, remarkably indifferent to historical circumstance. He displayed a reflective vision, therefore, that would be complemented by the narrative approach of the gospels. While his own communities and their immediate imitators continued to develop, other traditions asserted themselves, wedded to compatible but variant interpretations of Paul's Saviour. To these we must now turn.

Further reading

Paul has commanded enormous attention, and readers will find it easy to lay their hands on a multitude of studies. I omit here any detailed examination of individual letters, and include only those more recent books that have sharpened my own eye.

For well focused and stimulating study of the man himself, see (in order of publication) Alan F. Segal, *Paul the Convert: the Apostolate and Apostasy of Saul the Pharisee* (New Haven, CT: Yale University Press, 1990), Daniel Boyarin, *A Radical Jew: Paul and the Politics of Identity* (Berkeley, CA: University of California Press, 1994), Richard Wallace and Wynne Williams, *The Three Worlds of Paul of Tarsus* (New York, NY: Routledge, 1998), John G. Gager, *Reinventing Paul* (Oxford: Oxford University Press, 2000) and John Ashton, *The Religion of Paul the Apostle* (New Haven, CT: Yale University Press, 2000).

The Christian study of Paul's writings quickly affected devotees' understanding of transmission and interpretation, on which see, by way of introduction, David E. Aune, *The New Testament in its Literary Environment* (Cambridge: James Clarke, 1987) and the collection he edited, *Greco-Roman Literature and the New Testament: Selected Forms and Genre* (Atlanta, GA: Scholars

Press, 1985) and add more recently Elizabeth A. Clark, *Reading Renunciation: Asceticism and Scripture in Early Christianity* (Princeton, NJ: Princeton University Press, 1999). As an introduction to several major issues, see Bruce W. Winter, *Philo and Paul among the Sophists* (Cambridge: Cambridge University Press, 1997).

On the social context, see Wayne A. Meeks, *The First Urban Christians: the Social World of the Apostle Paul* (New Haven, CT: Yale University Press, 1983), Philip Esler, *Community and Gospel in Luke-Acts: the Social and Political Motivations of Lucan Theology* (Cambridge: Cambridge University Press, 1987) and Raymond F. Collins, *The Birth of the New Testament: the Origin and Development of the First Christian Generation* (New York, NY: Crossroad Publishing, 1993). A more specific field is admirably introduced by Jane Gardner, *Family* and Familia *in Roman Law and Life* (Oxford: Clarendon Press, 1998) and by A. Jensen, *God's Self-confident Daughters: Early Christianity and the Liberation of Women* (Leuven: Peeters, 1997).

Where to begin?
John Ashton, *The Religion of Paul the Apostle.*

Chapter 3

JESUS OF NAZARETH: PORTRAITS OF A SAVIOUR

By writing first about Paul and then about the gospels, we appear to take a backward step. It seems more natural to regard accounts of Jesus as a primitive tradition that Paul inherited later. In a way, that is true. Paul knew at least some anecdotes and sayings that were circulating before the formation of the existing gospels. However, to read what now survives is to enter a world of subsequent and wide-ranging reflection. We observe in the gospels a tendency that permanently marked Christianity's self-understanding. The momentum of its development was governed by a persistent desire to revisit the scenes of its origin. The life of Jesus, his temporal existence, always formed the basis of belief; but the further that life receded from view, the more it invited scrutiny.

Paul had begun the process of connecting memory with reflection. Jesus, vividly present throughout his preaching, was flesh and blood as well as a transcendent 'Christ'. Faith, Paul stressed, was more than faith in an idea. The gospels, however, provided a more tangible anchor for what had remained, in Paul's case, a leap of the mind beyond the visible. Amid their pictorial detail, they were equally essays in symbolism and transcendence; but it is hard to imagine Christians taking the path they did, without the image of Jesus in Galilee and Jerusalem, crucified and risen, speaking with Thomas in the locked room, or cooking breakfast by the lakeside. Later Christians continued to read Paul, but with those images before them. In the previous chapter, I attempted to suspend that awareness, to picture a community without gospels – certainly without gospels as we know them: those of Matthew, Mark, Luke and John (and I hasten to warn the reader that my use of those familiar and convenient names will at no point take for granted the existence of an identifiable or single author). By the end of the first century, however,

Christians were applying Paul's ideas to a figure more readily available in their mind's eye. The result was an essay in portraiture that reached beyond Paul's imagination.

As soon as a 'gospel tradition' was under way – and here was another feature that predated Paul, since much of his work responded to it – issues with a long future quickly came to the surface; issues of unity, authority and the status of the Scriptures. Jesus was made to pass comment on a world larger than he had known himself. His recommendations began to modify the communities of Paul's immediate successors. The gospels also provided fresh materials for the depiction of Jesus as Saviour, and Christians acquired as a result a coherent and widely shared view of their incarnate God. They did so, however, by constantly laying on the table of discussion, like parts of a mosaic, fragments of narrative and reflection – rearranging them, allowing them to reflect new light on one another, transforming them in the process; all of them fragments drawn from a rich storehouse of early memories.

THE 'HISTORICAL' JESUS

What can we know about 'Jesus as he really was' – which is to say, what do the gospels tell us about him? We have to interpret their apparent detail with caution. We are understandably eager to discover as much as possible about the character and actions of Christianity's central figure. The 'quest for the historical Jesus' is impelled by curiosity as well as by faith. But we cannot allow ourselves to be impelled uncritically. The gospels provide vivid impressions of town and village life, of the rural cycle and the bustle of trade and administration. They depict the developing world of the Pharisees and of the synagogue – its popularity, its rituals of interpretation, its rivalries and guarded dignity. We witness the teeming pilgrimages of the Jewish festal calendar and sense Jerusalem's antiquity and grandeur. We are made aware of the mercantile and imperial setting within which the inhabitants of both Judaea and the more independent surrounding territories were accustomed to flourish or fail. Our modern experience can appreciate both the advantages and the harsh injustices of domination by a great yet foreign power. We find unforgettable portraits – the learned and cautious Nicodemus, the volatile but generous Zacchaeus, the reticent centurion and the eager woman of Samaria. We gain access, it seems, to the society with which Jesus was familiar, and the fact that the gospel account tallies with other evidence reassures us that the depiction of Jesus himself deserves credence. His trade as a carpenter, the simplicity and forcefulness of his achievements as a healer and teacher, his distaste for the scrupulous observance of the Pharisees – all bear the hallmarks of his Galilean environment: warm-heartedness and practicality, spiritual intensity, charismatic leadership and a vigorous independence.

But another curiosity has been at work in those texts, antecedent to our own. 'Who do people say I am?' Jesus is supposed to have asked. Those words – destined to hang for ever in the Christian air – draw us into another landscape of contested opinions and beliefs. In the gospel texts themselves, Jesus seems to be content with the humble (though historically resonant) title, 'the son of man'. Herod thinks he might be the slaughtered Baptist John, returned from the dead. God, presented as a voice from the sky, corroborates a transcendent view and establishes a crucial relation: 'You are my beloved son.' Mark's gospel hints in this way at a range of possible answers, adding phrases like 'the holy one of God' and 'the son of God'. The line of thought reaches its climax in Jesus's final confrontation with the high priest: 'Are you the anointed one, the son of the blessed?' to which Jesus replies, 'I am.' Mark was eager to press his earlier question on his own audience: 'And you? Who do you say I am?' Peter is made to answer on behalf of every devotee: Jesus is indeed the anointed one, the Messiah. A choice was to be made; a response was demanded.

The quest for the historical Jesus must start with that demand. One cannot pare away reflection in the hope of finding 'facts'. To think otherwise is to risk an impoverished scepticism or to misjudge the genuine unity and self-conscious purpose of each surviving text. The clearest 'truth' we can learn from the gospels is that Jesus was a person who had to be taken seriously. He had been unavoidable in his impact. Nothing other than vividness of personality can explain the actual existence of the gospels, even though they proceeded to present that personality in traditional terms. In addition to their portrayal of Jesus, the gospels provide narratives of conversion, of surrender to the message of a striking preacher. The narratives may be embellished and weighted, but the initial shock of coming face to face with Jesus, a shock difficult to articulate but impossible to ignore, lies at the root of the literary process. The gospels offer us, therefore, a combined impression of character, anecdote and reflection. With the passage of time, it became easier to present that impression in narrative form, since it was less likely to be challenged by living memory. But the figure of Jesus was consciously and carefully constructed. It revealed in symbolic rather than descriptive form what his life and teaching were thought to imply.

So, we cannot regard the gospels as mere biographies. In addition to their crafted symbolism, they are imbued with a sense of the future. They do not achieve closure but point beyond themselves. To read a gospel is to be led out of Galilee, out of Jerusalem, into the church community of a later day. The huddled timidity hinted at in portrayals of the disciples after Jesus's death was transformed into confident and increasingly widespread proclamation of their belief in his resurrection. Luke was the most assured in achieving that transition, but the other evangelists were comparably expectant. Once one recognizes the quality, one is led to see each gospel as an essay in possibility. The argument is not linear but describes moments of commitment that invite the reader to face afresh the possibility of other choices; choices that are at the same time rejected. There is a constant sense of 'Where do we go from here?' Moreover, to help readers find their bearings and empathize with the 'right choice' (for 'orthodoxy' itself was born of this experience), each incident and each personality (especially the personality of Jesus himself) points beyond the frame of the text, evoking antecedents and models that would have automatically come to mind among men and women reared in the Jewish biblical tradition.

The symbols used in this enterprise are extraordinary in their range. They are also to some degree contradictory. Attempts to prove otherwise have not been guided by sound textual or historical methodology. One cannot believe all this at once, most of all because that was not the intention of the gospel writers in the first place. Even though they agreed that Jesus was significant, and even though they rehearsed a shared store of anecdotes, they argued (either with one another or successively) about the way in which that significance should be explained. If one is looking for consistency, it resides more in the motives of the observers than in the declared character of the man they observed. Although they varied in their solutions to what we might call the crisis of engagement – the shock of coming face to face with Jesus – they agreed about the quality of the shock itself. Many of those first touched by Jesus, whose changes of heart and intensified religious commitment take solid form in the gospel accounts, seem to have felt that a problem, an inadequacy, an estrangement in their lives had suddenly been rendered powerless by the presence of this man. He appeared to guarantee, by his personal authority, access to a new life, a new order of being, a release from time itself.

MODELS FROM THE PAST

How might one best describe such authority and power? The different gospel writers, drawing on different traditions and addressing different audiences, seem to have made a choice between available models of the authoritative and the powerful. Jesus, in Luke's account, does exactly that in relation to his cousin John. Here, he says, was no reed shaken in the wind, no man in fine garments, but a prophet – indeed, 'more than a prophet'. Just as Jesus stretches the available typology, so in relation to Jesus himself the gospel writers took the traditional images of Jewish authority and extrapolated beyond them in an attempt to encompass the apparent immensity of this Galilean.

Tradition has inclined us to focus first on the title 'Messiah'. Even at the time, there was debate as to what the title meant. A notion of kingship was commonly involved, but some emphasized or included a prophetic or a priestly role. The Messiah could also be a hidden figure and even suffer death. An honest reading of the gospels forces us to admit that, in the passages we can trust as history, Jesus was reluctant to accept such labels. Assertions to the contrary show that interpretation had already been built into the narrative. Jesus simply reflected attitudes prevalent in his time and place, involving no necessary claim to be the Messiah, let alone divine. The charismatic enthusiasts of Galilean Judaism were prepared to claim 'sonship' of God their 'father'. Yet Mark and the other evangelists made the title of Messiah, as the embodiment and instrument of God's justice, a doorway through which Christians could be led to a fuller range of exalted assertions. Their Messiah enjoyed a special intimacy with God. By the time John wrote the famous prologue to his gospel – 'In the beginning was the Word' – divinity affected not merely the dignity but the very nature of Jesus.

To call Jesus Messiah was to raise the question of the 'kingdom' (whether 'kingdom of heaven' or 'kingdom of God'). Was he – was any Messiah? – the herald or creator of a new social order? The so-called 'parables of the kingdom' are noteworthy, not only for their rural realism, but also for their indifference to grand notions of power and victory. They render inappropriate any question of political timing or political intrigue. The notion of 'kingdom', potentially strong in its social implications, was in essence spiritual. Its immediacy, its 'closeness', resided in a redefinition of inner experience. Some asked at the time whether the kingdom of God, as Jesus understood it, would arrive with dramatic suddenness, or whether they faced a long wait, during which a lasting community would be built with slow pain. We can see that debate circling the word 'kingdom', inevitably rendered ambiguous by the subsequent death of Jesus (and by the failure of Jewish rebels in the face of Roman autocracy). An optimistic zeal may have been current, even among Jesus's followers. We have the bold request for status voiced by the mother of James and John, the rash courage of the sword-wielding disciple in Gethsemane, and the question whether Jesus would 'restore the kingdom'. But those aspirations were set in a different light by Jesus's cautious and enigmatic replies. His association with Galilee would have made them paradoxical, since the region was a notorious refuge for guerrillas and subversives (and, in later rabbinic tradition, synonymous with undisciplined enthusiasm and careless attention to the Law). Rebellion, however, and a political interpretation of the Messiah's role are on the whole rejected in the surviving gospels. Since their view of matters for the most part post-dated the Jewish revolt of 66–69, that rejection represents a special judgement on those events, alluded to in several passages. It was not a view restricted to Christians. Although violent and subversive hopes were revived among the Jews – first, in the Diaspora, in 115 and then, within Palestine, in the 130s (the Bar Kochba revolt) – not all Jews resented Roman policy. By the end of the second century, most were willing to see themselves enfolded within the Roman system (enjoying, at least in Palestine, a limited degree of judicial and administrative independence). So the gospels, in this respect, reflected attitudes familiar to some Jewish contemporaries.

Willingness to see Jesus as 'one of the prophets' (like his cousin John) and to call him 'Lord' adds to our understanding. Some Jews of the period thought of the prophetic age as having ended – hence the pointedness of saying that John the Baptist was 'more than a prophet'. Yet the piety of Galilean peasants (so Josephus assures us approvingly) accepted that God's voice could still be heard, his inspiration felt and his power made visible. To think of Jesus in 'prophetic' terms, therefore, was not to indulge in a wishful conservatism. The same readiness to keep open that pathway to the Spirit of God continued to characterize many Christian communities in the future. As for the term 'Lord', *Kurios*, it was considered, as a common form of deference, particularly apposite to wonder-workers and teachers. However, more exalted – indeed, divine – connotations, such as we observe in Mark, and which Matthew, Luke and John developed, had equal support in Jewish tradition; and Paul had already made 'the Lord Christ', the anointed *Kurios*, virtually Jesus's proper name. What the gospels provided, by way of further sophistication, was an image of the Messiah designed to counter false hopes. That in turn allowed the title, especially in its 'peaceful' and 'interior' forms, to enfold (and thus reinterpret) more original but potentially more ambiguous features of Jesus's life.

Among them was Jesus the wonder-worker. Wonders in the gospels are proof of God's special favour, and even of divinity. There was also Jesus the sufferer, ultimately identified with the 'suffering servant' of *Isaiah* – an association made possible because Jesus was indeed misunderstood, opposed and persecuted, and then (worst of all) inexplicably defeated through a cruel execution. Similarly hounded Christians, in the decades that followed, found here a model to imitate, an experience that gave meaning to their own misfortunes and encouraged them to bolder disdain. *Hebrews* and *1 Clement* make that vividly clear. Earlier figures, like the 'Teacher of Righteousness' at Qumran, had founded movements, fought against enemies, demanded loyalty and left their followers grieving if not outraged at their death. Now, in the gospel account, with reflective hindsight, such experience fed directly the notion of what a Messiah might be. That skill set in train a lasting paradox for Christianity. Believers were invited to admire a man of initiative and power, whom even the winds and the waves obeyed, but also a man who was the object of other people's destructive antagonism. The tension between Jesus the chosen son and Jesus the rejected victim was central to the task of relating the divine and the human within him, a task that came to dominate the portrayal of the Christian Saviour. We can attribute to Mark and his immediate sources the original interpretation of the sacrificial meal, the 'last supper', which bridged the otherwise problematic gap between the physical failure of Jesus – the breaking of his body and the shedding of his blood – and the experience of victory enjoyed by his followers – the reality of his resurrection. Where Mark led, Matthew followed with more reflective detail. Thus the eucharist, as it was to become, brought about for believers a divine and triumphant presence amid human division and mortality. Bread and wine signalled fellowship and vitality but also brought to mind the fragility and brevity of human life. There was, finally, an atmosphere of postponement that was equally pathetic in a technical sense. If this was what 'kingdom' was now to mean – this ceremony of reminiscence, companionship and temporary weakness – then the freedom promised by Jesus, the 'salvation' or 'redemption', was obviously yet to be achieved. So the structure and atmosphere of the Christian community flowed, as in Paul, from the interpretations placed upon Jesus's life.

Messiah, king, prophet and wonder-worker: such qualities have, at various stages of Christian history, been combined to form the figure of Jesus the critic, the man who challenged the cultic and moral expectations of Judaism in his day. However, we have to be careful that the range of emphases in the texts does not encourage us to make too partisan a choice between them.

There is, first, the view that Jesus set himself up in opposition to a false legalism (unjustly attributed to the Pharisees) and to certain aspects of Temple worship (as it was alleged to have been practised at the time). Yet he clearly did not reject the Law outright, which would have been inconceivable, even in Galilee. To understand aright the 'charism' of Jesus, we have to recognize that it operated within a tradition of holiness and admiration. He and religious teachers like him were never dramatically subversive of the existing order. However, he may well have 'cleansed' the Temple, vigorously disrupting the commercial activity of its outer court. Some have regarded the act as the quintessential demonstration of his mission – the eschatological declaration of a new and prayerful intimacy with God – and the first immediate provocation that led to his trial and execution.

Second, we have the Jesus who embraced the constituency of the outcast, the alien and the impure, showing more than a simple regard for the 'ordinary person'. He seems on occasion to have qualified the need for strict Sabbath observance and ritual cleanliness. He may, in doing so, have simply asserted with sympathetic clarity the perfectly sensible scale of values in such matters defended by the stipulations of the Law. He is made to do so, however, in the name of a new order that rendered obsolete the anxieties and solutions portrayed by some as central to the Jewish covenant. Much of that reflects the later prejudices of the evangelists. If Jesus did attach priority to personal honesty and interior commitment, the gesture is used in the gospels to undermine a glib trust in visible observance.

Third, we have Jesus the teacher – the orator at ease in the synagogue; the exegete who interpreted the Scriptures with startling and straightforward novelty; the master who formed chosen disciples to become masters in their turn. There is no reason to suppose that he did not play such a role, teaching (as Mark put it) 'with authority'. But later prejudices are again evident. Jesus's supposed opposition to the Pharisees is designed to warn the gospel reader not to think of him as a 'rabbi' without careful qualification – a warning that reflected later clashes between Christians and their fellow Jews.

Fourth, it seems possible to identify subtle, inward shifts of attitude and terminology. They appear to affect in particular the interpretation of kinship and virtue (paralleled by the belief that the 'kingdom of heaven' or the 'kingdom of God' was 'within'). A new family was to be created, a new definition of parent and sibling, bound together not by blood but by dedication to 'the will of God'. That family would be recognized by the mutual affection of its members. 'Who is my neighbour?' asks the rich young man. In his strikingly illustrated reply – the parable of the 'good Samaritan' – Jesus reaches well beyond the expected boundaries of social responsibility. And the 'sins of the fathers' could no longer be either a burden or an excuse. Purity, that essential Jewish virtue, was to denote an interior, individual demand.

All those available models, with their varied impact, had to be measured finally, in Christian eyes, against the figure of Jesus raised from the dead. Much has been made of supposed parallels within other religious systems of the time; but we are dealing with more than the epiphany of some anthropomorphic god. The gospel writers did not invent the notion of resurrection, which was shared by the majority of Jews. It did not set Christians apart, except (as with other Jews) from the Sadducees. The specific contribution of the synoptic gospels resides in their exploration of bodily resurrection. Their imagery, consequently, gave fuller colour to Paul's portrait of the cosmic Saviour. Grand tableaux like the 'transfiguration' of Jesus on a 'high mountain' or (if we include Luke's *Acts*) his 'ascension' were subtly combined with moments of ambiguity, as when intimates failed to recognize him returned from the dead – Mary in the garden, two disciples on the road to Emmaus or his apostles gathered in Jerusalem and by the lakeside in Galilee. When we come to John's account, the harbingers of transcendent glory are more evident: the heavens would open; angels would 'ascend and descend on the son of man'; in Jesus, God had been glorified and would be glorified again. John also had a clear sense of the connection between Jesus's 'going' and the 'coming' of the Spirit: the resurrection released the Spirit of God upon the Christian community. And John (compared with Paul) shifted attention from an awareness of power to the enjoyment of understanding.

Eventually, therefore, the resurrection acquired a furnace-like intensity. It represented an act of faith whereby sense could be made of Jesus's suffering and failure. Within the gospels themselves, it was allowed to reflect its light backwards: earlier experiences were imbued with a reassuring prescience. The 'transfiguration' is a case in point. Mark, Matthew and Luke all describe how Jesus, as he prayed with Peter, James and John, was 'changed' – *metamorphōthē*, as they put it – so that his face, in Matthew's words, 'shone like the sun'. This ability of Jesus to be 'different', something 'other', was the crucial element, and affected descriptions of his post-mortem appearances. In the earlier account, he stood translucent on the boundary between human, material experience and the world of divinity and spirit. Given such a precedent, the specifically post-mortem anecdotes in the gospels are ultimately unsurprising. The believing writers have already dissolved the problematic distinction between the human figure and the divine: they have become fused into a single being, the risen Christ, who passes between the worlds of mortality and transcendence as easily as he passes through a Jerusalem door. The resurrection explained, therefore, as did the eucharist, God's paradoxical ability to allow his son to suffer. It was destined to create a problem, however, because it gave priority to a heavenly and remote Jesus, raising doubts as to whether so triumphant a figure could ever have been genuinely human.

TEXT AND COMMUNITY

This 'modelling' of Jesus did not follow a simple progression. The development of models cannot be matched exactly with the development of texts. While sophisticated reflections, like those in John's gospel, might suggest a later phase, the task of presenting Jesus as this or that type of leader or exemplar had already inspired the anecdotes and formulae predating the gospel texts. The images of Messiah, wonder-worker, teacher or critic were overlaid one upon another under the pressure of competition and debate.

A key to understanding such complexities lies in the relation between image and community. Behind each portrait of Jesus lay a particular group of believers. The endurance of conflicting or contrasting conceptions of the Saviour depended on the endurance of jealously guarded traditions in this group or that. Portrayal took social form. Only within a later, more homogeneous Christian community was there a shared vision of what Jesus meant, of what 'manner of man' he was. Early interpretations were precisely that – interpretations. The gospels available to us today – Matthew, Mark, Luke and John – have always tempted readers with access to all four at once (an option that became available only with time) to embark upon the misleading and dangerous enterprise of synthesis; and this in spite of their mixed sources and their mutual criticism. Given the complexity of the information they supply, a synthesis was bound to be unjust and to reflect the anxieties of later ages. Jesus the critic of the Law, Jesus the lover of the lowly, Jesus the rabbi, Jesus the master of the inner spirit – all such portrayals have come and gone in Christian history, telling us more about interpreters than about the figure they claim to respect. Even when the four 'canonical' gospels came to be read as a unit, by Christians more removed from their Jewish roots, their de facto diversity, so easily overlooked, inevitably provided ammunition for a number of conflicting agenda.

Nevertheless, we must be careful not to take too simple a view of the processes involved. Literary texts can challenge, as well as create or confirm, a community's self-image. Evangelists may have wished to criticize the values of their associates. Nor is debate always limited to acrimonious rivalry. We have to allow for less explicit but deeper doubt. The gospels are rightly described as documents of faith, but faith is often asserted in the aftermath of obscurity. 'Are you the one who is to come?' ask the disciples of the Baptist, 'or are we looking for someone else?' The answer reported by Matthew and Luke was precisely an attempt at assurance. Such logic is endemic in the texts. It governs the scepticism of Thomas, the hesitancy at Emmaus, the caution of Peter at the lakeside, 'not daring to ask him who he was'. The traditions that had gathered around Jesus remained at their heart problematic. Later critics knew well how to touch that nerve, how to ridicule so humiliated a god. Doubt, therefore, and the particular assurances by which it was countered, were in themselves a force behind the momentum of portrayal.

It is also possible that Jesus had not been able to bring himself into sharp enough focus in the eyes of his admirers – indeed, this may have been his genius. Apart from his gathering of disciples, no one portrayed him as an organizer. He inspired loyalty and formulated ideals, but he left to others the task of defining the community best calculated to maintain that loyalty and protect those ideals. If he was unique, his singularity may have resided, not so much in his having acquired over time a broad definition acceptable to all Christians, but rather in some original vagueness and ambiguity. The puzzles and choices revealed by the gospel writers could have sprung from the fact that he bore no resemblance to other religious leaders in first-century Palestine, or that he combined many elements of leadership. The most insidious of the false trails that beset the quest for the historical Jesus – the desire to present him as he 'really' was – is a readiness to restrict him to one category of religious behaviour – the zealot, the teacher the worker of miracles. Later history shows clearly enough how difficult it was to be precise in such matters.

Debate proceeded, nevertheless, and two processes were thereby set in train. What Jesus actually did – the exorcisms, the cures, the forgiveness of sin, the moral exhortation, the bold analysis of sacred texts, the criticism of established religious authorities – was eventually conceived as a single story. Later believers felt that they possessed a 'synoptic' vision, by which (in this case) three texts (Mark, Matthew and Luke) were thought to present a consistent narrative, which could then provide a basis for the gospel 'canon'. The original proclamation of each gospel, however, was designed to steer its audience through a labyrinth of choices. Taken by themselves, they are otherwise unintelligible. Those reading or hearing the separate accounts were expected to associate Jesus with a current tradition or pattern of religious behaviour, or to acknowledge that he had chosen to adopt it. And the later synthesis had to take account of that original tendentiousness. The grander and more complex figure of the Saviour had to appear presaged by the gospels, so that the later portrait gathered its threads from an earlier web of possibilities. The gospels mark neither the beginning nor the end of that process of interpretation. They were forced to take their cue from work already done, made their contemporary bid for acceptance and then flowed together (in other people's hands) to support an integrated portrait that the original evangelists might not have found either recognizable or convincing.

Another development complicates matters. Even though a gospel might reflect the attitudes of an enclosed or embattled community, often supported by an embittered estrangement from non-Christian Jews, there came a time when self-righteousness and expectation could survive only if the group attempted to win others to its point of view. Exclusive possession of the truth came to depend on the confirmation afforded by converts. Not all religious people isolated by their own exaltation of spirit will follow such a path; but most will at least reach out to replenish or stabilize their community of faith. We have seen the process at work in the world of Paul. Many gospel texts — acting, here again, as critics of their own milieu — betray the same missionary zeal, or rather the argued conviction that such zeal is demanded. From confirming a narrow self-identity, they moved to break down the boundaries of communities and to create the wider world within which the integration of their various emphases could take place.

I have adopted the view that Mark's was the first of our surviving gospels, and that it provides us with our earliest insight into a 'gospel community'. (The *Gospel of Thomas* may preserve equally ancient traditions but was written in its present form later.) Matthew and Luke adapted Mark's text, and may have been helped in doing so by a collection of sayings, oral or written, but now lost. Much ink has been spilled in the search for this 'source' — hence given the German name *Quelle*, or 'Q' for short. It is, virtually by definition, unavailable: yet many scholars have happily speculated, not only about its contents and character, but also about its social setting and independent impact. From a strictly historical point of view, the effort reflects an unavoidably frustrating and possibly dangerous endeavour, built as it is around textual material that may never have existed and that we do not require in order to explain what we do have at hand.

Mark's gospel has also been thought of as presenting Peter's point of view. We need not take the tradition literally; but Peter's reputation did call for later reinforcement, in texts that were not always accepted as orthodox. Mark's has also been thought of as a dramatic gospel, heralding the subversion of the old Jewish order and the imminent return of Jesus in apocalyptic glory.

His Jesus is a stunning wonder-worker, exorcist and healer, who foretells and symbolizes the end of an age. The account is certainly breathless, charged with expectation and a sense of triumph; but Mark's narrative of inheritance, reform and destiny is far from straightforward, and its complexity is directly related to the audience he had in mind.

His attitude was one of openness, in contrast to the caution and anxiety of the other evangelists. He emphasized the access to Jesus enjoyed by the despised, the impure, the alien – although he never disguised the presence in the Christian circle of the relatively prosperous and prominent. He had to cater for a diverse community: for Jewish Christians, for those who admired Judaism generally and for those outside the Jewish sphere; for the less privileged but also for the well placed. We do not hear in his gospel the small voice of a small group. By the middle decades of the first century, the undefeated scepticism of many Jews and the acceptance of the Christian message among the gentiles were firmly established features. Mark was prepared to live in Paul's world – indeed, he did so: he may have written his gospel in Rome; certainly beyond the confines of Palestine and Syria. Just as, in his account, we are thrown into the life of Jesus in mid-stream, so we catch sight of a Christianity already on the move. Even its patterns of eucharistic worship were echoed in Mark's account of miraculous feeding. As at the last supper, Jesus 'spoke a blessing, broke the loaves, and gave them to his disciples'. In his human form, he could earth the vivid lightning of Paul's cosmic Christ.

Mark's Jesus was also a prophet, whose preaching demanded new standards of behaviour and whose suffering betrayed the reluctance of others to live up to them. Those who submitted to his sway, therefore, could expect cruel opposition. Mark's Christians were not, however, beleaguered in a hostile world: rather, they were coming to terms with the rejection of Jesus by other Jews and they embraced with confidence a wider pastorate among the gentiles. Jesus's triumph was not limited to vindictive retribution but declared in universal terms. It was also to be a triumph for each individual believer. An arc of logic curves from the opening echoes of the prophecies in *Isaiah* through the ministry of John and the experience of baptism to the demand for repentance and faith. The transformation of the self would not be the automatic outcome of ritual observance but a change based on an inner shift of aspiration. For that reason, the message that 'time has reached its fulfilment' had to be immediately available to those outside the boundaries of the Jewish dispensation. To share in the new kingdom, one had only to recognize its presence – a species of enrolment that was potentially without limits but also based on individual perception; an almost secret achievement.

Mark had already understood the inseparable connection between personal commitment and universal destiny, between faith and salvation; and he set in place a paradigm that would at once inspire and frustrate every future generation of Christians.

When we turn to Matthew and Luke, we enter a more constrained and defensive world. It is also later – later than the tragedy of Jewish defeat in the war of 66–69. The divisions between the new sect and the ancient faith had become more marked and more embittered, especially in communities still close to the Jewish heartland. Preoccupation with those divisions was therefore more intense, a trend reflected in Luke's account of debates in Jerusalem. We cannot be surprised, therefore, that Matthew's gospel adopts a specific and calculated attitude towards the growing conflict. His basic message was that Jesus brought to completion the heritage of his community. He made sense of the Jewish past, as Matthew saw it. The analogy with Paul is arresting; but a difference of emphasis shows that Paul's view of Jewish history was neither exhaustive nor unchallenged.

In a way, Matthew had taken a stand against novelty. His portrait of Jesus as a sober and authentic interpreter of the Jewish Law represented a peculiar caution and reflected tension between his own affiliates and the Pharisees (who were too similar and too close for comfort). Perhaps as a result, his gospel presents a more brightly lit but more tightly articulated picture of a 'Jesus community' than we find in Mark. In the 'sermon on the mount' especially, every aspect of mutual responsibility is explored, so exhaustively as to make its fulfilment inevitably the achievement of a few. In later canonical collections, Matthew was placed first and was the most often quoted – perhaps because he provided hallowed and explicit antecedents to the developing structures of Christian communities.

Brotherhood was his own community's hallmark: shared concern and independence from, if not indifference to, the surrounding society. Brotherhood, however, now reached beyond family and kin. In this gospel, we witness the shift from household to association, where shared commitment to belief superseded loyalty to one's relatives. Matthew was the only evangelist to use (in a gospel) the inclusive term *ekklēsia*, which brings his believers closer to the traditional Roman vocabulary of burial and banqueting societies, the *collegia* and *sodalitates*. Social relations and the sanctions protecting them were based on mediation and forgiveness. Authority was vested chiefly in the 'good scribe' (for not all scribes were reprehensible), a man of action and missionary zeal. Believers were most accurately described as 'disciples'. Stability, therefore, was the overriding value. The Matthaean community was a *beth midrash*, a 'house of instruction', focused on the acquisition and formation of new members.

The 'Lucan community' is reflected as much in *Acts* as in Luke's gospel, and the urban and Hellenistic atmosphere of the later work can influence our reading of the earlier. We cannot assume, however, that either text was addressed generally to a non-Jewish world. There is a universal tenor to Luke's account (his genealogy of Jesus reaches back to Adam), but a broad message can still be addressed to a narrow group. Luke's Jesus cares for a 'little flock' and exhorts them to a courage they have yet to possess. What most undermines their assurance is a degree of separation from their fellow Jews. Luke opens his account of the public ministry of Jesus by describing an address that he gave in the synagogue at Nazareth, which was promptly followed by an attempt to lynch him. The anecdote was the epitome of Luke's convictions. The immediate audience of his gospel, if it were to make sense of the story, could not have been even extensively gentile. The group's chief bond may have been its exclusion from local synagogues. Luke catered specifically for their pain in his treatment of the Temple. His measured respect for a place of cult that was now (by the time of his writing) destroyed could at once guarantee a reassuring heritage and compensate for a recent loss.

We need not deny, however, that Luke and Paul were addressing similar audiences. Inspired by a Jewish tradition that they were also prepared to modify, they were rooted in the urban world of Hellenistic culture. Setting was not all that contributed to their sense of isolation, but it provided (in Luke's eyes) an important range of social and economic opportunities for the working out of a Christian commitment. The centralized and moralistic polity created by Augustus and his family had begun to crumble at the hands of more brutal men. Survival within the framework of the old *pax Romana* called for the infusion of a new spirit into the wealthy cities that the vision of Augustus had helped to foster – a new identity, new patterns of mutual support. Luke's gospel depicted, therefore, in symbolic form a pattern of social engagement that would break down barriers, not only between Jew and non-Jew but also between potentially antagonistic sectors of the typical urban community. On the one hand, he presented readers with an intimate world of shared meals, an image reinforced by Isaiah's transcendent image of the 'messianic banquet'. On the other hand, he portrayed Jesus, in his Nazareth address, as a champion of the destitute – a clear message to the 'middling sort' of the Pauline communities and another attack on barriers that had long been taken for granted.

The Early Christian Centuries

Luke's Christians, therefore, had moved one step away from their seed-beds in Galilee and Jerusalem. Operating in a larger and more varied world, they were by necessity dedicated to a less dramatic questioning of their environment. The salvation of society would be achieved by the reformation of the individual. Prayer and renunciation would inform the heart, succeeding to the honour of sacrifice in the Jewish Temple. And the enduring sense of debt to the past (appropriate to a man of Luke's historical temper) would more readily embrace the prospect of future effort and a less imminent end.

A different mood pervades the gospel of John, which seems to have been written for an even smaller group. It is not a 'synoptic' gospel, and John's profoundly reflective account has been explained by a late date (our earliest surviving Christian document is a second-century fragment of this text). However, there is every sign that his portrayal of Jesus was based on early and partly independent sources; and his often divergent account reinforces the view that the loyalty of Christians and the social forms that loyalty gave rise to varied from the outset. We should not imagine, therefore, that the fourth gospel was addressed to an elevated group of mystical ascetics. Such a view has been encouraged by the treatment of the 'Word' in its famous prologue and by its profound discourses and rich symbols – the shepherd, the vine, the path. But it is a mistake to think that such intensity and concentration could not have gone hand in hand with a recent experience of Jesus's company. The gospel is full of drama as well as meditative calm, and peopled with vivid characters.

The great prologue, in fact, provides an immediate clue to the nature of the Johannine community. The way Jesus is presented 'in the beginning' (echoing *Genesis*) reflects the self-understanding of the writer and his audience. Jesus 'comes down', only to 'return', to 'go back', to be 'raised up'; and he comes to 'his own', a chosen group that will eventually share in his return to God. 'His own', therefore, could recognize in their social circumstance a reflection of the distance between the Jesus who was 'from above' and the antithetical 'world' that enveloped them. The immediate cause of their estrangement was likely to have been expulsion from the synagogue, which Jesus is made to foretell. The resulting pain is more intense than in Luke, and the strategy demanded, the stark choice to be made, is more forbidding and divisive. John's well-known antagonism towards 'the Jews' (creating already an artificial and misleading contrast) may have been strengthened by an enduring sense among those expelled that they had lost what they had deemed most precious, most peculiar to themselves.

In addition to the overarching theory of Jesus's coming and going, John creates a series of confrontations that highlight the distinction between his community and the society around it. John the Baptist represented a mild but important threat – from those who interpreted baptism differently and saw Jesus only as a prophet. The dialogue between Jesus and Pilate allowed John to make political distinctions (probably of earlier relevance than those in Matthew or Luke); to evoke a sovereignty alternative to that of Caesar, 'not of this world', but equally at odds with the anarchy and violence of Barabbas. But the chief confrontation is with Nicodemus – not a man of secretive faith but symbolic of another community that, while ready to acknowledge a significance in Jesus, was incapable of understanding what it was to be born 'from above'. Alienation from other Jews is always present in such dialogues; but no less obvious are the divisions among those who admire Jesus. John brooked no compromise or obscurity. His circle was represented by the man born blind, who, seeing for the first time, boldly affirmed before the Pharisees, 'If this man did not come from God, he could not do anything.' He reaches that level of confidence precisely in his confrontation with prejudice and ignorance.

The chief issue facing the Johannine community, therefore, was whether one should keep one's loyalty secret. Public witness was an obligation, but the necessary courage fostered an inner intensity. John's Christians were eager to convince others; but they were also withdrawn, and felt that they had already experienced the salvation of the new age. They were most clearly marked off by their interpretation of baptism, which they associated with God's Spirit (and therefore with birth 'from above'); a Spirit that stood not so much for wisdom as for truth – an important concept for John. Truth, in its turn, brought freedom. And because Jesus was the 'Word', he could be thought of as speaking a word; a word that his followers were sworn to keep. They were made more than a brotherhood of disciples. John understood more deeply than Matthew the loving nature of their bond; a love that reflected the greater unity achieved in creation by the Word of God. The sense of privilege reflected in such a view, the note of affection, and the complexity and refinement of thought, would allow later gnostics to echo John in many ways. But his understanding of the Word affected Justin and Irenaeus more than those they opposed – a development I shall discuss shortly. John's Word was present at and instrumental in the creation – a notion entirely strange to most gnostics. 'All things came into being through him: apart from him, there came into being not a single thing.' And Jesus imparted to 'those who believed in his name' the ability to understand the nature of the cosmos and the role of the Word within it.

Those gospel communities were probably small and certainly not the only ones easing themselves, under the banner of Jesus, away from their Jewish contemporaries. Particularly elusive, in the surviving material, is the Christian community in Jerusalem, under the leadership of James, whom we met in the previous chapter, but who seem not to have produced a gospel of their own – certainly not one that was allowed to survive. This was, in a sense, the Pentecost community, the community left behind by Jesus risen from the dead and ascended into heaven: nervous about its 'difference' from the Jews around it, but made unavoidably public and visible by its novel interpretations of scripture and ritual. What makes all those communities important for us is the way they demonstrate the harnessing of texts to social ideals and the variety of ways in which one could do so. Paul and Luke betray the competitiveness involved; a propensity to fragmentation that was born of the very speed with which groups were distanced from the Palestinian heartland. As for those who stayed behind, John and (to a lesser extent) Matthew offer clues to their particular difficulties. Rivalry among the earliest Christians is exposed by Paul's description of Apollos and by Luke's reference to James as a challenger of Peter (and perhaps an example of the compromise that John abhorred). A written record, authenticated as a living witness to Jesus's life and focused perhaps on a leading disciple, could at once define a group and provide for its survival.

FROM GOSPELS TO 'THE GOSPEL'

So much for the arguments at work within the earliest gospels – their creative fusion of Jewish memories, their exploration of Jesus's personality, and the different emphases that characterized the groups that lay behind them. But there is much to be learned additionally from the preservation and transmission of the gospel texts themselves and from the ways they were gradually interrelated. From being disparate instruments of initially local debate, they became a single hallowed archive, providing in the eyes of later generations a coherent basis for order and belief. This is what we mean by 'the formation of the canon'. How was that transition achieved and what was its effect?

The notion that the gospel narratives, together with other Christian documents, could be made to form a whole was encouraged by the integration of the Christian churches. As they became (very slowly) a single 'church', they more readily appealed to a single body of authoritative writings, which they could use to express and justify their developing self-awareness. Individual gospels thus shook off whatever association they may once have had with a narrow group and joined forces with other parts of what came to be called the 'New Testament'. The resulting corpus – for a long time, far from stable in its content – began to underpin broader reflection throughout (and beyond) the Roman world. Seeking to deepen and enrich their understanding of their faith, succeeding generations of believers appealed to that heritage with increasing subtlety. The appeal depended, however, on the possibility of comparison, of bringing one text to bear upon another – which included a comparison with what could now be called, by contrast, the 'old' Testament. The resulting exegesis modified in its turn the texts upon which it claimed to depend. The collection as a whole thus came to reflect an attempt to sharpen and reshape not only the record of the earliest Christian experience but also the riches of the Jewish scriptural tradition.

The phrase we use to describe that process – the 'formation of the canon' – is misleadingly tidy: for the 'canon', the ostensibly single archive, took in fact a variety of forms. Some communities knew of and appealed to only a fraction of what was later thought of as the 'New Testament'. Others happily included texts that were later regarded as uncanonical (the most famous being a work called the *Shepherd*, which I shall discuss below and in the next chapter). Historians have long attached importance to the so-called 'Muratorian Fragment' – part of an eighth-century Italian manuscript published by Lodovico Muratori in 1740. It presents (in somewhat confused Latin) an obviously incomplete list of canonical Christian texts, together with some commentary on their origins and character. Familiar portions of the modern New Testament are omitted (for example, *1* and *2 Peter*); other texts are included (the *Apocalypse of Peter*, for example, but not the *Shepherd*). Some scholars are prepared to believe that its probably Greek original was drawn up, perhaps in Rome, at the end of the second or at the beginning of the third century; but others continue to argue for a fourth-century date. In no way can we regard the Muratorian Fragment, whatever its date, as a sudden, universal or binding declaration. On the contrary, it only serves to prove how slowly agreement was reached on issues of authenticity and how varied the agreement could be.

Several factors made the development of the canon gradual. Small combinations of Christian documents were compared – 'read together', as it were – differently at different times and in different places. It would have taken decades to gather the texts into larger collections; and the earlier and more tentative associations offer comment on the piecemeal and geographically varied distribution of early documents. However, an appeal to more than one text undoubtedly gave additional force to a writer's reflections. Clement of

Rome and Ignatius of Antioch, for example, refer to Paul's writings in some detail, bearing witness to the continuity of Pauline traditions, in the West as well as in the East, at the turn of the second century. Ignatius had also begun to develop a sense of 'the' Gospel, alluding briefly to both Matthew and John. There may be echoes of Matthew in the liturgical text known as the *Didachē*, written almost certainly in Syria, although exactly how early is open to dispute. At least as reported by Eusebius, there were similar echoes in the writings of Papias, bishop of Hieropolis, who died around 130. The *Shepherd*, as difficult to date as the *Didachē* but perhaps as early, shows an Italian familiarity with a range of material. The *Letter of James* was clearly a favourite of the author, Hermas; and there are at least recollections of (although no direct quotation from) the *Gospel of John*, the synoptic gospels more vaguely, and the Pauline *Letter to the Ephesians*.

So, in the period of the 'Apostolic Fathers' — that is, the heyday of those who were thought to have known the apostles — memory played as large a part as reading, and churchmen depended on oral as well as on written tradition. Clement and Ignatius are often, as we would see it, 'inaccurate' in their quotations and more familiar with phrases than with sentences. Papias prefers to comment on 'sayings' as the guarantee of a living testimony. Polycarp, bishop of Smyrna, gives a similar impression. He is richer in his use of the gospels and the apostolic letters, and looks back as an older man over the head of his mentor Ignatius. So, he recognizes the emergence of a longstanding textual tradition, but still mixes the written and the oral. Such sustained memory continued to feed the Christian mind, even after individual gospels had acquired their textual definition. Justin, using the word 'recollections', was obviously thinking of written records; but not until we reach *2 Clement*, in the later second century, do we find an unambiguous attempt to fuse the implications of actual texts — and even there, a memory of oral tradition is still evident.

With the passing of the generations, however, some Christians felt that oral tradition was no longer enough. We cannot explain that shift as mere bookishness, a scholarly concern for accuracy and preservation. In order to prove their authority authentic, church leaders needed to find in reputable texts a reflection — indeed, the origins — of their leadership. Their possession of and loyalty to a primitive record underpinned their claim to orthodox inheritance. They felt their hand additionally forced by the daring of thinkers who were ready to challenge their status. I shall discuss those challengers more fully in later chapters. Montanus, the great Phrygian prophet of the later second century, believed that fresh evidence of divine wisdom was constantly made available to the inspired Christian. Marcion, a native of Pontus in what is now northern Turkey (d. *c.* 160), rejected the Old Testament as a document unworthy of Christian attention, and was deeply suspicious of the gospels, throwing his weight in favour of Paul and undermining in the process many other bases of authority.

Yet even the more 'orthodox' students of the Scriptures were not always precise in their reference to the components of their canon. (I shall have more to say about all these figures later.) The earliest surviving Christian 'apologist', Aristides, allowed his defence of Christianity to stand upon philosophical argument alone. Justin (d. *c.* 165) displayed his knowledge of John and of the synoptic gospels more by paraphrase than by quotation, often alluding rather generally to the apostolic record. Athenagoras, a decade or so after Justin, still contented himself with unattributed words and phrases. When we come to more prolix theorists of the late second and early third centuries – Irenaeus and Tertullian, Clement and Origen – there is clearer evidence of system. Irenaeus, chiefly as a blow against gnostics, began to insist more formally on the coherence of Christian and Jewish Scriptures, and explicitly restricted gospel authority to the canonical four. (He bears witness, in the process, to an abundance of scriptural texts in the later second century as far west as Lyon.) Tertullian, on the other hand, continued to measure the canon against something greater and more ancient, which he called the *regula fidei*, 'the rule of faith', and which guaranteed the endurance of other traditions. (His delight in coining Latin words for Greek ideas produced our familiar word 'testament', which represented a shift from covenant to legacy and encouraged in the West a desire for a tighter and more exclusive corpus.) Clement of Alexandria was more ready to acknowledge the claims of different scriptural traditions, different senses of antiquity and value. Origen drew up a list of authoritative documents closer to what we would now regard as canonical, and was followed by Eusebius and Athanasius of Alexandria in the fourth century. But Eusebius was still reluctant to give his selection (which included the four gospels) any quasi-legal status, preferring to defend it by strictly historical evidence and widely received and longstanding opinion.

The Muratorian Fragment, therefore, whatever its date, can only be taken as a marker along the way. Harmony of interpretation was actually impeded by the popularity and proliferation of scriptural material. The production of texts reflected the varied interests of different regions and the texts themselves were written in different languages. It may be possible to improve our understanding of early practice by arguing backwards from later textual compilations. Any confident sense of order is almost certainly deceptive; but three separate enterprises usefully illustrate the processes involved. According to Luke in *Acts*, the term 'Christian' was first used in Antioch; and the Syrian church has bequeathed to us some of our earliest witnesses to the preservation of gospel texts: for what came to be known as the 'Old Syriac' version may have drawn upon material dating as far back as the middle years of the second century. The character of that Syriac tradition has to be deduced, however, from its later revisions – the fifth-century 'Peshitta' and the subsequent translations and editions by Philoxenus of Mabbug and Thomas of Heraclea. Contemporary with the Old Syriac, perhaps earlier, was the *Diatessaron* of Tatian, which harmonized the four gospels in a single text. It is striking that so original an example of Christian scholarship should have been by a Syrian whose orthodoxy did not fit neatly into a Greek mould. Having begun the work in Rome, Tatian carried it back to his native East and translated it from Greek into Syriac. A conflation of the gospels implies that there were gospels to conflate. (Tatian's single version opens with the first section of John, whose gospel provided him with a framework within which to place the synoptic accounts.) The various Syriac versions raise many problems – their relation, for example, to Greek antecedents and (in Tatian's case) to gnostic texts like the *Gospel of Thomas*. Yet they suggest that, by the middle of the second century, copies of the four canonical gospels were available to scholarly Christians and accorded equal authority.

Egypt presents us with a slightly different picture. It is hard to tell whether Paul's difficult colleague Apollos, originally from Alexandria, offers proof that Christianity had already gained so early a foothold in the city. Eusebius of Caesarea, writing at the turn of the fourth century, was forced to admit that a clear picture of the Egyptian church emerged only with the episcopate of Demetrius, less than a hundred years before his own time. What he also makes clear is that the Christian message had begun to reach well beyond the confines of Hellenistic, Greek-speaking culture: hence (perhaps as early as the late second century) the development of 'Coptic' Christian literature, which included gospel texts. ('Coptic', a word derived from a later Arabic equivalent, simply means 'Egyptian'.) Clement of Alexandria, writing at the turn of the third century, lamented the fact that Egypt in his day witnessed a bewildering variety of opinions and traditions. These are reflected in surviving additions to the gospel corpus – the *Gospel of the Egyptians*, the *Gospel of Truth*, the *Gospel of Thomas*, the *Gospel of Philip*. So we find in Egypt not only the careful preservation of older gospel texts but also a rash of new creations, the nature of which will call for more attention shortly.

The Latin text of the Bible, to come to our third endeavour, is inescapably associated nowadays with the name of Jerome. But Jerome was not responsible for the whole of the Vulgate. Indeed, in his own day, he was viewed as a disturbing revolutionary, too ready to rob worship of its familiar rendering. There reached back before him some two hundred years of Latin translation, the time of the so-called *Vetus Latina*. In spite of the fact that 'Latinisms' began to affect Christian writing in the western church from an early stage, Greek continued to be its chief literary language down to the time of Hippolytus in the third century. The earliest surviving Christian manuscript in Latin contains work by the Roman priest Novatian, martyred in the late 250s. Before him, however, came the towering figure of Tertullian. It is possible that Christian Latin experienced its first significant development not in Italy but in North Africa. The *Acts of the Scillitan Martyrs*, for example, composed there shortly after 180, imply established familiarity with a Latin text of the Pauline corpus. Marginally earlier but more obscure in its implications is a letter from Gaul reproduced by Eusebius (at the beginning of the fifth book of his *Church History*). Some of its Greek phrases may hint at Latin originals.

Those three scholarly enterprises – the Syrian, the Egyptian and the Latin – show how the geographical extent of Christianity's reach meant that the New Testament canon was inevitably constructed in a variety of ways. The same applies to a gradual shift in attitude towards the Jewish Scriptures. Both the writings of Paul and the gospel tradition were rooted in the Jewish past, but the first Christian writers had already put their own gloss on the ancient heritage. The *Gospel of John*, more than others, had been additionally belligerent. Clement of Rome's possibly earlier and certainly independent appeal to ancient Jewish models was not so hostile and reflected the extent to which a majority of Christians continued to formulate their religious practice in Jewish terms. Only with time did quotation from the Jewish Scriptures become more antagonistic in tone, asserting a new relation between the parent faith and its novel offspring. Yet use of the older texts also reflected the effort required to justify Christian literature's claim to respect. Too great a readiness to supersede the Jewish past could affect the stability of the Christian documents themselves, undermining their fulfilment of prophetic promise, and calling into question their sufficiency as keys to the meaning of salvation and to the proper order of the Christian community. Paradoxically, the increasing status of the gospels and of the letters of Paul made it all the more important to redefine the implications of the Old Testament, without (like Marcion) abandoning it altogether.

RESISTANCE TO CLOSURE

Nowhere was that paradox more painful than in the controversy over *gnōsis*. By showing (with time) an exclusive favour towards Matthew, Mark, Luke and John, those who favoured the establishment of a gospel canon asserted the belief that 'revelation' had come to a close. About Jesus, there was nothing more to be learned. Others, however, resisted that view. They did not always wish to displace earlier accounts, but they thought those accounts could be augmented. I described in the opening chapter how unwise it would be to take 'gnosticism' as a principle of coherence in early Christianity, and I shall have more to say about the reaction it provoked in the chapter that follows. Here I want to focus only on what are commonly referred to as 'gnostic gospels' (most of them written in the second century). These did not constitute a normative corpus of texts revered by a specific group, but provided accounts of Jesus that reflected a distinctive species of confidence – in general, a claim to preserve his 'secret sayings', his conversations with disciples (held most often after his resurrection); but more particularly, an assertion that immediate access to the transcendent presence of the risen one remained an option.

The attachment to individual enlightenment that is commonly associated with *gnōsis*, and the number and geographical distribution of those who shared that attachment, made for variety of emphasis. Nevertheless, they also shared the uncertainties that made salvation seem necessary, even to their opponents. Theodotus, in the second century, asked familiar Christian questions (at least as reported by Clement of Alexandria): where do we come from, where do we find ourselves, where are we destined to go? For Theodotus, baptism was not enough. Only the added benefit of *gnōsis* guaranteed release from fate. That amalgam of fear and hope led some Christians to enfold both the saved and the Saviour in a specific mythology. It included what we might term the prehistory of Jesus, not least his relation to the Jewish Scriptures, which affected all Christian understanding of salvation. Those mythologizing thinkers, therefore, attempted a particular redefinition of the Jewish past. Their epic drama, enlivened by the frustration of the creator's plan by an evil 'demiurge', recast the account of creation in *Genesis*. The God of the Jews, the maker of the material world, was seen as a usurping power, either limited in his understanding or arrogant in his pretensions. A more exalted divinity wished to win back its rightful domain, and Jesus was the instrument and guarantor of that victory, both within the believer and within the cosmos generally. Jesus the 'son of man', Jesus the 'new Adam',

Jesus annulling on the cross the curse of the paradise tree: such images (in the *Gospel of Philip*, for example) defined the only worthwhile type of investment in the Jewish Scriptures. 'Valentinian' texts from Nag Hammadi similarly place Jesus at the heart of a great restoration – in the *Gospel of Truth*, for example, the *Tripartite Tractate*, and the *Valentinian Exposition*, where he brings to fruition the primeval intentions of the supreme God.

A poetic and symbolic vision and a shift from the horizontal of scriptural narrative to the vertical of spiritual ascent transformed the 'history' of Jesus, as Mark and others had presented it, into a series of tableaux, windows onto the cosmic realm within which the 'real' Jesus operated. Even the surviving canonical gospels, built as they are around striking events, retain something of that dramatic structure, which may predate the formation of the synoptic accounts. The literary staging of the crucifixion is a prime example, demonstrating (in the *Gospel of Truth*) how the world of error, dominated by its lesser creator, reacted to the coming of its Saviour. At the climactic moment, the Word rescued Jesus from the wood of the cross, reversing (in the so-called *Trimorphic Protennoia*) the effect of Eden's forbidden fruit. The *Gospel of Philip*, on the other hand, and *The Testimony of Truth* attributed greater significance to Jesus's baptism in the Jordan – the opening of the heavens, the descent of the Spirit and the voice of God. Those events, for the *Valentinian Exposition*, marked the moment when Jesus, and the world with him, began the cosmic journey of return. Once one recognizes the 'gnostic potential' in such a passage, one can see embedded in all the gospels many other moments when time stood still and observers engaged with a different order of being.

I used the phrase above, the 'real' Jesus. Patterns of thought commonly regarded as gnostic – the frustration of the creator, the original 'Mind', and the reinterpretation of *Genesis*, suspicious of unbroken Jewish history – all served to divorce Jesus from human experience. The constricting effect of his birth into the present world, his hardship, betrayal and death, were vain blows struck by a lesser God. The Saviour, the Jesus who spoke to gnostics, could not be limited by such misfortune. So we have another tableau, another dissolution of the barrier between the divine and the human: Jesus hangs on his cross in the lower frame of the picture, but above him the victorious Saviour laughs. The *Second Treatise of the Great Seth* and the *Apocalypse of Peter* provide the most vivid versions of this famous scenario. The laughing Saviour – laughing at the powerless ignorance of his tormentors – is the living and genuine Jesus, rising above the Jesus of the flesh, untouched by humiliation and defeat. Opponents were outraged by this suggestion that Jesus did not pass to victory through death. Paul, for all his transcendent emphases, had avoided that artifice of escape; was, for all his focus on resurrection (in *1 Corinthians* especially), unequivocal in attributing significance to Jesus's physical death. The comparison makes clear at once the divisions of opinion, the varieties of emphasis, that dogged inquiry into the nature of the Saviour.

The wish to achieve and maintain a vertical access – access to a transcendent Saviour, to Jesus as a present force rather than a figure in the Galilean past – was in no way facile. Jesus died, even for gnostics. His death was in their eyes the moment of his fullest self-discovery. Privileged believers would live through comparable pain and loss. Self-understanding based on affinity with the divine demanded death of a sort – escape from the prison of the body. Those who took the gnostic path called for unlimited commitment, which could not be exhausted in this present life. As the *Gospel of Thomas* put it, one had to bring forth what was within and be saved by it. To fail in that release of inner power was to court destruction. The synoptic gospels had made similar emphases – that the 'kingdom' was within, that the heart was the measure of virtue. For the *Gospel of Thomas*, however, the 'kingdom' was a kingdom of knowledge – a prize that one might obtain at once, not a social utopia yet to be achieved.

The writers and readers of gnostic gospels saw themselves like the disciples talking with the risen Jesus, hearing from his lips fresh wisdom as yet unrecognized; the corrective of others' misunderstanding, of a literal-minded weddedness to Jewish tradition. That image of a circle of attentive followers carried its social message – confident of its rectitude, suspicious of outsiders and harsh in condemning apostasy. Gnostics were supposedly dismissive of rigid hierarchies, the instruments of status and control; but the evidence of their opponents and of 'Valentinian' documents in particular make it clear, for example, that they celebrated the sacraments. Like John and the synoptics, their gospels illustrate the link between community and text. Their new dialogue with the risen Jesus reopened the issue of who might command obedience. John and the Synoptics, as also *Acts*, had confirmed the authority of certain apostles, Peter and Paul especially. The declared allegiance of these later accounts was to Philip, Thomas and (in a more direct way) John himself. Their subversion of what threatened to become, in their eyes, a received and unquestioned ancestry represented a claim to alternative authority. They beat the canonical gospels at their own game.

A striking example is the *Gospel of Mary*. Mary Magdalene was doubly subversive in being a woman, but was no less a 'witness' to the earthly life of Jesus than his famous male followers. Many ancient anecdotes linked her closely with the Saviour, and the dossier could be extended if one conflated all the gospel Marys into one figure. In the *Gospel of Mary*, she is shown arguing with and getting the better of Peter, who is criticized by his male colleagues also. She had received confidences withheld from them. The text takes the opportunity to put its own gloss on the concept of 'witness', referring in a special way to those who had 'seen' the Saviour. The link between vision and *gnōsis* was close. The implication was that even women who had encountered the risen Jesus, in their rigorous self-discovery and their repudiation of a fleshly life, could, like Mary, claim an authority comparable to that of any man.

That portrait of the Magdalene, especially when conflated with the sister of Lazarus, is no more than an extension of the way in which she is treated in the *Gospel of John*. One is not surprised to find, therefore, that the Nag Hammadi text *The Second Treatise of the Great Seth* can describe the cosmic destiny of Jesus in quite Johannine terms: 'I came to my own and united them with myself.' 'After we went forth from our home and came down to this world and came into being in the world in bodies, we were hated and persecuted, not only by those who are ignorant but also by those who think that they are advancing the name of Christ.' In the closing discourse of John's gospel (echoing many earlier addresses), Jesus declares to his Father, 'I have revealed your name to those you gave me from the world. They were yours and you gave them to me. . . . I appeal on their behalf. I make no appeal on behalf of the world but on behalf of those you have given me.' And earlier, to his followers, he says, 'If the world hates you, know that it hated me before you. If you were of the world, the world would love its own. Because you are not of the world – for I have singled you out from the world – for that the world hates you.' Those passages, when combined, recall Paul's famous image in *Philippians*: Jesus 'emptied himself, taking the form of a slave', returning, in that case by way of a real death, to share glory with the Father. Paul and John carry their message to their audience, demanding that they emulate the submission of the Saviour and support one another in love. If the Nag Hammadi text is different, it may be only in preferring confidence to effort: 'They persecuted those who have been liberated by me', and 'In the uprightness of our love we are innocent, pure and good.'

TOWARDS A UNIVERSAL SAVIOUR

The task of reflection and leadership in the field of doctrine, therefore, as some conceived it, was to rescue Jesus from partisan interest; to draw together the best from different traditions. As I suggested earlier, it was the genius of Christianity to keep so many options open, while fusing them into a portrait greater than its parts. We have seen what forces drove Christians to more formal reflection: a desire to 'make sense' of a charismatic figure; to place him within the stream of Jewish history; to link his career with the formation of communities; and to set in place a textual tradition that underpinned continuity. Fuller debate followed – about the humanity and divinity of Jesus; about the use of Jewish Scripture in the service of Christian history; about the need to counter the fluidity of textual inventiveness – all of which I shall consider in due course. Yet Christians never failed to respect the potential breadth of 'salvation' as an idea. Jesus overcame the cosmic power of evil and the power of sin within the humanity he shared. He overcame ignorance, prepared believers for final judgement, and exemplified the moral path they should follow. One could choose between those images, but more was gained by asserting their compatibility.

The ability to think of Jesus as a Saviour depended on a wide agreement that salvation was both necessary and possible, that there existed a traffic between humanity and its gods. That belief was common, but Christianity had a specific view of the matter. The intimacy and assurance that characterized gnostic thought was allowed its place, but the 'real humanity' of Jesus and the link that could be established between himself and the Jewish Scriptures gave a particular quality to the personal experience of salvation – were, indeed, its prerequisites. On the other hand, there was an increasing resistance to a more apocalyptic view, such as we found in *2 Thessalonians*. Dramatic expectation pulled Jesus away from the world, making him an imminent threat ('coming in the clouds', as Mark put it, 'with great power and glory'), rather than a reassuring presence (as in the *Letter to the Hebrews*, 'always interceding for us'). The imagery of *Revelation* and analogous texts map in symbolic terms the place of fulfilment (the 'new Jerusalem'), in which the figures of the saved appear stilted and hieratic, while the presence of God is luminous but ill defined. The experience of striving to reach such a place is hardly mentioned. The portrayal of the 'son of man', as also in *Daniel* and the *Similitudes of Enoch*, lifts Jesus out of the narrative. In Mark's account, there is a certain mobility – people rush to escape, 'false Christs' tumble over one another to deceive, the moon is darkened, the stars fall – but John imposes stillness, as angels pass up and down beneath the open heaven, and Jesus, lifted above the earth, draws humanity to himself.

All those choices and distinctions hinged upon a central question: how to describe the effect of the Saviour and the mechanisms of salvation – the channels, the links, the affective bonds between Jesus and believers. The earliest images of Jesus were of one who overcame death through the power of the Spirit. Paul, as we have seen, developed the notion at length. Baptism meant identifying oneself with that victory and coming into contact with that Spirit. It is only later that we find a more metaphysical notion of Jesus as God incarnate, as one whose coming changed the make-up of human beings and of the whole natural world. To be associated with Jesus was to release into one's person and circumstance a new current of divine life. The difference is not startling, but nevertheless important. To 'put on Christ', as Paul put it, was to experience at once an inward and an upward thrust. The intensification of commitment recorded in the gospels has a similar quality. In the second instance, Jesus became an event in history and in the world. This belief had been essential to Paul, but the gospels helped to set Jesus more vividly within the context of human and natural experience.

We need to ask what triggered the change of perspective. There was a reach beyond individual experience. Such breadth of vision demanded a common style of discourse; one that extended between and across communities hitherto sustained by narrower loyalties, and that could be disseminated or imposed by authoritative teaching. A common discourse of that sort had been characteristic of the Roman world for a long time. Members of the élite, drawn from disparate provincial societies, each with its own past, felt bonded in the service of the empire and in their adhesion to the aesthetic and moral values of the Greek tradition. 'High culture' is found in all complex societies. When that sense of a shared investment or dependence is lost, people revert to tribal myths and partisan prejudice.

The so-called 'docetist' controversy – testing the notion that Jesus only 'seemed' to be human, from the Greek verb *dokein* – was the first debate that demanded the attention of the whole Christian community. Because it was concerned with Jesus's nature, it brought into the open divergent arguments that would affect in different ways any theory of salvation. What use was a Jesus so far beyond human reach? The gospels contributed to the confusion. Jesus the man is at times transfigured, clothed with the raiment of divinity, elevated beyond the human level. That was not a comment on his actual appearance but a symbolic vocabulary calculated to explain his behaviour. Thus, the gospels devised a way of overcoming the supposed embarrassment of his limited humanity. They allowed disciples to betray doubt on occasion, faced with a Jesus transformed – on Mount Tabor, for example; in the upper room; by the lakeside; on the road to Emmaus – but they relentlessly assured their own readers by continuing to make transcendent statements about apparently ordinary situations. As a result, the material circumstance of Jesus's life became diffused with a light from elsewhere.

Here was a species of disembodiment that some wished to question. But, turning to other texts, we see how slowly Christians became clear-headed about the balance between humanity and divinity in Jesus. Hermas's *Shepherd* is a perfect example. Written (in Greek) at or near Rome by a former slave, it was concerned chiefly with the issue of appropriate conduct. The work is divided into three major sections: 'visions', 'mandates' (i.e. commands) and 'similitudes' (or more properly 'parables'). In the midst of its other concerns, it develops some remarkably complicated ideas about Jesus – and this in a document that gained almost canonical status.

Hermas adopted a theory of creation that kept the believing community in view. The world had been made for that community's sake. He attempts in his first three visions to describe those who presided over that providential act: God, but also the 'church' (conceived of as an old woman), and then the angels who govern the created order. (Hermas's personal mentor, the 'shepherd' of his title, is one of those angels.) Strands interweave further in the eighth similitude: the angel Michael sets the Law in people's hearts, yet presides over the universal proclamation of God's Son. A transition from Jewish Law to gentile Gospel was no doubt intended. Hermas now adds that God wishes to save all those called through his Son. In the next similitude, this Son becomes entwined with a 'holy Spirit', who 'spoke with you in the form of the church' (the old woman): 'that Spirit is the Son of God'. In the fifth similitude, the Son, along with the angels, is accepted by God as a 'counsellor', because he has not defiled the Spirit in his flesh: he has taken flesh with the Spirit as a colleague. All flesh in which the Spirit dwells will be rewarded in a similar way. A clear bond was thus forged between the Son and other humans.

Hermas saw that link between Jesus and believers as the basis of religious practice, of conduct in daily life. It was established by 'taking the name'. The association of ideas (here in the ninth similitude) is again complicated. 'Taking the name' helps Christians pass into the 'kingdom' through a new gate in the 'church' (now seen as a tower rather than a woman). The gate symbolizes a new order: the Son of God is an ancient figure, through his involvement in the creation, but also points forward, as one who will be manifested at the end of time. 'Taking the name', however, is not a simple act of identification. Christians, if they wish to pass through the gate, must wear garments inscribed not only with the Son's titles of power but also with the names of virtues. They become associated not only with the victory of Jesus on the grand scale but also with the acquisition of temperance, simplicity, joy and understanding. The 'name' remains essentially the name of the Son, rock-like in both its magnitude and its mysterious impenetrability; but its power resides also in the daily support it offers those who bear it 'with all their heart'.

Hermas's ideas, for all their obscurity, remind us that the nature and the effect of Jesus were seen as inseparable qualities. They also show that at least some Christians were far from understanding clearly how the connections were to be made, or what they implied about either Jesus or the human beings who depended upon him. Nevertheless, Hermas provided a secure future for certain concepts, building on the speculations of earlier Christian writers: the eternity of the 'Son' and his relation to the 'Spirit'; the place of the 'Spirit' in the lives of believers; and the historical involvement of the 'church' in the process of salvation. Moreover, the popularity of the *Shepherd*, even after clearer formulations had emerged, suggests that it made engaging sense of the relation between Jesus and the individual.

A more secure judgement is reflected in the letters of Ignatius of Antioch – almost certainly because contrary and popular opinions were deemed more dangerous. Ignatius is famous for his insistence that Jesus was truly human – that he did not merely 'seem' to have lived, suffered and died. Ignatius did not deny a divinity in Jesus. In his letter to the church at Ephesus, he declared his belief in 'one physician, fleshly and spiritual, born and not born, God in man, truly alive in his death, from Mary and from God, suffering at first and then without suffering'. But his statement was designed to dispel any suspicion that a spirituality free from suffering might override or annul the reality of Jesus's birth and death. He could trust his friend Polycarp not to misinterpret his suggestion that Jesus lay beyond the reach of the human senses; was in himself incapable of suffering; was made visible and subject to death only 'for our sakes'. To the broader community, Ignatius was adamant: Jesus was truly born, truly died, truly rose again. That was why, as he put it to the church at Philadelphia, to take refuge in 'the Gospel' was to take refuge in the flesh of Jesus. It was the record of his bodily coming, dying and rising. A fair number in Polycarp's Smyrna had failed to understand the import of history and prophecy, the dramatic victories in the gospel narratives, and the sufferings of people like Ignatius himself, soon to be martyred. No one would surrender to hardship, pain and death for the sake of a mere phantom. His own view of fulfilment in the cosmos was summed up in the concepts of peace and hope: a purging of flesh and spirit through a sharing in the death of Jesus and a firm trust in the resurrection.

We find a significantly more developed set of ideas in the writings of Justin. Hellenistic in culture, although a Samaritan by birth, he adopted a Christian view in his adult years. He displayed the characteristic philosophical syncretism of the Middle Platonist school, but he was steeped in the biblical tradition and judged other systems of thought in that light. His understanding of salvation and of the nature of Jesus was most clearly expressed in dialogue with a Jew, Trypho. He went to great (and sometimes improbable) lengths to show that Jesus fulfilled what he himself interpreted as prophecies in the Jewish Scriptures. (He proves how essential to the defence of Christian claims that kind of exegesis had become.) Against the background of Jewish history, however, he posed questions entirely proper to a Christian perspective, which counts for more than the Jewish and philosophical bric-à-brac he made use of in conducting his inquiry. Justin defined what he thought were the appropriate links between Christianity and other cultures. Christian preoccupations came first and the useful paradigms of the non-Christian world were appealed to later.

Justin thought of Jesus as the *Logos*, the 'Word' – an apparent echo of John's gospel, though Justin never quoted him. The *Logos* was both a component of God's mind and the expression of his creative will; something thought, something spoken; a principle, and an act. And Jesus of Nazareth was to be wholly identified with that *Logos*. The *Logos* did not merely assume a human form but became a human being – body, spirit and soul. Justin confirmed the notion that Jesus was not just a manifestation of God's rationality but a complete person in his own right. He safeguarded, on the other hand, the unity of the godhead by asserting that Jesus had been associated with the *Logos* since before the creation of the world. His birth had simply brought into the world of time a union of the divine and the human sustained from eternity in God's mind.

Two difficulties are created by Justin's approach. First, he took the *Logos* to be a necessary mediator between God and his creation. The *Logos* enabled human beings to understand how God's order functioned. There is a gnostic touch to the view – indeed, the saving revelation that the *Logos* embodied could heighten the sense of God's remoteness. Justin wrote also of fallen angels, who caused havoc in the world – a havoc from which the *Logos* rescued those whose understanding he empowered. Justin was set apart from gnostics, however, by his belief in the unity of creation – a point taken up by Irenaeus. The creative *Logos* and the human mind were related within a single system, and the gift of understanding did not break the world apart or prompt a wish to escape from the circumstances now made more intelligible.

Justin had been able to see the matter from God's point of view, to sympathize with a creator's wish to retain a link with his creatures. It was true that one could not speak of God independently of the *Logos,* but that did not mean that God had lost control of his creation: it was simply that human understanding was placed at some distance from the divinity and needed the enlightenment that the *Logos* guaranteed. The nature of the creator, therefore, the nature of humanity, and the nature of the one who mediated between them were all part of a single economy subject to the will of God. Thus, Justin was able to offer opponents of the gnostic view an alternative and durable definition of *gnōsis.*

The second difficulty affects what later came to be thought of formally as 'the doctrine of the Trinity' (although Justin was less tidy in his terminology). The effect was thoroughly concrete. When one considers the flood of words, the ruined lives, the spilt blood that marked subsequent debate, it is instructive to see how Justin, two hundred years before the height of the Arian conflict, identified – indeed, fostered – puzzling obscurities as well as possible solutions. He was particularly imprecise in his treatment of God's Spirit. Like Hermas, he ascribed inspiration to God's 'Word', and therefore to Jesus; and he set up a temporal succession from God, through Jesus the eternal *Logos,* to the prophetic Spirit of the ancient Jewish era. In other words, he did not tie the Spirit into his overall argument as a distinct but eternally divine figure, and did little to discourage a notion of the Spirit's inferiority. Here was the seed of many later difficulties. On the other hand, he insisted that Jesus the *Logos* reawakened a rational power that had been natural to humanity from its inception (a view that proved attractive to Clement of Alexandria). Because the *Logos* was eternal, those who had lived by reason had always been de facto devotees of Jesus. Moreover, the reawakening was a process that defined one's whole life. Baptism signalled a genuine rebirth, which allowed a gradual liberation of spirit; a spirit enlightened in its turn by a lasting infusion of the *Logos.* Jesus was a teacher, but the dynamic of rebirth and enlightenment depended on more than his words. He had shared in human suffering and had conquered death; an achievement no less essential to the enhancement of created nature. The relation between Saviour and saved, therefore, was intimately grounded in a shared experience of both sorrow and triumph.

Justin's train of thought was given added substance by Irenaeus. A vigorous opponent of gnostics, Irenaeus rose above polemic to develop theories of his own. Born in Smyrna about 115, he had (according to Eusebius) links with Polycarp and traced his spiritual ancestry to the apostle John by way of Polycarp's associate Papias, bishop of Hierapolis in Phrygia. He spent some time in Rome, as a pupil of Justin. By 177, he was a priest at Lyon and soon afterwards became the city's bishop. He symbolizes, although he did not initiate, the westward expansion of Christianity beyond the Greek-speaking communities of Italy. He is also important for having developed patterns of thought that were independent of the Egyptian traditions inherited by Clement and Origen.

Irenaeus snatched from his gnostic opponents the building blocks of their mythology and fashioned them into a system of his own, focused on creation, salvation, and the role of Jesus. He made much of a passage from the first chapter of *Ephesians*, which gnostics glossed in their different way. God had a 'plan', an *oikonomia*; a plan that had in mind a 'fullness', a *plerōma* ('the fullness of time'); a fullness that would be achieved by 'recapitulation', *anakephalaiōsis*. As a follower of Justin, he was naturally attracted to the coherence of that Pauline formula. The same sense of unity affected his vision of a community bound together by what he called 'the principle of truth'; a concept that inspired also his belief in the coherence of Scripture. But it was the historical dimension of Pauline thought that Irenaeus made most of. Reaching further than Justin, he emphasized that humanity as a whole had to grow towards divinity – not just by recognizing some inherent quality within the individual or regaining a lost paradise, but by moving as a race through historical stages of re-engagement with the creator. Preoccupation with gnostics allowed him to restore a greater sense of drama to the account of human recovery. The species had been created in God's image, which defined its destiny; but between creation and fulfilment there stretched a pilgrimage of the flesh – flesh that was also created in God's image. Jesus, the eternal Word made flesh, was related to the entire passage of time and to each person within it – a relation that sprang from the part he played in creation; a relation that would have been forged, therefore, even if Adam had not sinned.

For Irenaeus, the key word in the passage from Ephesians was *anakephalaiōsis*, 'recapitulation'. Its original connotations were literary – it meant the summary of a plot – and its use by Irenaeus, and probably in *Ephesians*, implied that human history was a narrative that Jesus encapsulated within the compass of a single lifetime. He did more, therefore, than link the *Logos* with the human spirit: he engaged, as only a human could, with every human experience. In particular, he defeated every human enemy, even suffering and death. His 'recapitulation' had to include identification with bloodshed, especially the ancient and enduring bloodshed imposed upon the just. His flesh had to experience the pain of all flesh. In his moment of loss and defeat – the loss and defeat of humanity throughout time – God gave his victory a lasting stability. 'The glory of God is the living man', as Irenaeus put it in his fourth book *Against Heresies*, 'and the life of man is the vision of God.' The Incarnation of the Word represented at once the revelation of God's image in its human fullness and the fresh imprinting of that image on the saved. The individual believer could recognize a promised destiny, a guaranteed escape from the limits of sin, and could experience by a gift of God's Spirit what Irenaeus called a 'mingling' with the Word.

Debate about Jesus did not stop in the second century (we shall pick up the thread in later chapters), but Irenaeus provides a natural resting place in our account. The philosophical elevation of his theories, like those of Justin, carries us some way (as do gnostic texts) from the apparent realism of the gospels; but the need for salvation, the nature of divine intervention, and the accessibility of the Saviour had affected all Christian speculation throughout that early period. History and humanity had become the crucial themes. Jesus was firmly embedded in time and flesh. To gain advantage of his salvation, it was necessary only to be human, to experience temporal limitation, and to acknowledge the difference that Jesus had made in both respects. Irenaeus lived and worked at an important moment of change. Interpretative choices had become clearer, but so had their dangers. He laid just claim to a living link, through Polycarp, with the apostolic age – the last major figure to do so convincingly – and he and Justin between them prepared the agenda for conflict in the centuries that followed.

Now that we have absorbed both the message of the gospels and the message of Paul, we can see how they combined to bequeath something greater than either. They were like two images projected on a single screen, each constantly colouring and shaping the other. The memory of Jesus, as a result, and the example of the communities he influenced and inspired, were endowed with richer meaning and greater force in the minds of later generations. The chemistry that compounded those various traditions helped to explain and preserve the shifting but guarded balance between the 'historical' and the 'cosmic' Jesus – categories more representative than 'human' and 'divine'. They referred not so much to *what* Jesus was as to *where* he was. They focused on the lines of communication between Saviour and saved. They affected relations more than arguments and the experience of salvation more than its definition. Later debates about 'substance' and 'nature' never quite captured that more personal intensity, which owed its force to the combined impact of Paul and the evangelists.

Further reading

For general reflections, see Christopher Rowland, *Christian Origins: from Messianic Movement to Christian Religion* (Minneapolis, MN: Augsburg Publishing House, 1985), Bruce J. Malina, *The Social World of Jesus and the Gospels* (London and New York, NY: Routledge, 1996) and Michael L. Humphries, *Christian Origins and the Language of the Kingdom of God* (Carbondale, IL: Southern Illinois University Press, 1999). Older but still influential and stimulating is John G. Gager, *Kingdom and Community: the Social World of Early Christianity* (Englewood Cliffs, NJ: Prentice-Hall, 1975).

When assessing the Jewish context of Jesus's career, a look backwards at the world of the Dead Sea Scrolls is always informative, on which see Florentino García Martínez, with Julio Trebolle Barrera, *The People of the Dead Sea Scrolls: their Literature, Social Organization and Religious Beliefs* (Leiden: Brill, 1994) and Israel Knohl, *The Messiah before Jesus: the Suffering Servant of the Dead Sea Scrolls*, translated by David Maisel (Berkeley, CA: University of California Press, 2000). In English, two writers have been particularly helpful (and I mention only one work by each, although both have been prolific): Geza Vermes, *The Religion of Jesus the Jew* (Minneapolis, MN: Fortress Press, 1993) and E.P. Sanders, *The Historical Figure of Jesus* (New York, NY: Penguin Books, 1996). Much can still be gained from Bernard J. Lee, *The Galilean Jewishness of Jesus: Retrieving the Jewish Origins of Christianity* (Mahwah, NJ and New York, NY: Paulist Press, 1988); and see his more recent *Jesus and the Metaphors of God: the Christs of the New Testament* (Mahwah, NJ and New York, NY: Paulist Press, 1993). A useful collection of essays: James H. Charlesworth and others (eds), *The Messiah: Developments in Earliest Judaism and Christianity* (Minneapolis, MN: Fortress Press, 1992).

On the shift from Jesus to 'the Christ', see (in order of publication) Ithamar Gruenwald, Shaul Shaked and Gedaliahu G. Stroumsa (eds), *Messiah and Christos: Studies in the Jewish Origins of Christianity* (Tübingen: J.C.B. Mohr, 1992), two books by Paula Fredriksen, *From Jesus to Christ: the Origins of the New Testament Images of Jesus* (New Haven, CT & London: Yale University Press, 1988) and *Jesus of Nazareth, King of the Jews: a Jewish Life and the Emergence of Christianity* (New York, NY: Knopf, 1999) and (forthcoming) Daniel Boyarin, *Making a Difference: the Logos and the Language of 'Christianity' and 'Judaism'*. For a foretaste of later developments, see Rebecca Lyman, *Christology and Cosmology: Models of Divine Activity in Origen, Eusebius, and Athanasius* (Oxford: Oxford University Press, 1993).

For general literary reflections, see Burton L. Mack, *Rhetoric and the New Testament* (Minneapolis, MN: Fortress Press, 1990) and, for a particular study of Mark, his *A Myth of Innocence: Mark and Christian Origins* (Philadelphia, PA: Fortress Press, 1988), together with Howard Clark Kee, *Community of the New Age: Studies in Mark's Gospel* (Philadelphia, PA: Westminster Press, 1977). On Matthew, two books by J. Andrew Overman, *Matthew's Gospel and Formative Judaism: the Social World of the Matthean Community* (Minneapolis, MN: Fortress Press, 1990), and *Church and Community in Crisis: the Gospel according to Matthew* (Valley Forge, PA: Trinity Press International, 1996); and see also David C. Sim, *The Gospel of Matthew and Christian Judaism: the History and Social Setting of the Matthaean Community* (Edinburgh: T. & T. Clark, 1998). On John: John Ashton, *Understanding the Fourth Gospel* (Oxford: Clarendon Press, 1991) and *Studying John: Approaches to the Fourth Gospel* (Oxford: Clarendon Press, 1994), together with John Painter, *The Quest for the Messiah: the History, Literature, and Theology of the Johannine Community* (Edinburgh: T. & T. Clark, 1993). Still useful is Raymond E. Brown, *The Community of the Beloved Disciple* (New York, NY: Paulist Press, 1979).

On the development of the 'canon', the classic and authoritative studies are those by Bruce M. Metzger, *The Early Versions of the New Testament: their Origin, Transmission, and Limitations* (Oxford: Clarendon Press, 1977), *The Canon of the New Testament: its Origin, Development, and Significance* (Oxford: Clarendon Press, 1987) and *The Text of the New Testament: its Transmission, Corruption, and Restoration* 3rd enlarged edn (Oxford and New York, NY: Oxford University Press, 1992). See also Harry Y. Gamble, *The New Testament Canon: its Making and Meaning* (Philadelphia, PA: Fortress Press, 1985) and, more recently, Arthur G. Patzia, *The Making of the New Testament: Origin, Collection, Text, and Canon* (Leicester: Apollos, 1995). An older but helpful view is supplied by Helmut Koester, *Ancient Christian Gospels: their History and Development* (London: SCM Press/Philadelphia, PA: Trinity Press International, 1990). Now indispensable is Philip Burton, *The Old Latin Gospels: a Study of their Texts and Language* (Oxford: Oxford University Press, 2000). For more specific comment on the 'Muratorian Fragment' see Geoffrey Mark Hahnemann, *The Muratorian Fragment and the Development of the Canon* (Oxford: Clarendon Press, 1992).

We shall be looking at Justin and Irenaeus more fully in following chapters. For a straightforward if somewhat old-fashioned account of Justin, see L.W. Barnard, *Justin Martyr: His Life and Thought* (Cambridge: Cambridge University Press, 1967) and on Irenaeus, Robert McQueen Grant, *Irenaeus of Lyons* (London and New York, NY: Routledge, 1997).

Where to begin?
Paula Fredriksen, *From Jesus to Christ*.

Chapter 4

INDIVIDUAL VIRTUE AND ITS SOCIAL SETTING

Two enterprises had now been set in train: Paul's redefinition of Judaism and the gospels' portrayal of a Saviour. Paul depicted his communities as fields of energy powered by the impact of God's Spirit; the gospels attempted to explain and define that energy's source. The two sets of texts were closely related – Jesus is present in Paul's letters and the Spirit moves throughout the gospels – but reflection followed experience. Moreover, the towering Christ of Paul was given, in the gospels, a human, Galilean face. An intense acknowledgement of inner release could now be projected on an individual who had both known and overcome the contradictions of life. Exhilaration and admiration are likely to have been fused in the lives of individuals, but the written distillation of that discovery and commitment was bequeathed to the next generation in separate forms. While Christians of the early second century may have recognized their own communities in those inspired by Paul, their inner sense of loyalty, their awareness of needs at once painful and assuaged, could now be focused on Jesus the man – sympathetic, vulnerable and triumphant.

Both the communal styles and the reflective emphases were contentious from the outset, and remained so as they gathered momentum. Paul preserved elements of Hellenistic Judaism that laid his cosmology open to misinterpretation, and he failed to resolve all issues of observance, sinfulness and renunciation, even though he offered the insights that a resolution would require. As for the writing of gospels, Christians continued to judge in different ways how human Jesus might have been and how he was related to the Father. Division of opinion was inevitable; and so, therefore, were different conceptions of what a church should look like. The motives that had governed Paul's converts were still at work, but arguments about authentic belief continued to affect the structure and expansion of the Christian communities. The opinions preserved in what has come to be called the New Testament were not yet available in condensed form, as a universally accepted and coherent account of right doctrine. Clement of Rome and Ignatius of Antioch wrote before that corpus was complete, and they defended their style of authority and order in the face of contrasting opinion.

While earliest Christianity exhibited, therefore, with surprising speed, characteristics of thought and behaviour that would mark later centuries, agreement was never one of them. Many doors remained open, many choices had yet to be made, a range of futures was available. The Christian imagination was still vivid, creative, even fevered. Christians were excited and uncertain, still not hedged about by the narrowing sobriety of longer experience. It is true that the writings of the Apostolic Fathers reflected the world of Paul and reinforced the insights he had made attractive. The breadth of Ignatius's correspondence and his easy progress from church to church, during his journey to martyrdom in Rome (sometime during the earliest years of the second century), mirrored the network of Pauline communities. The early gospels, for their part, had further defined the religious values deemed appropriate to believers, and had provided additional and enduring insights into the meaning of divinity, redemption and history. Ignatius, in his letter to Philadelphia, referred to the gospel as 'the flesh of Jesus' and wished churches like that of Ephesus to be 'of one mind with the apostles'. None of that yet represented, however, rigid church discipline. The challenge for us is to explain how, even when the sense of heritage was fractured and adapted to differing views of religious obligation, Christianity could still have begun to acquire in this period a coherent profile in the Mediterranean world.

Three themes have traditionally been seized upon as keys to that coherence – three victories: over error, idolatry and the Roman state. The identification and condemnation of heresy (victory over error), the assimilation of Greek and Roman culture (victory over idolatry) and the triumph of the martyrs (victory over the state) seem to have guaranteed the unity, appeal and eventual dominance of the Christian religion. This and the following two chapters will weigh and adjust those lines of thought, suggesting a different triad. A move towards unity, first at a local level and then more generally, was both prompted and sustained by the asking and answering of a simple question: how should one live? Unity demanded, therefore, a formative discipline, which drew upon the cultural practices of the non-Christian world. That dependence encouraged in its turn an engagement with the state that reached beyond a heroic confrontation between persecutors and martyrs. However, we cannot develop those themes in a tidy sequence. We shall observe from three heights, as it were, a single plain of endeavour. The goals, the formation and the circumstances of Christians cast three kinds of light on their endeavours. The quality of institutional and spiritual ideals hints at the processes by which they were expressed and maintained. The development of a Christian culture served the interests of doctrine as well as of conduct. The pressure of relations with the 'world' affected its stability and its ideology.

UNITY WITHIN AND AMONG THE CHURCHES, AND THE DEVELOPMENT OF AN 'ORTHODOX' TRADITION

Unity has always held a dominant place in the Christian mind. Failure to achieve it reinforces its desirability. The prayer of Jesus in John's gospel, 'that they may be one', has rung down the centuries with moral force, prompting continuously the question of what kind of unity Christians should work for. It is possible to argue that, between the writing of the *First Letter of Clement* (*1 Clement*, written in AD 96) and Cyprian's treatise *On the Unity of the Catholic Church* (written in AD 251), a single 'Church' had come into being, although in a sense that we shall have to define with care. The fact remains surprising because Christian communities were small, scattered, and parochial. In the early second century, one would have found in some cities only dozens of believers. Even in larger groups, Christians occupied no more than forty or so urban centres and made up barely one in a thousand of the empire's population. Nevertheless, the witness of Pliny the Younger, governor of Bithynia around 110, and of Justin and Irenaeus in later decades, suggests a wide diffusion, including (by the later period) a predominance of gentile converts, varying levels of education and a presence in country areas. The *Acts of the Scillitan Martyrs* imply the same for Africa, and Tertullian (in his *Apologeticum*) applauded (even if with some exaggeration) Christianity's penetration of 'cities and islands, forts and townships'. After barely a century and a half, some of its leaders were beginning to think in terms of a world-wide movement – a single household, as Irenaeus saw it, in spite of persistent regional tones and emphases; recognizably 'Christian' everywhere, exhibiting a homogeneity of belief and expression that older cults were unable to attain.

Do those confident assertions express an ideal, or relate an achievement? As I suggested in Chapter 1, we are certainly dealing with more than unity of doctrine. The Apostolic Fathers describe for us concerns at once more local and more diverse. *1 Clement*, written by a leader of the Christian community in Rome (and traditionally regarded as the city's bishop), was designed (like Paul's letters earlier) to resolve tensions in the church of Corinth. The letters of Ignatius, distributed some ten years later, displayed a similar concern for the spiritual morale of other churches – those at Ephesus, Magnesia, Tralles, Philadelphia and Smyrna, as well as at Rome. He also wrote a personal letter to the bishop of Smyrna, Polycarp; and Polycarp himself wrote to the church of Philippi. A range of other documents, to which I shall refer again, are clustered in the same period, although hard to date precisely: Hermas's *Shepherd*, probably written in Rome; the *Letter of Barnabas*, possibly written in Alexandria (an important cultural centre for Jews as well as Greeks); and the *Didachē*, so valuable as a witness to early Christian worship, and probably written in Syria. Those texts, together with the letters to Timothy and Titus, those attributed to Peter, James and John, the *Letter to the Hebrews* and *Revelation*, give a vivid but tellingly fragmented picture of church life in the two or three generations after Paul.

Since *1 Clement* was written in the face of Corinthian division, it was natural that harmony should be its chief preoccupation. Without attacking a specific error, the writer betrayed a feeling that jealousy and persecution had infected the developing community. Some of its enemies were to be found in its own ranks. Clement's ideal – based on Jewish antecedent – was a single household of the saved, called together by God. Failure to achieve that stability would undermine the goals of the community: immortality, justice, honesty, faith, discipline and understanding. We find in the *Shepherd* the same regard for close-knit loyalty. Hermas was particularly worried about hypocrisy. It was no longer easy to distinguish the honest from the pretenders. For that reason he attacked 'foreign' teaching, which he saw as precisely the contribution of the hypocrite. The fundamental problem, however, was self-aggrandizement. Hermas reveals a community already divided into grades – as much by its vices as by its institutions. His surest antidote may have been hospitality (recommended also in *1 Peter*), which gave clear evidence of a promising cohesion – 'receiving into their houses with gladness the servants of God'. Unity was a goal achieved, therefore, not by obedience or conformity but by purity of heart.

Ignatius deployed in his letters, it is true, a broad and forceful range of words against those in error, castigating 'evil teaching' that was 'strange' (in the sense of 'other') and using (in his letters to Ephesus and Tralles) the Greek word 'heresy'. He described such doctrines as 'offshoots', making clear their supposed novelty and deviance. (His friend Polycarp exhorted the Philippians to 'turn back to the teaching given us from the beginning'

– appealing to the paradigm that Walter Bauer questioned.) But Ignatius also wanted a generous community. His most specific attack – when he used the Greek word 'heterodox' to describe 'strange ideas about the grace of Jesus Christ' – was aroused by a failure in Tralles to show 'grace' to the needy. Like Hermas, he wished for those in error a chance of repentance more than all else. (Polycarp voiced the same desire, perhaps recalling *2 Thessalonians*.)

In spite of an anxiety, therefore, about right and wrong doctrine (no less present in Paul), and in spite of an appeal to authenticity based on unbroken tradition, Ignatius mounted his attacks within a framework designed to guarantee the cohesion of this or that community and to invigorate their senses of purpose and destiny. Orthodoxy was not the same as unity: in that much, Bauer was correct. Merely adhering to one set of ideas as 'right', while rejecting all others as 'wrong', would never have guaranteed social cohesion – indeed, it could have hinted at beleaguered self-righteousness. It was not, therefore, the gradual ascendancy of an orthodox position that created the unity we are trying to identify: rather unity, achieved on other grounds and by other means, created a climate within which orthodoxy could assert itself. There was, we must agree, a change in the relationship between opinion and community. As Christians acquired a sense of forming one church, diversity of opinion could no longer take refuge in social isolation. Conflicting views were forced to fight for their corners within a single community. Yet the process was a slow one, and social cohesion and doctrinal agreement were not the result of uncomplicated convergence. Christian conduct in the later third century and beyond shows us clearly that the churches continued to develop along a variety of paths, defined particularly by regional cultures; and no one saw that as a necessary threat either to their shared values and common practices or to their universal creeds.

AUTHORITY AND LEADERSHIP: THE RISE OF THE BISHOP

Let us explore, therefore, the notion that the increasing order of Christian communities and, in particular, the emergence of stable styles of leadership were orientated less towards doctrinal rectitude and more towards social cohesion in the cause of spiritual growth. (It needs saying at once – and the point will recur – that even that adjustment of perspective depends on the witness of texts that often calculatedly defended one pattern of leadership against another, and a pattern of leadership that may not have been widely accepted.) The community in Corinth, according to *1 Clement*, was 'called and made holy by the will of God'. Its hallmarks were faith, devotion, hospitality and 'knowledge'. The author stressed a need for tolerance. A church was a community of mercy, because all were tested in the same theatre of spiritual combat. And mercy, both human and divine, operated over time: resurrection was at once anticipated and experienced. Christians, lodged in the company of the devout, were living through a segment of the grander history that reached, as it had for Paul, from Adam to the coming of the kingdom. Clement's particular time-line ran from creation, through the coming of Jesus, the calling of the apostles, and the preaching of the Christian message, to end with the appointment of 'superintendents and their helpers' – the familiar Greek words *episkopoi* and *diakonoi*. (He alluded also to 'leaders' (*hegoumenoi*) and 'elders' (*presbuteroi*) and confused matters slightly by calling his *episkopoi presbuteroi* as well.) What did Clement hope or suppose that those men would do? They certainly did not represent, at that early stage, a calculated safeguard against error, but rather performed a service (Clement used the Greek word 'liturgy', meaning the fulfilment of a public obligation); and they were expected to do so 'with the consent of the whole church'. Specifically, they were linked with worship. The *episkopoi* 'present the gifts . . . without blame'. History had culminated, therefore, in the act of worship, a natural response to the redeeming sweep of time.

Unfortunately, Clement's particular interests prevent us from assuming that the practices he referred to were clear-cut and stable, let alone widely accepted. Even his own prescriptions betray a looseness of vocabulary. Only in later texts does the bishop appear to gain a more secure position in the ecclesial landscape. 'Elders' in *1 Timothy* 'labour in preaching and teaching', and so do 'bishops'. There is a similar link in the letter to Titus between bishops and elders (to be appointed 'in every town'). Their responsibilities seem to have been, therefore, still in part liturgical; but the preoccupation in these texts had become broader. A bishop should be 'well thought of by outsiders', while acceptance within his own community sprang from the 'prophetic utterances' heard (in Timothy's case) 'when the elders laid their hands upon you' – a combination of inspired perception and ritual gesture that recalls the 'commission' of Paul at Antioch, as described in *Acts*. A candidate had also to prove himself directly, making 'confession in the presence of many witnesses'. He had to manage his church as he would his own household. Similar demands were placed upon the deacons who assisted him. Their skill in household management was directed more to material affairs than to guidance and command: yet a deacon's faith and conscience had also to be 'tested' – a sign that candidates were sifted.

The fact that such straightforward and assured statements sought to nestle under a Pauline umbrella may reflect a fragile, defensive position, adopted well inside the second century. Ignatius of Antioch reflected a comparatively local and possibly personal interpretation of episcopacy, which we cannot assume was universally accepted. He was writing to bishops, after all, expressing consistently the view that the bishop was, in a sense, the church. Obedience was crucial – Ignatius used the language of subjection (which was demanded equally by 'the presbyterate'). He based those convictions on what he saw as a close link between bishops and Jesus, whom he described to the church of Magnesia as 'the bishop of all'. That quickly implied a unity among the bishops themselves, established 'throughout the world'. So we have the striking phrases addressed to Ephesus and Smyrna: 'We must regard the bishop as the Lord himself', and 'It is good to know God and the bishop'. On that foundation, Ignatius hoped to build a series of complex associations, particularly between church leadership and the persons of the Trinity. Jesus had fulfilled the will of his Father, and bishops were to fulfil the will of Jesus. The bishop would represent grace, the presbyters law; or the bishop would represent God, the presbyters the apostles. And, by safeguarding the unity of the church, Ignatius's bishop would validate its worship. There could be, according to him, no baptism or *agapē* when the bishop was absent.

There is a theoretical polish to those images that make one wonder how representative they may have been of actual practice. Certainly, one should avoid the temptation to arrange such declarations like a line on a graph, rising from Clement through Ignatius to the deutero-Pauline letters. There was no such simple curve. Other texts create a more blurred impression and hint at ways in which the surviving assertions of the Apostolic Fathers may have been resisted. A 'presbyter', for example, wrote *3 John*, and claimed sole authority over Gaius, the letter's recipient. Gaius, for his part, exercised comparable authority over the 'brothers'. He was dedicated to the ministries of love and truth (in contrast to his rival Diotrephes, who 'likes to be first'). Here, as in *2 John*, we are dealing with second-century Asia Minor. *1 Peter* calls senior church figures *presbuteroi*, making them, like the author, witnesses to the sufferings of Jesus, and exemplars more than rulers. Polycarp referred to 'leaders' at Philippi, where Paul had earlier written of 'bishops and deacons'. The *Didachē*, for all its cultic preoccupations, bestows most praise on 'prophets', 'your high priests', and only subsequently mentions bishops and deacons, who fulfilled the same ministry as prophets and teachers. The *Shepherd* also links bishops and teachers – men who 'listen to one another' and 'agree with one another'. Otherwise, like *1 Clement*, Hermas referred to

Individual virtue and social setting

'leaders' and thought of bishops chiefly as hospitable men, who welcomed strangers and cared for the widowed and the destitute. All such references belie the confident prescriptions of Ignatius. The variety of emphasis and preference in the second century warns us against hasty definitions.

What recurs is a wish to maintain unity, first within the local church; a unity desirable in itself, not merely the safeguard of a doctrinal position. Ignatius recommended harmony between bishop and presbyterate, using the analogy of strings in a harp. A bishop was exalted by the source of his authority, which rested (for Ignatius) neither in himself nor in his community. At the heart of that conviction lay a sense of service for the common good, which raised the leader above faction; and bishops and presbyters were supposed to provide an example – as he put it to the Magnesians, 'a lesson in immortality'. Unity and morality were thereby wholly intertwined: division was the root of evil, and Ignatius combined his taste for order with the hope that Christians would be temples of God, imitating Jesus as Jesus had imitated his Father. Hermas and the *Letter of Barnabas* describe a similar bargain struck between leaders and communities, underpinning their sense of shared responsibility for the virtue of the group. Those claiming authority should be visible in the performance of good deeds. Prescription and advice were, according to Barnabas, to be shared among equals and not merely handed down from above. Hermas was instructed by his 'shepherd' – no cleric – precisely so that he could return to 'God's chosen' and urge them to purge themselves of wickedness. He could expect to exercise a temporary authority, even over his own bishop, as well as over the disadvantaged of his community and over 'the elders who have charge of the church'.

And what of worship? As we move through the second century, developments heralded by Paul, in relation both to the eucharist and to leaders, continued to converge. Responsibility for the conduct of Christian worship seems to have been placed increasingly on the shoulders of *episkopoi* and *presbuteroi*, although the process remained gradual and uneven. The *Didachē* is a major source of information, although we have to bear in mind both its weighted interest and its possible restriction to Syria. It discusses baptism (preferably in running water), fasting (on Wednesdays and Fridays), and daily prayer; but its central demand is that the community should gather on Sundays and, after public confession and reconciliation, offer prayer over the bread and the cup, in thanksgiving for unity and knowledge. The unbaptized are specifically forbidden to participate, which may indicate that some communities had allowed them to do so. (An extended baptismal liturgy is first described fully in the *First Apology* of Justin, in the middle of the century.)

'Prophets' should be allowed to 'offer thanks as they wish'. *Eucharistein*, offering thanks, seems to mean here celebrating the eucharist, but it is not clear whether a special concession is implied. No instructions are given otherwise as to who should preside over the ceremonies. Hermas was even more vague in his references, which concern chiefly private prayer (at home and in the countryside) and fasting. When we reach the period of Justin, the conduct of worship is similar to that recommended in the *Didachē*. Anticipating Dionysius in Corinth and Hippolytus in Rome, Justin refers also to the reading of sacred texts, together with more recent letters and treatises, as part of the regular worship. He retains in his *First Apology*, however, a vague term for governance or leadership (found also in *1 Timothy*). It is only in the letters of Ignatius that we find a precise and early correlation between hierarchy and worship. Once again, the preoccupation of the letters should make us cautious. Ignatius was not always specific, pursuing his more general point about unity within each church. But he did emphasize the importance of assembling frequently as a community. He thought it dangerous to imagine (as some presumably had done) that one could offer God suitable service on one's own or in small groups – perhaps a gibe at the 'prophets' of the *Didachē*. The binding presence of bishop and presbyterate was an important safeguard – indeed a touchstone, since meetings held apart from a bishop flouted authoritative commandments. Those stipulations supply us with an extended context for Ignatius's single reference to the celebration of the eucharist (in the letter to Philadelphia), which draws together the notions of one flesh, one cup, one altar and one bishop.

ACQUIRING A FUTURE

Leadership was dedicated, therefore, to the preservation of social harmony and the ordering of formal prayer. Concern about specific doctrinal error and a corresponding defence of consensus were less evident. Later writers still accepted that argument would persist. The leader's task was not to identify principles but to resolve disputes. Even Irenaeus's respect for Rome was couched in those terms. Each of the original churches – close-knit groups, focused on the demands and promises of God – aspired to more than accurate belief. A powerful image in *Acts* presents us with the apostles in their upper room, bewildered about the timing of the coming kingdom, then seized by the spirit of God and confidently proclaiming to thousands their faith in Jesus. This shift from expectation to mission, from 'looking up into the sky' when Jesus was taken from them, to 'preaching the Gospel to the whole of creation' under the impulse of God's Spirit has provided an attractive tool of sociological analysis. It is taken to represent the transition from the charismatic leadership of a founder to the establishment of a stable religious movement. Among the earliest Christians, so the argument runs, the final days were thought to be imminent – the *eschaton*, which would herald the coming of Jesus in glory. It dawned on them, however, that the end had been postponed or was at least unpredictable. Heightened expectation was thus undermined by a species of 'cognitive dissonance' (nothing seemed to be happening), and a longer task presented itself, extending over generations and demanding a more detailed attention to order and continuity. Mission was at once the condition and the fruit of that altered view.

Evidence gleaned from the letters of Paul shows how swiftly the current of expectation could swerve. Paul was too much a Jew to have escaped, not just the expectancy – specifically, the messianic hope – of Judaism, but also its apocalyptic temper. However, as a Roman citizen reared in the Pharisaic tradition, as a Hellenized Jew not unfamiliar with the religious traditions of Rome's easternmost provinces, he had been able to impart to the apocalyptic view a degree of abstraction that carried it beyond the narrow anxieties of a localized conventicle. He stood for mission, therefore, as perhaps no other Christian pioneer. He allowed his images of fulfilment to be set once again in creation's past, making them historical and slow-moving in ways that would counter more fevered hopes and assurances. Clement, equally attentive to Jewish traditions, developed a similar sense of extended triumph, of a resurrection happening day by day. *1 Peter* had been ready to declare, 'It is time for judgement to begin.' *2 Peter* was designed to counter a subsequent doubt, 'Where is the promise of his coming?' That was a question posed (as Ignatius also suggested) by deceitful and hypocritical teachers, with their 'ruinous heresies'. The 'day of the Lord' would come. The insistent pressure of God's apparent slowness reflected only his eternity and his patient readiness to provide (as Hermas believed) a time for repentance. (The *Shepherd*, in its fifth 'similitude', provides a clear echo: 'the absence of the master represents the time left to us until his coming'.)

The interpretation of such a change, the particular readiness to make it sociologically significant, can take its cue from a misunderstanding of apocalyptic thought. The Jewish documents associated with the persons of Enoch and Daniel came from a variety of social settings and were not always inspired by a sense of alienation, threat, or millennial excitement. The same may be said of later exemplars, like *4 Ezra* and *2 Baruch*. Even the literature of Qumran shows that heightened expectation could be combined with a clear sense of community, rigorous discipline and a carefully ordered system of priestly instruction. The so-called *Similitudes of Enoch* (which may be Christian, at least in their final form) present a vision of the future useful to any community in any crisis, just like the eschatology and transcendence of Paul, of the *Letter to the Hebrews* and of *Revelation*. Moreover, when we think in terms of charism and institution, we should not assume that all apocalyptic visions were inimical to social order and religious cult. Constant reference in the Jewish texts to the heavenly temple and to an everlasting priesthood was carried over into Christian material. Such imagery allowed the worshipper to envisage another liturgy, enfolding but reaching beyond the Sunday eucharist. A growing institutionalization has to be interpreted in that light. Liturgical practice, closely linked with leadership and focused on the eucharist as an instrument of unity and a validation of authority, carried its own cargo of expectation. Those who waited waited now in prayer. The imminent presence of Jesus as a final judge in glory gave way to the presence of Jesus 'in the midst' of his community and 'in the breaking of bread' (as the Emmaus story in Luke's gospel had already begun to suggest). So the pulse of apocalyptic expectancy may have slowed and become more regular; but it beat still, as Christians settled down for a longer haul.

We need to be comparably cautious about the 'status inconsistency' I mentioned in Chapter 2. That may have affected the Pauline communities, but it cannot explain all further growth. A loss of advantage in politics, wealth and traditional religion was assuaged, according to sociological theory, by the consolations of an age to come. The stratagem proved less necessary, given new and lasting opportunities for honourable recognition within the Christian community: the exercise of priesthood, of patronage, of exceptional virtue. Those opportunities were sustained by a hierarchical structure and an increasing air of confidence. A keen sense of 'the coming', of 'the final days' could now endure alongside not only resolute proselytism but also the readiness to breed the next generation of believers.

There was one event that acquired an apocalyptic dimension, and helped to shift the emphasis of Christians: the suppression of the Jewish revolt of 66–69. The desecration of Judaism's holiest shrine, the Temple, and the brutal imposition of Roman authority in Palestine provided a new model of persecution. *Revelation* is probably the fullest witness to the adaptation achieved. This undeniably Christian document invited the churches to see themselves as the true Jews, who would survive all current and future turmoil (its vitriol recalls the isolated paranoia of some Qumran material). It described a period of oppression preceding the consummation that Paul and

Individual virtue and social setting

the gospels had foreseen. The genius of the work, however, perhaps not entirely conscious, resides in the symbolist obscurity of its descriptions, which allowed later generations to see their own oppression in *Revelation*'s terms, and to adjust its consummation, the 'new Jerusalem', to fit their immediate hopes and fears.

It was within this new framework of humiliating oppression, therefore, that authoritative structures protected communities against the fear that all was about to be dissolved. That pattern of thought reached forward through the centuries. It affected the interpretation of martyrdom, for example, which might otherwise have stood merely for the liberation of the individual. Persecution brought also its crop of defectors and pretenders, who threatened to render almost invisible the boundaries of shared belief. Ultimately, after Constantine, citizenship itself would be redefined, to be enjoyed within the 'city of God'. Some Jews were slow to abandon all hope of political triumph – their own apocalyptic literature was given a new boost by their misfortunes at the hand of Rome. Christians, on the other hand, were able to combine a sense of impending doom with a vague and more distanced impression of how persecution might end. As for any associated impulse to proselytize, the unavoidable swing away from Palestine towards the communities of the Diaspora gave fresh urgency to Jewish relations with the Hellenistic and Roman worlds and a greater prominence to 'godfearers' – gentiles attracted to Judaism, although not necessarily to Christianity. Imbued with a growing sense of mission to the whole of humanity, Christians felt able to herald the coming of a new age of universal significance, while effectively postponing its fulfilment.

We must concentrate, therefore, on the characteristic paradox of the new religion – its ability to combine a sense of destiny with an acceptance of failure. This was felt most keenly, as by Paul in *Romans*, within individuals. The Christian community served to assure its members of God's mercy, and mediated that mercy's application. Belief endured in the coming of God's judgement and kingdom: Christians were living, as Ignatius expressed it to the Ephesians, in 'the last times'. Hermas, however, and the *Letter of Barnabas* describe a more intimate anxiety: believers wanted to know what was going to happen next. Christian time began to stretch ahead as well as behind. For Hermas, in his conversations with his 'angel of repentance', there was a time remaining, limited but generous. It was to be a time of persecution as well as of conversion, a time of 'blood and fire' that would purify Hermas like gold and bring him and others to the bright glory of 'the coming age'. The blood and the fire, like other images in the *Shepherd*, recall the vivid prognosis of *Revelation* and find their parallel in the *Didachē*. Now, however, prophecy passed through the human heart, setting it upon a bridge between past and future. The hopes that marked Christianity were ancient but only distantly fulfilled. The past, in the *Letter of Barnabas*, one might know of, but understanding of the future was not yet available. The present, meanwhile, was the domain of wisdom, the knowledge of self.

The weakening of the community of expectation, therefore, ushered in the community of repentance. The notion was central to the work of Hermas. His Christians were quietly putting into practice the change of heart demanded amid the greater clamour of *Revelation*. He also placed a telling emphasis on the household. The tower being built in his visions (which he called the 'church') was recognizably the community of a later generation (the generation, perhaps, of the *Didachē* and certainly of Polycarp), within which children could be reared in the fear of God and slaves and women could be kept in their place. It was also the forum within which virtue was exercised. 'Virtue' here meant the care of widows and orphans, of the destitute and the distressed, the honouring of the poor as powerful advocates before God, and a generosity made possible by fasting. Here we begin to see how Pauline society might actually have affected its members. The households of Paul's authentic letters, with their almost proprietorial leadership and their domestic patterns of worship, had become more than convenient or well-endowed places of assembly: they were now a major force for spiritual formation. The angel of repentance made Hermas personally responsible for the failings of his family and for their spiritual improvement – not unlike the bishop in *1 Timothy* and the elders in the letter to Titus, each 'the husband of one wife', with children who were also 'believers'.

Seeing the household as the arena of redemption provoked anxieties about sexuality, marriage and the place of women. Hermas's handling of purity and adultery and his preference for the single life found their parallel among the churches inspired by Paul. Some had repudiated marriage altogether, in the belief that the end of the world was at hand. Others, while appealing to Paul's authority, resisted such extremes. *1 Timothy* sees exaggeration as the work of 'deceitful spirits', the 'doctrines of demons'. That caution reflected a desire to embed sexuality within a protective set of community structures. The same motives prompted respect for widows, offering them more than a choice between remarriage and oblivion. Women of sound reputation, advanced in years and faithful to the memory of one husband, soon became an integral and honoured part of every Christian group. (Those younger, however, were allowed less independence and were recommended to remarry.) Widows are already singled out as a group in *Acts*, the beneficiaries of pious generosity. *1 Timothy* demands later that they be 'enrolled', and relatives were given first responsibility for their maintenance. Both emphases persisted. The scope made available to such women was still governed by existing convention: they were to behave 'as befits women who profess religion'. Their enthusiastic piety was thought liable to founder on female weakness, exposing them to male exploitation. They were 'weighed down by sins', in the words of *2 Timothy*, 'and driven by a range of desires, constantly learning and never able to reach an understanding of the truth'. The movement involved here, from exhilaration to control, echoed perfectly a more general decline in the spirit of expectancy and a corresponding demand for order and continuity. While exalted destiny might content itself with simple abnegation (for men as well as women), postponement of the *eschaton* demanded more a carefully controlled fertility.

Some enduring ironies resulted from that interweaving of priestly leadership, moral urgency and familial pressure. Writers confidently stipulated practices that might have struggled, in fact, in a contentious atmosphere, to gain acceptance. Some deacons, for example, may have been women – taking in that sense the phrase in *1 Timothy*, 'the women likewise [i.e. like other deacons] must possess dignity'. This possible association of women with others in authority was destined to cause confusion, and shows that the authority was claimed as well as contested. The use of the word 'elders' contributed to the tension. In the letter to Titus, reverence is demanded for 'older' women, as well as men, and more seems implied than mere age. *1 Timothy* has traditionally been taken as depressingly specific: 'Let a woman learn in silence with all submissiveness. I permit no woman to teach or to have authority over men. She is to keep silent.' Yet in Titus's world the 'older women' clearly taught, even if under restriction – taught 'what is good [or were perhaps "the best of teachers"]' to 'train young women to love their husbands and children, to be sensible, chaste, domestic, kind and submissive to their husbands'. So judgements varied, even where liberty was limited. One can detect, in these orthodox texts, the pressures against which males would have to fight, without always winning.

THE QUEST FOR VIRTUE, AND ITS SOCIAL SETTING

Our inquiry into the nature of second-century Christianity has already carried us a long way from episcopal autocracy and doctrinal rigidity. Social cohesion and a clearer sense of historical continuity seem to have been of greater significance. One should highlight, above all, the culture of repentance. Christians were intent now upon a long-term task: the achievement of immortality through the conquest of vice and the acquisition of virtue. That urge remained the chief engine of ecclesiological growth, the basis of both community and hierarchy. Social motives – the chance of escape or betterment, for example, in the face of political or economic disadvantage – can lie behind any conversion; but we should not underestimate the sense of sin, of corruption, of imprisonment in matter, of distance from God – painfully felt in heart and psyche, and not always catered for by traditional religious affiliations. Explanation of the pain ranged from God's anger to the machinations of one's enemies. Christianity represented, correspondingly, either freedom from personal weakness, or a key to the cosmic and psychic maze, or perhaps just a talisman against malevolent intrigue. For many, it must have meant that expectation could become interiorized: the portents and vindications of apocalypse could be taken to stand for the drama of more intimate threats and stratagems. One no longer pinned one's hopes exclusively on a final day of reckoning, imminent or otherwise: one awaited a transformation of the self as much as of the world. Neither nature nor history nor birth nor disposition any longer defined what was possible. Weakness and inferiority lost their power to limit life. It was not just a matter of turning one's world upside down, choosing white instead of black. Christians sought a new order entirely, and thus combined their sense of a postponed ideal with dedication to moral effort. They did not want simply to exchange one 'kingdom', one political system for another: they wanted power and community to be redefined. In the process, they overrode the deadening polarities of disobedience and obedience (made obsolete by liberty), of body and soul (transcended by spirit and resurrection).

The keys to effecting this rite of passage were faith and repentance – optimism in response to promises, and a shaking off of the past. The social envelope catered for the inevitable precariousness that faith and repentance could induce, and ensured their visibility and permanence. Baptism constituted the bridge between individual and community – indeed, created and defined the community itself. It channelled and symbolized the individual act of faith and provided a corporate setting within which that faith could be protected. It demanded in particular an austerity and selflessness of life that could be policed at the same time by a controlled tolerance of backsliding. Yet faith and repentance remained deeply personal, the root of religious life. The individual Christian was one orientated anew, embracing change on the basis of trust. Moreover, 'faith' was faith in Jesus. For that reason, we can see how the competing images of Jesus discussed in Chapter 3 could affect in varying ways the conduct of the Christian life during subsequent generations. Was he the guarantee that repentance was possible? Was he himself the model of repentance, or indeed of faith? Was he the source of one's own regret? If so, by what perceptible mechanism? Was he the one who promised victory and reward, even at the cost of his own humiliation? Did one appeal to Jesus in this cause of redemption, or was he the one who appealed? Was baptism a symbol merely of one's commitment to the new way, or was it part of the process of 'salvation'? Jesus was, of course, no longer accessible, except by prayer and hope. His absence could be taken to portend his victory ('He has been raised, he is not here'). Yet his 'spirit' still struggled to gain a hold in individual lives. Was it the spirit that brought promises to fulfilment? And what was the role of one's fellow believers? Were they accidentally, so to speak, on the same path as oneself, or did one's association with them have some organic role to play in the process of one's own salvation? Could one be saved alone? There might be as many churches as there were hopes. That was why growth in unity depended on Christians acquiring a shared view of what they could hope for under God's dispensation.

So the passage from theory to practice depended on three factors: subjective intensity, a shared sense of need, and the support of an ordered group. Abstract theory was articulated with surprising speed. Faith in Jesus meant believing not only truths about the man himself but also that he had been born to redeem believers. One acknowledged either personal or historical failure, either the 'Fall' of humanity or one's own alienation; perhaps both. One believed equally in a new engagement with God, either by personal divinization or by a reordering of the cosmos. But ideas promptly directed conduct: as in the gospels, choices were demanded. In the *Didachē* (echoing *Deuteronomy*) there were two 'ways', good and evil (or, in the *Letter of Barnabas*, light and dark). One had to adhere to a 'teaching' and step out on the appropriate path. A vigorous, radiant, truthful, trusting and disciplined life would bring, in Clement's eyes, immortality, righteousness, sincerity, assurance and holiness. The most striking feature of the *Shepherd*, with its overarching emphasis on repentance, is its readiness to develop a spirituality, a mapping of human nature as conceived by God. Its complex programme of self-improvement, especially its imagery of good and evil 'spirits' or 'angels', anticipates later masters of Christian spirituality such as Evagrius and Cassian, which makes its survival and popularity among Christian readers doubly important. Its definition of faith focuses on the discernment of spiritual conflict within the heart, and is sustained by the conviction that God wished his creatures to achieve spiritual fulfilment. Like *1 Clement, 2 Peter*, and the *Didachē*, Hermas provided exhaustive lists of the virtues he wished to foster, especially in his third 'vision'. He showed a particular interest in *enkrateia*, ascetic self-discipline (best explained in the sixth 'mandate'); but he regarded it as a discipline for all. *Enkrateia* came to be seen in time as attainable only by a few; and even in earlier days, degrees of commitment varied. For Hermas, however, it was inspired by a healthy fear, which he identified simply with the purified desire for good. Equally important as witnesses to such early Christian sensibility are the so-called *Sentences* or maxims of Sextus (which I shall discuss more fully in a moment). Difficult to date and ascribe, the original collection had been made by the early decades of the third century: Origen noted its popularity. The late fourth-century Latin translation by Rufinus demonstrates its remarkable endurance, comparable to that of the *Shepherd*.

The early Christian quest for virtue was marked by interiority, humility, attractiveness and a sense of social obligation. The world of the *Shepherd* is lit from within: thoughts and desires define the arena of endeavour. The shepherd, in the fifth 'mandate', inspires Hermas to courage, so that the 'holy spirit' within him might remain 'pure', unimpeded by evil, free to range within his body, serving God with joy. We witness the ease with which Christians continued to believe that their private victories offered the best assurance of their religion's universal significance. Clement, Barnabas and Ignatius shared that view. God was perceived 'with the eyes of the soul': 'See', wrote Clement, 'how near he is: none of our thoughts escapes him.' God, granting time for repentance, was seated within. 'God really lives in us', wrote Barnabas; 'we are his dwelling-place.... He prophesies within us, dwells within us. By opening to us the door of the temple (that is, his mouth), he grants us repentance and leads us ... into the incorruptible temple.' *2 Peter* recognizes well the intimacy of this vocation: the message of the prophets was 'like a lamp shining in a dark place until the day dawns and the light of the morning star shines in our hearts'. A remarkable interiority inspired Ignatius also, colouring more richly his attachment to church order. In his letter to the Ephesians, for example, he wrote, 'He who has the word of Jesus for a true possession can also hear his silence ... Let us therefore do all things as though he were dwelling in us, that we may be his temples.' The virginity of Mary and the birth and death of Jesus ('hidden from the Prince of this world') were 'three mysteries of a cry which were wrought in the stillness of God'. There was in him, as he put it to the Romans, 'no fire of love for

Individual virtue and social setting

material things, but only water living and speaking in me and saying to me from within, "Come to the Father"'.

It is instructive to see how soon tension developed between confidence in self and dependence on God. 'A Christian', according to Ignatius, writing to Polycarp, 'has no power over himself but rests in the presence of God.' The *Didachē*, on the other hand, was assured enough to declare, 'If you can bear the whole yoke of the Lord, you will be perfect; if you cannot, then do what you can.' Hermas regarded trust in human potential as baseless without God's 'power'; but simply to acknowledge that power was to dispel debilitating fear. The act of creation had placed all things under human authority. Anyone who had God in their heart would master with ease the shepherd's régime. Indeed, believing that to be the case was half the battle. The shepherd wanted no mournful pessimism, which dragged the holy spirit down. Hermas's famous critique of *dipsychia* – 'double-mindedness', duplicity of soul – referred above all to an inner hesitation about God's mercy; and the appropriate and contrasting confidence, essential to repentance, demanded 'simplicity' (a strong and positive self-possession) and purity of heart. This subtle interplay of human and divine, of the potential and the dependent, essential to the notion of the Incarnation, although at times clouded or betrayed, would endure at the core of all that was best in Christianity. It is reflected also in the *Sentences of Sextus*. A humane and social sympathy is central to the collection – qualities not restricted to Christians, but presented by the author as the essential components of their life and community. The compiler of the maxims rejects submission to fate and makes God's providential care for individuals the chief characteristic of divinity. Faith, as in the *Shepherd*, means recognizing that fact; and faith and election by God are linked in the opening maxim: to believe was to be chosen. The implied mutuality pervades the collection. It was natural for human beings to aspire to and achieve likeness to God; it was natural for God to dwell in the human mind and heart. Freedom, understanding and acknowledgement of one's own nature: those were the instruments whereby God and creature were made present to each other.

Prophetic figures were not alone in presenting this new or freshly fashioned vision. There was a heightening of both anxiety and fervour in Mediterranean religion generally at this time, and Christianity would not have seemed the only available path to insight and self-possession. The interplay between Christian and non-Christian thought will concern us further in Chapter 5; but the *Sentences* make a particular point. Although we cannot ascribe the original maxims to Sixtus II, bishop of Rome in the late 250s, the compiler of the collection as it now stands was clearly a Christian. Jerome thought otherwise, and his hasty and tendentious judgement has carried considerable weight; but there are too many Christian sayings to make his opinion tenable. Nevertheless, the writer borrowed from beyond the Christian circle. The philosopher Porphyry was happy (towards the end of the third century) to draw upon the same sources; and much of the material would have seemed natural to Stoics and Pythagoreans. A reluctance to attribute positive value to the body, a readiness to endure hardship in a higher cause, a prejudice against hasty advice and overconfident speculation – all had a long past in Mediterranean culture. Yet there is, as a result, a striking and twofold ease about the text: the original compiler was ready to make 'foreign' wisdom his own; but later readers took for granted the Christian character of the result. Eventually, each judgement fed upon the other, and one can see why. We find foreshadowed, in the special formulae of the *Sentences*, a long Christian future: a preference for the celibate life, so soon to become entangled with the exaltation of virginity; the toughness of the martyr, capable of scorning tyrants; a sense that the truth about God was either inexpressible or unfitting for the ears of the majority and that curiosity and eloquence were conducive chiefly to error and pride. All these recall the inclinations of Paul and echo the prescriptions of the gospels. The tradition as a whole serves as a paradigm for the vexed issue of Christianity's relationship with, or distinction from, 'pagan' or 'classical' culture. It is unwise to explain the *Sentences* merely as an exercise in late imperial syncretism. The compiler's intention was not so much to borrow as to subsume; to place moral truth in a destined Christian setting.

That setting was social. In the *Sentences*, the inner colloquy of the moral agent was not a solitary indulgence. Efforts that were made alone would come to nothing. God would not listen to anyone who did not listen to the needy or pray for the salvation of others. There was no good that could not be shared. 'Concern for others', as the compiler put it, 'is the basis of religion.' The Christian writers of this post-apostolic period naturally took their cue from the 'great commandment' of the Jewish tradition and from the Johannine emphasis on love. The *Didachē* opens on that note, underlining the social responsibilities that follow. Hermas kept his rigorous ideals firmly embedded in a social framework. Ignatius encouraged those at Ephesus to 'seek who may suffer the more wrong, be the more destitute, the more despised'. 'The beginning is faith and the end is love' he added, 'and when the two are joined together in unity it is God, and all other noble things follow after them.' One of Christianity's most arresting features was this early insistence that virtue was a social achievement. Its system of formation and control was marked by a public coherence. Individual growth depended on that encouraging environment. Such a state of affairs was not peculiar to Christianity; but its special interpretation of personal relationships allowed it to define on its own terms the limits of a believer's freedom and responsibility. Repentance and virtue were brought to their peak among others. When the *Shepherd* describes *enkrateia* in detail, for example, the reader is plunged into a range of social disorders – adultery, pride and deceit. As an antidote, one must strive for harmony. The care of widows, orphans and the destitute; the encouragement of the distressed, especially those with weak faith; reverence, hospitality, justice and brotherhood – such were the fruits of self-discipline. The knowledge proper to the indwelling spirit would be declared when the spirit willed it, but would be declared within the community, 'the meeting of righteous men', where 'intercession is made to God'. Only the falsely inspired prophesied 'in corners'. The *Sentences*, for all their formal emphasis on discipline, recognized the same need. The author, as well as being open to the principles of other thinkers, was steeped in Christian sentiment and coupled confident self-discipline and self-respect with a humble and compassionate regard for others, making that the touchstone of effective religious practice, the guarantee that faith and redemption could represent the fulfilment of genuinely human values. That such a view developed so soon and remained popular for so long does much to explain Christianity's success.

ENDURING SEEDS OF CONFLICT

The disputed importance of history

Writers later regarded as orthodox remained for a long time at ease with 'knowledge language', but they distinguished one type of knowledge from another. The deutero-Pauline letters to Timothy attacked speculation and a craving for controversy, precisely because of their association with myth and fastidious asceticism. Hermas promised converts understanding, but he most often used the word *sunesis,* meaning shrewd perception rather than privileged insight. One was entitled to inquire into God's purposes and to question the state of one's soul, but one should recognize what lay beyond knowledge and concentrate on immediate tasks rather than remote speculations. Clement of Rome could adopt an exalted tone – 'Through [Jesus] the eyes of our heart have been opened, through him our foolish, darkened understanding leaps up to the light, through him the Lord allows us to taste immortal *gnōsis*' – but with the promise went a warning: 'the greater the *gnōsis* we have been granted, the greater the risk we run'. *Gnōsis* could be linked also with cult and hierarchy: having 'looked into the depths of the divine *gnōsis*', Christians should 'perform in due order and at appointed times the sacrifices and services the Lord has prescribed'. Barnabas, finally, packed about his use of *gnōsis* with other terminology – wisdom, understanding, and instruction.

That kind of 'knowledge', therefore, veered towards self-discipline and self-improvement. Among the Nag Hammadi codices is a document called *The Teachings of Silvanus*, which helps us to appreciate what lay behind that preference. Roughly contemporary with the *Sentences of Sextus*, it shares with other Nag Hammadi material certain images of the self and of the world that would be opposed and to some extent overridden within later Christian communities. It rehearses the dangers of ignorance and forgetfulness; asserts a belief that 'this whole world has come into being deceitfully' and is subject constantly to the influence of 'powers'; accepts that the soul is female, that wisdom is a 'mother'. There is, on the other hand, a focus in the *Teachings* on the engagement of the believer with the process of redemption. Christ remains a cosmic victor, but God (as Justin believed) is brought within the compass of human understanding (for Jesus is God's image, making his power visible). The victory, therefore, is achieved within the confines of self-discipline. The cure for sensuality is seclusion: 'release yourself', the text declares, 'from every bond' (including marriage); be sparing in friendship and cautious in choice of counsellors; 'if you wish to pass your life in quiet, do not keep company with any one'. The self is a stronghold defended by 'words' and 'counsels', by 'mind as a guiding principle'. As in the Jewish tradition, it is a temple within which one wears wisdom like a priestly garment. Nevertheless, each individual is provided by the *Teachings* with a social context. 'The divine teacher is with you always', but the text itself represents human instruction. Mastery is guaranteed by 'the teaching'; submission depends on a genuine humility. The reader is warned against those who peddle 'strange kinds of knowledge'. Behind every high principle – frugality, aestheticism and indifference – the contrary conceit can lurk – hypocrisy, greed and vanity – and only the judgement of others will protect one from illusion.

The instruction offered in the *Teachings* straddled, therefore, boundaries of conflict. Its ambiguities can help to clarify the distinctions aimed at by reflective or belligerent minds. The exalted 'knowledge' of speculative élites and the practical earnestness of less complacent devotees were divided along axes of opinion more profound than terms like 'gnosticism' and 'orthodoxy' can reasonably represent. Some appealed to a series of spiritual guides and to

Individual virtue and social setting

proven methods of instruction. They believed that even individual redemption was extended in time. Others appealed to an immediate relationship with the Saviour, which plucked the individual out of temporal sequence and away from the human institutions that had been developed within it. I have already described these as horizontal and vertical views of redemption. The *Teachings* offered elements of both. Inclination towards the more historical view, however, came to be identified with orthodoxy, while heretics were thought of by the orthodox as more sudden and independent in their sense of religious achievement. That contrast is more instructive than a supposed tension between order and anarchy, between episcopal rigour and spiritual enthusiasm. Patterns of church leadership were developed to serve a historical emphasis. Order was not considered valuable in itself but was designed to safeguard an accurate interpretation of the believer's past.

The struggle with the less historically minded was an important stimulus towards the development of authority. It made Christian leaders inevitably apologetical. What were regarded later as ancient, inevitable, divinely founded forms of government were in reality gradual responses to the ideologies and ambitions of others. In the *Clementine Recognitions* of the early third century, Simon Magus, Peter's antagonist in *Acts*, admits that the apostle attracted followers by teaching them what was 'customary', what they had grown used to. Simon himself was confident of an immediate power and taught what was 'new and unheard of'. The eternal purposes of the creator, therefore, the redemption that overcame estrangement from God, the tested doctrines and practices of the Christian community, the gradual, hesitant, even painful improvement of the individual – all were, in a sense, 'pasts' that required, for Simon's opponents, a different definition. The past explained what one might have cause to regret and offered assurance that regret could be transcended.

Paul had both represented and resolved the difficulties entailed. His letters provided a channel through which an old *gnōsis* could be inherited by a new – challenged and modified, nevertheless, by his characteristic judgements. His appeal in *1 Corinthians* to personal revelation was taken up later in a variety of guises; but he tested it by the shared rituals that (according to Luke) authenticated his claim and by caution in the face of prophetic utterance. A liberating sense of being plucked out of temporal sequence was analogous to the release from sin that Paul described in *Romans* and *Galatians*; but he did not encourage uninhibited indulgence on the strength of it. He knew well that an easy but deluded conscience was no substitute for spiritual victory. As he put it to the Corinthians, true wisdom was yet to come; and he countered alternative understandings of the word by the richer context within which he used it.

The keystone that secured Paul's strategy was his appeal to the past. The purposes of God 'in Christ' had been effective before the creation of Adam and reached across the ages to the day of glory. Baptism embedded an individual life in that wider arch of time. And the history was a Jewish history. Paul's evocation of Abraham, Moses, and the prophets was a genuine act of loyalty to the past, reordered by the perceived significance of Jesus. 'Authentic' Christianity modified *gnōsis*, therefore, by placing itself, with calculated precision, in Jewish history. Later writers understood how the transition was achieved. *1 Timothy* undermines 'false knowledge' with its own 'great mystery', the manifestation of Jesus 'in the flesh'. The author of *2 Peter* emphasizes the importance of an eyewitness encounter with the living Jesus. He reaches back to the words of the prophets as a counterweight to personal interpretation and supplies a long history of God's judgements. There will be, at the end of time, not only a new heaven but also a new earth. *2 Peter* claims a place in the Pauline tradition by insisting that Paul had judged rightly, even though his obscurity may have lent itself to misuse: careful attention to his words will confound 'the ignorant and unstable'. Similar points were being made in the gospels. The attack on docetism attributed to Jesus an extended historical reality, which undermined any tendency to mythologize him or to denigrate his human, bodily nature. For Ignatius of Antioch (writing to Smyrna and Tralles), not only did Jesus live, suffer, and die 'truly' – only that reality could justify martyrdom – but those who believed otherwise were flying in the face of a tradition that included Moses and the prophets, as well as the gospels. Paul had made the same point to the church in Corinth. There was a historical context to his famous remark, 'If there is no resurrection of the dead, then Christ was not raised; and if Christ was not raised, our preaching is hollow and your faith also.' He juxtaposed, in the same passage, death in Adam and life in Christ, looking backward and forward along the time-line of salvation. The whole period down to the end of the second century, therefore, can be seen as a debate about Paul's significance. He was not just the pioneer of community life but a thinker who exposed dangerous alternatives.

Bodies, women and the last things

So, those who exercised a more tightly structured authority and fostered the development of a scriptural canon tolerated a degree of *gnōsis* but excluded much else. Two attitudes claimed their particular attention: apocalypticism and asceticism. The apocalyptic tradition in Jewish thought could easily take a gnostic turn. The expectation of an immediate consummation could encourage a belief that only a few were privileged to understand its nature and timing. That attitude governs *Revelation*, traditionally associated with 'Johannine' documents, all of which are marked by a regard for *gnōsis*. But Christians gradually moved away from that immediate and esoteric emphasis and made the end of time part of a long history, with its own past and future. One could develop an eschatology, in other words, a theory of the 'last things', without being apocalyptic in a stricter sense. Indeed, religious dedication might be best sustained by postponement of the *eschaton*. The crucial fear to be countered was that there might not be an end. Gnosticism might be defined by its feeding upon that doubt – by a readiness to individualize, interiorize and mythologize the apocalypse; by asserting that the end had already come, or rather was part of the present that *gnōsis* created. The same attitudes underpinned a certain style of asceticism – one that despised the body and wished to live at once the life of the angels. *1 Timothy*, in its opposition to false knowledge, wished also to counter extreme views on marriage and dietary scruple. *Colossians* had already made a similar point. The scene was set for a long tussle, therefore, in which the developing hierarchy of Christian leadership made every effort to place ascetic enthusiasts under their own control; a campaign pursued with new vigour after the accession of Constantine, but never with total success.

Ascetic concerns about the body, passion and the material world clustered naturally around issues of sexuality. Here we have access chiefly to male opinion and male fears, and there is something condescending in their supposed liberality. The place of women in Christian society was contested at the level of theory. The earliest believers, even when suspicious of *gnōsis*, may have allowed women a degree of independence not always available outside their own communities. They were alarmed by ruthless repudiation of the body, and therefore of marriage, based on spiritual élitism or a sense of imminent fulfilment. Their admiration for widows, whose rights were defended throughout the early centuries, implied neither rejection of marriage nor extreme renunciation. As for those women still married, the chief concern was to safeguard their fidelity and curb male lust. Virginity appears to involve a more obvious disdain for the body, for social convention, and for biological continuity, all of which feature no less prominently in the *Odes of Solomon*, for example, or the *Acts of Philip*; but female virginity as an ordered way of life, defining permanently a distinct social category, was still a distant feature of church discipline. The *Symposium* of the bishop Methodius, written in the late third century, provided the first full theoretical treatment of the subject.

It is clear, nevertheless, that many churchmen were afraid of women's power – the power, for example, of the 'Jezebel' of Thyatira, whom *Revelation* describes as a 'prophetess' learned in the 'deep things of Satan'. Which was more worrying, her womanhood or her inspiration? Irenaeus and Tertullian were horrified that gnostics should tolerate such leadership in their women – clear evidence of their subjection either to evil powers or to sexual desire. They even suggested, perhaps with exaggeration, that women exercised priestly as well as prophetic roles in those communities. It is often suggested that the specific quality of gnostic asceticism did indeed break down the gender barrier. Males and females were seen as equal in their transcendence of sexuality. Those so inclined, however, could still succumb to the prejudices of their age. In the *Gospel of Thomas*, Jesus assures his disciples that Mary Magdalene can be saved. Obviously, some people thought differently. In the text, the disciples declare that 'women are not worthy of Life'. Even Jesus says of Mary that he will 'make her male': for 'every woman who will make herself male will enter the kingdom of heaven'. Small consolation, perhaps; but the passage may have attempted to justify a liberty already (and to the alarm of some) acquired. The *Gospel of Thomas* is not peculiar in its ambiguity. The feminine cosmological elements that we find in some of the Nag Hammadi texts is evident enough (although not peculiar to that collection) – the figure of *Sophia*, of wisdom itself, for example. But *Sophia* was also the root of all that was corrupt in the cosmos. She had wanted to produce offspring without the consent of the Spirit. As the *Apocryphon of John* puts it, 'a thing came out of her which was imperfect... the consequence of her desire'. This was the first Archon, the demiurge, the creator-god of Genesis. After the forming of Adam, Eve also became a handy symptom of division. Fundamental to many systems of thought represented at Nag Hammadi was the belief that Eve had been Adam's partner in regaining knowledge from the tree of paradise. The pair's expulsion from Eden had been only the work of the jealous creator-god, from whom Jesus the Saviour would rescue them. But nothing could disguise Eve's weakness, her need of rescue. According to the *Gospel of Philip*, it was her emergence from Adam's side, her difference from her partner, that had brought death into the world. To take the path of mythologized return meant not only 'forgetting the difference' but also escaping from female qualities.

Champions of the orthodox cause

The best-known ancient critics of a gnostic world-view tended to systematize what their opponents interpreted more loosely. Their abstract and conflated attack obscures the social behaviour of those whom they criticized. Justin, to take the first obvious example, was clearly antagonistic to any understanding of salvation that divorced God from the act of creation. Thanks to a complex demonology, he felt able to address the problem of evil in the world without impugning its goodness. Similarly, he distinguished the evil of idolatry (again, a ploy of demons) from the goodness of Platonist philosophy. Even more important were Justin's ethics and his calculated attempt to explain their evolution from the Jewish past. His understanding of human freedom, of the human capacity for choice, was deeply antagonistic to fatalism, either as a cosmic principle or as a moral excuse. Historically, he distinguished between tradition (reaching back to the apostles) and the novelties of more recent upstarts (Marcion, Valentinus and others). Christians constituted a long-standing and universal community, possessing (as he put it in his *Dialogue with Trypho*) 'one soul, one synagogue, one church'. For Justin, therefore, other opinions were deviations from an ancient norm.

His references to his fellow Samaritan Simon Magus are of special interest. Simon came with time to represent not only the purchase of authority but also an underlying arrogance, the notion that God could be controlled and his power harnessed by human guile. Justin, in his *First Apology*, supplies a moderately trustworthy account of Simon's supposed successors – Menander (who died *c.* 180) and Saturninus (less easy to date but clearly Christian). Justin clothed Simon himself in gnostic garb; and that was the view of the man, and of his admirers, taken up by Irenaeus and Hippolytus. It also coloured the Petrine apocrypha of the third century, in which Simon was consistently presented as Peter's doomed rival. But the picture becomes increasingly gnostic. Simon embodies a remote God (he called himself the 'great power'); he teaches the fall of the primal Thought and its successive imprisonment in human bodies (symbolized by his mistress Helen); and he practises magic (a common Christian insult).

In judging Irenaeus, we should notice the titles of his major works – *Against Heresies* and *The Demonstration of the Apostolic Teaching*. His purpose was to oppose error. He also took seriously the questions raised by those he dubbed gnostics. His polemic was based in part on the assertion that they formed a school, or rather a series of schools. Their teaching represented mere opinion and was vitiated by inevitable variety, reflected in its chaotic dichotomies. The 'Valentinians' in particular were perfect examples of tradition gone awry. Irenaeus relied by contrast, first, on his theory of recapitulation: not only had Christ restored what Adam had lost, but the restoration was part of the history that it transformed. Second, bishops safeguarded the inheritance of a unified and traditional dogma. (Irenaeus foreshadowed the later 'church historian' Eusebius, by producing lists of bishops.) He was far from thinking of tradition, however, in monolithic terms. His attachment to Polycarp, John and the church at Ephesus implied that there was more than one path leading back to the apostles (a useful key to his occasionally critical treatment of the bishops of Rome).

His slighting reference to differences of opinion had a polemical air; but Irenaeus distinguished usefully a number of supposedly erroneous groups. To place alongside Simon, we have Cerinthus, a contemporary of Polycarp (he died in the mid-150s). In him and in Saturninus, at least as described by Irenaeus, we can see obviously Christian elements. Saturninus dispensed with personified concepts like *Sophia* and *Ennoia*, 'wisdom' and 'thought', and presented Jesus as the single redemptive intermediary between God and humanity. He adopted an ascetic élitism. Cerinthus, again according to Irenaeus, believed in a distant, unknown Father and in creation by a lesser demiurge. Jesus was born and eventually suffered as a man, but it was Christ who did the redeeming, descending as a dove and making known his Father. Cerinthus seems to have moved in the world of John's gospel. We stumble, secondly, upon a full-blown system — what Irenaeus described as that of the Barbelognostics. The texts from Nag Hammadi prove that there were different refinements, even of this tradition. ('Barbelo', the first emanation of the Father and identified with the feminine element *Sophia*, was an obscure Semitic neologism.) We have a debilitated cosmos, in which humanity is trapped in a system of aeons and archons, while *Sophia* plays a key role in helping it to climb back to its destined level, challenging the forces pitted against it. There is an obvious link with texts like the *Apocryphon of John*. Finally, still in Irenaeus's account, we have the Sethians, who were even less ambiguously Christian. Their aeons bear the names of Father, Son and Spirit; Christ and church have comparable symbolic significance; and it is Christ who descends through the heavens to bring back humanity in triumph. A Nag Hammadi analogue in this case would be the *Book of the Great Seth*, probably originating in the region of Antioch.

Tertullian is justly regarded as the father of Latin Christianity, but he worked in a community still profoundly influenced by the Greek-speaking churches. In opposing gnostics, therefore, he owed much to Justin and Irenaeus; but his awareness of eastern developments also helped to encourage his gradual move towards Montanism. The combination explains how a rigorist who eventually rejected the world of non-believers could also mount so forceful a criticism of other rigorists. Like Irenaeus, he saw the gnostics as

Individual virtue and social setting

philosophers. In his *Scorpiace*, for example, he derided them as too eager to speculate in the traditional mode, too readily disdainful of heroism in the face of the state's demands. He was particularly critical of the followers of Valentinus. He attacked Hermogenes for dividing the soul between spiritual and material faculties. (Hermogenes had already been opposed by Theophilus of Antioch and was subsequently included by Hippolytus in his list of heretics.) Tertullian was inclined, like Irenaeus, to limit the word 'doctrine' to the teaching of Jesus and the apostles (this in his *De praescriptione haereticorum*, best translated as *A Ruling against Heretics*). Subsequent catechesis should conform to that or be deemed false. At one stroke, argument with opponents was rendered unnecessary. Priority was all that mattered. Tertullian was working here in the tradition of Paul, reaching back to the language of *Deuteronomy*, judging insight and ardour by a *regula* from the past. In the passage of the *Ruling* in which he made his famous contrast between Athens and Jerusalem, he declared that 'our teaching derives from the Portico of Solomon, who himself taught that men must seek the Lord in simplicity of heart'. 'Simplicity' was contrasted with the intellectual curiosity of ancient culture. He was sharp enough to spot a general failing among those he attacked: their optimistic aggrandizement of individual potential at the expense of the created world within which they were placed. Thus he grappled with a problem Paul had faced more than a century and a half before.

Hippolytus produced, or has been associated with, a substantial body of work, much of it exegesis. (I shall continue for the moment to refer to a single 'Hippolytus', as if he wrote everything that later generations attributed to him; but matters are not that simple, as I explain in Chapter 6.) He is chiefly famous for his opposition to Callistus, bishop of Rome from 217 to 222; but the argument between them had broad implications. Hippolytus was trying to balance a respect for institutions with a modified anticipation of the Second Coming. Order was necessary, for the end was not imminent, but one should not promise oneself too long a future. Hippolytus's understanding of the godhead helped him to that view. Retaining elements of Irenaeus's 'recapitulation', he still awaited a fulfilment of the divine plan. Collaboration with the empire could be presented, therefore, as redundant if not harmful. In that joint espousal of eschatology and social distinctiveness, Hippolytus developed a bold and uncomplicated interpretation of scripture. He would not soften his exegesis with allegory. He delighted in the images of deliverance afforded by the Jewish scriptures – Noah, Jonah, Susannah and Daniel. So straightforward an appeal had little time for mythology. But Hippolytus's understanding of the *Logos* (founded as much on Justin as on Irenaeus) displayed a caution that opponents could exploit. He felt that, if Jesus were the divine Son, then his humanity implied a shift in his relationship with the Father. Creation, Incarnation and redemption formed, therefore, a single cycle. We are brought back to the problem of how the *Logos* was generated. Because Hippolytus was willing to include in his discussion terms like *nous* and *sophia*, he came closer to a gnostic viewpoint than his reputation for biblical conservatism might suggest.

Nag Hammadi and Christian gnōsis

What happens when we relate the emphasis on historical continuity, together with the specific bugbears of our four 'champions', to the material from Nag Hammadi? I stressed in Chapter 1 that the majority of the Coptic treatises make no sense outside a Christian context. They illustrate variety more than they constitute an alien threat, even though opponents would later be inclined to label that variety 'heretical'. But they enrich our historical understanding in other ways. First, they raise the issue of how specifically Egyptian Christian gnosticism may have been. Second, they provide an explanatory context, within which to place the more famous proponents of the views that Justin and others rejected. Third, they sharpen our sense of what we should look for as distinctive – namely, their weaker attachment to history.

As I outlined in Chapter 1, the Nag Hammadi tractates were written in Coptic in the late third or fourth centuries and were, for the most part, translations of earlier sources. They confirm, therefore, the importance of Egypt as a centre of gnostic speculation, but their dependence on antecedent texts suggests that the tradition of thought they represent was more widespread and more ancient. Since Christianity – even given its specific novelties – was not an entirely original system of thought, it is neither surprising nor disturbing to find that many of the particular theologies preserved in the tractates had old and distant roots. Christians did not invent the notion of *gnōsis*, for example, even if most of the surviving gnostic material from the first century and later bears a Christian mark. Nor would it be odd to look for a link with Judaism, or to suggest that an immediate source of these Egyptian enthusiasms lay within Syria. Such have been the more fruitful lines of inquiry among scholars.

The first great 'Christian gnostic' was Basileides – an obscure figure of the late first or early second century, who may have come from Syria but is equally likely to have been Egyptian. It is even more probable that, at the height of his teaching, he was based in Alexandria. His influence is attested by Clement. Predominantly an oral exegete, with a strong inclination to asceticism, he was not as schematic as his successors. His early date and his clear wish to be considered a Christian thinker exemplify the relative ease with which one could combine at that time speculation and an appeal to the traditions of the apostles. Basileides believed, however, that Jesus was one of the great spiritual 'powers', who had come to rescue human souls from the control of the creating angel, whom he identified with the God of the Jews. He distinguished, as a result, between what he saw as Jewish ignorance and gospel wisdom (anticipating, to some degree, Marcion). Although there is no direct connection between Basileides and the Nag Hammadi material, the mythological dramas of the Egyptian tractates provide an illuminating context for his work.

The same is true in the case of Valentinus – again, almost certainly Egyptian. He acquired a Greek education in Alexandria, where he was converted to Christianity. He spent some years in Rome (c. 135–65) and may have lived for a while in Cyprus. The proliferation of his ideas through a number of disciples (Ptolemaeus and Heracleon in the West, Theodotus and Marcus in the East) hinted to a limited degree at what would later become a clearer division between Greek and Latin Christianity. For actual fragments of Valentinus's work, we depend chiefly on Clement's *Strōmateis* and *Excerpts from Theodotus*. (I shall discuss the *Strōmateis* further in the next two chapters.) What Nag Hammadi adds are works hitherto unknown that can be labelled 'Valentinian', although it is uncertain whether any were written by Valentinus himself. The most important are the *Gospel of Truth* (in Codex I, the 'Jung Codex'), *The Letter to Rheginus* and the *Tripartite Tractate* (also in Codex I), and the *Gospel of Philip* (in Codex II). The most obvious antecedent of the Valentinian system is the *Apocryphon* or Secret Book of John. Characteristic of Valentinus himself was a division of humanity into those enslaved by material passion (the 'hylics'), those touched by repentance (the 'psychics'), and those purified and enlightened by the Saviour (the 'pneumatics'); categories that corresponded roughly to body, soul and spirit. Movement from one state to another represented a shift from ignorance to knowledge, both in the individual and in the cosmos as a whole. Later commentators disagreed with him about the mechanism whereby this return to the *plerōma* could be achieved; but Valentinus readily included sacramental worship as an aid in reaching that spiritual goal. The *Gospel of Philip*, for example, establishes a firm link between reception of the eucharist and union with Jesus triumphant on his cross. Valentinus and his followers, therefore, were far from being placed at an extreme in the spectrum of Christian thought at the time.

Basileides and Valentinus reflected perfectly the Christianity of Alexandria: still close to the Hellenized Jews of the Diaspora, attentive to both the exegesis of scripture and the formation of a spiritual élite, and adventurous in its taste for philosophical speculation. Here was a city in which one could combine an apocalyptic emphasis with a world-weary cynicism, precisely because it was riding the wave of Hellenistic culture, challenging the ancient cultic traditions of the city-states that Alexander had conquered. Alexandria, like Antioch, also encouraged an intertwining of Jewish and Christian history. The exciting mixture of peoples and cultures in those new super-cities produced exactly the combination of rootlessness and ideological fertility that underpinned religious novelty. That had been a key element in Christianity's early understanding of its universal destiny, symbolized (at least in *Acts*) by the varied audience of Peter's sermon at Pentecost. In that instance, the audience had been predominantly Jewish, made up of pilgrims. Paul had quickly discovered other social groups that no longer felt tied to local and traditional cults. Their rootlessness and searching independence could lead as much in a gnostic direction as in any other. They were of the 'middling sort' I mentioned in Chapter 2, cultivated and prosperous, but alienated from the power structures of the Roman system. Such was the world that Basileides and Valentinus shared with Clement and Origen.

The sharing is what matters most. I shall have more to say about it in the next two chapters. Here I want to bring out the religious and social implications of the dialogue that Alexandria so characteristically fostered – a dialogue particularly crucial to our appreciation of Clement's career, during the early episcopate of Demetrius (189–232). Clement's attachment to *gnōsis* reflected his genuine hope that he might bridge a gap between different social groups. He wanted to rouse his fellow devotees to a greater degree of subtlety, so that they might acknowledge what was valuable in the arguments of apparent opponents. Tertullian demonized his enemies, while Clement favoured reconciliation. That readiness to negotiate across a narrow divide made him seem ambiguous in the eyes of less reflective purists, then and later. His attempt to address on their own ground those of a gnostic inclination – and even to adopt their vocabulary – encouraged a mystical and élitist bent that not everyone subsequently welcomed. But Clement's importance resides more in his being a thoroughgoing moralist. He believed that people's ability to return to God was based on their being created in God's image. That concept of *homoiōsis*, of 'likeness to God', became central to Greek theological discourse and provided an agenda for Christian optimism. Clement

Individual virtue and social setting

supported his conviction by appealing to Paul and to the apostolic tradition, as he had been taught by his Alexandrian mentor, the converted Stoic Pantaenus. But he considered that the best elements in Greek philosophy were desirable in themselves and a forceful weapon against obscurity and confusion; and his renowned openness to traditional *paideia* was firmly grounded in his concern for correct behaviour. To clarity of argument he wedded respect for rules of life, too readily dispensed with by the overconfident. When he referred to 'true *gnōsis*', he implied that Christianity offered a genuine knowledge that was calculated to expose the errors of more sectarian believers; but it was a knowledge acquired by stages under the guidance of teachers. The degrees of renunciation that Clement admired and recommended were correspondingly balanced, and described with subtlety. It was the intrinsic goodness of the created order that rendered indulgence unacceptable. Virginity and continence were authentic and constructive aspirations; but marriage was both necessary and honourable, and its difficulties and limitations made it a school of virtue. Not far below the surface of Clement's philosophical tolerance and moderate élitism, therefore, we can detect the typical weapons of those who opposed more extreme forms of *gnōsis*: respect for the gospel tradition, belief in the goodness of creation and provision for progress in the spiritual life.

Clement's endeavours, with their amalgam of generosity and caution, show how difficult it remained, at the turn of the third century, to dismiss in simplistic terms those who thought differently from oneself. Anyone who could reasonably claim to be Christian might be open to attack because of their supposed lack of logic; but it was harder to overlook the predilections they shared with those intent upon challenging their orthodoxy. Christians who were attacked as gnostics had ethical ideals. They celebrated liturgies little different from the liturgies of those by whom they were suspected. They valued the experience of community that was symbolized by the word 'church'. They even paid court to history. Irenaeus and Tertullian regarded gnostic churchmanship, however, as a calculated pretence. Gnostics, they asserted, were fomenters of division. They favoured an educated, prosperous élite and looked down on less disciplined, less perceptive groups, upon whom, nevertheless, they depended for their social and economic advantage. The heresy-hunters lamented what they thought of as the chaos of gnostic discipline, which (as they put it) confused priests with laity, catechumens with initiates, idolaters with believers. The attack foundered, however, on a contradiction. It overlooked the fact that the variety of social forms in the earliest churches had allowed room for gnosticizing Christians in the first place. As Paul had already found at Corinth, the so-called gnostics were simply challenging their co-religionists to put their house in order. One might despise their obscurity and suspect their claim to privileged insight or a continuing attachment to prophetic inspiration; but the persistence of such antinomian views simply proved that there were still many believers who refused to pass quietly from charismatic enthusiasm to sober discipline.

Historians have to accept, therefore, more ambiguity than a man like Irenaeus could afford to stomach. Plenty of those pilloried as gnostics used institutional vocabulary. 'Church' and 'bishop' were words familiar to them, even if they interpreted them differently. 'Church' in the Valentinian system may have been seen as part of the *plerōma*, a community limited to 'pneumatics' (as in the *Tripartite Tractate*), but it was a community, nevertheless, and took its shape within time and space. For all their rejection of the Jewish dispensation, Valentinians echoed *Deuteronomy* in linking dedication of heart to the formation of a 'people of the Beloved'. The *Gospel of Philip* and the 'Sethian' *Gospel of the Egyptians* made comparable emphases. The *Tripartite Tractate* happily usurped Paul's words in *Galatians* – 'neither Jew nor Hellene, neither slave nor free, neither male nor female' – but diverged in its explanation, rejecting historical reference to 'descendants of Abraham, his promised heirs' and substituting 'knowledge of the truth that existed before ignorance came to be'. That anarchic use of institutional terminology, held in quite different respect by the orthodox, was the boldest sign of a gnostic disdain for the ordered régime of their opponents.

Gnostics took equally seriously the traditional invocation of brotherhood. Once again, the quality of communal relations counted for more than regimentation. Among the orthodox, brotherhood came to be subsumed under a Stoic ideal of integration with the cosmos and the state. Gnostics retained a more literal sense of equality, which depended on their readiness to bypass intermediate definitions of order. The harmony of the regained *plerōma*, the 'wholeness' to be achieved in the 'fullness of time', implied for them an imperative, the urgency of which the orthodox were willing to postpone. The *Gospel of Thomas* makes its own gloss on 'love thy neighbour as thyself': Jesus says, 'Love your brother like your soul, guard him like the pupil of your eye', which immediately draws the recommended bond into association with the soul's enlightenment. Similar exhortations are embedded in the *Apocalypse of Peter* and the *Book of the Great Seth*. A vivid expression of primal equality, prior to and superior to human institutions, is preserved in Clement's *Strōmateis* from the treatise *On Righteousness* attributed to Epiphanes. The passage parodies Paul's lament in *Romans*, 'If it had not been for the Law, I should not have known sin.' Epiphanes was thinking more of human law (although he implicated the Jewish God of *Exodus*). Law parcelled out the common inheritance of nature and fostered envy and theft. The gnostic kiss, by contrast, which opponents would highlight sensationally, symbolized an ability to transcend the vulgar possessiveness of the tenth commandment. The attachment to liberty that went hand in hand with so precarious a rejection of the world meant in practice that a compromise had to be struck between, on the one hand, complete indifference to convention and, on the other, admission that obligations (social and otherwise) were unavoidable. How else, for example, might one attract devotees? That may explain the Valentinian conviction (reported by Origen) that one should serve those who are still unenlightened. As the *Gospel of Philip* put it, 'He who is really free through knowledge is a slave because of love for those who have not yet been able to attain to the freedom of knowledge.' The sentiment was not far removed from Paul's position in *1 Corinthians* – he made himself 'a slave to all, that I might win the more'.

Finally, for all their elevated detachment from time, Christian gnostics paid court to history. They valued in their own way the apostolic tradition: for gnostic gospels claimed to reproduce 'the secret sayings which the living Jesus spoke'. That written record could be taken, it is true, to reflect a transcendent book in the mind of the Father. Similarly, Jesus himself wavered in gnostic thought between his timeless role in the cosmic mythology and his appearance among his disciples on earth; and 'appearance' was often taken in a docetic sense. Yet the historical circumstances were of genuine significance. There had been a man called Jesus. His baptism in the Jordan and his crucifixion on Calvary had, as I explained in the previous chapter, a special place in gnostic Christology. They represented the moments when Jesus was taken up into the greater drama of the Word's return to the Father. So, their historical reality was integral to the conflict between divine power and the archons of the fallen world. And the individual retained a temporal identity. Simon Magus (according to Hippolytus) thought in terms of primeval, present and future ages, which were mirrored in his own life as one who 'stood, stands and will stand again'. Texts from Nag Hammadi adopt the same dynamism: 'Know who you are and how you were or how you shall be'; 'I have come to teach you what is, and what was and what will come to pass'. The *Letter of Barnabas* expressed itself no differently, thanking God for 'knowledge of the past, wisdom for the present and . . . understanding for the future'.

MARCION AND MONTANUS

Neither Marcion nor Montanus were strictly speaking gnostic, nor indeed akin to one another; but each man's challenge to the orthodox cause was related to his use of the past. Marcion rejected the Jewish scriptures entirely, while Montanus regarded tradition as a species of unfinished business, continually modified by the inspiration of the Spirit. Of the two, Marcion offered the greatest threat, from an orthodox point of view – at least to the formation of a historical literary tradition. Tertullian complained, with some exaggeration, that his heretical communities 'filled the world'. He aroused the fury of Irenaeus in southern Gaul and of Bardesanes in eastern Syria. His rejection of the Jewish past, which he saw as being at odds with Jesus's message of love, had a gnostic tone. The Law, he thought, was the work of the demiurge, whom the God of Jesus would overthrow. He diverged from gnosticism, however, in his distaste for mythology, and interpreted simply and strictly the biblical texts he was prepared to study. He thought of his heritage chiefly in Pauline terms, and it was this admiration that made him dangerous. The evangelists (with the partial exception of Luke), and indeed the apostles themselves, had been deluded, he said, by their Jewish heritage. Paul, on the other hand, had a sound understanding of what redemption meant. Only by God's mercy could the human soul gain salvation. There was no 'natural' path to its restoration. Even Marcion's missionary energy and administrative skill echoed Paul's career, and his followers may have been the first to translate Paul's letters into Latin. His Christology was essentially docetic, but he believed that Jesus had truly suffered on the cross (an apparent contradiction that Tertullian ridiculed). He encouraged an ascetic régime, based in part on the Sermon on the Mount, and rejected sexual intercourse as a particularly vicious ruse on the demiurge's part. Again, one can see gnostic parallels. Disciples like Apelles adopted a more obviously gnostic position, which helped contemporary critics to cast Marcion's enterprise in a gnostic light.

Montanus rejected the world more in the name of prophecy and apocalyptic. A new age of the Spirit was about to dawn, to be followed promptly by the descent of the heavenly Jerusalem. As with many gnostics, we meet again a readiness to believe in the accessible presence of divinity: the attention of the believer is directed upwards, as it were, rather than along the axis of inheritance. The images that Montanus could have found in *Revelation* were, in his own mind, about to become a reality in the village of Pepuza near Philadelphia. From an objective point of view, one can recognize an unbroken Christian history in Lydia and Phrygia that linked the communities castigated in *Revelation* with those later warned and encouraged by Ignatius and those now captivated by this 'New Prophecy'. Montanism did not revive convictions that had waned – attachment to spiritual charisms, for example, or defence of the dignity of women. It was not an anti-clerical movement, reflecting distress at increased institutionalization and at some Christians' readiness to compromise in the face of the world's expectations. Rather, the Montanists adopted practices and attitudes that had always been acceptable in some communities, and injected into them a new sense of urgency and obligation in the face of more recent threats. There is enough in Christian texts to explain how a 'Montanist view' might have developed, long before Montanus. As John's gospel put it, 'When [the Paraclete] comes, he will prove the world in error about sin, justice and judgement' (an accusation levelled against 'the archon of this world'); 'he will guide you into all truth: for he will not speak on his own initiative but will speak what he hears and will announce to you the things to come.' Montanism's arguably 'traditional' character, as heir to such convictions, made it particularly dangerous in the eyes of its opponents.

Yet literal eschatology (including physical resurrection) distinguished Montanism sharply from gnostic belief – in spite of the gnostic echo in John's words. It owed more to Jewish apocalyptic, like that in *4 Esdras*, and its dependence on Jewish models of prophecy distinguished it also from Marcion's system. Its intensity, however, encouraged a 'pneumatic' vocabulary. The orthodox were dismissed as mere 'psychics'. Montanists demanded also a radical asceticism, partly in the name of spiritual exaltation, partly in anticipation of the coming end. That stricter imperative had much to do with increasing persecution by the state, although the resulting élitism reflected only the fact that Montanists made compulsory what other Christians had long admired or recommended. The pressure of powerful opponents will always call into question the propriety of tolerance and compromise. The heroic can be unforgiving in their disdain for the cowardly and the cautious. Women were among the heroes, and Montanism was notable for including them. Two indispensable associates of the prophet, Prisca (or Priscilla) and Maximilla, achieved great status; and there is evidence that Montanist women in general exercised something approaching priesthood, although so prophetic a movement placed less emphasis on the eucharist. Their eminence in a cultic context, as in the case of men, may have been the fruit of their having suffered under persecution. The North African martyr Perpetua is presented in her *Passion* in Montanist terms and independent of the clergy. It may have been courage like hers that made Tertullian throw in his lot with the rigorists. He persuaded himself that the Montanists (at least of North Africa) were the most authentic Christians of his day. The orthodox found it hard to fault Montanism on the score of doctrine. The threat it presented was more a matter of discipline, leadership and morality. Its enemies could not endure the way it bypassed priesthood (by making the prophet the mouthpiece of God) and implied that fresh revelation was still possible (thus denying a stable authority to the gospel tradition).

This account of experiment, variety and debate leaves us with several loose ends and will be developed further in the two chapters that follow. It is clear, however, what meaning we should attach to unity. Geographical expansion in the second century, combined with enduring traditions that can be labelled priestly, gnostic, apocalyptic, philosophical or ascetic, encouraged believers to regard themselves as part of a single body. There was more than one tradition, but Christians could rise above parochialism. The episcopate and the sacramental liturgy may have given the orthodox an edge when it came to maintaining a stable community; but gnostics and Montanists led a cultic life also (the later philosopher Plotinus described the chants of gnostics) and gave meaning of their own to baptism, priesthood and the eucharist. Orthodox leadership and liturgy were designed more to foster a historical consciousness, to emphasize that cosmic order and personal virtue would be realized over time and on the basis of past achievement. It was still not agreed, however, whether cultic acts or moral endeavour offered the best pathway to understanding and spiritual success. Those who favoured rigorous discipline still constituted a sizeable proportion of believers.

Other themes reach forward into later sections of our inquiry. The past included the Jewish past and was used to counter the timeless mythologies of gnostics. Jesus, placed firmly in the physical and historical world, was related to that past. Both convictions governed the authenticity afforded by Christians to scriptural texts. Suspicion of matter, of the body and of sexuality was not restricted to gnostics. By attributing the progress of gnosticism to the influence of Satan, the orthodox supported in their own way a temporal dualism that failed to combat effectively the imputed pessimism of their opponents. A more general ascetic tendency, which could include fasting, isolation and élitism, threatened to narrow Christianity's appeal and fracture its communities. Prophetic and apocalyptic traditions had comparable effects – the notion that they died out is misplaced, and reflected only orthodox optimism. Finally, moral rigour and spiritual exaltation coloured the Christian's attitude to civil society, especially when the suspicion or distaste of outsiders brought pressure to bear and fomented defiance. We must concern ourselves next, therefore, with discipleship and martyrdom. The first reflected the scale and intimacy of Christian communities. The second tested both their rigorism and their capacity for compromise and accommodation.

Further reading

On the social structures of early Christianity, see Rodney Stark, *The Rise of Christianity: a Sociologist Reconsiders History* (Princeton, NJ: Princeton University Press, 1996), together with Philip Francis Esler, *The First Christians in their Social Worlds: Social-Scientific Approaches to New Testament Interpretation* (London and New York, NY: Routledge, 1994) and the collection Esler edited, *Modelling Early Christianity: Social-Scientific Studies of the New Testament in its Context* (London and New York, NY: Routledge, 1995). Also stimulating is Howard Clark Kee, *Christian Origins in Sociological Perspective: Methods and Resources* (Philadelphia, PA: Westminster Press, 1980). More general issues emerge from the essay by Peter Brown in Paul Veyne (ed.), *A History of Private Life*, 1: *From Pagan Rome to Byzantium*, translated by Arthur Goldhammer (Cambridge, MA and London: Belknap, 1992).

Social structures carry theoretical implications, on which see Howard Clark Kee, *Who are the People of God? Early Christian Models of Community* (New Haven, CT & London: Yale University Press, 1995) and Lewis Ayres and Gareth Jones (eds), *Christian Origins: Theology, Rhetoric, and Community* (London and New York, NY: Routledge, 1998). Of lasting value are older studies by Wayne A. Meeks, *The Moral World of the First Christians* (London: SPCK, 1986), and Rowan A. Greer, *Broken Lights and Mended Lives: Theology and Common Life in the Early Church* (University Park, PA and London: Pennsylvania State University Press, 1986). See also Everett Ferguson (ed.), *Doctrines of Human Nature, Sin, and Salvation in the Early Church* (New York, NY: Garland, 1993).

On the issue of 'mission', see Martin Goodman, *Mission and Conversion: Proselytizing in the Religious History of the Roman Empire* (Oxford: Clarendon Press, 1994) and Robert W. Hefner (ed.), *Conversion to Christianity: Historical and Anthropological Perspectives on a Great Transformation* (Berkeley, CA: University of California Press, 1993).

For further reading on Christianity's relations with Judaism, background information is supplied by John M.G. Barclay, *Jews in the Mediterranean Diaspora: from Alexander to Trajan (323 BCE–117 CE)* (Berkeley, CA: University of California Press, 1999), Martin Goodman (ed.), *Jews in a Graeco-Roman World* (Oxford: Oxford University Press, 1999) and Steven Fine (ed.), *Sacred Realm: the Emergence of the Synagogue in the Ancient World* (London and New

York, NY: Oxford University Press, 1996), together with H.L. Strack and G. Stemberger, *Introduction to the Talmud and Midrash*, translated by M. Bockmuehl (Edinburgh: T. & T. Clark, 1991); and more specific issues of relationship with Christianity are treated by Jack T. Sanders, *Schismatics, Sectarians, Dissidents, Deviants: the First One Hundred Years of Jewish-Christian Relations* (London: SCM Press, 1993) and James D.G. Dunn (ed.), *Jews and Christians: the Parting of the Ways, AD 70 to 135* (Tübingen: J.C.B. Mohr, 1992).

On the internal order of Christian communities, see Henry Chadwick, *The Circle and the Ellipse: Rival Concepts of Authority in the Early Church* (Oxford, 1959) and *The Sentences of Sextus: a Contribution to the History of Early Christian Ethics* (Cambridge: Cambridge University Press, 1959), John S. Kloppenborg and Stephen G. Wilson (eds), *Voluntary Associations in the Graeco-Roman World* (London and New York, NY: Routledge, 1996), Alexandre Faivre, *The Emergence of the Laity in the Early Church*, translated by David Smith (New York, NY: Paulist Press, 1990), James Tunstead Burtchaell, *From Synagogue to Church: Public Services and Offices in the Earliest Christian Communities* (Cambridge: Cambridge University Press, 1992) and Paul F. Bradshaw, *The Search for the Origins of Christian Worship: Sources and Methods for the Study of Early Liturgy* (Oxford: Oxford University Press, 1993). A comparative study of great value is James A. Francis, *Subversive Virtue: Asceticism and Authority in the Second-Century Pagan World* (University Park, PA: Pennsylvania State University Press, 1995).

For viewpoints that suffered gradual exclusion under the impact of 'orthodoxy', see two studies by David E. Aune, *The Cultic Setting of Realized Eschatology in Early Christianity* (Leiden: Brill, 1972) and *Prophecy in Early Christianity and the Ancient Mediterranean World* (Grand Rapids, MI: Eerdmans, 1983), together with Christopher Rowland, *The Open Heaven: a Study of Apocalyptic in Judaism and Early Christianity* (New York, NY: Crossroad, 1982). Specifically on Montanism, see Ronald E. Heine, *The Montanist Oracles and Testimonia* (Macon, GA: Mercer University Press, 1989), Christine Trevett, *Montanism: Gender, Authority, and the New Prophecy* (Cambridge: Cambridge University Press, 1996) and William Tabbernee, *Montanist Inscriptions and Testimonia: Epigraphic Sources Illustrating the History of Montanism* (Macon, GA: Mercer University Press, 1996).

Gnosticism has inspired an enormous scholarly output. I mentioned some general studies at the end of Chapter 1, and of Justin and Irenaeus at the end of Chapter 3, to which one might add Denis Minns, *Irenaeus* (London: Chapman, 1994). See also John D. Turner and Anne McGuire (eds), *The Nag Hammadi Library after Fifty Years* (Leiden: Brill, 1997), Michael Allen Williams, *Rethinking 'Gnosticism': an Argument for Dismantling a Dubious Category*

(Princeton, NJ: Princeton University Press, 1996) and Alastair H.B. Logan, *Gnostic Truth and Christian Heresy: a Study in the History of Gnosticism* (Edinburgh: T. & T. Clark/Peabody, MA: Hendrickson, 1996). On the subject of women and gnosticism, see Jorunn Jacobsen Buckley, *Female Fault and Fulfilment in Gnosticism* (Chapel Hill, NC: University of North Carolina Press, 1986), Karen L. King (ed.), *Images of the Feminine in Gnosticism* (Philadelphia, PA: Fortress Press, 1988) and Daniel L. Hoffman, *The Status of Women and Gnosticism in Irenaeus and Tertullian* (Lewiston, NY: Edwin Mellen Press, 1995).

Turning to the subject of women more generally, the corpus is again enormous. I have omitted most general studies of women in antiquity, although one might note in particular the work of Elaine Fantham, Jane F. Gardner, Barbara Levick, Sarah B. Pomeroy, Beryl Rawson and Rosemary Radford Ruether, together with the collection edited by Averil Cameron and Amélie Kuhrt, *Images of Women in Antiquity* (London: Croom Helm, 1983). Wide-ranging reflections are contained in Aline Rousselle, *Porneia: on Desire and the Body in Antiquity* (1983), translated by Felicia Pheasant (Oxford: Blackwell, 1988) and Leonie J. Archer, Susan Fischler and Maria Wyke (eds), *Women in Ancient Societies: 'An Illusion of the Night'* (London and New York, NY: Routledge, 1994). The work of Ross S. Kraemer has been influential: *Her Share of the Blessings: Women's Religions among Pagans, Jews, and Christians in the Greco-Roman World* (New York, NY: Oxford University Press, 1992), together with two edited collections, *Maenads, Martyrs, Matrons, Monastics: a Sourcebook on Women's Religions in the Greco-Roman World* (Philadelphia, PA: Fortress Press, 1988) and (with Mary Rose D'Angelo) *Women and Christian Origins* (Oxford: Oxford University Press, 1999). For later developments, see Gillian Clark, *Women in Late Antiquity: Pagan and Christian Lifestyles* (Oxford: Clarendon Press, 1993) and Antti Arjava, *Women and Law in Late Antiquity* (Oxford: Clarendon Press, 1996). Other useful and in some cases classic studies are Kerstin Aspegren, *The Male Woman: a Feminine Ideal in the Early Church* (Stockholm: Almqvist & Wiksell International, 1990), Jo Ann McNamara, *A New Song: Celibate Women in the First Three Christian Centuries* (New York, NY and Binghamton, NY: Harrington Park Press, 1985), G.S. Nathan, *The Family in Late Antiquity: the Rise of Christianity and the Endurance of Tradition* (London and New York, NY: Routledge, 1999), Deborah F. Sawyer, *Women and Religion in the First Christian Centuries* (London and New York, NY: Routledge, 1996), D.M. Scholer, *Women in Early Christianity* (New York, NY: Garland, 1993) and Ben Witherington, *Women and the Genesis of Christianity* (Cambridge: Cambridge University Press, 1990).

Where to begin?
Howard Clark Kee, *Who are the People of God?*

Chapter 5

CHURCHES AS LEARNING COMMUNITIES

I have suggested that the momentum of a church's growth was governed not by its institutions but by its spiritual aspirations; that institutions developed in the service of more abstract principles. I want now to explore an implication of that argument — namely, that codes of behaviour and systems of belief depend on patterns of formation, whereby people learn what they have to do and why they have to do it, and find their efforts sustained by the example and encouragement of those around them. It was the function of a Christian community to teach. Commitment to Christianity resulted in a distinctive style of behaviour, a distinctive skill in self-discipline, which was based on tradition, acquired over time and shared with one's fellow believers. Christians subscribed to a culture of expertise. It identified the well informed. Its most characteristic and effective leaders defined ideals, guarded the resources upon which their development and preservation depended, and imparted to new generations the insights and convictions of the past.

INSTRUCTION AND COMMUNITY FORMATION

Christianity involved more than the transfiguration of individuals by the impact of God's presence. Paul, after his experience on the road to Damascus (as *Acts* presents the affair), was instructed by Ananias; the Ethiopian eunuch (again, in *Acts*), reading *Isaiah* in his carriage, needed the guidance of Philip. Those anecdotes sum up perfectly the labour of Christian initiation. Intense reorientation had to be protected within a living tradition. One might be seized by Jesus transcendent but one was instructed by Jesus the man, his teaching preserved and handed down by his followers. The conviction could be expressed in exalted terms. In the *Gospel of Truth,* Jesus the tactful and

A learning community

patient 'guide' opened 'the living book of the living' in the hearts of believers; a book 'written in the thought and mind of the Father'. Justin, in his *Dialogue with Trypho*, described the words of Jesus as more brilliant than the sun, penetrating 'the very depths of the heart and the understanding'. Clement of Alexandria played on the ambiguity of 'Word' and 'word': the incarnate *Logos* could only have been a teacher. Origen saw teachers as the high priests of the Christian dispensation, sharing out the *Logos* like a victim from a spiritual altar, revealing its inner meaning. Jesus's humanity, however, made the effect less abstract. In the course of his 'recapitulation', Jesus had been, as Irenaeus put it, first instructed, then an instructor. For Justin, he fostered reason, virtue and happiness. Clement portrayed him as unassuming, generous and cheerful. Only his humanity, according to Hippolytus, made his teaching intelligible and acceptable.

In committing oneself to Jesus, therefore, one accepted a formative discipline. Most churches housed more listeners than heroes. Clement, in his *Paidagōgos*, was the great theorist of instruction. 'The church here below', he wrote, 'is a school [a *didaskaleion*] and the bridegroom its only teacher'; and 'piety is pedagogy [*paidagōgia*]' – although he never imagined that in either phrase the second term exhausted the meaning of the first. In all this, he echoed Justin's *Apology*. Justin had trusted intelligence. Once they had seen the practical fruits of faith, he felt, and had given them honest attention, people would be bound to recognize the truth. Christians were not the only ones to think in those terms, but they were convinced that their religion was more effective in such a cause. In the first place, they saw life's varied circumstances as tests of virtue. For Clement and Origen, affliction itself was a *paideusis*, an education, which made assurance more secure and lasting, precisely because it had been painfully acquired. To overcome the limitations of the body and return to the realm of the spirit was, in Origen's eyes, to respond to the instruction of experience. Thus, in his *Peri Archōn*, 'On First Principles', he joined in his characteristic way the workings, on the one hand, of the mind and the will, which drew the believer back to the level of true humanity, and, on the other, the great ladder of the cosmos, which stretched from God's heights to demonic depths.

Belief in discipline and progress served to distinguish Clement and Origen from their gnostic rivals. There was always more to learn. Simple faith was not enough: one struggled to grasp the deeper meaning of Scripture and prayed for spiritual progress. At the same time, initiative was dependent on God's aid. A constant urge to better oneself by choice, to exercise freedom, was central to their spirituality. Gnostics congratulated themselves on natural powers received from the outset. Origen made freedom a precarious prelude to God's rewards. The gnostic tendency to stillness gave place to an exhilarating momentum, a longing to regain what was not yet possessed. Justin was the pioneer here also. Christianity was not just a name, he said, or a state achieved suddenly: it was a pattern of behaviour, the constant exercise of virtue. Justin the 'philosopher', moving from school to school, had seen his acceptance of Christianity as the conclusion of a process. Successors stressed equally the need for prolonged effort. Origen, about whose methods we know most, offered his pupils clear stages of enlightenment. According to his pupil Gregory the Wonderworker, he stimulated them in the Socratic manner, prompted their belief in a providential God, described and encouraged virtue, and finally opened their minds to more complex theology. Building on the insights of Justin and Clement before him, Origen did most to unravel in symbolic form the various stages of Christian progress, anticipated in the single experience of baptism. The eucharist, similarly, operated on two levels. With each ritual encounter, new understanding was achieved; but the sacrament contained, on each occasion, its fullest possible complement of meaning. Individual and subjective experience was, again, enfolded within the single system of God's creation.

The theory demanded a language – a language of motive and understanding, of the inner self. And masters and disciples, even bishops and their churches, depended on an oral etiquette to formulate and impart their beliefs. The religious language of early Christians – their techniques of presentation, assertion and assent; the way in which they made authority and deference audible – was borrowed both from within and (increasingly) from outside Jewish tradition. Justin exemplified the shifts that soon made the language of Christianity more specifically its own. He took, for example, the philosophically familiar notion of the *logos spermatikos* – the intellectual principle embedded like a seed in each human being – and limited its complete embodiment to the *Logos* Jesus. Only 'in Christ', as Paul would have put it, could each person fulfil their *logos* potential. The associated idea of 'seed' had formative implications: it was the task of the teacher to bring latent reason to maturity. Reason is endorsed in many texts, such as *The Teachings of Silvanus* or *The Testament of Truth*; but a specific engagement with Jesus broadened Justin's view. The *Logos* represented power as well as enlightenment, and a release of freedom. Clement, who inherited those notions, made teaching Orphic in quality, a seduction, the weaving of a spell, as well as a healing demonstration of *philanthrōpia*. That was why, in Origen's thought, freedom had to be set loose, had to be the source of inner growth. Gnostics stuck to a more rigid, hierarchical view of nature, of body, soul and spirit, whereas, for Origen, nature was raised to its proper level by the exercise of freedom. *Paideusis* depended on persuasion, therefore; a persuasion based on the power God gave to speakers, to 'men of proven wisdom and the unquestionable ability to teach others the truth'. Each act of understanding, charged with a potential of cosmic proportions, was coloured by the circumstances in which it was awakened.

Christianity gained enormously from the range of languages in which it was expressed, especially because, with time, it was able to conflate the insights and nuances of different speakers under the governance of a single set of ideas. To achieve such harmony, texts were essential. Although the century after 150 would assure a common culture, the move from word to text had taken place sooner; and the motive behind the move had been immediately connected with instruction. Christians came only slowly to rival the pedagogic literature of the rabbis, but they inherited at once from their Jewish and biblical matrix the deeply ingrained habit of basing religious formation on the mastery of a text. The letters of Paul are the earliest surviving examples of that facility. Letter writing lent itself to a certain breathless disorder, which only gradually settled into a genre. But the period of the Apostolic Fathers presents us with a network of letter-writing communities. They continued to read Paul, whose letters were grouped in collections. By the time of 2 Timothy, the apostle seemed both a herald and a master, which hints at a transition from the riveting call of a great missionary to the 'healing words' of an experienced pedagogue. Others were eager to join that tradition: Ignatius of Antioch, for example, and the writer of *Revelation*. The second genre of note can be loosely called biographical: the gospels, but also novelistic dramas like Acts and its imitators. Literary tradition regarded such works as formative in their impact. As we have seen, they could start by reflecting the loyalties and convictions of particular groups, but soon inspired the discourse of a wider community and shaped its hymns and prayers. The preservation of everything, therefore, that we explored in relation to Paul and Jesus was designed to enthuse and direct the later generations of believers.

To talk of letters, of reading letters and writing letters, is to talk of the settings in which they were composed and received. The sound of language filled a social space. Texts played a central role in creating, reinforcing and modifying the relation between ideas and communities. Modification proved the most significant aspect – a shift of weight, a major turning of the wheel in Christianity's progress. Several types of social structure could have emerged, but certain emphases better guaranteed stability and endurance. A major feature of early Christianity was each generation's ability to inherit ideas and practices from the last. By describing its evolution in those terms, we make its future more intelligible. The key to its success was not the quality of its doctrine – orthodoxy's triumph and the marginalization of heretics – but its effort to establish continuity. The doctrine that served that continuity best would prove to be the doctrine that survived. As the Christian library grew, so it nourished new learners. Divorced from partisan and local roots, where such existed, Christian literature sustained a common and ever more widespread view. The formative usefulness of available texts brought together groups that might otherwise have remained isolated or distinct. A fruitful bargain was struck between the learned, the Christian 'scribe', and the as yet uninformed enthusiast. Texts also supported a missionary thrust, and the centres in which they were copied were likely to have been the centres of such expansion. Paul had led the way, but Marcion knew the wisdom of the technique, as did the Manichees after him. The community at prayer, finally, was a community nourished by texts. The celebration of the liturgy as Justin described it was like a reading circle, at once philosophical and religious. After Scripture and other documents had been read and discussed, the eucharist was celebrated, and then all departed to apply what they had learned. The liturgy was an integrated gesture of informed and powerful conviction, and its participants were *logoi spermatikoi* in action. The ripples that moved outwards from valued writings, through expert instruction and missionary zeal, to a broad audience of potential adherents served to emphasize the static sterility of gnostic élites. Thus, each church became a series of concentric chambers, and its erudition was designed to counter the contained enlightenment of complacent minorities.

Learning and instruction defined the leadership of each community. The authors and chief recipients of early Christian letters, and of gospels, either possessed or aspired to high status. A mastery of written material and the ability to explain it to others became the hallmarks of revered authority. *2 Timothy* described 'a pattern of healing words'. Timothy was exhorted to be 'gracious towards everyone, a handy teacher', 'instructing opponents with soothing words', so that God might lead them to 'repentance and recognition of the truth'. The writer recalled the recipient's youth in exactly the terms we have described. 'Hold fast to what you have learned and believed in, seeing who they are from whom you learned it. From infancy, you have been familiar with the sacred writings, which can give you the wisdom that brings salvation through faith in Jesus the Christ. All Scripture is inspired by

God and helpful for instruction... so that the man of God may be perfect and equipped for every good work.' The contrast was with the familiar bugbears of orthodoxy – namely, teachers who 'turn aside into myths' (*1 Timothy* had added 'interminable genealogies'). The flow of thought from the written word to its practical application made the asceticism of the scholar a paradigm of Christian commitment. To preserve and interpret, to create with effect: those who could not rise to such a task were unlikely to command respect. And those who could, regardless of their title, might challenge the authority of any priest not similarly gifted. Tension resulted (which the deutero-Pauline letters to Timothy were anxious to circumvent in the name of episcopacy), but it could be resolved. Priests and scholars strove to acquire each other's dignity and virtue. A tension was there, however, which affected the ways in which a community went about instructing its members. We have to take that tension into account, when we try to envisage such communities. Were they always gathered around their bishop, their sole instructor in practice and belief? Or did they also gather around a range of other figures – catechists, moral exemplars, charismatic interpreters, inspired prophets? Such figures could equally claim to respect the past and mould the future.

THE SCALE AND STYLE OF INSTRUCTION

The small group

Does the notion of a 'learning community' provide a social model capable of embracing all or most believers? Few would have appreciated the higher flights of allegorical exegesis; but we should not expect to find a mass movement. The demands of both proselytism and catechesis favoured the smaller scale. Jesus and the apostles may have addressed large crowds, but the 'feel' of the gospels and the letters of Paul is intimate and domestic, reflecting and encouraging a comparable social practice. Christian art, liturgy, exegesis and theology were not products of a thought-world spread evenly across the empire. Each text, although it may have gained a place in an increasingly common library, started life in limited circumstances. Its initial character and effect must be measured in relation to its immediate audience. Its eventual usefulness in a wider setting depended on earlier and local success. The speed with which, for example, passages from Irenaeus of Lyon could turn up on an early third-century papyrus in Egypt reflects not the size or rapid expansion of a universal church but rather a network of messengers, hurrying with texts and letters from group to group.

We have to take seriously (in the writings of Justin, for example) unambiguous references to small circles of inquirers. We have to believe, moreover, that Justin taught what inquirers wanted to know. Only those already informed and interested (together perhaps with their friends and family) were likely to seek instruction and incorporation. Justin is a crucial figure in part because of his ability to reach beyond his Judaism. Gentile Christians, sharing with the 'godfearers' an attraction to Jewish belief and culture, albeit interpreted in their special way, were now able to extend a welcome to nonbelievers outside the Jewish orbit; but their own attractiveness was likely to be limited to persons of similar piety and openness of mind. When Celsus, criticizing Christianity, made (according to Origen) his famous statement about the religion's appeal to slaves and women, he not only seized upon a traditional instrument of satire but also betrayed a mandarin's typical inability to credit such persons with intelligence. Christianity's extended purchase may explain his own culture's eventual failure. Social class was not a controlling factor: rather, intensity of interest and the availability of satisfying answers. Such loyalty was not gained among crowds on street-corners, however. When Origen surrendered the instruction of the less advanced to his colleague Heraclas, we should not imagine the latter plunging himself into some noisy classroom of youthful beginners. Heraclas's curriculum was less speculative than Origen's, but equally demanding. He was, as Eusebius put it, 'very learned and not unacquainted with philosophy'. It was no accident that he and his associate Dionysius became bishops of Alexandria. Their polished addresses were pastorally inspired, but their avoidance of élitism did not make them elementary. When we hear, therefore, that hundreds of bishops presided over the churches of North Africa in Cyprian's day, contemporary with Dionysius, we should not imagine a teeming world of Christians, whatever the level of confidence the figure suggests, but rather hundreds of small groups attentive to the words of their masters; perhaps a few thousand persons all told. The earliest surviving Christian 'church', at Dura-Europos on the Euphrates, dating from the 240s, consists of two rooms knocked into one in a private house, together with a tiny baptistery. (A similar 'house-church' existed in Carthage in Tertullian's day.) While we recognize the formality implied by liturgical use, we cannot ignore the size of the Dura-Europos complex, capable of holding comfortably no more than a few dozen people.

The small group has been taken as a hallmark of heresy. Irenaeus even used the word 'school' in that negative sense. Numbers, however, have never been a guarantee of truth. Second-century and third-century Christian

A learning community

groups could still have been small, without being either eccentric in their demands or disdainful in their attitudes. When one group imputed such qualities to another, they did not base their rectitude on the larger size of their congregations. Nor was ascetic rigour essential to the coherence of the smaller group: the elevated spirituality of Clement left room for marital virtue. Tatian rejected the Hellenistic sympathies of his associate Justin; but his encratite extremism, abhorring sexual intercourse as a deceit of the devil, aped, as it deplored, the intimate régime that Justin encouraged. Groups similar in size, therefore, could foster different attitudes and rest upon different models of virtue and leadership. Not all of them were pulled in an esoteric direction.

That forces us again to be cautious in our description of gnostics. Their abundant literature is not a measure of their numerical strength: for their complex theology demanded the private attention of patient readers, and must have remained accessible to relatively few. Truth, according to the *Gospel of Thomas*, welled up from within. So privileged a view, however, would have been fed by an awareness of rivals. The competitiveness demanded of the gnostic élite immediately made them part of a larger world. In taking their cue from cultic associations or philosophical schools, they were no more recherché than their critics. They were open to the variety of social models available. What mattered first to each group was faith, whether conceived in speculative terms or not. Hellenistic philosophy, together with its social forms, proved convenient to a number of parties but had to be adapted to the faith of each. The social model by itself, therefore, was not the essential clue to a group's convictions. Only when a significant body of believers laid claim to the open spaces of Roman society was it enough to castigate error on the grounds of its secrecy or seclusion. In the second century, gnostics were too similar for comfort. The most dangerous and least distinctive example, as we have seen, was Valentinus. He, like Tatian, had been a product of Justin's Rome. He moved in a world of teachers. Origen said of Valentinus's pupil Heracleon that he admitted to an early dependence on instruction. There were many like the gnostic Ptolemy, who acknowledged in his *Letter to Flora* a succession of masters reaching back to the time of Jesus. Valentinus saw himself in the same category, continuing the tradition of the 'teachers' in the letters to Timothy. He was a catechist, interpreting Scripture and encouraging prayer through use of the psalter and of his own hymns. He, no less than Clement, saw his endeavours as a supplement rather than a challenge to the bishop's church.

The Apocryphal Acts

Much can be learned from the so-called *Apocryphal Acts of the Apostles* – chiefly those of Paul (and Thecla), Peter, John, Andrew and Thomas, written in the late second and early third centuries. (Others, like the *Acts of Philip*, are later.) They are not complete fiction, at least in their incidental detail; they are not homogeneous, although at times conscious of one another; and they are not exclusively gnostic. The *Acts of Paul*, *Peter* and *John* were probably written in Asia Minor; those of *Andrew* perhaps in Greece; those of *Thomas* in Syria – a range of origins that explains their range of emphasis. *Peter* is marked by openness to men and to ecclesiastical office. *Andrew* is a 'philosophic' work, preoccupied with language and with relations to Jesus the Word. *Thomas* has all the rigour and drama one expects from Syria. *Paul* is sharp in its mistrust of gnostics who peddled false views of resurrection. *John*, on the other hand, is happy (at least in part) to espouse the docetism gnostics approved of. The corpus displays, in other words, considerable diversity.

It interests us here in two respects. It allows us to reflect on the scale and purpose of instruction, and helps us to relate instruction to institutional forms. Both the sources and the reliability of the *Acts* have generated debate, a debate interwoven with and confused by an analysis of the Greek novel. Novels, like the famous *Daphnis and Chloë*, for all their romantic abandon, reinforced the expectations of city élites – their expectations about marriage and status in particular. The *Apocryphal Acts*, therefore, which espouse continence and disrupt family allegiance, appear to reflect the novelistic genre by a process of deliberate inversion. However, the *Acts* may have been more conservative than at first appears. Nor is it certain whether they were predominantly literary creations or whether they were based on popular oral themes. There is even deeper doubt about the usefulness of such apparent fictions. Nevertheless, their imaginative detail is likely to have echoed social realities. More important, the care devoted to their literary construction betrays both the tastes of their intended audience and the ideals that the audience was expected to sustain.

Speaking generally, the *Acts* present a three-sided drama, featuring a wandering apostle, a determined woman (who is swayed by his teaching) and an angry husband (who resents the estrangement of his wife). Each narrative identifies Christianity in some degree with the renunciation of marriage. The renunciation, however, is chiefly a challenge to the foundations of civil society. The *Acts* contrast, therefore, with novels; but their different answers address the same set of questions – questions about the appropriate relation between sexual mores and the conduct of the citizen. They are not interested in the practicalities of sexual abstinence, but more in the status that continent men and women can justly claim in the public sphere.

The characterization of the apostle is of special interest. Similar figures, intrusive and charismatic, appear in Justin's *Apology* and arouse ire in some 'Clementine' texts. Origen, writing *Against Celsus*, mentions preachers who travelled from village to village. In the *Acts*, the reputation of Jesus's first disciples attempts to justify that style of leadership. They impute at times virtual divinity to their heroes (as the citizens of Lystra had to Barnabas and Paul). They present them, on the other hand, as mediators between a virtuous woman and her outraged husband, and therefore as both the source and the focus of intimate emotion. In each respect, the figures are at once distant and alarming – drawn from an earlier age but capable of disrupting current order. The disruption mattered most. 'Apostles' had already been viewed in the *Didachē* as threats to church discipline, not least because there were those who still valued their capacity to startle. The danger persisted, as Irenaeus made clear in his description of the gnostic itinerant Marcus in Lyon decades later. Critics were not just deploring the overthrow of family relations, but responding to a subversion of the discourse of power. While aping a genre that channelled young ardour towards civic conformity (the novel), the *Acts* admired an ironic parody of marital virtue that threatened to question the purpose of such a tradition.

The threat seems most evident when we turn to the 'disciple' in this scenario – the woman launched on her new path of self-identity. Loosed from male expectations, she sits at the apostle's feet, embraces continence and gains new influence. How much are we dealing here with a 'woman's world'? Were the *Acts* written by women for women? Do these texts corroborate a view that male teachers were helpless without women's independent interest and support? The view has been widely defended, and embraces more than the *Acts*. Clement was happy to include women among his pupils, and appealed to their example. Origen employed them as scribes, and depended on female patrons. We have plenty of second-century evidence for earnest groups of women sharing an ascetic life or, as 'widows' especially, serving the needs of their community. There is no denying such realities, a ready-made venue for stories of this sort; and features of the *Acts* point firmly to a female perspective. Thecla, in *Paul*, became the most popular example. During her second exposure in the arena, a lioness protects her, driving off the male beasts, to the wild delight of female spectators. Her contest is brought to a prudent end when Tryphaena, a kinswoman of the emperor, swoons in horror. Men, by contrast, are (apart from the apostles) not only villainous but also wooden. They do not grasp the preacher's message. However, their stupidity rests in their failure to accept that the apostle's teaching is ultimately to the city's advantage. It is perfectly possible to argue, therefore, that the real heroes of the *Acts* were men who were prepared to deny themselves children in order to gain a wider family. The real dialogue took place between the masters of households and cities, on the one hand, and the apostles who were able to create and inspire a different sense of community, on the other.

The woman, therefore, spectacular in the narrative itself, was, as a reader, potentially more docile. It was her loyalty the text was after, not her spirited capacity for drama. She was to switch from one male master to another. Tertullian (in his work *On Baptism*) disapproved of women who claimed like Thecla the right to baptize and teach. Harsh though he could be, he may have judged correctly the authors' intentions. The genre itself, even when inverted, made its demands. The *Acts* addressed a world in which households were still forceful instruments of cultural identity and political ambition. Christians' increasing desire for public recognition had to be fostered within them. The social displacement of the heroic female was just as much a ploy in the *Acts* as it was in the novels; not an end in itself, but designed to awaken staid or restricted readers to alternative patterns of engagement with the people around them. The shift of perspective demanded an enduring social context. For all the liberty of a Thecla or a Maximilla, the *Acts* expected readers to support such women, as they had long supported widows and other committed devotees; and support required wealth and continuity.

The groups portrayed in the *Acts* were stable enough to practise a regular liturgy, and to place their leaders within it. The wandering apostle achieved his effect in that setting. Marcellus entertained Peter in his own home, where Scripture was read, homilies preached and prayers recited in the dining room. One is reminded of Dura-Europos, but also of the liturgies described by Justin. In just such a room, Thecla in her window-seat listened to Paul. It was often the hope of the audience, moreover, that the apostle would remain in their settled world. Those who failed to do so were not obvious role models for the people they left behind. Thomas is portrayed as understanding the contrasts involved. He appointed the deacon Xenophon to take his place – a man who would not fail like Aaron in the absence of Moses; a man who 'preached Jesus' no less than had Thomas himself. Thus the passing excitement generated by an outsider could be preserved by the long-term leader who stayed behind. Teachers with staying power catered for a world only lightly touched by the passing charismatic, who may have become an archaic figure, no longer genuinely subversive. An apparent conclusion to the *Acts of Andrew* (its original structure is not easy to determine) hopes that by listening to the apostle (or by reading the text) the community might achieve firmer 'fellowship'. Here, one suspects, was a church capable of producing the type of text it was invited to applaud; the source rather than the recipient of missionary endeavour.

What may we deduce from this material? First, that the early Christians were divided less between orthodoxy and gnosticism and more by their methods of forming settled churches. The *Apocryphal Acts* wanted to harness unpredictable enthusiasm to the preservation of groups; to make the virtues of liberty the guarantee of order; to bottle, as it were, the pure spring waters of the gospel era. The result was not communities blown asunder by individual 'conversion', but churches drawn together by the attraction of shared and novel goals. Measured and prolonged instruction was the essence of the enterprise. That was the world of Polycarp as described by Irenaeus (to Florinus) and of Irenaeus as described by Eusebius; of Justin, pitted against the Cynic Crescens, with Tatian, Marcion and Valentinus in the background; of the *Letter to Diognetus*, where the text became the teacher. It was the world of Origen. In the house of a rich patron, he attended prayer meetings with men and women of dubious or varied opinions. He accepted the support of the repentant gnostic Ambrose, employed his stenographers, sat (in his own words) 'at the master's desk', and built a small community of students.

There could be some loose-footedness. Justin taught in places other than Rome (his *Dialogue with Trypho* was probably written at Ephesus). Clement came to Alexandria from Athens via several masters, and was forced north again by persecution in 202. His mentor Pantaenus was from Sicily, and may have travelled as far as India. The opening book of the *Strōmateis* describes pockets of scattered souls who preserved and handed on the timeless truth that was the source of Clement's wisdom. Origen, for his part, made several journeys to Greece, Palestine and Syria, as well as to Rome. Yet those men bear little resemblance to the heroic apostles of the *Acts*; and the clue to the difference lies in their firm association with the bishop. The possibility of that association is implied by the ordered liturgies of the *Acts* themselves. Clement and Origen provide the most richly illustrated instances. Clement understood in what respects he needed to counter an exaggerated gnosticism. He built up in his disciples a sense of spiritual priesthood, but kept it within ecclesial bounds and linked it firmly with the need to love others. Origen may appear less successful. His later reputation for theological error was provoked as much by a spiritualizing élitism as by his readiness to speculate. But we should not confuse his frustrations with his principles. Clement's world was undermined, not by an exalted emphasis but by the persecution of Septimius Severus. Origen took up, therefore, under his bishop's direction, a tougher task, and was then left to his own devices by his bishop Demetrius's temporary withdrawal from his see. It was difficult, when peace had been restored in 211, to revert to Clement's style. Origen's acceptance of his new responsibilities had coincided with a radical reassessment of what 'teaching' might mean; and a man of his talent could not rest content with heroic repudiation of the classics. His search for a new vocation inevitably affected his relations with authority. Clement had been practical in his approach to the Alexandrian clergy. Origen, with his taste for allegory, saw human institutions shot through with light from more spiritual levels of reality – not always to the advantage of the institution. Where Hippolytus interpreted the *Song of Songs* as an image of the church's union with the Word, Origen focused on bonds between the Word and the soul. Yet that intimacy could induce tears of repentance; and tears would demand in their turn confession 'to one of the Lord's priests', seeking the 'remedy' of his spiritual direction.

SCHOLARSHIP AND 'ORTHODOXY'

Clement and Origen: the Alexandrian achievement

It is useful to have considered first the formation of the wider community. It helps us to avoid the supposition that Christian history is a history of thinkers and ideas. Scholarship operated, however, at a variety of levels and, in the hands of a few, contributed directly to theological development. Here the big names come into their own. Paul and his successors, and the writers of the gospels, were already dealing with conceptual issues; and the preservation and dissemination of their work represented the formation of a culture capable of dealing with intellectual difficulties. *2 Timothy* had already appropriated the term *paideia*. Justin, Irenaeus, Clement, Origen and Tertullian gave the trend a secure future, and carried debate to a high level of reflection and analysis. Nevertheless, they retained a specifically Christian motive – to reach out to an audience of more than academic disposition. The title 'apologist', which all five deserve, hints at a desire to explain oneself to the less convinced. The writings of such early 'fathers' served as tools for the less erudite, guides for the perplexed, weapons in a busier struggle against error and in the rougher commerce of persuasion. They addressed both

A learning community

opponents and allies, and served to supplement a bishop's efforts to instruct and protect his charges.

The reading and writing of such literature familiarized Christians with the notion of learnedness itself. The Bible was an indispensable aid, but the techniques of traditional *paideia* were as necessary to Christians as they were to the interpreters of Homer and Plato. Even deeper was dependence on a Christian past, which had to be defined and enlarged upon. 'What you have heard from me before many witnesses' – so Paul was made to say – 'entrust to such men of faith as are equipped to teach others.' That kind of pedigree, however, was not without its problems. To a more sophisticated mind, it might appear to inhibit the originality of thought essential to scholarship of integrity and worth. The resolution of the paradox soon became, and has long remained, a central feature of Christian theology. At the end of the first book of his *Strōmateis* or 'ragbags' – an offhand evocation of 'miscellanies' that scarcely does justice to the collection's profundity and length – Clement of Alexandria, reflecting on the meaning of history, ascribed to tradition in the richest sense a timeless quality that preserved amid shifting circumstance the essential secrets of God's nature and purpose. The teacher, in his eyes, inherited what he called the 'apostolic seeds' of eternal and transcendent truth. Too much trust in mere antiquity, therefore, hobbled the understanding. A genuine appreciation of timeless truth depended, for Clement, on making the transition from the tribal world of the Pentateuch to the 'pneumatic' state, the exalted spiritual perception, of the Christian *gnōstikos*.

The implications were radical. The integrity and fruitfulness of scholarship was neither constrained by nor antagonistic to an orthodox view. To a man like Clement, habits of mind were no more valuable than habits of discipline and practice. The past that one had to respect was not a past defined by custom, even the custom preserved in Scripture. The Christian scholar experienced a species of 'modernity' – a fresh but disturbed understanding of what the past had led to. Only in those terms could authority and morality be legitimized. Those who considered themselves orthodox had to measure themselves by the same standard. 'Orthodoxy' could not survive as a form of outmoded intransigence, but responded to the shock of the present. It involved attachment to the past, but from a viewpoint that had outlived custom. It preferred system to disordered memory, but it etched on the copperplate of tradition a calligraphy modelled by its own anxieties. That explains why orthodoxy could change. It also explains why people from other religious backgrounds found Christianity at first so difficult to make sense of. It was constantly ahead of its time.

Yet the 'modernity' of Clement depended on inherited skills. The increasing complexity of rabbinic thought and the lawyer's skill in preserving and interpreting documents formed, along with philosophical and literary criticism, a respected, exemplary and accessible community of scholarship. It possessed in addition a genealogy of named authorities. Because Jews like Philo had already been influenced by Hellenistic methods of interpretation, Christian Hellenists like Justin and Clement found it natural to appeal to Jewish antecedent. Justin may have been formerly a 'philosopher', but he insisted (in his *Dialogue* and not just *ad hominem*) that Jewish prophets were equally possessed of wisdom. Clement's reach was even longer. He attributed wisdom to the enduring inspiration of God, and found its traces in Orpheus and Plato no less than among Jews and in the gospels. A crucial effect of that catholicity was a readiness to accept more than one interpretation of a text. Clement (like most of his contemporaries) was eclectic. His views of God, the cosmos and the soul were influenced by Plato; his logic and psychology owed more to Aristotle; his morality was Stoic at heart; and his understanding of the last things was almost Pythagorean. It is remarkable, therefore, that his writing remains identifiably his own. The same was true of Justin and Origen. Given the dominant role of Platonism in the contemporary trend to synthesis, Clement's masterly coherence is all the more notable for avoiding the pitfalls that trapped so many gnostics. He recognized in Plato a deep attachment to notions of beauty and goodness, which far outweighed his ambivalence about matter and his pessimism about knowledge, hindered by the illusion of the senses. From Aristotle, he inherited an unshaken belief in reason. In the second and fifth books of the *Strōmateis* especially, he fathomed Aristotle's keen understanding of how the mind assents to evidence, taking for granted, by necessity, certain principles of judgement. It proved for Clement that faith was not irrational, and could be enhanced by practised perception. Origen displayed the same confidence. One could always find a reason for what the apostles said, even if they had not provided it themselves. What they did not say, on the other hand, one was free to investigate as one could. The crucial caveat was that reason set to work on what was given, and did not appeal to new authorities. It also needed God's help in the task. One is reminded how much rational thought was tolerated in the second and third centuries, under the protection of Aristotle's name. Within the broader context of philosophical syncretism, that cautious realism did much to safeguard the practical aspects of religious commitment, raising its sights above literary technique.

Allegory was a major aid to practicality. Philo and Origen are the best-known allegorists. Their enthusiasm, sometimes strained in its ingenuity, is often thought of as irresponsibly disregarding the plain meaning of Scripture. They had found, however, the means to rise above the temporal restraints of ancient documents. Allegorists are interested in deciding what a text can mean now, as opposed to what it might have meant then. They make texts contemporary – 'modern' in the sense I suggested above. They gain thereby a greater freedom of interpretation. In Origen's case, the freedom was controlled by the concept of 'foreshadowing'. One read the text in a present setting, where both clearer understanding and visible fulfilment justified implications glimpsed less directly by the original author. The Jewish Scriptures could now be read in circumstances that gave them added sense – a sense, Origen felt, that the inspired writers would have acknowledged, had they been present. Exegesis by itself, therefore, was not enough – which, in the light of later disputes, was a crucial assertion. It is true that gnostics were also masters of exegesis. Their opponents had to defend, therefore, interpretation of a different sort. Allegory rescued them from the illumined speculations of an esoteric coterie. Based on the tested skills of authoritative forebears, and deployed in the interest of a cumulative understanding, it channelled the implications of the text into the daily lives of believers. Gnostics, on the other hand, were drawn away from the moral quandaries of earthly existence, and allowed themselves to trust in the reality of what was exclusively symbolic. Those eventually regarded as orthodox used their scholarship to preserve exactly the texts they had inherited. How else could the implication, the foreshadowing, remain reliably available? Gnostics, on the other hand, created documents that were essentially new, in which older elements were allowed to meld with their inventive commentary.

The refinement of such issues may tempt us once more to think of Clement and Origen simply as theological giants or exemplars of a single 'Alexandrian' culture. They represent the first intellectual peak of Christian history, but they worked in a city that teemed with teachers of varied persuasions – most of them not Christians. Although markedly different in both circumstance and ideology, it was as teachers that they sought their own fortunes and as teachers that they aroused resentment. Both were widely read, and Origen appreciated the importance of books for research. They were at the same time surprisingly disorganized in their productivity. Clement started well, with his *Protreptikos* and *Paidagōgos* – careful treatises that explained why one might wish to embrace Christianity and submit to its moral tenets. The *Strōmateis*, on the other hand, for all their bulk and wisdom, hint at a man overtaken by circumstance. They were accumulated notes, as he put it himself, 'stored up for my old age'. Origen was aware of Clement's unfulfilled promises. His own *Peri Archōn* attempted a task that Clement had left unaddressed. But he also kept bundles of notes that never found their way to an independent order (although they must have sustained him in his sermons and commentaries).

Haphazard methods were a symptom of their practicality, of their desire to face whatever challenge came to hand. Nowhere is that more obvious than in their response to gnosticism. Fundamental elements of what we now think of as their 'theology' were set in place under the pressure of debate with rival teachers. Clement used 'faith' to inspire a yearning in the pupil that 'knowledge' by itself might dispense with – a psychological rather than a systematic emphasis. His understanding of time was coloured, therefore, by the future; a future one could know of but never (in this world) complacently possess. And his understanding of morality was correspondingly designed for living now, although governed by the demands of a destiny as yet unfulfilled. Even that, in Origen's eyes, surrendered too much to gnostics. He never used *gnōsis* terminology, preferring allusion to *pneuma*, the spirit. He addressed anxieties about providence more than understanding. His Christian was a swimmer rather than a sailor; less guided by charts or a canny sense of wind and sail, and more swept onward by the deep currents of God's creative energy. The clue to Origen's reassurance was cosmic rather than interior, and he recaptured the astringency of Justin's thought. If one could appreciate how creation worked (and that dynamic emphasis was crucial), the purpose of Jesus's life and the nature of the salvation he offered would at once become clearer. The humanity of Jesus was the indispensable sign of the invisible *Logos*, in whose image his fellow humans had been made. The life of Jesus was an invitation to become more like the *Logos* and so to reach the transforming threshold between the absolute singularity of God and the dispersed imperfections of created multiplicity. That was no facile exercise in 'spiritualization' but an exhausting struggle to recognize one's 'logical' nature, and to climb beyond the restrictions of visible existence.

Neither man, however, took his cue entirely from his rivals. Clement and Origen did not try to build preferable theories by rearranging elements in the theories of their opponents. What gave their work its ultimate coherence was their independent rootedness in Scripture. They were exegetes rather than speculators, and their arguments with gnostics focused on the meaning of texts. Their grander achievements in spirituality and theology had their origins in that analysis. In Origen's case, the enterprise reached in the end well beyond polemic. His *Hexapla* or 'sixfold' version of the Bible remained for well over a century the greatest example of scriptural scholarship. Reaching

A learning community

beyond Tatian's comparison of gospels, Origen set side by side the Hebrew text, a transliteration, the Septuagint Greek and three other Greek versions (plus extra passages here and there). The resulting object must have been huge and was never entirely copied, although Eusebius and Jerome are witnesses to its survival over the best part of two centuries. The three translators set beside the Septuagint were Aquila, Symmachus and Theodotion. Aquila was a Jew from Pontus, who adopted and then abandoned a Christian viewpoint. His literal translation was an attempt to supplant the Septuagint, which (by his time, in the 130s) had been, as he saw it, appropriated by the Christians. He was deeply influenced by the rabbis of Palestine. About Symmachus (a decade or so later) we know less, but he was probably a convert to Judaism also. His translation was looser than Aquila's. Theodotion (perhaps a little later again) was more an adapter than a genuine translator. He may have been Jewish, or a follower of Marcion. All three illustrate the traffic between Hellenism, Judaism and the various species of Christianity, and illustrate how much biblical scholarship relied on fluid loyalties and a constant exchange of ideas. And Origen was far from content with his six columns: the *Hexapla* was valuable most for its meticulous comparisons. Over some words or phrases, he placed an *obelos* (a dotted stroke), over others an *asteriskos* (our familiar star). The first denoted passages that were not in the Hebrew but had become familiar or revered. The second identified material that was not in the Septuagint but was in the Hebrew and could be added from the other versions. Origen thus subjected the text to the standard critical methods of, for example, Homeric scholarship (which also made use of allegory). In addition, he authoritatively recommended and painstakingly made easy a direct appeal to the Hebrew text. Jerome and the Latin church applied the principle further. It also became virtually the rule, after Origen, to read one part of Scripture in the light of all others. Unreliable memories and irresponsible novelties could now be judged by careful reference.

Origen, a 'sign contradicted'

We are right to find Origen fascinating. His scholarly breadth and the grandeur of his vision influenced Greek and, indirectly, Latin Christianity to an extent impossible to unravel, in spite of later condemnation (in the sixth century especially). We are able not only to gauge his principles as a teacher but also to view his career in detail – thanks chiefly to the special admiration of Eusebius. He was probably born into a Christian family, or his family turned to Christianity when he was very young. Unlike Justin or Clement, he had always experienced that faith from within, and viewed other traditions accordingly. His father Leonides exposed him to the Bible as well as to the traditional curriculum: so his characteristic taste for the 'hidden meaning' rested on years of familiarity. Leonides was also a martyr. Origen, then in his late teens, was able to place his personal grief at his father's death within a living tradition of heroic witness. His troubled relations with Demetrius his bishop were born of those harsh years under Septimius Severus, and were intensified by his sense of pastoral responsibility towards those outside the Christian community. His experience of priesthood (bestowed while visiting Palestine) was made at once bitter and determined by Demetrius's resulting outrage and by his exile from Alexandria in the early 230s. (He had already proved his independence of spirit by visiting Rome, where he heard Hippolytus.) All the more striking, therefore, is his remarkable balance of character. His devotion to Jesus as *Logos*, and his confident acceptance of the Saviour's suffering as a cosmic defeat for the powers of evil, gave to his spiritual vision a degree of humanity. The gentility and charm of Clement disguised a reserve that leaves him almost unknowable. Origen's impetuosity, by contrast, was openly generous, and his frequent embroilments rarely disturbed his transparent calm.

It would be naive, however, to overlook the anxieties that Origen aroused. His use of allegory was deemed excessive, his exaltation of the *pneumatikos* (the 'spiritual one') élitist and his moral rigour dismissive of the body. I have already said a little about Origen and allegory. He placed the technique at the service of spirituality and fulfilment. He laid history along a rising plane, from the shadows of the Jewish past through the images of the Gospel to the mysteries (that is, the realities) of eternity. His wonderful capacity for coherence allowed an essentially literary skill to colour the whole of experience, so that both other people and the world that contained them became texts of spiritual significance. He was an exegete of the cosmos. And allegory in Christian hands could not afford to be merely inventive. The ability of a figure from the Jewish past, for example, to stand as a 'type', to which the future could attach more meaning, was not the result of creative skill in the reader, but a quality built into the figure itself by the providence of God. The 'types' were neither portents nor symbols. When the early Christians painted on their walls and carved on their sarcophagi the figures of Noah, Jonah or the 'three young men', they proclaimed an enduring release at the hand of God. The figures were not quaint, but enlarged. As Paul had understood well, their Judaism was transformed rather than abandoned. The release experienced by the Christian had been rehearsed in those ancient liberations from the flood, the whale, and the 'burning fiery furnace'.

Origen's élitism is a trickier issue. It is important to emphasize his belief in freedom (which led to his incautious, ad hoc and isolated assertion, in the late 220s, that the devil had fallen by choice; an assertion taken by critics, with even greater carelessness, to imply that the devil could be saved as much as any sinner). Origen's complex cosmology was designed to provide a setting in which humanity could respond profitably to the providence of God. Division, imperfection and even embodiment were themselves the result of bad choices, some made long ago; but a pathway from the limitations of the flesh to an expansiveness of spirit was in theory open to all. The fact that Clement and Origen pioneered a catechetical system, and held out the sure hope of a return to God, must counter any suggestion that they fostered a species of religious privilege in the minds of the few. It is false to suppose, for example, that Origen reserved sacramental observance for the 'simple', while feeding the more advanced on words. He lamented attendance at the liturgy for love of ceremony rather than of Scripture; but the distinction between shadow and reality meant for him, in worship as in other matters, acting out symbolic ritual with the spiritual understanding of a 'true worshipper'.

It remains true, nevertheless, that both men could adopt what seems a haughty tone. Clement, commenting in the sixth book of the *Strōmateis* on Peter's recognition of Jesus as Messiah, mused that a certain level of spiritual insight was required to make such a declaration. Origen, for all his suspicion of *gnōsis*, inherited that realism. His own work *Against Celsus* was designed, he said, for those who wanted to understand what they believed – a characteristic emphasis, also shared with Clement. He defended his writings against charges of error by suggesting that less perceptive readers found heresy where none existed. He also believed, however, that people could reach beyond their present incapacity and could be prompted to spiritual progress. He veered towards belief in the eternity of the individual soul and therefore in its pre-existence, and he described its restoration as a contemplative recovery of its 'likeness to God'. But all creatures were equal in their fundamental separation from God, however successful their individual preservation of his 'image'. While the complexity of Origen's ideas, therefore, rather than any snobbery on his part, may have encouraged an apparent hierarchy in his audience, he was far from condemning individuals to an inescapable ranking on a scale of excellence. The blame for confusion here lies with the contemporary enthusiasm for Plato, which set up two levels of perception and demanded (among Origen's pupils) that belief – in the Incarnation, in biblical prophecy, in the power of the sacraments – should rise from a lesser to a greater understanding. Worshippers as well as readers were thus inevitably open to discrimination, judged by their success or failure, albeit temporary, in making the necessary change.

It is easy to see how such attitudes could encourage a relative indifference to the body. Origen certainly did not mean by 'spirit' what he thought gnostics meant by 'knowledge'; but he could be accused of sharing with gnostics a distaste for the world of the flesh. He may have lost the surer sense of humanity that had inspired Ignatius of Antioch and persisted in the theology of Justin. The soul's reclamation of the image of God did not, for Origen, depend unwaveringly on a literal resurrection. That weakness, or lack of precision, had a lasting effect. Origen influenced at the deepest level the subsequent Christian understanding of the ascetic life, especially through the writings of his two later admirers, Evagrius of Pontus and John Cassian. He could be just as clear as Clement about the value of marriage. In that, he was faithful to Paul, and made the point against Marcion and Montanists in particular. But his enthusiasm for virginity involved a sense of the body's impurity. Virginity stood coupled with the other virtues in an undivided contrast to the physical world. Virginity was also a quality of the Christian community, springing from its association with Jesus; a quality, therefore, that transcended created time and bore the mark of God's eternity.

Origen's own dramatic embrace of the virginal life, involving perhaps self-castration, occurred at the time of his father's martyrdom. The resulting link in his mind between death and purity was profound and lasting. The link was ironic: for Origen lived most of his life in periods of relative toleration. The development of his rich exegesis and cosmology depended on the scope toleration allowed. Fidelity to his early sorrow and heroic commitment demanded, therefore, an intensity that could come only from within. As a younger teacher, preparing pupils for baptism in the years before Septimius Severus's death in 211, his catechesis could be presented as a preparation for martyrdom. In spite of changed circumstances, he never lost that conviction. His *Exhortation to Martyrdom* of the late 230s (when Maximinus seemed less accommodating than Alexander Severus) had all the adamantine quality of his youth. Commenting on the prophet Jeremiah in the 240s, he lamented the loss of Christian fervour in the absence of faith's harshest test. Although he escaped execution, his privations under Decius (which hastened his death) made his life an honest preparation for the sacrifice he had seen others make. The combined effects of his rigorous continence and his physical courage coloured later experience of both martyrdom and abnegation.

A learning community

Tertullian the 'Christian sophist'

Tertullian may not seem at first an obvious exemplar of patient and reasoned instruction. The *Ruling against Heretics* voices deep suspicion of argument: faith is enough. In his later work *On the Flesh of Christ* (against the supposed docetism of Marcion), Tertullian described faith (specifically faith in the Incarnation) as if it were a startled affirmation in the face of paradox. As for disbelief, the *Scorpiace* (the 'antidote' – against gnostic scorpions) recommended force over persuasion in the face of obstinacy. A certain logic in the line of thought does not make it more humane. The *Ruling against Heretics* argues that inquiry never reaches a secure goal, can never therefore lead to faith, and thus has no place among Christians. All of which may encourage us to read in a pessimistic light one of Tertullian's more famous assertions: 'What has Athens to do with Jerusalem? What has the academy in common with the church?' (a sentiment expressed in both the *Ruling* and the *Apologeticum*). In one of his earliest works, *On Idolatry*, Tertullian judged the teaching profession harshly. Yet he insisted in the same tract that *divina studia* could not survive without their 'worldly' equivalents. The contradiction permeates the whole of Tertullian's œuvre. But there was a particular inflexion to his complexity that separates him from Clement and Origen. The Alexandrian exegetes had been prepared to infuse into their commentaries and speculations not only the language but also the substance of Greek philosophy, even though they remained rooted in the scriptural tradition. Tertullian displayed an analogous dependence, but was more pragmatic and clear-sighted in his tolerance of *saecularia studia*. He adopted with a surer touch the view that one could separate method from content. His skill as an educated man was marshalled in defence of a truth derived elsewhere.

We must assess his undoubted learning in that light. Carthage was a cultivated city, capable of nurturing and reclaiming the great Apuleius. Its schools reflected the enduring influence of Greek culture. Tertullian was informed, like most contemporaries, by convenient florilegia of extracts from famous writers. But he was clearly widely read, and may betray an independence of erudition that outstripped even the later Jerome. Most important, his formation was literary rather than philosophical. He was a master of style, of rhetorical structure, which helped him to isolate the usefulness of technique from the purposes it might be put to. There was nothing hollow or specious about such facility, nothing 'sophistical' in a less welcome sense; but it commended a readiness for instruction that was less curious, less speculative, less enthusiastic than one might have found among the pupils of Justin or Clement. The human soul, untouched by philosophy, was *naturaliter Christiana*, disposed by nature to recognize the truth of the Gospel. As Tertullian put it famously in his *De testimonio animae, The Evidence of the Soul*, its disposition 'bore witness' to that truth. One placed before such a soul the *doctrina* first sown by the apostles. The pupil mastered the gospel texts as one might master Homer or Virgil, applying traditional methods to the interpretation of Christian literature. In his intriguing treatise *On the Pallium* (an African garb he distinguished from the toga), Tertullian displayed the confident inversion involved. Not only was the pallium a worthy garment for African Christians emancipated from idolatry: it was also a teacher's dress, and symbolized their right to appropriate that dignity. 'The fact that you have begun to clothe Christians [here Tertullian addresses the pallium itself] makes you all the more worthy of philosophy.'

A Christian context, therefore, governed one's acceptance of tradition. Tertullian himself espoused in the end the 'New Prophecy' of Montanus. His estrangement from the wider Christian community in Carthage may have resulted from his wife's death and his strong disapproval of second marriage. He may have wished to protect himself against natural weakness by consorting with the highly principled. More generally, he had shown increasing disapproval of what he took to be the moral laxity of the Carthaginian clergy and their leniency towards sinners. We need not suppose, however, that he 'became a heretic'. We have no evidence that the Christians in Carthage were divided by formal schism; and Tertullian's 'Montanist' companions may have provided no more than the congenial company of radical critics. He may seem to us to have crossed some kind of divide in 206; but he continued to express, albeit more forcibly, opinions he had held for years.

Tertullian maintained a down-to-earth view of church affairs. He was less inclined to idealism than to authenticity. He accepted that no community could be perfect, but felt required thereby to resist false claims and careless pretence. Christianity was more than a product of history, which could prove embarrassing to its sense of values and limit its significance. It was not idolatrous in spirit or form, but nor was it entirely Jewish. The question to be asked in current circumstances was, what were the proper channels by which one could safeguard the active presence of God? It was here that Tertullian's 'Montanism' had its chief effect, as a critical stance and as a commitment to God's Spirit. Only the Spirit could underwrite authentic power, especially the power to forgive sin (too frequently indulged, in Tertullian's opinion). So strict a view led inevitably to disdain for mere 'psychics' – an echo of Origen's problems. But Tertullian also opposed gnostics and Marcionites, presenting in the process the argumentative face of an abiding defence of the Trinity. His 'Montanist' devotion to the Spirit was immediately placed in a wider context. The churches formed a single 'body of Christ' – virtually a continuation of the Incarnation. The Word continued to be made flesh, and the Spirit could be present only where the body lay. There is a touch of Justin here, but some contrast with Origen, whose sense of 'spirit' was at once more interior and more dispersed. The Incarnation, therefore, had two functions for Tertullian. It interrupted, or rather allowed one to see from the Father's point of view, the historical line that ran from Law to Gospel. It also stood as the enduring guarantee of contact between God and his people. The two functions were brought together by the presence of the Spirit.

This skilful and influential theology deserves our attention for several reasons. It shows how a cautious and honest thinker could preserve his individuality without slipping into partial exaggeration. It suggests that 'Montanism' was not a static or monolithic set of ideas (Africa was not Phrygia). It proves that 'spiritual' enthusiasts were found in various forms; that Alexandria did not monopolize their definition. Above all, it confirms that small groups did not have to be gnostic. If Tertullian has anything to tell us about teachers in Carthage, both his hesitations and his convictions clarify the context of their activity. The *Passion of Perpetua*, indubitably 'Montanist' in tone, adds to the picture: it reflects independent criticism of the clergy, trust in inspiration, openness to the counsel of the virtuous, a broad range of social types, and a keen sense of mutual responsibility and respect. While we have to remember both his strict judgement and his practicality of intellect, Tertullian did operate as a teacher in that setting. Several of his early works, dating from the 190s, bear the marks of catechetical discussion in a liturgical context: works on baptism, prayer and repentance. In his later work *On Purity*, the rebirth achieved in baptism, the formative impact of the spoken word, and the scriptural basis of morality constituted the essence of Christian integrity. In the end, we are brought back to the world of Justin and Clement, modified by the self-reliant intensity of Perpetua, preserved in a stylized document that has at least some affinities with the *Apocryphal Acts*. Worship, instruction and insight combined to set Tertullian apart as an 'elder' of his community, exactly like his peers in Italy and Egypt. In both his ideas and his practice, therefore, he protected himself, like Clement and Origen, against the isolation of heresy, offering his understanding and integrity to the community in which he lived.

THE VIEW FROM THE FUTURE

As far as later Latin Christians were concerned, Tertullian represented the outer limits of their historical knowledge, their remotest native ancestor; and they often saw his Greek antecedents through his own eyes. All the more striking is the abundance of his output and his stylistic poise. He suddenly presented the West with a rich, profound and polished corpus. He was visibly the master of Cyprian and of an African tradition that included Arnobius and Lactantius and reached forward to Augustine. Not until the fourth-century figures of Hilary, Ambrose and Jerome could other parts of the West mount a comparable display, and then with heavy dependence on Greek models. It is impossible to overestimate the importance of that commanding authority. The accidental intersection of Tertullian's upbringing, temper and controversial setting formed over time an unchallenged paradigm of theological insight. He had to be, in every Latin inquiry, the point of departure.

The situation in the East was more varied and more ambiguous, and perhaps for those reasons more fertile. Origen was just as disturbing as Tertullian, but even harder to escape. His Greek successors could more easily see beyond him, and were forced to subject him to more subtle historical judgement. He had drawn up an indispensable and inventive agenda for the future study of Scripture, for theology and for asceticism; but he also summed up well-documented developments in the second century, and could be accused of carrying less desirable emphases to exaggerated conclusions. To claim him as a master, therefore, was stimulating but dangerous. The talent of later Christian Greeks was forever stretched between building upon his insights and avoiding a share in his condemnation. In the West, only Augustine succeeded in generating even remotely comparable embarrassment. Fortunately for the Greek church, it was able to shield itself from the full glare of Origen's complexities by admiring more directly the tactful dependence of the Cappadocian Fathers – Basil of Caesarea, his brother Gregory of Nyssa and their friend Gregory of Nazianzus.

Acknowledgement of older masters was inflected differently in each generation. Theology did not flow from the insights of Origen and Tertullian alone. Eusebius did more than most to 'tidy' the account of the Alexandrian 'school'. Himself a disciple of Pamphilus, who had known and admired Origen, he wanted to safeguard his credentials as a scholar and theologian just as he safeguarded the credentials of bishops – by suggesting an unbroken succession from the shadowy Pantaenus through Clement and Origen to the men of his own generation. But Christian culture represented an increasingly complex dialogue between the living and the dead, which constantly affected its understanding of its ancestry. The 'fathers' looked backwards, their capacity for original thought modified by respect for the authority of those who had gone before them. Nor should we find in Origen and Tertullian the roots of a supposed divergence between eastern and western Christianity. Variety of subsequent experience had a greater impact. The resumption of bitter persecution after 250, the contrasting exhilaration of Constantine's reign, the factiousness provoked by the Arian controversy, the moral and spiritual crisis exacerbated by barbarian settlement and weak government – each factor varying in its impact in different parts of the empire – all adjusted in their way the lenses through which Christians scrutinized the values and achievements of their past. In the West, after Augustine and down to the time of Gregory the Great, theology was widely subordinated to a homiletic outreach focused on peasants and barbarians. Opportunities for meditated composition in the style of Augustine were most often solitary and plucked from the hours of a busy life. In the East, after the heyday of the Cappadocians and Chrysostom, and prior to the challenge of Islam and Iconoclasm, theology was harnessed more to structural adjustments, conciliar debate and cautious negotiation between religious and secular powers. Only the great ascetic writers had the leisure (although not always the inclination) to diverge from those paths.

Origen's legacy remained the most problematic. More than any other Christian writer, his taste for Platonist hierarchies invited the less astute either to adopt or to deplore a series of distinctions – between cult and study, 'psychics' and 'pneumatics', tradition and speculation – all of which had the potential to undermine unity of belief. Not only was Origen obstinate in his loyalty, however: those who came after him could not dismiss him from their minds. Their respect proved both the indispensable wealth of Origen's ideas and the injustice of lesser men's simplicity. The clue to Origen's honesty and productive genius was his unwavering attachment to Scripture. The significant poles of his career were exegesis and homily, and a constant field of energy played between them. Meticulous and perceptive as a scholar, he applied the fruits of scholarship to the instruction of those who wished to understand the sacred text. He combined visible precision, fidelity to the received document, with an exciting originality of interpretation. After Origen, the task of the Christian rhetor was clear: to facilitate a pastoral use of the Bible; to help others grasp what one had grasped oneself.

His achievement was symbolic in another way. His 'capacity for coherence', as I called it, helped him to integrate time with truth, the historical with the absolute. In doing so, he held in unison the diversity of Scripture, and unwittingly secured for himself an unassailable and essential place in Christian history. Before Origen, writers had worried in different ways about the usefulness of the Bible – an anxiety inseparable from the practicalities of competition and from the ambiguity of Jesus as at once a temporal and a transcendent figure. Origen sealed the alliance between historical continuity and symbolic reference; and he sealed it – or rather believed that God had sealed it – within every phrase of Scripture, which was both inherited and illumined, an ancient heirloom and a fresh discovery. At exactly the moment when history expanded for Christians, leading them to embrace more openly a non-Jewish world, Origen turned their minds away from timorous apology and provided them with an integrated framework of ideas, within which they could relate their diverse traditions and achieve a single focus of attention, contemplative but articulate. The experience would be harsh and divisive, but an indispensable stepping stone to the Christian empire.

It will be useful to provide at this point a brief summary of the general argument. Having in Chapter 1 explored issues of method, viewpoint and coherence, we identified in Chapter 2 the central components of Paul's thought and influence, emphasizing liberty, community and the redefinition of Judaism. In Chapter 3, we examined the human and historical roots of Christianity in the life of Jesus, and then traced the process whereby his transcendent significance as Saviour was associated with the early records of his teaching and mission. In Chapters 4 and 5, we set in place two of three analyses of early Christian society. The first asserted the priority of a theory of virtue, which subjected debate about unity and authority to the demands of individual growth. The second gave an associated priority to teaching, which affected further both the scale of the Christian achievement and the criteria of leadership. Now, in Chapter 6, we must mount a third analysis, which will suggest how both religious ideals and pedagogic techniques brought Christians into closer contact with the world of non-believers: not only with their standards and models of virtue but also with their principles of organization, status and control. These three central chapters not only describe the world in which the ideas of Paul and the gospels made their mark, but also detect a momentum that carried believers from a world of intense sectarianism to a publicly respected and thoroughly Roman identity in the urban communities of the empire.

Further reading

A significant proportion of the books mentioned at the end of Chapter 4 touch upon the issues treated here. On the background to the intellectual life of the time, see Graham Anderson, *The Second Sophistic: a Cultural Phenomenon in the Roman Empire* (London and New York, NY: Routledge, 1993) and *Sage, Saint, and Sophist: Holy Men and their Associates in the Early Roman Empire* (London and New York, NY: Routledge, 1994). Older but important studies: Glen W. Bowersock, *Greek Sophists in the Roman Empire* (Oxford: Clarendon Press, 1969) and Marcia L. Colish, *The Stoic Tradition from Antiquity to the Early Middle Ages* (Leiden: Brill, 1985). A particularly brilliant account is provided by Maud W. Gleason, *Making Men: Sophists and Self-presentation in Ancient Rome* (Princeton, NJ: Princeton University Press, 1995).

On more specifically Christian connections, see Henry Chadwick, *Early Christian Thought and the Classical Tradition: Studies in Justin, Clement, and Origen* (New York, NY: Oxford University Press, 1966), Patrick Henry (ed.), *Schools of Thought in the Christian Tradition* (Philadelphia, PA: Fortress Press, 1984), Robert McQueen Grant, *The Greek Apologists of the Second Century* (London: SCM Press/Philadelphia, PA: Westminster Press, 1988), Richard Valantasis, *Spiritual Guides of the Third Century: a Semiotic Study of the Guide–Disciple Relationship in Christianity, Neoplatonism, Hermetism, and Gnosticism* (Minneapolis, MN: Fortress Press, 1991) and Harry Y. Gamble, *Books and Readers in the Early Church: a History of Early Christian Texts* (New Haven, CT: Yale University Press, 1995). There is much of value in Angelo Di Berardino and Basil Studer (eds), *History of Theology*, 1: *The Patristic Period* (Collegeville, MN: Liturgical Press, 1996).

For a general view of the Egyptian milieu, see C. Wilfred Griggs, *Early Egyptian Christianity, from its Origins to 451 CE* (Leiden: Brill, 1989) and Roelof van den Broek, *Studies in Gnosticism and Alexandrian Christianity* (Leiden: Brill, 1996). On individual figures, and first Clement, there are old studies by Salvatore Lilla, *Clement of Alexandria: a Study in Christian Platonism and Gnosticism* (Oxford: Oxford University Press, 1971) and H.B. Timothy, *The Early Christian Apologists and Greek Philosophy, exemplified by Irenaeus, Tertullian and Clement of Alexandria* (Åssen: Van Gorcum, 1973). More recently, Denise Kimber Buell, *Making Christians: Clement of Alexandria and the Rhetoric of Legitimacy* (Princeton, NJ: Princeton University Press, 1999) and John Behr, *Asceticism and Anthropology in Irenaeus and Clement* (Oxford: Oxford University Press, 2000). On Origen there are classic studies, translated from the French, by Jean Daniélou, *Origen*, translated by Walter Mitchell (New York, NY: Sheed & Ward, 1955) and Henri Crouzel, *Origen*, translated by A.S. Worrall (San Francisco, CA: Harper & Row, 1989). See also Nicholas de Lange, *Origen and the Jews: Studies in Jewish–Christian Relations in Third-Century Palestine* (Cambridge: Cambridge University Press, 1976), Charles Kannengiesser and

W. Petersen, *Origen of Alexandria: his World and his Legacy* (Notre Dame, IN: Notre Dame University Press, 1988) and Joseph W. Trigg, *Origen* (London and New York, NY: Routledge, 1998).

For Tertullian, see the classic study by Timothy D. Barnes, *Tertullian*, revised edn (Oxford: Clarendon Press, 1985) and add David Rankin, *Tertullian and the Church* (Cambridge and New York, NY: Cambridge University Press, 1995) and J.B. Rives, *Religion and Authority in Roman Carthage from Augustus to Constantine* (Oxford: Clarendon Press, 1995).

Finally, on the *Apocryphal Acts*, I have been guided most by Kate Cooper, *The Virgin and the Bride: Idealized Womanhood in Late Antiquity* (Cambridge, MA: Harvard University Press, 1996). See also Stevan L. Davies, *The Revolt of the Widows: the Social World of the Apocryphal Acts* (Carbondale, IL: Southern Illinois University Press, 1980), Virginia Burrus, *Chastity as Autonomy: Women in the Stories of Apocryphal Acts* (Lewiston, NY: Edwin Mellen Press, 1987) and François Bovon, Ann Graham Brock and Christopher R. Matthews (eds), *The Apocryphal Acts of the Apostles* (Cambridge, MA: Harvard University Press, 1999).

Where to begin?
Harry Y. Gamble, *Books and Readers in the Early Church*.

Chapter 6

HEROES AND SURVIVORS: CHRISTIANS ENGAGE WITH THE WORLD

When one considers relations between Christians and the wider world, traditional images can arise in the mind. The history of those relations has often been divided into two eras, one of suffering, one of triumph. Jesus foretold that his followers would suffer as he had. Suffering would be the inevitable result of courage in causes that others regarded as scandalous; but it would also be the instrument whereby God would either overwhelm or enrapture those who imposed it. The 'age of the martyrs' (of the 'witnesses', in Greek) represents the fulfilment of the first prediction, the 'conversion of the Roman empire' the second. Before Constantine, therefore, catacombs and circuses (both seriously misunderstood) can seem to be the proper settings for Christian self-assertion. Huddled believers await the savagery of approaching lions, while an audience of thousands roars with lust and hatred.

The previous two chapters have uncovered, by contrast, an earnest pursuit of virtue, an increasing degree of scholarship and close-knit, unobtrusive communities that were able, nevertheless, to attract recruits and retain loyalty. Such ideals and bonds were unlikely either to invite or to bring down automatically the wrath of the state. They were typical of their time and characterized similar associations, both Jewish and otherwise. Those associations were by their nature calculated to create for their members pathways into the wider community, an access to status, a public clarity of definition. Temperate behaviour, exegetical learning and religious brotherhood were valued throughout the Roman world and dignified with public honours.

There were probably, even so, thousands of early Christian martyrs. Their 'witness' upheld the principles of the gospel, displayed great courage in an age of excessive judicial brutality and served to inspire their fellow-believers for centuries. They were, however, the victims of intermittent antagonism, misunderstanding or prejudice, normally local. Not until the reign of Decius (249–51) was there a universal persecution, undertaken on ideological grounds. In that instance, the emperor's shallow nostalgia was pitted fruitlessly against an irreversible assurance. Martyrdom cannot stand alone, therefore, an emblem of estrangement or intransigence. A Christian community's relations with the wider world were established on two fronts, both public in character. Martyrs met their deaths either, like many criminals, in the city's customary site of corporate entertainment or in normal places of execution. They were tried before authorized magistrates and in the courts that all Romans frequented. Those who sought a less dramatic access to public respectability and influence were equally tied to custom – to the roles of philosopher, priest or rhetor, for example. Martyrdom was not a prelude to acceptance, but its accompaniment; a note of doubt and sometimes of outrage in a gathering polyphony of visible success. The presence of martyrs was a symptom of both courage and hesitation: for it implied directly that the majority were not prepared to go that far. One person's outstanding sacrifice shone out against a broader background of alternative commitments. Among the martyrs' admirers, guilt could be combined with exaltation. There were always tasks left over for the living, for those who survived; tasks that were by definition long-term and dependent on tolerance. Martyrs offered a challenge to their fellow Christians, therefore, as much as to non-believers.

DEATH AND GLORY

The antecedents of martyrdom were predominantly Jewish. Accounts in *1* and *2 Maccabees*, describing the conflict between Jewish traditionalists and the Seleucid and Hellenizing king Antiochus IV Epiphanes (215–164 BC), provided a powerful model for later self-sacrifice. The famous mother and her seven sons – the sons killed horribly one by one, the mother after them – represent the important elements of heroic 'witness': fidelity to one's religion, attachment to the traditions of one's people and the ability to transcend the imperatives of kinship. Courage in the Maccabaean era was directed against the dominion of a foreign power and the insidious influence of an alien culture. By the time of Jesus, the Romans had supplanted the Seleucids in Syria and Palestine, but Jews continued to suffer in defence of their traditions, and their defiance retained at times a political form, as in the great revolts of the first and second centuries. Christians, with their talk of a 'kingdom not of this world' and their repudiation of the imperial cult – they refused even to throw incense on an altar – might seem to present a similar threat to Roman hegemony. Nor were Jews and Christians alone in a defiance of civil authority. The so-called *Acts of the Pagan Martyrs* describe judicial proceedings and executions that resulted from demonstrations of Egyptian resistance in the late second and early third centuries. The material helps one to appreciate the range of eccentricities and resentments that the imperial government occasionally had to face. It provides a context for the particular 'witness' of Christians. It also brought into play a more general tradition – the critique of tyranny – mounted by radical ascetics and philosophers, and by historians, poets and dramatists, as well as by those bent upon more concrete subversion. The Christian martyr was not an isolated and obstinate misfit, therefore, but one among many symbols of resistance to bad government.

Yet Christian heroism reached beyond politics. To understand martyrdom, one has to understand Christian attitudes towards death. Torture and mutilation were the casual norm in Roman courts. For every criminal killed horribly as a public spectacle, hundreds perished in secret, or dragged their broken bodies through state quarries and mines. Life expectancy was short, disease endemic. A bad harvest might reverberate in a region for a decade, while unscrupulous landowners hoarded grain against a rise in prices. Little wonder that, among the leisured and reflective, only marginally protected against misfortune, the cold tranquillity of Stoicism formed a dominant philosophical culture. In such a setting, how did martyrs view their sacrifice, and what afterlife did they hope for? Was it a 'risen life', an experience comparable to the resurrection of Jesus? Most Romans thought of their dead as inhabiting a ghostly and impersonal world, often on the outskirts of their towns. They were revered by rites designed to ensure them a modicum of peace, but few were thought to enjoy a genuinely personal survival. The underworld of dead spirits was far removed from the heavenly setting of the gods. Only a portion of the better educated trusted in the immortality of the soul, a philosophical rather than a religious belief, derived from Greek (and especially Platonist) tradition. Did Christians, who could hardly remain untouched by such attitudes, subscribe to a more obviously different view?

Their Jewish forebears had been surprisingly divided in their beliefs about survival after death. The followers of Jesus were able to choose among several options, and made up their minds slowly. It is arguable that they never reached a single, coherent conclusion. Their attitudes were most often influenced by the twentieth chapter of *Revelation*, which asserts that those who bear bloody witness to Jesus, or at least refuse to honour idols, will 'live' and 'reign' with Christ for a thousand years – what the text calls 'the first resurrection'. Only after the thousand years will there be a final judgment; and the 'new Jerusalem', the 'new heaven' and the 'new earth' foreshadowed in *Isaiah*, comes later again. What kind of 'reign' was envisaged here, and what kind of 'resurrection'? Justin, Irenaeus and Tertullian suggested that a majority of Christians believed in this 'intermediate' period between death and general judgment; and they themselves appear to have accepted the same view. Origen discussed the *Revelation* passage more than once, although, in line with his distaste for literal exegesis, he regarded the 'thousand years' as a metaphor for some spiritual state. All those writers make it clear, however, that other Christians, whom they regarded as equally orthodox, believed that death would bring swifter access to the presence of God. Whichever option one chose, 'resurrection' remained an open question. One could believe in both the postponement of reward and the eternal destiny of the body.

The Jesus of the gospels seems equally complex in his allusions. *Revelation* was heavily influenced by Jewish apocalyptic traditions and, like *Daniel* and *1 Maccabees*, closely tied to a moment of national trauma, the destruction of the Temple. In his 'eschatological discourse', recorded by all the synoptic gospels, Jesus evokes the same connections. He refers, for example, to 'the abomination of desolation', the *shiqqusim meshomem* of *Daniel*; a term applied to idolatrous shrines and altars placed in the Jewish Temple (as, for example, by Antiochus in *1 Maccabees*). Here, the gospel writers were reflecting on the fact that the Romans had behaved in a similar manner, during the harrowing events of the year 70. Jesus does not describe, however, the changing state of individuals during and after the final 'affliction'. He speaks simply of the Son of Man 'gathering his chosen ones together from the four winds'. *2 Maccabees*, even amid its political allusions, had expressed a clear interest in the future fate of its heroes. The death of Eleazar is described straightforwardly as an act of honour, a 'good death' endured for the sake of the Law; but the seven brothers and their mother die confident of unending life to follow, which will entail the restoration of their bodies. Such were the ancestral exemplars of faith that the Christian *Letter to the Hebrews* had in mind, the 'enfolding cloud of witnesses', who had preserved their hope in God's promises while suffering humiliation, privation and death. They were assured explicitly of 'resurrection'.

We have to look in less apocalyptic passages for comparable reflections on Jesus's part. His more dramatic prophecies are veiled in Mark and Matthew with the warning that only the Father knew 'the day and the hour' of the Son's coming. Luke made the point at the opening of *Acts*, with added talk of 'witness'. The command now was simply to 'stay wake'. The interpretation of portents merged into a trusting ignorance (and the expectation of the Spirit).

Elsewhere, Jesus rebukes the Sadducees for a sarcastic scepticism about the afterlife. Women remarkable, he says, for having outlived seven husbands (so runs Mark's account) will hardly worry about which one to claim in the next life: they will all be 'like angels in the heavens'. Luke (although only Luke) has Jesus promising the 'good' thief crucified beside him, 'Today you will be with me in paradise'. Another type of eschatology is at work here. Mark sums up many implications in his account of Jesus's reply to James and John. 'Allow us', they say, 'to sit with you in glory, one on your right hand and one on your left.' (In Matthew, their mother does the asking, and adds the phrase 'in your kingdom'.) Jesus rebukes the brothers for their presumption, but also warns them of the price of such privilege – sharing his 'cup' and his 'baptism'; all in the context of his 'going up to Jerusalem' to face his death. Jesus's resurrection is interwoven by the writer of the fourth gospel with a symbolized treatment of the Temple's destruction – 'Break down this temple and in three days I shall raise it up.' John displays otherwise a strange reticence, as if going out of his way to avoid a 'literal' interpretation. Mary Magdalene, on Easter morning, thinks Jesus is a gardener. He walks through walls. He invites Thomas to touch his wounds. The oddest story comes at the gospel's end. Faced with a figure on the beach in Galilee, Peter and his companions 'did not dare to ask him, "Who are you?" knowing that it was the Lord'.

The gospel tradition, therefore, did not supply Christians with a simple tool that helped them to sort out the implications of more apocalyptic imagery. What about other sections of the New Testament? Paul's interpretation of personal survival may have been too specific for some Christians. In *Philippians*, when he must have known that his death was imminent, he prayed to escape 'weakness', so that Christ might be 'magnified in my body'. 'I long for release and to be with Christ', he wrote, implying that union might quickly follow release. In earlier letters, he had been almost hesitant in describing what he believed. If there was no resurrection, Christian faith crumbled: that, as he wrote in *1 Corinthians*, was beyond dispute. The raised Jesus, however, was only the 'first fruit'. Those who were to share in his triumph – those who were, as Paul put it, 'of Christ' – gained their victory only 'in his coming'. They would be 'brought to life . . . in their proper order'. Then came the issue of what resurrection would be like. Paul's fundamental point was that 'flesh and blood cannot inherit the kingdom of God'. Belief in resurrection, therefore, was belief in a 'change'; a change brought about by a shift from *psychē* to *pneuma*, by the transformation of 'soul' into 'spirit', each demanding a bodily envelope different from the other. It would take place 'in a moment, in the twinkling of an eye'. A further ingredient of Christian belief was supplied by Luke's account of the stoning of Stephen, which carried the convictions of Paul and the gospels into a new age. After a long speech, which is at once a judicial defence and a complete reinterpretation of Jewish history, and in which Stephen sets himself within a long tradition of rejected prophets (the tradition preserved in the *Letter to the Hebrews*), the protomartyr has a vision of 'the glory of God' and declares to the outraged Sanhedrin, 'I see the heavens thrown open [as had the writer of *Revelation*] and the Son of Man standing at God's right hand.' A vision of God in one form or another was familiar to both the Jewish and the gospel tradition, and the 'open heaven' suggests immediate access to a better world.

So, a complicated stage was set for martyrs. Those images had to sustain them, in the first place, in the face of pain and horror. Martyrs were not suicidal fanatics; but the drama of sacrifice invited vivid anticipation and in some cases a genuine longing. Ignatius of Antioch foretold his suffering with almost lurid satisfaction. He would be ground by the teeth of lions like the flour of the eucharistic bread. Such a frisson of combined fear and excitement was probably essential, but implies nothing specifically about its expected aftermath. Jesus had provided the model. With his phrase, 'Now we are going up to Jerusalem' – recorded by Mark, repeated by Matthew and Luke, and hinted at by John – a die was cast: now we bring matters to a head, now we face up to those who oppose us. 'It is not fitting for a prophet to die outside Jerusalem.' He says defiantly to Pilate, 'For this I was born and for this I came into the world: in order that I might bear witness to the truth.' Equally credible, however, and redolent of genuine revulsion, is his prayer in the garden of Gethsemane: 'Father, everything is possible to you: take this cup from me.' Like anyone facing an imminent and painful death, a martyr could either collapse under the weight of such terror, or else seize upon some other view of both self and time, endowing his or her particular death with a lasting significance. The condemned 'witness' was lifted above the limited world of trial and torture. Anyone brave enough to die on behalf of others must experience to some degree the same exalted affirmation.

Yet a well-grounded hope need not have depended on immediate fulfilment. Some of the earliest physical evidence of Christianity is associated with the funerary culture of the catacombs. It is wrong to think of them as secret sites: they were extended and decorated, in ways that would have made secrecy impossible, during those decades of the third century that witnessed a growing assurance among Christians. Nevertheless, alongside the 'house church', there had long been a 'cemetery culture' among Christians. Prayers for the dead, especially prayers offered in the presence of the dead, coupled with a sharing of food and drink, could strengthen the bonds of the community and reinforce its faith in resurrection. Outsiders like Celsus were right to suppose that Christians had a special relationship with the dead. For the Christians themselves, however, the dead were their kin; the bond between them and the living was unaffected by the threats and uncertainties of mortal existence. Anticipated martyrdom might have seemed, in such company, at once a less abrupt and a more social experience. In Christian hands, therefore, the traditional model of the funerary society extended beyond burial, coloured by rich ceremonial and a particular theology. Such *collegia* were, in their Christian form, 'obscure and secret', as Celsus put it, only because their members refused to engage also with their city's public cult.

The physical setting for that 'communion of saints' was also enlivened by a religious art – some of the earliest known to us – that emphasized future victory. The most popular biblical images were those of Noah and Jonah – Noah saved from the flood and Jonah rescued from the belly of the whale; both symbols of resurrection. Mark's Jesus had refused to give his generation a 'sign'. Matthew, more sensitive to Jewish hopes, made him appeal precisely to Jonah – three days in the whale, as Jesus would be three days in the tomb. Such were the images now interpreted in the presence of buried forebears – forebears whose access to glory might still be incomplete. The 'orant' figure, so common in Christian frescoes, with arms raised in prayer, was ambiguous in its reference, symbolizing individual tension in the face of death, intercession for those who had passed beyond it, and the suspended expectancy of the dead themselves, as they waited patiently for what might be a postponed reward.

THE LITERARY IMAGE: PURPOSE AND EFFECT

Martyrdom was also a literary phenomenon. Texts helped to create the martyr ethos and governed its interpretation. Historians now distrust many surviving accounts. They are often demonstrably late: incidents that occurred in the second or third centuries are recorded in documents written in the fifth or sixth. The surviving *acta*, *martyria* and *passiones* shroud their early components in a complex interweaving of heavily edited material. Some of them seem to be based, however, on *hypomnēmatismoi* or *commentarii* – the records of trials drawn up by official scribes and then obtained, at least in copy form, by the martyrs' supporters. Many such records provide priceless insight into the legal system that brought martyrs to their end. They identify, in many cases, the date of a hearing, the name of the magistrate, the nature of the charge, the process of verbal investigation, and the verdict of the court. In the case of the martyrs, they disclose the court's determination either to coerce the defendant to an act of cultic obeisance or to remove the possibility of deceit or hypocrisy. The magistrate demanded at least some formal veneration of the reigning emperor, either by solemn praise or by the burning of incense (he might exempt the defendant from eating sacrificial meat). Failing that, he would want it made clear that a martyr's refusal was based on an explicit attachment to Christianity. The motive in either case was never religious in a narrow sense – such a limitation would have been unintelligible at the time. The courts wished, rather, to use certain types of religious gesture to verify political loyalty and, less directly, to undermine or defuse any local tendency to public disorder.

Three early examples offer illustration. The *Acts of Justin Martyr* have been edited beyond the limits of a court record, but are obviously based on a hearing before Rusticus, prefect of the city of Rome between 163 and 168. It is hard to judge whether Justin was being subjected to an inquisition mounted in the name of the emperor (a possible but uncommon procedure), or whether he had been formally accused by his Cynic opponent Crescens (a more frequent method of bringing a person to trial: the imperial government rarely prosecuted criminals, responding more often to the petitions of plaintiffs). The involvement of Crescens gives the *martyrium* a philosophical air, as does the presidency of Rusticus, the admired Stoic tutor of Marcus Aurelius. There are echoes of the trial of Socrates and of dispute over the appropriate influence of teachers. Several literary genres are thus conflated, especially *consolatio* and the philosophical dialogue. The second example, the *Martyrdom of Polycarp*, dates at its heart from the years 155–58 but was added to and adapted, partly perhaps by the Decian martyr Pionius, who, like Polycarp, came from Smyrna. It shows less dependence on the *commentarius* form, although a philosophical note is introduced, when Polycarp engages the proconsul in 'argument' and 'apology'. (Pionius did the same with his own accusers – Smyrna being noted for its sophists, including in his later years Aelius Aristides.) But the text also draws on Christian models. One is reminded of the letters of Paul and the Apostolic Fathers: for the *martyrium*, both in its surviving form and perhaps from the outset, was placed within a letter – in this case, from the Christians of Smyrna to their colleagues in Philomelium (on the main route across south-central Turkey). Gospel images are also evident. Polycarp enters the city on an ass, like Jesus on Palm Sunday. There is a reminiscence of Jesus facing Pilate in the martyr's reference to 'my king who saves me'. And the presence of what is disparagingly referred to as a 'lawless mob' recalls the disorderly accusers of Jesus, but may also disguise a legally formulated plea — in which case, the proconsul (like Pilate) may have been as eager to prevent a riot as to win Polycarp's acquiescence. In the third example, the *Acts of Ignatius*, dating is more open to dispute, and variations among different versions are more marked. Like historical chronicles, those different versions reflect the interests of different locales — in this case, Antioch and Rome: the central scenes of Ignatius's heroism are transferred from one city to another. Both had a claim to association with the bishop's witness; but it is likely that any early account of a martyrdom was designed in part to reflect some glory on its setting. In the Ignatian material, there is also a parallel with Paul's journey from his trial before Felix in Caesarea to his imprisonment and death in the empire's capital. Not surprisingly, therefore, the account in its final form has acquired, like Luke's *Acts*, novelistic traits.

Confrontation with the state, therefore, gave Christian writers a new confidence. They developed distinctive literary genres of lasting influence. One can better appreciate the artistry of Tertullian, whose *Apology* was forged in the face of Septimius Severus's limited but vigorous repression. Through a long line of African imitators, both his conviction and his style put a lasting mark on writing by Latin Christians. Another phase then followed in the textual presentation of the Christian hero (and heroine), from the *Passion of Perpetua* through Pontius's *Life of Cyprian* to Eusebius's lost life of Pamphilus. Perpetua, martyred under Septimius Severus in 203, contravened as a catechumen the emperor's attempt to prohibit conversion. Cyprian, having survived the persecution of Decius, died under Valerian in 258. As a bishop, he fell foul of the emperor's wish to forbid the assembly of Christians and to cull their leaders. Pamphilus died under Maximin Daia in 310. He probably knew Origen and was deeply influenced by him, not least as a man who had schooled himself for sacrifice. Pamphilus was also learned, Eusebius's instructor and hero — a reminder that Eusebius was equally a child of persecution.

In those third-century and fourth-century accounts, martyrdom was increasingly associated with biography and history. Pontius's portrait of Cyprian is generally regarded as the first Christian biography in Latin. Thus martyrdom was folded back into the bigger story (as had already happened in the gospels). The moment of death was made significant not only by courage but also by a relation to the martyr's life as a whole. The *Passion of Perpetua* makes a hesitant but undisguised effort to explain the heroine's steadfast capacity by adding to the account of her death a discussion of her family background, her circle of admirers and supporters, her religious convictions and her privileged visions. The eventual compiler of the text provides in the process an invaluable description of the Carthaginian church (although Perpetua undoubtedly wrote some elements of the text herself). Half a century later, Pontius felt that Cyprian would have had a lesson to teach, even if he had not been martyred. He begins his account with Cyprian becoming a Christian, and emphasizes the usefulness of his hero's having survived the ravages of Decius (just as Ignatius, in his *martyrium*, had escaped the hand of Domitian). Only four of his nineteen chapters narrate the eventual trial and execution. Pamphilus, while in prison, felt that the best way to justify Origen's frustrated hopes of suffering for his religion was to present a full account of his thought and writings – a priceless *Apology*, now for the most part lost.

The most remarkable account of third-century martyrdom is the *Acts of Pionius*. Although revised and embellished over many centuries, it retains a substantial core of third-century material, which Eusebius knew about (but misdated). The account is informative about persecution generally, about Smyrna and Pionius, but also about the preservation of a martyr's memory. Pionius was clearly a man who lived in the hope of ultimate sacrifice. When it came, he was ready. He had already taken a hand in safeguarding the memory of Polycarp. Now, while in prison, he wrote with the deliberate aim of creating texts that would sustain other Christians, then and later. His long and carefully recorded discourses were an important supplement to the terse, idealized description of his end. They proved how prolonged and open a 'martyrdom' might be. Given the notorious lethargy of legal proceedings, imprisonment provided a martyr with frequent visitors. There was as much opportunity for philosophy as there was for bloodshed. An element of *consolatio* was also involved. Those left behind had to be comforted in the sudden violence of their imminent loss. Although created in part by those who did not survive, *martyria* were designed for those who did. They sprang from the intersection of one person's dramatic apotheosis and the more extended experience of their spared admirers. In their later form, they could cater, like the *Apocryphal Acts*, for audiences and needs quite different from those they appeared to describe. If (as Tertullian put it famously, in his *Apology*) the blood of martyrs was the 'seed of the church', the accounts of their deaths were among the bonds that held churches together.

The future thus created for 'martyr literature' was a long one. The message of past suffering was being constantly washed up on the shore of future toleration. It was natural that the courage of Polycarp should have encouraged

Pionius. A different force was at work when the beneficiaries of Constantine's dispensation found it useful to venerate the victims of less generous emperors. For a long time, in a corridor of mirrored reflections, each text caught the light from older accounts and models, and cast it forward onto the imaginations of future writers. In that sense, persecution had prepared the Christians for their eventual triumph. Augustine, in his *City of God*, thought so. Eusebius, who lived on the cusp between darkness and light, adopted a reverse order, seeing persecution as an antidote to complacent ease. Origen and Cyprian had done the same before him, and the argument helped Christians to make sense of subsequent crises. Simply to rejoice in persecution as an antecedent was a luxury permitted only to people living in less anxious times, or in times charged (like the times of Augustine) with a different anxiety. It represented a degree of wisdom after the event that Eusebius, at least in his younger years, was unable to enjoy: for the bulk of his *Ecclesiastical History* was, as we shall see, written before Constantine's conversion.

Two tendencies were at work, therefore. At one moment, martyrdom helped Christians to explain their new fortune; at another, it provoked a lament for lost virtue. Modern war memorials and the prestige of the military hero may help us to appreciate the difficulties involved. The defeat of Nazism or the fall of an 'evil empire' may seem grounds for congratulation; but guilt and admiration will frequently compete in the minds of survivors who enjoy an advantage purchased by the death of others. The justification of the sacrifice and even the nature of the debt can be obscured and called into question by the passage of time. The language of heroism, on the other hand, is a symbolic tool that allows one to overlay with selflessness and courage the cruelty and horror of war. The balance achieved within any one society between revulsion and reverence will vary; but heroes themselves are normally hard-headed about their supposed heroism, and confident admiration of the living for the dead survives best when those with the recollection of experience have died. During the century that spanned the accession of Constantine, running from Decius to Julian, attitudes gradually but irreversibly changed in exactly that way. Pontius had already praised unbloodied survivors. They may have been disappointed, he wrote, in their desire to share Cyprian's fate; but anyone who longed inwardly for martyrdom, under the eye of Christ and in the presence of the priest, would be heard by God: their devotion was martyrdom enough. Persecution under Diocletian, and even more under Maximin Daia, represented a new development. It was less preoccupied with individual assent and focused more on the material resources of the Christian community (continuing a trend begun under Valerian in the 250s). Books were special targets: they enabled that community not only to sustain its cultic assemblies but also to pass on its teachings. The effect of those policies was to foster a remarkable degree of disunity among Christians themselves, which took decades to heal. This was the age not only of the *lapsi*, the weak backsliders of Cyprian's day, but also of the *traditores*, those who willingly surrendered priceless texts and vessels into the hands of the state. The challenge was not only to receive back waverers, by processes of repentance and absolution long set in place in the Christian rituals of the third century, but also to define authentic leadership, legitimate succession in episcopal sees and the appropriate communion between them. Synods and councils, already an established feature of third-century life, were now troubled by such 'political' issues more than they ever were by doctrinal dispute.

The relation between martyrs and monks casts light on the changes. A simple interpretation suggests that monks were the heroic witnesses proper to an age without martyrs. The monk's witness was heroic because it involved physical suffering, and it was a witness because it involved a refusal to be part of society. Some argue further that the refusal constituted a judgement on the corruption of a now tolerated and privileged church. But there are dangers and difficulties in so straightforward an explanation. In the first place, the Constantinian Empire did not end persecution. It readily punished those who were reluctant to conform to its principles, religious as well as political. In an age when the freedom to be 'different' was severely limited, anyone who 'withdrew' from society (for that is what 'anchorite' meant) was just as likely to be avoiding martyrdom as aping it. The frequently exiled bishop Athanasius, of whom we shall hear more, was prepared to defend such a policy in writing (his *Apologia de fuga sua, In Defence of his Flight*, written in the late 350s). The character of monastic withdrawal was, in the second place, paradoxical. It allowed its own species of engagement with society. Radical ascetics were admired and appealed to because they were familiar and accessible figures in villages and towns. 'Withdrawal', *anachōrēsis*, simply redefined the distinction between witness and integration. It was not a matter of accommodating oneself to the loss of an old opportunity. Rather, Christians of every sort continued to measure with care their willingness to take advantage of the secular world. That world was in some respects beguiling in its capacity to be generous and in other respects dangerous in its material indulgence and willing brutality. In negotiating an appropriate response, neither martyrs nor monks had a monopoly of virtue.

PERSONAL SACRIFICE AS A PUBLIC SPECTACLE

The surviving accounts of martyrdom were often coloured, therefore, by the beliefs and needs of later readers and compilers. People like Perpetua and Pionius could not have foreseen such developments. What pressures affected the immediate experience and earliest narratives of martyrdom? One may dismiss at once the simplistic notion that Christians needed an enemy in order to thrive. *Acta* and *passiones* were not desperate attempts to place in a favourable light a sense of powerlessness in the face of a tyrannical society. The martyr's defiance of the state represented another species of confidence. Tertullian, in his *Scorpiace*, provides the first of two important clues. Writing at a time of real danger, he rounds upon gnostics who flourished while the orthodox died. He worried about them more than about Septimius Severus. Heretics were the typical escapees, the collaborators with oppression. Martyrdom, by contrast, was a test of orthodoxy. In the search for a common theology (mounted against Marcion, Montanus and the gnostics), martyrdom was a powerful instrument of cohesion. As Ignatius of Antioch had already asserted a century before, no one was going to die for a docetist phantom. Martyrs not only displayed their trust in salvation but also identified their sacrifice with the death of Jesus. Peter and Andrew, according to tradition, had been crucified like their master. Out of humility, they had asked to be fixed to the cross in a different position; but reminiscence was unavoidable. Blandina, one of the martyrs at Lyon in 177, hanging upside down with her arms spread loose, still reminded her fellows of the dying Jesus. The shedding of blood, therefore, the ending of bodily existence, was seen as the inescapable path to risen victory. Match that, the gnostic was made to hear; match that understanding of both the value and the instability of earthly existence, and that assertion of historical continuity with the Jesus of the gospels. Martyrdom was a proof of the Incarnation, a living formula of Christology, a symbol of humanity and divinity conjoined. It made present in the community, as much as any eucharist, the saving effect of Christ.

Martyrs, male and female, were also allowed to claim the role of the authentic *paidagōgos*; allowed to teach what they symbolized. Both a 'philosopher' like Justin and a bishop like Polycarp were, in that respect, perfect archetypes. Hence the importance of the martyrs' rhetorical address – their debates with their opponents and their instruction of their admirers. From the time of Tertullian onwards, the martyr's cell was not merely the antechamber to death but a virtual pulpit, where the condemned were surrounded by admirers, disciples and petitioners. Those whom they could not instruct, comfort or advise directly were encouraged by their letters (like those preserved in Cyprian's correspondence) and their virtual diaries (like the reflections at the heart of the *Passion of Perpetua*). Anyone prepared to die for their faith must be sound in their ideals: it would have been too paradoxical to find courage and error combined in one person. Perpetua, in spite of her sex but also in spite of her Montanist leanings, was quickly accepted into the canon of martyrological literature, with a role as much instructive as exemplary. The circumstances of her death were taken to justify her opposition to her father, her admonition of the clergy, and her privileged visions and spontaneous reflections – all potentially dangerous encroachments upon authority, whether traditional or religious. Origen was equally honoured. The loss of his father, the rigour of his catechesis under Septimius Severus, his *Exhortation to Martyrdom* in the face of Maximinus Thrax, and his cruel treatment under Decius, all dissolved any suspicion that might have attached to his passionate asceticism and spiritualizing speculations. He himself linked martyrdom with baptism, giving it central significance in Christian formation. He stressed not only its agonistic element but also its alliance with the dying Jesus and its firm trust in a single God.

The second clue to the martyrs' incontrovertible claim to public significance and regard was the setting within which they faced their accusers and met their end – the courts and amphitheatres of the Roman world. Martyrdom was open for all to see, and the openness was an essential feature of the experience. The legal proceedings and the cruel spectacle may have been designed to make martyrs seem outsiders and to reinforce a contrasting unity among those who opposed them. The lonely criminal in the arena was placed beyond the social pale, while the watching crowd represented a political norm, the 'people' rather than the 'mob'. But the martyrs themselves and the accounts that survived them were making another point: that the Christian hero embodied contemporary values in a more authentic form. Tertullian, in his *Ad Scapulam* of 212, warned that persecution could bring widespread disorder to Carthage, reminding the proconsul (albeit with some rhetorical guile) that Christian penetration of the city had become extensive. The claim is confirmed by the crowded scenes in many *martyria*, where Christians on their way to execution, accompanied by unabashed and unimpeded supporters, jostled and bantered with surrounding non-believers. Ignatius had travelled to Rome in triumph, greeted everywhere by formal and fearless gatherings. He was intensely aware of being a part of a great community (whose love, ironically, might hold him back from his journey). In a comparable way, Pionius, in the third century, not only teaches in prison but also speaks publicly, with telling erudition, in the great colonnaded *agora* of Smyrna. The speeches in *martyria* carry a forceful message. Much about them was specifically Christian. Justin's discourse in the *Acts* that bear his name, although conducted with the learned prefect Rusticus, is most like a sermon, built around what is virtually a creed. Ignatius, addressing Trajan (in his *martyrium*), discusses sin and the theology of the godhead. But the emperor accuses him, like Socrates, of 'seducing' his hearers. The discussion between prisoner and judge revolves around their understanding of *nous* and *kardia*, of 'mind' and 'heart', and of the indwelling divinity (a topic touched upon also by Perpetua). Those concerns echo a longstanding philosophical debate about protection and inspiration, charged here by an added disagreement over the meanings of *daimōn* and *theophoros*, 'demon' and 'god-bearer'. Ignatius, or the writer, wanted to capture traditional 'pagan' terminology and give it a Christian meaning sufficiently different to be startling. Pionius taunts the rhetor Rufinus with a partially subverted appeal to his values and heroes (again, Socrates included). He quotes Homer at the expense of the poet's Smyrniote admirers (Homer was imagined to have come from that city). He acknowledges the people's applause for his *paideia*, but shifts the weight in the word from literary polish to ardent self-discipline. He argues over the true meaning of 'vainglory', a problem for a martyr just as much as for the honoured leaders of a great city. One could seek too eagerly for martyrdom's assumed reward. Even the death scenes of martyrs were translated into a more broadly intelligible language. Perpetua's vision of her triumph, the night before her execution, still takes the form of a tussle in the arena, during which she successfully throws a demonic wrestler and receives from Christ the traditional prize in the Carthaginian games of Apollo.

MARTYRS AND APOLOGISTS

Everything said so far serves to draw the martyrs into a broader setting. It is not surprising, therefore, that their link with the Jewish past acquires fuller meaning when related to the Apologists, who bore at the same time their own species of witness. Christianity's earliest ventures into a wider society had demanded a reassessment of its claim upon Jewish history, which was in part a claim upon Jewish heroes. The Apologists, in the service of their characteristic defence, were similarly beholden to Jewish antecedents and values. Their approach to those who were not Jews was affected by their sense of distance from the Jewish community: for their literary culture was underwritten in part by a proprietorial hold over the Jewish Scriptures. That continued allegiance to the Old Testament familiarized Christians not only with the Maccabees but also with Jews who had shown an easier regard for Hellenism and had been willing to adjust their ancient loyalties as well as reaffirm them. Christians were now presented with a similar agenda.

Jewish martyrdom had often been endowed with Messianic and political significance, and Jews thought differently about sacrifice and about the veneration of the dead. Traditions concerning ritual purity would have made later attitudes to the handling of martyrs' bodies seem unhealthy, if not abhorrent. Christians, for their part, had continued to honour the notions of priesthood and sacrifice; but Jesus's one sufficient sacrifice enveloped the individual 'witness' of the martyr and gave it its entire meaning. The *Letter to the Hebrews* placed Christian witness within the tradition of Abraham and the prophets, but devoted most of its discourse to the timeless intercession of Jesus before the throne of God. By the end of the second century, however, new circumstances began to have their effect. The blossoming rabbinic culture was different from the Judaism that Christians had rejected a hundred years before, and challenged in new ways their study of the Old Testament. Their culture of learning would always have half an eye on the rabbi's educational and exegetical practice.

Martyrdom was an essential part of the apologist culture, which began to gather strength at the same time. Justin was himself a martyr. Many of his colleagues affirmed or aspired to the martyr's status. In other respects, the early Apologists were a varied group. Some we know little about: Quadratus, who wrote to the emperor Hadrian in the 120s, survives only in the comments of Eusebius; the works of Miltiades, from the other end of the century, are lost but, according to Tertullian and Eusebius, attacked heretics and non-believers alike. About others, we are better informed. Aristides was an Athenian philosopher, who wrote to the emperor Antoninus Pius (138–61) early in his reign, suggesting that only Christians had true understanding. He showed a remarkable ability to see his own religion with an outsider's eye. (The fullest record of his thought has survived in Armenian and Syriac.) Tatian, the compiler of the *Diatessaron*, showed the reverse inclination: his *Oration to the Greeks* presented Christianity as a radical and superior alternative to Hellenistic thought. Athenagoras (*c.* 177) directed his defence to the emperor Marcus Aurelius, but his philosophical explanation of the Trinity had more than the emperor in mind, responding to wider criticism. By his time, the apologist's audience had acquired a more precise conception of Christian belief. Theophilus, bishop of Antioch in the later second century, compared the Christian God with the polytheist pantheon (in his treatise *To*

Autolycus) and stressed the organic link between the Old Testament and the gospels, avoiding the sharper contrasts characteristic of Marcion. (A reading of the Old Testament had underpinned his own acceptance of Christianity.) He carried the Christian understanding of the Trinity and the *Logos* to a further level of clarity, developing a terminology that distinguished more effectively between the unity of the *Logos* with the godhead and his role in creation. Melito, bishop of Sardis († *c.* 190), like Athenagoras, appealed to Marcus Aurelius. More interesting is his treatise *On the Pasch*, which highlights a preoccupation with gnostics as well as Jews.

In spite of contemporary martyr heroism, most apologists were eager to persuade the persecutors to a Christian point of view. In the process, they continued to uphold the principles that had already been espoused in *1 Peter* (precisely to defuse the resentment of those outside the Christian community): 'Be subject to every human institution (the emperor, the governors) for the sake of the Lord.' Their challenge resided in their ability to be Greek in their cast of mind without their religion being tainted. The theoretical reflections set in train by Ignatius, who formed the clearest bridge between the human passion of Jesus and the sufferings of the martyrs, were thus enfolded within a more complex ideology promoted by a dialogue with traditional philosophy. The Apologists were also concerned with the methods whereby ideas were shared and bequeathed – the concern that inspired the 'learning church'. Again, the 'pedagogic' status of the martyr was enfolded within that larger development. Like the discourse between a Christian philosopher and his students, martyrdom provided the whole of its audience with a series of persuasive *exempla*. So, the seeding of the church in martyr blood was less a paradox or stunning immolation and more a strategy among strategies, whereby believers encroached ever further upon the consciousness of the wider society. It was the intermittent spark or tremor that accompanied the deeper transformation of two cultures in unrelenting friction. The martyr's death did not represent a stubborn repudiation of an alien world, but offered in bolder tones the same invitation as the patient theorist.

Justin was a pivotal figure in the process. His martyrdom capped a lifetime of varied engagement on the threshold of a new, 'post-apostolic' phase of experience. Addressing, like Aristides, the emperor – whose régime seemed rational and tolerant, during one of those long periods when Christians escaped serious condemnation – he described how he and his fellow believers offered prayers for the ruler and for the peace of the empire, reflecting their readiness to obey the law, pay taxes and serve in the army. Christianity was a seedbed of good citizenship. One need not fear its notion of 'kingdom', since that kingdom was in heaven. Justin's invaluable account of Christian worship and community life – the reading of the Scriptures, moral exhortation, the eucharist and care for the needy – was included within his *Apology* as an important part of what he wished to explain to outsiders, a feature as attractive as doctrine. Such details were now more familiar to informed outsiders.

But Justin was equally conscious of a Jewish audience. In his *Dialogue with Trypho*, he made the habitual Christian assertion that moral worth was superior to legal conformity; but he acknowledged that the Old Testament preserved a comparable scale of values, and he made careful distinctions between prescriptions and ritual. He preserved, in so doing, the tone of the *midrash pesher*, in which analysis of the sacred text was interwoven with reflections upon it. While less attracted by apocalyptic and even typological forms of exegesis (although he respected Philo), he did not abandon Judaism for the classics but (like may Jews) shifted the focus of his loyalty within the Jewish past. A correct understanding of the relation between Judaism and Christianity depended, for Justin, on understanding historical development. The prophecies of the Old Testament allowed one to interpret correctly the life of Jesus – a bridge between two covenants that was built upon the fact that the Old Testament writers, harbingers of Christianity, were inspired by the same Spirit that dwelt in Jesus. (Justin may have used 'proof texts' like those that informed the gospel of Matthew, but he also had a mind of his own, often making independent interpretative appeals.) Non-Jews were now invited to share that history. Justin, eclectic in the Middle Platonist tradition, made that tradition more readily available to Christian writers; but the *Dialogue with Trypho* worked in the other direction, making Greek philosophers beholden to the older prophets, and the *First Apology* presented Plato as dependent upon Moses (an assertion long-lived in the Christian mind thereafter). So, no one needed to feel that, in passing from their own revered thinkers to the teachings of Jesus, they were abandoning their past completely. Acceptance of Christianity, for Justin, implied nothing so dramatic.

The amalgam represented in Justin – the readiness to die, the sympathetic familiarity with traditional philosophy, the sensitive adjustment to the Jewish past – can be found in many writers of the persecution period. Tertullian and the Alexandrian theologians, archetypes of a Christian rapport with 'classical culture', are cases in point. Tertullian knew relatively little about contemporary Judaism, or even about the rabbis of Carthage, which distinguishes him from Origen. One is inclined to take at face value, therefore, his famous distinction between Athens and Jerusalem. The reference to Jerusalem, however, continued to associate Christianity with Judaism. Tertullian said explicitly that Christian wisdom could be traced back to the portico of Solomon. Yet his treatise *Against the Jews* appealed in the first place to those who were not Jews: he wanted to dissuade them from joining the Jewish community. His assertion that the New Testament had superseded the Old was designed to undermine a regard for ancient cults in general. The twists of his argument signalled a new phase in Christianity's competition with Jewish counterparts. Tertullian's work also reveals how 'public' Christianity had become, how irreversible was its immersion in city life. His attacks on idolatry were a warning to Christians as much as a challenge to the idolators. He felt a need to regulate in detail, down to the level of clothing and coiffure, the customs they could adopt, and the relations they could enter into. The concept of *idololatria* covered more than participation in cult. Roman society was stained through and through with its religious allegiances. In contrast to Justin, Tertullian felt that no Christian could hold public office or undertake military service. Yet the caution with which the believer now had to venture into this or that sphere of public life was itself a sign of involvement. Moral rigour, rather than repudiating the transition, catered for it.

In the case of Clement and Origen, there was a comparable breadth of reference, extending beyond debates about Greek philosophy. Alexandria was not only a Hellenistic city but also part of a Jewish sphere that reached north into Palestine and Syria – the route traced by Origen's career. Esoteric texts like the *Gospel of the Hebrews* and the *Gospel of Peter* drew Christians into a new dialogue with Judaism throughout the region. Clement picked up the relation between Plato and Moses to underpin a new species of independence for his own creed. Traditions of every sort were worthy of respect but truth could be distinguished from those who uttered it. What had remained, in Justin's hands, a past to be shared became, in Clement's, a universal wisdom, a transcendent value. He, no less than Tertullian, was distressed by 'demonic' cult, but shared thereby in the polytheists' critique of their own tradition. He thought it useless to abandon mythology, if materialism was the proposed alternative. He was a willing partner in the broad philosophical trend of the time, Platonist in inspiration, that reached out to a single God who gave meaning to the variety of the visible world. In that enterprise, the unrelenting monotheism of the Jews was an invaluable ally, if only interpreted correctly. Philo had pointed the way, symbolizing the natural bond between philosophical judgement and biblical reflection. Some Christians, on the other hand, had besmirched philosophy with gnostic associations. Irenaeus had considered gnostics irrational, and Clement was determined to draw a line against gnosticism without appearing an enemy of intellect. Origen, for his part, was similarly engaged in a dialogue with Jewish learning (while as eager as Tertullian to steel himself for martyrdom). His laborious tabulation of biblical texts, for example, as he declared to his colleague Julius Africanus, was undertaken chiefly to aid discussion with Jewish scholars, so that he and they might not find themselves arguing over a disputed text.

THE PRESERVATION OF INTEGRITY: HIPPOLYTUS AND HIS RIVALS

Certain aspects of martyrdom and of the apologist culture, therefore, illustrate the ability of Christians both to maintain their own cohesiveness and to increase their openness to Roman society. The two categories – 'martyr' and 'apologist' – did not exhaust between them the ways in which one might relate to the wider world. The differences between martyrdom and other forms of commitment were contained within a broader debate.

Martyrdom implied the rejection of certain options. In contrast to the Jews, Christian martyrs avoided ethnic or political aspirations. But that helped them to rise above any tendency to isolation. Orthodox martyrs were also seen as standing in judgement on gnostics. But the distinction was simplistic, since gnostics were less opposed to heroic witness than some of their enemies admitted. They merely resisted (as in the *Testament of Truth*) the notion that it brought automatic forgiveness, or that it represented specifically a sacrifice demanded by God. Many of those who thought of themselves as orthodox would have felt the same. More adamantly antignostic was the martyrs' belief that their physical experience had theological significance. But that proves that they did not represent a 'hatred of the world' or an escape from circumstance: rather, they signalled a need to reassess the impact of circumstance on religious demands.

The 'broader debate', of which martyrdom and apologetics were partial reflections, had been going on since apostolic times. There had been initial resistance to the pressure of 'outside' values; and the boundary between church and world (which resistance implied) had encouraged a high level of observance in both behaviour and worship, and constantly challenged a community to reconcile itself to those who slipped across that boundary. In spite of tensions, however, the Pauline and later churches continued to push their boundaries outwards. Strict observance was not thereby abandoned but acquired a different force and operated according to different strategies. Martyrdom was not a simple conflict between those who continued to put their trust in the integrity of an ancient culture and those who sought a more personal, withdrawn or antinomian sense of religious identity. Contrasts came to seem less stark. Christians began to feel that the best way of dealing with the 'otherness' of non-Christian culture was to imitate it. That applied to social structures as much as to philosophy or rhetoric. Tertullian's characteristic strictures acknowledged that immersion and accommodation were already under way. Clement of Alexandria's moderation and tact instructed a wider audience how far they might reach into the non-Christian world.

Thus, dialogue itself helped to determine the path of Christianity. It preserved ancient habits of thought and behaviour, but enlarged the social space within which they were expected to function. No duplicity was involved. The Apologists' assertion that Christians prayed willingly for universal peace and order was not a cover for some secret and feverish desire to hasten their own end and the end of the world. They did not behave in one way among themselves and in another when facing outsiders. The essence of Christian 'apology' was the assurance that they had nothing to hide. They demanded neither more nor less in private than they did when the world was watching. Martyrdom, in particular, was not a rigorist stance adopted to impress outsiders. At the moment of trial, the whole Christian community presented itself to view, with its different levels of obligation and its varied catalogue of roles and spiritual gifts. And martyrdom was not superseded by alternative commitments. It represented just one of the ways in which the Christian community redefined virtue and discipline. A single set of values enfolded all believers. During the long periods when there was no direct persecution, Christians continued to prepare themselves for the physical test of immense pain. Their assurance would never shake off or elide its twin components of ecstasy and horror: it was 'fostered alike by beauty and by fear'. But the martyr became enveloped in a long-term and more widely shouldered task. Christians were not to be caught unawares. Anyone might be called upon – those who died were distinguished from those who did not more by God's choice than by their own. Everyone was a potential *agōnistēs*, a competitor, an athlete, an ascetic; one who subdued his body to the needs of the future contest (and women laid equal claim to that typically male accomplishment). Paradoxically, by keeping in mind a test that was only rarely imposed, Christians prepared themselves for acceptance and security. The *ascēsis* or training demanded by martyrdom inspired the belief that fasting and virginity were the best preparations for the ultimate defence of principle. Tertullian thought of the church as a virgin – an image that went well beyond the bridal language of *Ephesians*. Christians sought constantly for a balance between martyrdom and the expectant discipline and inner purity of other believers. The bulk of ascetic practices, therefore, was gradually distinguished from the culture of self-sacrifice. Asceticism, whether mild or extreme, became an ideal for the living as well as for those facing imminent death. And that more humdrum pursuit of goodness was never seen as second best. While Christians may have found heroism more often than not uncalled for, they bore its possibility in mind and admired it when realized.

The career of Hippolytus offers a special illustration of the tensions involved. Confusions about his identity, which I have mentioned already, are symptomatic of the third-century increase in the production of texts. One simple solution to a complicated problem is to suggest that two figures lie behind the numerous works now associated with Hippolytus's name. One was the opponent of Pope Callistus in the early 220s. He was probably at some stage a schismatic bishop, but also the author of the *Refutation of All Heresies*. The other was a presbyter, who died in a Sardinian mining camp during the persecution of Maximinus Thrax, in the company of Pontian, recently bishop of Rome (230–35). Their joint endurance may have represented a reconciliation of the factions led by Callistus and the earlier Hippolytus. Certainly, the second Hippolytus must have had a hand in the preservation and partial editing of the works of the first.

If that account is in any way accurate, what caused later confusions? First, there exists a statue of a seated figure long regarded as Hippolytus, because a catalogue of works traditionally ascribed to him (including the *Refutation*) is carved on the chair. It has seemed to offer proof of a single author and an extensive œuvre. The statue was at an early stage substantially altered, however, and, more recently, was heavily restored. It may have been originally allegorical and even female in form; in which case, the listed works on the chair may have been the products or admired resources of a 'school' rather than the work of one individual. The significance of that possibility will become clearer shortly. Some scholars have believed that the statue was originally of a specific woman, the philosopher Themista of Lampsacus (praised by Clement of Alexandria). It could have been destined for the new library in the Pantheon, being designed at that time by the Christian Julius Africanus. That would connect the list of works carved on the chair with a supposed rapport between the church in Rome and the emperor Severus Alexander (222–35), about which Eusebius wrote with enthusiasm. The emperor's relative tolerance of Christianity, shared with his immediate Severan predecessors, may have been influenced partly by his mother Julia Mamaea, who showed a keen interest in philosophy and eastern religions. A famous story in the later and partly fictional *Historia Augusta* describes a shrine in which the emperor had included a figure of Jesus. There is undoubtedly room for that sort of speculation about the relaxed religious atmosphere and varied interests of the period; but, as far as the Hippolytan statue is concerned, allegorical or not, it was probably the property of a Christian group. Eusebius, for his part, exaggerated in Severus Alexander the unfulfilled anticipation of Constantine's later favour.

The second source of confusion was the ignorance of later authors, particularly of Eusebius in the East and of Prudentius and his contemporaries in the West. Their account of antagonism followed by reconciliation was an attempt to combine the regrettable errors of an otherwise admirable figure with their own understanding of episcopal authority. Both the opportunities and the dangers that affected the papacy of Damasus, for example, bishop of Rome from 366 to 384, would have been incomprehensible to Callistus and his peers. Damasus enjoyed a leadership among other bishops that was at once enlarged by imperial favour and challenged by theological division. That defined both the opposition he faced, in Rome itself and among the bishops of the West, and the powers he possessed to resist it. In addition to the distracting character of their own systems of government, post-Constantinian writers looked back on the 220s through the period of conflict between the Roman presbyter Novatian and his bishop Cornelius. Novatian was intransigently rigorist in the face of laxity during the persecution of Decius, consecrated as a rival bishop and then redeemed by martyrdom under Valerian (258). The parallels were tempting but the circumstances were different.

Hippolytus's 'politics' have to be related to his fundamental ideals. The *Refutation* and associated works ended the dominance of Greek in the western church, but retained a special respect for eastern tradition. They also brought to a close a phase in theological development; one associated with Justin and Irenaeus, focused on the *Logos*, and respectful of the Johannine tradition more generally. Close bonds of love within a tightly knit group, and a heightened sense of exclusive destiny (both Johannine hallmarks), might have been modified, but were not superseded, by social engagement and official toleration. The thrust of Hippolytus's eschatology postponed the end of the world, but still fostered a lively hope in fulfilment. He allowed room for both order and anticipation, each entailing strict discipline; but he suspected compromise where others found opportunity. His fidelity to John extended to his historical analysis of the last days of Jesus, which may have kept alive older disagreements about the dating of Easter – the inscriptions on the famous statue include reference to the issue – and may therefore have provided further cause for discord among the Roman communities. Finally, Hippolytus's enduring reflection on the nature and role of the *Logos* and his respect for the historical processes involved dissuaded him from fudging distinctions that characterized the 'monarchian' theology of his eastern contemporary Noetus and his fellow theologian in Rome, Sabellius. (Sabellius and his imitators believed that the Father and the Son were distinguished only in that God performed at different times different tasks – a view sometimes known as 'modalism'. Praxeas, attacked by Tertullian, had similar ideas.) Here was another invitation to stormy argument.

Fidelity to Greek tradition, anxiety about a lax response to the temptations of a tolerant empire, calm but literal expectation of final judgment, deep antagonism to Trinitarian as well as gnostic error, and devotion to a small band of friends and followers – all provided a perfect background to Hippolytus's dislike of Callistus (and of bishops of Rome before and after him). Callistus had made human weakness too easy to assuage; his lenient response to sin made him dangerously attractive, not least to heretics – so ran Hippolytus's complaint. But what institutional form did his opposition take? According to him, Callistus was leader of a *didaskaleion*, a school. He was also a bishop. Hippolytus, according to tradition, was created a rival bishop (and therefore the first 'antipope'). Does that mean that the Christian church in Rome, hitherto a unity, was divided between two claimants to the same jurisdiction? So fourth-century observers might have supposed; but Hippolytus, himself a teacher, a *didaskalos*, seems to have been more concerned with Callistus's opinions than with his jurisdiction. The essence of his outrage may have been precisely that Callistus claimed authority beyond his own circle. Had he remained, in Hippolytus's eyes, orthodox in his judgements, there would have been no grounds for division. The unity of the church in Rome was built more on doctrine than on territorial rights.

That possibility casts light on Irenaeus's famous reprimand of Pope Victor (189–98) for his harshness towards those who dated Easter differently. In the previous generation again, Polycarp of Smyrna had tried to persuade Pope Anicetus to retain the old Jewish *Pasch*, the Passover, as the day on which to celebrate Easter (the fourteenth day of the month *Nisan*; hence the label 'Quartodecimans'). Most eastern churches did so, then and for more than a century after. Victor tried to impose on the easterners the contrasting practice of celebrating Easter on the Sunday after the Jewish festival, and was roundly resisted; but Irenaeus, in his rebuke, was thinking as much of Victor's need to reconcile himself with opponents in his own city – pointing to divisions that would have been still recent in Hippolytus's day. Another associated development is reflected in the textual tradition of Hippolytus's works, which became interwoven with the so-called 'Clementine literature' (named after the Clement of the 90s). Those fictional accounts of early church history were greatly expanded at precisely this time, and were designed to reinforce a 'Petrine' interpretation of papal authority at the expense of a looser pattern supposedly sanctioned and represented in earlier times by James of Jerusalem. So, both the 'Easter Controversy' and the conflicting interpretations of the papal past suggest that Callistus's position (and the position of any pope) was never as clear-cut as later historians and theologians were ready to imagine.

The adaptation of the Hippolytan statue and its inscribed catalogue may have represented a parallel mythology, designed to enhance Hippolytus's reputation as a 'philosopher' rather than an 'antipope'. Two impressions would have been created thereby: either Callistus played a similar although, in his case, misguided role, or Hippolytus opposed him as a teacher rather than as a bishop. The reality behind those carefully orchestrated reinterpretations (not to mention later reinterpretations of the reinterpretations) is almost impossible to capture. Hippolytus's own vocabulary suggests a philosophical context. The teaching authority of both men, and the apparently visible distinction of their followers and supporters, is entirely akin to philosophical practice, then and later: teachers and pupils gathered in urban households (just as Christians had done for nearly two centuries, when celebrating their liturgies). Hippolytus's group may even have wished to declare a specific if modified allegiance to the traditions of Epicurus: for Themista of Lampsacus – supposing she was in any way associated with the statue's history – had been an adherent of the Epicurean school.

Nevertheless, the atmosphere that surrounded Hippolytus, even in his own works, was inescapably 'ecclesial'. His discussion of philosophical issues was designed to protect his church from error. His opposition to Callistus, his belief that leaders should be respected for their moral quality and their adherence to tradition, his independent rigour (reminiscent of Tertullian the Montanist), were nonetheless judgements about status. He was equally interested in ceremonial. His account of it, as it now survives, depends on a complicated series of translations and adaptations; but there is no doubt that Hippolytus lies at the root of the *Apostolic Tradition*, a rich source of information about the ordination of bishops and priests, the administering of baptism, and the celebration of the eucharist. He also describes how Christians celebrated the *agapē* or communal meal, distinct from the eucharist. They met together on Saturday evenings to prepare for the Lord's Day following. They made offerings of fruit and flowers. They were encouraged to pray at regular hours. It is useful to compare this vivid record with the roughly contemporary *Didascalia apostolorum*, written in Greek in northern Syria, and surviving in a Syriac version and in extracts inserted in later documents (especially the fourth-century *Apostolic Constitutions*). Its tone is less exacting but its detail no less instructive. Worshippers are strictly organized by rank and sex. The writer has a lot to say about women, and particularly about deaconesses, who had specific roles to play in baptism, and ministered to the needy in ways not readily open to men. Hippolytus reserves his fullest account for ordinations and baptism, and therein lies the chief importance of his liturgical legacy. Like Tertullian and Origen, he was anxious to control the doorway of initiation that led from the world of unbelievers into the 'holy church'. Control depended both on the authority of the baptizer and on the explicit wording of the ceremony. Numerous categories of person were forced either to renounce their employment or withdraw their candidacy. The exclusion of pimps and prostitutes may not surprise us, but painters, actors, gladiators and charioteers were also recommended to rethink their careers, together with soldiers and magistrates (because they exercised power over life and death). Preparation, the 'catechumenate', lasted for as much as three years, rounded off by exorcism, washing, anointing and the laying on of hands – practices that would endure for centuries, and seem to have been already fully developed in Hippolytus's day.

A UNITED CHURCH IN A UNITED EMPIRE

It seems paradoxical that a high degree of religious sensibility and a carefully contained group consciousness, both designed to foster some distance from the non-Christian world, should in fact have encouraged a contrary engagement. The paradox fades when one recognizes that a genuine attempt was being made to forge new patterns of leadership and unity at a time when several options were still open that would later be closed. There would always be rigorists, suspicious of status and honour, fearful of diminished standards. The belief endured for a long time – a belief characteristic of Hippolytus, Tertullian and Origen (and of many heterodox groups) – that virginity and associated styles of renunciation were appropriate markers by which to distinguish Christians from non-believers. Origen provided a rich basis for such a view. Unlike Clement, he carried fervour beyond the world of the flesh. Yet those architects of Christian integrity shared their world with more moderate, even hesitant figures, who were equally representative of Christianity's development and equally assured of future imitators. Julius Africanus, with connections reaching from Edessa to Rome, enjoyed favourable relations with the emperors Elagabalus and Alexander Severus, helped to develop the new Pantheon library and wrote five books of *Chronographies* that placed 'salvation history' within an ordered history of the whole world – an enterprise that would influence Eusebius. Origen wrote both his *Against Celsus* and his *Exhortation to Martyrdom* with the encouragement of the ex-gnostic Ambrose, an anxious man only half-assured in his adhesion to Christianity, reflecting the far from sharp distinction between Origen's own circle and those he sought to influence.

Origen's characteristic movement from *psychē* to *pneuma*, with its associated emphasis on free choice, owed as much to Paul as to Plato. He believed in both the 'futility' and the 'corruption' of the present order, but also in 'the hope of deliverance'. That sense of both individual and cosmic potential helped him to solve tensions that had defeated Hippolytus and Tertullian. The contingency of existence imposed its demands. But Origen enjoyed a longer experience of persecution and toleration – from Septimius Severus to Decius via Maximinus Thrax; the other Severi and Philip the Arab (244–49) providing intervals of calm. As a result, he more readily appreciated the variety of circumstances in which the Christian life might have to be preserved. There was an intrinsic breadth to his thought. He judged other cults not only by their dangers but also by their failure to match what he saw as universal principles in creation. His greater wisdom was directly bequeathed to Eusebius, and it is doubtful whether a church limited to the heritage of Tertullian and Hippolytus could have accommodated itself to the impact of Constantine.

Hippolytus, Tertullian and Origen, for all their strictness, were also symptomatic of a looser church order, of an enduring elasticity in styles of leadership. Their indignation highlighted the ambiguities of contemporary practice. They carried into another generation the disciplines of the household and the philosophical circle that had held sway under Justin. But Hippolytus's liturgical interests, deliberate and detailed, laid down foundations that would last well into the fourth century; and the instructor of his community was permanently identified as the *proestōs*, the leader of the eucharistic celebration – more 'priestly', even, than Irenaeus's bishop. Tertullian had also taken direct issue with church leaders in Rome. His *Against Praxeas*, late and in that sense 'Montanist', attacked the Sabellian tendency that Callistus seems to have favoured (although we cannot be sure that he was thinking of Callistus personally). His *De pudicitia, On Purity*, almost certainly had an African target in mind – a man he addressed ironically as *pontifex maximus* and *episcopus episcoporum*, 'high priest' and 'the bishop of bishops'. There is no reason to suppose that he would have used the terms more happily in addressing a bishop of Rome. His local opponent, however, was imposing the policies of Callistus, perhaps at his command – issuing an *edictum peremptorium*, a definitive decree that (for example) adultery could be forgiven. The criticisms made by Hippolytus in his *Refutation* were similar, although not identical. Yet, in spite of his strictures, Tertullian was perfectly prepared, in his *Ruling against Heretics*, to appeal to the doctrinal authority of Roman bishops as guardians of the heritage of Peter and Paul.

Although the process was slow and not without its critics, Christians were acquiring a clearer sense of unity and universal mission – a sense that demanded in turn more hierarchical control. The pressures exerted by the proximity of other faiths had driven them at first to a stark revulsion; but the relatively simple social structures that resulted became in the end administratively more complex and theologically more refined. Origen's influence contributed significantly to those changes, at least in the East. His successors Heraclas and Dionysius, both bishops of Alexandria (Dionysius from 247 to the mid-260s), brought Eusebius's *Ecclesiastical History* to a new threshold of intelligible episcopal succession. Dionysius became embroiled with both Cyprian in Carthage and his own namesake in Rome (bishop there from 259 to 268), partly over the *lapsi* and the reconciliation of heretics, and partly over the relation between the Father and the Son. The correspondence between three leaders so widely flung is the first major demonstration of how far a bishop's authority might now reach. The church in Rome itself had benefited from the long episcopate of Fabian (236–50). According to the *Liber Pontificalis* (not always reliable), the city, now recovered from the divisions of the 220s, began to take on the administrative shape that would last beyond the end of our period. It symbolized the robust confidence that defeated Decius. Fabian's immediate successors, notably Stephen I (254–57), were invited to deal with supporters of Novatian in Gaul and Spain, thus enhancing the influence of the papacy, at least in the West. So, the influence of the bishop of Rome between the accession of Fabian and the death of Dionysius grew to be markedly more effective than it had been under Victor and the contemporaries of Callistus; and the city survived the intransigence of Novatian more easily than it had that of Hippolytus. Yet the issues remained the same – laxity in the face of persecution and theological dispute over the Trinity. Those two sensitivities continued to govern episcopal diplomacy and Rome's claims to leadership well beyond the accession of Constantine.

Behind the new and spectacular eminence of Rome, Carthage and Alexandria, we find a more general pattern of development. Every city with a significant number of Christians was moving, as Rome had done, from loose groups, such as Paul addressed in *Romans,* to formal parishes, such as we find in the *Liber pontificalis* during the fifth and sixth centuries. In making such changes, Christians were always inventive to a purpose. Their needs might have been served in the second century by 'schools' like the small circles that gathered around Justin and Valentinus, or around Clement and Origen. But such circles began to overlap. While still stamped with their own loyalties and styles of conduct, they had functions in common – the care of the poor, for example. And even a man as intransigent as Hippolytus recognized that agreement over doctrine demanded tighter leadership. That conviction widened in turn into the need to exchange views and information among different churches, a sign of their awareness that they had ideals and problems in common. Letters to other churches, already characteristic of the Pauline mission, had to be based on representative discussion and on the literary skill and personal charism of an organizing spokesman. Clement of Rome, Ignatius of Antioch and Polycarp of Smyrna were exactly such men. More is involved, therefore, than seeing one bishop achieve leadership among others: our first attention must be directed at the ways in which episcopacy emerged within each city. Nor should we jump decades or centuries. Eusebius, for example, was too tidy in his suggestions. He slipped easily from agreement within an individual church to a juridical decree by its leader and then to the formal voting that characterized the councils of his own day. Certainly, early debates and experiments set in place the machinery of order and communication that would later make possible more formal organization and authority; but that machinery was not yet stable enough to impose effective authority on a figure like Hippolytus.

There was more at stake, in any case, than effective jurisdiction. The development of the episcopate reflected, and was designed to protect, qualities intrinsic to the notion of 'church'. We are observing the next stage in the process outlined in Chapter 4, the creation of structures within which to foster virtue. By the third century, it was possible to think of 'the church' on a grander scale; a church that was able to describe with clarity and detail not only its transcendent origin and inner purpose but also the singularity of its social forms. The clarity was not simply born of oppression, as if the difficulties of the persecution era brought a new church into being. Rather, a deeper and more ancient confidence allowed it to overcome new difficulties. At least to that extent, we can believe in a 'primitive' conception of Christianity that was one within itself and relevant to the destiny of all humanity. It seems natural to ask whether such a conception did not drive an irrepressible urge to dominate the world, an urge to integrate on its own terms alone. If 'domination' in that sense was ever envisaged or attempted (and Constantine's empire and legacy seems an obvious instance), it was likely to prove a failure, a phase from which Christians would have to recover. But such a misinterpretation could arise only when Christianity's universal mission had become more visibly attainable. The nature of that mission was more accurately discerned by the theologians of the age. Their predominantly Platonist enthusiasms meant that the Incarnation, the interpretation of Scripture and the celebration of the sacraments were approached at two levels – to put it at its simplest, the visible and invisible. True knowledge, true understanding, true devotion and true virtue demanded that one should rise from one level to the other. That dynamism, inspiring effort but also distinction, affected not only the elevation of individual spirit and clarity of insight but also the relative merits of different believers. Text and community were still bound together. One could hardly debate the issue of engagement with the world without bringing into play the cosmic destiny of Jesus the *Logos* and Messiah, which Origen did so much to elaborate. Enduring preoccupation with the Father and the Son, and especially with the latter's distinctiveness and purpose, created in the minds of Christians a truly universal context for their endeavours and destiny; and the preoccupation would long outlive any sense of self-satisfaction at the conversion of Constantine. If new patterns of administration and authority were designed to foster and protect religious ideals, they did so in the light of that fuller notion of the invisible world and of cosmic fulfilment. Clement of Alexandria's patient pedagogy, Tertullian's *anima naturaliter Christiana*, and Origen's exalted view of spirituality translated the thrust of individual aspiration into an all-embracing anthropology. It was the human being as such, made in the 'image' of God, that could now achieve *homoiōsis tou theou*, 'likeness to God'. The achievement depended on adhesion to Jesus, sealed in baptism, and to Jesus understood as being himself the 'image' of God. Once again, the nature of relations within the Trinity affected directly what human beings could hope for themselves, and the social order that would bring hope to fruition. Beneath the heady triumphs of the Constantinian church, that theology continued to generate its deeper anxieties.

The temptation to ally the vision of Origen with the ambition of Constantine may have been encouraged by an independent sense of unity in the

Roman Empire more generally. The question arises whether Christianity could attribute its eventual favoured status to its perceived usefulness as an instrument or symbol of such unity – a possibility frequently mooted in relation to Constantine. It would be ironic, on the other hand, if a more favoured status signalled the victory of the persecuting state – because Christians eventually decided to join forces with an increasingly unified empire. At no time, however, were the boundaries of the Christian world – even when conceived of as a single 'church' – regarded as coterminous with the boundaries of the Roman state. No one had considered that they could be in the earliest days, and no one wished them to be so under or after Constantine. One should be sceptical about Roman unity in any case. It may seem suggestive that church developments in the early third century coincided with the famous 212 *constitutio Antoniniana*, which made the free inhabitants of the empire Roman citizens. The cynical point to the tax advantages thus gained by Caracalla. However, he may have defined his move partly in religious terms, and it undoubtedly contributed to a greater unity in Rome's legal system, reinforced by the brilliance of contemporary lawyers like Domitius Ulpianus and even Aemilius Papinianus, executed soon after Caracalla came to power: for Caracalla's opportunities owed much to the long reign of Septimius Severus, his father – indeed, Tertullian's boasting about the vigour of the church coincided with the military and political triumphs of the earlier emperor. Caracalla himself, sole emperor from 211 to 217, anticipated Constantine in remarkable ways, his career reaching similarly from northern Britain to the frontiers of Persia, inspired by the achievements of Alexander the Great. The first three decades of the century were marked by a literary flowering, symbolized in the work of the Athenian sophist Philostratus, author of the *Life* of the archetypical 'holy man', Apollonius of Tyana, and of the *Lives of the Sophists*. The writers of the age stood on the cusp between two phases in philosophical development – a new synthesis of Stoic, Platonist and Pythagorean thought, and the beginnings of a Neoplatonist tradition that would culminate in the achievements of Plotinus and his pupils (Porphyry especially) at the end of the third century. (Plotinus died in 270, Porphyry *c.* 305.) Stoic attachment to cosmic order and the mastery of passion was wedded with the Platonist sense of a transition from the natural to the divine. The Stoic's characteristic sense of political obligation was thus enfolded within a less empirical, more transcendent system, amenable not least to the Pauline ideal of shared citizenship with the saints.

The optimism (if that is what it was) of Caracalla's reign was, however, short-lived. There was no ascending curve to carry a single church to its

Constantinian destiny. Clement and Origen more accurately reflect the shape of events. Clement, living in Septimius Severus's more stable reign, saw the tensions between church and empire declared in a straightforward way. Origen, surviving into the middle years of the century, witnessed the empire's ensuing political and strategic insecurity. Rome faced a more vigorous enemy in Persia, after the victories of the Sassanian usurper Artaxerxes I Ardashir (224). Not until the campaigns of the Caesar Galerius, completed in 298, was that threat diminished. After the Severan dynasty ended in 235, a series of largely unsuccessful emperors exposed the provinces to pillage and adventure. Decius the persecutor may have intended to restore Rome's ancient institutions, but his ineffectual conservatism was, as I have said, a compliment to Christian resilience. By 260, an emperor, the persecutor Valerian, had been captured and humiliated by the Persians. Only in the late 270s was a strong hand evident again at the centre of Roman power. Even then, provincial self-interest and an occasional readiness to rebel or secede, in both Gaul and the East, showed that the unity of the empire and the stability of its administration were far from assured. That variety of local ambition echoed more accurately Christianity's enduring idiosyncrasies.

The chief conclusion to be drawn from this account is that the 'Christian Empire' got under way in the first decades of the third century; but in a special sense. Theological dispute, moral discipline and patterns of order and authority began to acquire the forms that Constantine and his contemporaries would take advantage of; but none of them were developed with such an end in view, which no one at the time could have foreseen. Constantine was not predictable, even in theory. Christianity's sense of its past and future, already a conscious component of its identity, had first to pass, as we shall see, through the minds of Lactantius and Eusebius, whose characteristic understanding of history and fulfilment were articulated before Constantine's accession. Lactantius in Latin and Eusebius in Greek, each building on the legacy either of Tertullian or of Origen, provide us with a thoroughly third-century reflection on the essence and momentum of Christian experience. The experience included martyrdom; and neither writer, in his earlier and major works, saw martyrdom as a prelude to some tranquil and glorious era. Eusebius interpreted Christian suffering under Diocletian and his colleagues as a necessary antidote to the dangerous and complacent tranquillity of earlier decades.

The account has also bound together elements previously separated. The engagement of churches in public life was interwoven with their own increasing cohesiveness. The religious earnestness and pedagogic structure of the earlier communities acquired new relevance to both inner development and external relations. The Jewish heritage and the riches of other ancient cultures further inspired Christian habits of thought, but also provided new models of leadership and authority – and, by the same token, made the churches more visible and intelligible as institutions in the cities of the Roman world. The pressures of persecution had induced weakness and failure, which demanded in turn both formal instruments of reconciliation and authorities strong enough to make them work. Persecution also helped to identify a growing community of less heroic believers – orthodox, admiring and susceptible – whose pastoral needs had to be catered for, and whose style of piety was gradually becoming the expected norm. The conversion of Constantine may have surprised them; but it did not sweep their world away.

Further reading

Again, the suggestions at the end of the previous two chapters have a bearing on this one. I concentrate here on martyrdom. The standard study in English, although modifed by a generation of scholarship, is still W.H.C. Frend, *Martyrdom and Persecution in the Early Church; a Study of a Conflict from the Maccabees to Donatus* (Garden City, NY: Anchor Books, 1967). A sense of the changes that have taken place since that book's appearance will be gained from Daniel Boyarin, *Dying for God: Martyrdom and the Making of Christianity and Judaism* (Stanford, CA: Stanford University Press, 1999). Texts are splendidly produced and discussed in Gary A. Bisbee, *Pre-Decian Acts of Martyrs and Commentarii* (Philadelphia, PA: Fortress Press, 1988), although still indispensable is Herbert Musurillo, *The Acts of the Christian Martyrs: Texts and Translations* (Oxford: Clarendon Press, 1972). On the attitudes of martyrs themselves, see Eugene and Anita Weiner, *The Martyr's Conviction: a Sociological Analysis* (Atlanta, GA: Scholars Press, 1990), Arthur J. Droge and James D. Tabor, *A Noble Death: Suicide and Martyrdom among Christians and Jews in Antiquity* (San Francisco, CA: Harper, 1992) and Judith Perkins, *The Suffering Self: Pain and Narrative Representation in the Early Christian Era* (London and New York, NY: Routledge, 1995). A stimulating series of reflections is provided by Glen W. Bowersock, *Martyrdom and Rome* (Cambridge: Cambridge University Press, 1995).

Other topics covered in this chapter are additionally discussed by Allen Brent, *Hippolytus and the Roman Church in the Third Century: Communities in Tension before the Emergence of a Monarch–Bishop* (Leiden: Brill, 1995), L.V.

Rutgers, *Subterranean Rome: in Search of the Roots of Christianity in the Catacombs of the Eternal City* (Leuven: Peeters, 2000) and Polymnia Athanassiadi and Michael Frede (eds), *Pagan Monotheism in Late Antiquity* (Oxford: Clarendon Press, 1999).

Where to begin?
Daniel Boyarin, *Dying for God.*

Chapter 7

THE CHRISTIAN EMPIRE, A CONTESTED EXPERIMENT: CONSTANTINE AND HIS SUCCESSORS

It would be silly to suggest that the conversion of Constantine in 312 made little difference to Christian fortunes; but, unless one bears in mind the developments I have described in the previous chapter, it is difficult to appreciate just what the difference was. Both his own antecedents and those of his new religion carried considerable weight. Constantine did not invent a new type of Christianity, but submitted to an existing set of beliefs and practices. He may not have understood them aright. He may have been selective in what he accepted. He may have continued to display older habits of mind. All that is possible. The major point, however, is that he identified himself with an ideology and a community already of considerable antiquity; an ideology and a community both complex and self-assured. Historians have justifiably admired his innovative genius. That there was innovation, inspired by the emperor's convictions, is not open to doubt; and innovation implied, among other things, Christian status, wealth, display, privilege and power. It is equally true, however, that the major features of fourth-century Christianity – its resources, organization and doctrine; its spiritual values and aspirations – were substantially in place by the late third century. For that reason, they were to some degree independent of the emperor's change of heart. As I said earlier, no one could have seen Constantine coming. Even by 306, with the abdicator Diocletian safely removed, few churchmen would have pinned their hopes on a usurper who had yet to confirm his position. (Ossius of Cordova, a long-lived and trusted adviser (d. 357), was a notable exception.) For usurper the young Constantine was; and, after his mastery over the western provinces was assured, he was compelled for more than ten years to share power in the empire as a whole with the non-believer Licinius. His conversion induced, in fact, a powerful but unstable fusion of two tendencies: a defence of tradition and a disturbing excitement in the face of unexpected opportunity. The same tendencies affected other aspects of his policy. He proved as volatile in secular affairs as in religion. His adhesion to a new faith became part of a larger plan, which sucked Christians into the maelstrom of his unpredictable intelligence and limitless ambition. Many gained from the chances thus offered, and worked hard to preserve them. Many more came with time to doubt the wisdom of the whole experiment.

BISHOP AND COMMUNITY: A NEW PHASE

Of all the features of the Christian religion calculated to impress a man of Constantine's experience and ambition, the most striking may have been the increasing eminence of the urban bishop. Trying to sum up in later years his own role, the emperor declared a cryptic wish to be 'the bishop of those outside'. While the phrase may have betrayed some misunderstanding of ecclesial structures, it made obvious his admiration for the bishop's standing and influence. As he moved towards his own conversion, some fifteen years previously, it had been bishops of his new western domains, like Ossius, that had encouraged and clarified his growing adhesion to the Christian faith. It has been common to suggest that Constantine was attracted to Christianity because it seemed a ready instrument of unity. The notion undoubtedly grew in his mind, as we shall see; but so tidy a motive would have been out of place during his first bid for power in the West. Never a man to find abstraction easy, he understood perfectly, however, the mechanics of leadership and loyalty; and he knew that wide-ranging power depended on the gradual accretion of local control. Christian bishops, for their part, continuing on the path of their third-century development, were able to recognize in Constantine's unpredictable but stunning success a further guarantee of their own cohesion and stability.

The progress of Christianity between 250 and 350 represented, therefore, a further phase in the history of bishops. The successful transition from small groups of teachers and disciples to the commanding authority of a single pastor, symbolized in Rome by the changes that took place between the time of Hippolytus and the time of Fabian, did much to prepare churchmen for their 'triumph'. Christianity was able to collaborate with developing imperial ambitions, once Constantine had acceded to power, in part because of its doctrines and cults, which provided attractive answers to current questions; but, equally important, it had continued to shape itself according to fundamental social patterns in the Roman world. Far from being a single body, lying in wait to support an emperor greedy for universal power, the Christian *oikoumenē* at the beginning of the fourth century still consisted of urban communities enfolded within local economies and networks, marked by the patterns of patronage and subordination typical of the wider society in which they operated. Bishops understood the dynamics of that urban system: the attachment of the *polis* or *municipium* to wealth, privilege, office and Greco-Roman culture, and its relationship with the surrounding *chōra* or *territorium*, the sphere of the landowner and the peasant. There had always been something inherently universal in Christianity's claim and appeal; but we must not read back into the world of the young Constantine the perceived opportunities and evident achievements of later decades; and we must acknowledge the degree to which churches never lost their 'local' character, even when those achievements were in place.

GREAT CITIES, OLD AND NEW

Rome

In an effort to appreciate the character of those local communities, it is natural to focus on the great cities of the empire, for which evidence is more plentiful. Both the loyalty and the scepticism of later centuries have made Rome seem of greatest importance. While there is no doubt that the opinion of its bishop, because of his association with the apostle Peter, carried great weight among his episcopal colleagues – we have seen that eminence developing already in the previous chapter – it is unwise to think of 'papacy' in the early fourth century as comparable to the authority wielded two hundred years later by Gregory the Great, or even by his predecessors Gelasius (d. 496), Leo (d. 461) and Damasus (d. 384). Contrary to later tales about the baptism of Constantine by Sylvester (a calculated but groundless myth), the bishops of Rome suffered from the fact that their city was no longer the centre of the imperial system. The emperor Diocletian and his colleagues had hastened that process, both by their division of the empire and by their focus on its frontiers; and Constantine altered the balance of power even more by his establishment and patronage of Constantinople after 324. As accounts by the historian Ammianus Marcellinus reveal, the bishops of Rome were now thrown much more into the arms of an aristocracy that was becoming, at the same time, increasingly frustrated by its isolation and impotence. As those aristocratic families were converted, they took a growing and sometimes inconvenient interest in the control of their own pastor. That reflected to some extent jealousy and suspicion of the bishops of Milan, who had a certain advantage (dangerous in its own way) in being close to the western court – Ambrose being the most famous example (d. 397). Close interaction of such a sort, between bishops and local élites, would characterize the religious politics of most cities in the next two centuries. The new 'aristocracy of service', fostered at the expense of older families, reflected by contrast a fresh and territorially more extensive series of opportunities for wealth and aggrandizement. It formed also a more natural constituency for Christianity, and patronized ambitious churchmen who were eager to escape the stifling competitiveness of their local churches and to seek support, followers and fame on a wider stage.

Carthage, Constantinople, Alexandria, Jerusalem

During the fourth and following centuries, other major cities built upon their ancient status and produced churchmen of great character and lasting influence. In the West, Cyprian's see of Carthage, although lacking an 'apostolic ancestor' and therefore intent upon retaining the approval of the church in Rome, still stood at the apex of a rich sector of the western empire. It honoured Cyprian's memory, took pride in his intellectual legacy, and presided over a fertile tradition of speculation and debate. Lactantius (d. *c.* 320), a major influence on later thought, sprang from the same milieu. Augustine (d. 430), bishop of nearby Hippo, was a close friend of Aurelius, bishop of Carthage in his own day. Meanwhile, in the East, Constantinople gradually claimed for its bishop the status that seemed appropriate to a seat of government, gaining for him the title 'patriarch' in 451. Paradoxically, however, its most famous pastor in the early period, John Chrysostom (d. 407), came from Antioch. Alexandria, steeped in the still fascinating heritage of older religions, maintained its reputation as a hotbed of theological enthusiasms. It was the city of Athanasius and Arius, and visited by the hermit Antony; and it would generate a bitter contest with the bishops of the new capital, particularly during the episcopates of Theophilus (d. 412) and his nephew Cyril (d. 444). As political power became focused on Constantinople, so Egypt's exported grain encouraged close imperial control. A new Coptic culture, inventive in both literature and art, helped to define, on the other hand, its singular Christian identity. Finally, Jerusalem, the focus of many Jewish traditions, awakened in the new Christian emperors a passion for building and, among an increasing number of devout pilgrims, a curiosity and a readiness to spend money, all of which brought the city new status and wealth. This catalogue of city-based achievement seems to encompass the heart of Christian history in the century of expansion inaugurated by Constantine; but it also emphasizes the extent to which the 'church' remained a constellation of local communities, rivals as often as they were friends.

Antioch

If one wished to pick out one city that represented the temper of the new Christian world, it would have to be neither Rome nor Constantinople (nor indeed Alexandria, so rich a source of theological inquiry) but Antioch. This was the city where, according to *Acts*, the followers of the new religion had first been called 'Christians'. It had numbered among its bishops Ignatius and Theophilus. It symbolized the frontier between Greek and Syrian Christianity and mingled traditions as potently as Alexandria. In the third century, it acquired a new and broader significance: for, with the establishment of the new Sassanian dynasty in Persia in 224 and its almost immediate aggressiveness towards Rome, Antioch became the headquarters for the imperial forces on the eastern frontier and the occasional residence of the emperor himself. New strategic imperatives – the improvement of roads and fortifications – also had the effect of bringing more within the Roman orbit even those Syrian cities close to the frontier (as also happened in Armenia). As far as Christian history is concerned, Antioch, from the later third through to the fifth and sixth centuries, became both an emblem and a motor of change. It symbolized, more than its later rival Constantinople, the effective supplanting of older religious traditions, proven so forcefully during the frustrated residence of the 'apostate' emperor Julian (361–63). It is no surprise, therefore, that the central literary figures of that older world were from Antioch: Ammianus Marcellinus, writing in Latin, and Libanius, writing in Greek. The ecclesiastical conflicts within the city lay, as we shall see, at the heart of the Arian controversy in the East. Its church leadership was remarkably fractured. Rival bishops (at one point five in number) were at loggerheads there for much of the fourth and early fifth centuries. The schism caused pain and fear among their colleagues, and epitomized the dangers that could infect any community under the stress of theological dispute and imperial scrutiny. Two key bishops of Constantinople in the fifth century had been Antiochene priests: Chrysostom (already mentioned) and Nestorius (d. *c.* 451). As I shall suggest in the next chapter, failure to resolve the crisis that those men had helped to precipitate drove a wedge between Antioch and other Christians in the East. The intellectual precocity and passionate antagonisms of the city did much to undermine, therefore, the effects of Constantine's conversion: for his notions of religious unity and of how best to balance religious and secular authority foundered chiefly on Arian politics and the shifting religious emphases of his successors (Julian included) – both crucial influences upon Antioch's development.

PROVINCE, TOWN AND COUNTRYSIDE

Cities, increasingly dominated by and identified with their bishops, continued, therefore, to constitute the heartland of Constantine's Christian empire. At the same time, the nature of any 'city-based' church had been inevitably modified by developments both within and outside the Christian community. Speaking generally, there was an increased 'bunching' of regional traditions (just as there was in the political and economic life of the empire). The process predated the more marked division between Greek, Latin and Syrian cultures in the fifth century, and continued far beyond it. It was exemplified and reinforced by local synods, in which bishops found themselves raised above the interests of a single city; able to articulate ideas, disciplines and practices that bore the hallmarks of a wider community and a more complex past. It is difficult to discern the origins of such assemblies. They may have been first convened as a move against Montanism in Asia Minor; but the obscurity of their roots bears witness to their antiquity, and they had become habitual long before Constantine.

Each region had a character of its own. Cyprian, for example, and Carthage with him, represented a North African theological genealogy reaching back to Tertullian (Cyprian is said to have read him daily), culminating in Augustine, and including prominent thinkers of the Donatist community (one thinks particularly of the layman Tyconius, whose exegetical methodology Augustine admired, copied and disseminated to posterity). The impact of that Latin school of thought on subsequent western theology was at once fundamental and ironic, given the collapse of Roman North Africa itself beneath the weight of Vandal conquest in the fifth century, Justinian's destructive retribution in the sixth and the eventual assertion of Islamic settlement in the seventh. Similarly, in the East, the tradition that we have already seen represented in the work of Tatian and in the 'Old Syriac' version of the Scriptures allowed the development of a Christian mindset somewhat distinct from (and older than) that of the neighbouring Greek culture. The Syrian church's linguistic resources allowed it to maintain close links with the most ancient forms of Palestinian Christianity and with Jewish culture generally. It was characterized by a deeply ascetic piety, exemplified in the early fourth-century (largely theological) writings of Aphraates – the 'Persian sage', as he was later called. It blossomed further in following decades, not least in the person of Ephraem (d. 373), the great poet, theologian and deacon of Nisibis and (subsequently) Edessa. Amid the controversies of the fifth century and beyond, Syrian Christians were able to maintain their cohesion and self-confidence. The pattern was echoed on a lesser scale within the similarly distinctive Coptic church of Egypt, which was also enriched by its own literary and linguistic tradition, and blessed with a comparable leader of distinction, the preacher–abbot Shenoute of Atripe (d. *c.* 450).

Beyond the confines of the church communities themselves, new relations were developing between cities and their surrounding country areas. The decline of slavery as a component of the agricultural economy, together with fiscal changes, and shifts in patterns of small-scale freehold and estate ownership, all affected the life of cities: for they depended on the productivity of their immediate *territoria*, and were unavoidably sensitive to the social hierarchies established among peasants and landowners. None of that had anything to do with either Constantine or Christianity. It did determine, however, the resources open to a bishop in terms of both economy and status – the wealth he might draw upon and the alliances he might forge. Was his city dominated by the aristocratic masters of extensive properties, many with residences in towns, or by more modest, more numerous, but more remote peasant farmers? Was the surrounding land fertile and fully cultivated, or was it underpopulated and devastated by drought or ruthless taxation? Was there a resulting dearth of exchange and artisan employment and a corresponding increase in the numbers of the migrant and the hungry? Were the 'better sort' in his community civilian or (as was in many places increasingly the case) military? Did they see themselves as potential servants of the imperial system, steeped in Greek or Latin culture, or did they identify more readily with other cultural traditions? Did his city lie near the frontier – an area that was often, thanks to the retirement of successful soldiers and the opportunities for embezzlement and trade, remarkably rich. It is easy to see how such questions might press upon a bishop, defining his pastoral and material chances and responsibilities. In particular, his specific circumstances would govern his sense of his natural audience, constituency or clientele. How much responsibility did he bear, for example, in terms of a mission to those, both peasant and landowner, beyond his city walls; and who would aid him in such projects? Carefully selected priests and (in some places) *chōrepiskopoi* or 'country bishops' were essential to any such project; and similar divisions of the pastoral task were called for in bigger towns and cities. Finally, both townsfolk and countryfolk contributed in their different ways to the growing alliance between bishops and the 'poor', which coloured the placing of buildings, the content of homilies, the provision of hospitals and other material support, and the leverage that the affection of the 'people' might give a bishop in his negotiations with those more powerful.

So, on the eve of toleration, Christians did not form a single community, awaiting its destiny, but continued to display complex and overlapping ambitions. The longstanding struggle to define and protect the authority of bishops themselves, the need to foster and control intellectual insights that transcended individuals and could be gathered more securely into broader traditions, and the enduring desire to enfold heroic commitment within an arena of more lasting influence and respectability, all continued to circumscribe the policies of local communities and their leaders. The changes brought about under Constantine's influence provided new opportunities, certainly, but opportunities that expanded old convictions. A city within which Christianity could now express itself without reticence or fear still contained challenges to episcopal leadership, still generated rival and idiosyncratic proponents of theology and exegesis, still encouraged a subtle submission of a martyr's recollected eminence to the less excited and more cohesive cult of a whole community. Constantine might claim to have channelled Christian activities in new directions, but he observed more than he initiated. Old habits were impelled by a momentum of their own.

A NEW DIALOGUE WITH NON-CHRISTIANS

Growing confidence

It is dangerous to suppose that Constantine's conversion heralded the end of a debate with the defenders of other cults. His shift in religious allegiance is better seen as a further stage in that debate. Constantine defined his Christianity by adjustment as much as by rejection, and was no less honest for that. The false view, therefore, is that, after the age of the Apologists, when the essential components of Christian doctrine had been set in place, believers were faced only with a frustrated and harsh intransigence among traditional worshippers. Origen may have engaged with (the long-dead) Celsus, and Arnobius (to be followed by his pupil Lactantius) may have speculated about the truth lodged deep within the non-Christian mind. (Celsus's point had been, of course, that Christians had copied from the cults they despised, and had misunderstood them in the process – a possibly conscious

The Christian empire

inversion of Justin's account.) Those, however, willing to be wise after the event see only the coming dawn, already casting a bolder light on such meticulous discussions. 'Pagans', according to that view, knew their time was up. They admitted that persecution was ineffectual and, in Gilbert Murray's famous phrase, succumbed to a 'failure of nerve'.

The truth was different. The growing confidence of Christians, during the third century, and their adoption of a more public profile, enabled others reared in the traditions of Greek and Roman philosophy to take a greater interest in their ideas. They were better informed than predecessors like Celsus. Although still unconvinced, they were nevertheless impressed by the antiquity of Christian writings (when coupled with the Jewish Scriptures) and by the philosophical complexity of the Christian world-view. A range of developments within their own world had contributed to that interest. The systematized cosmology and anthropology of Stoicism and the elevated insights generated within the intellectual revolution that we now call Neoplatonism conspired to enhance the attractiveness of a monotheistic viewpoint. Plotinus, the founding figure of the Neoplatonist tradition (born in Egypt at the beginning of the third century), shared with Origen the formative influence of Ammonius Saccas – a man who may himself have been a Christian, but who abandoned that faith in favour of more traditional beliefs. If one is looking for symptoms of destiny, therefore, that conjunction – of an increasing social visibility on the part of Christians and a reflective taste for religious syncretism on the part of Romans generally – counts for as much as Constantine's conversion, which would have been unintelligible without it. And the conjunction, set in motion before his accession, continued to govern the development of Christianity as the fourth century understood it. Almost everything we might associate with 'tolerated Christianity' – its privileges, controversies and wealth – was born of an argument within the cities of the empire about the true meaning of the singularity and all-encompassing providence of God.

Porphyry, Iamblichus and Eunapius

The temper of polemic in this new phase of interaction was governed in part by the calibre of those who spoke for the Roman past: for it is striking that, as the intellectual eminence of Christian advocates (the 'Fathers of the Church') increased, so the corresponding stature of their opponents was made all the more clear. They certainly kept abreast of Christian declarations, and at times set the pace of the debate. Towering above all others was the philosopher Porphyry, Plotinus's best-known disciple. (Plotinus died *c.* 270,

Porphyry *c.* 305.) He had a paradoxical impact on Christianity. He edited Plotinus's lectures, which had considerable (although sometimes exaggerated) influence on a number of Christian thinkers — in the Latin adaptations by Marius Victorinus as much as in their original Greek. He was also, in later medieval eyes, an important mediator of Aristotelian thought. On the other hand, he was the author of a substantial work *Against the Christians*, which so disturbed its targets that it not only called forth a number of extended replies (by Methodius of Olympus, for example, and in the work of Eusebius) but also earned the eventual distinction of being burnt (in the late 440s), so that only fragments have survived in the writings of its Christian critics. Porphyry was slow in adopting a forceful stance. He shared with Plotinus some regard for Christian principles and ethics, and certainly for the character of Jesus himself; but he found it impossible to make any sense of Jesus's apparent failure (a powerful argument, he thought, against the man's divinity), and he criticized his followers for their refusal to share in the religious revival of his own age. That judgement reflected his understanding of the policies of Decius and his immediate successors, and did not draw upon earlier accusations of disloyalty. Many of the principles that Porphyry brought to bear upon Christian beliefs and sacred texts were comparable to those he held (in his *Letter to Anebo*, for example) against the contemporary naivety and inconsistency of popular religion. He favoured a properly instructed reform of traditional rituals rather than their rejection (he showed an enduring interest in symbolism, oracles and theurgy), but he considered that Christians had missed the opportunity (embodied in the emphases of Plotinus himself) to create a truly spiritual and universal pathway to salvation.

Porphyry's critique set the tone of debate for the coming century, not least because of his standing among those prepared to share his views. The most notable were his own pupil, the Syrian Iamblichus (d. *c.* 325), and Iamblichus's admirer and subsequent chronicler of the Neoplatonist 'school' (or, more correctly, of some of its proponents), Eunapius of Sardis (d. after 414). Iamblichus was a sensitive and inventive thinker, and he carried forward Porphyry's search for an ideal marriage between elevated metaphysics and the drama of cult. His most notable work in that cause was *On Mysteries*, which explored the traditional religious beliefs of the Egyptians and responded to cues in Porphyry's *Letter to Anebo*. His regard for a strict morality among practising philosophers was reflected in his works on Pythagoreanism, and he left behind him major commentaries on the works of Aristotle and Plato that Christians were to find invaluable. His closing years coincided with Constantine's final rise to universal authority at the expense of his colleague

Licinius, and exemplified the level of abstraction and devotion that the new emperor and his supporters had to counter among those who remained loyal to older custom. Eunapius, in a later generation, looked back on Iamblichus as a fount of excellence among Neoplatonists, and gave priority in his *Lives of the Sophists* to those whom Iamblichus had most influenced (his own teachers among them). As a biographer, he may have responded in part to the challenge of Christian admiration for holy men like Antony (whose *Life*, written in the middle years of the century, had already become a model of the hagiographic genre). He was also a historian of his own era, producing a text focused firmly on his hero Julian, and bitter in its judgement on the baneful influence of Christianity, in both its emperors and its more ardent devotees. In that, he was more like the Antiochene orator Libanius and less like his fellow historian Ammianus Marcellinus – although both were admirers of the 'apostate'.

The Emperor Julian

Julian was a crucial figure in the shifting dialogue between Christians and non-believers. The former were able to present his premature death as proof that Constantine's achievement was irreversible, but his accession to power had proved entirely the opposite. Constantine's father was Julian's grandfather, and Julian married Constantine's daughter: he lived at the heart of the imperial family. He was brought up a Christian, well instructed in theology and outwardly devout. He showed open favour towards the ancient cults only during his final push for supreme power. That shocking reversal served, as we shall see, to reinforce other misgivings about the security of his family's faith: for Constantine's son Constantius (emperor from 337 to 361) became in the end an open supporter of the Arian cause. But Julian played a pivotal role in more sympathetic minds. Especially among the followers of Iamblichus, he harnessed the energies of a generation that had already steeled itself in the face of Constantine's tolerance and conversion, and had reassessed the central tenets of its own faith by contrasting it with the assertions of a now more openly articulate and better understood opponent. If Constantine could create a single empire under a single God, then so, in their own terms, could they. Julian's religious policy, for all its asserted conservatism, was different from that of Diocletian, governed by a need to challenge the characteristic features of Christianity, while relegating the religion itself (as in his tract *Against the Galilaeans*) to the status of a tribal sect. The emperor claimed for his own theology (unfolded in his oration for the festival of the sun) the right to define the supreme God and to assert his intimacy with 'King Hēlios'. At the same time, he exhorted his collaborators (famously, Arsacius of Galatia) to outdo the Christians in reverence, austerity and the care of those in need. His failure to achieve his ends, through the tragic curtailment of his reign, made him nevertheless (in the mind of Eunapius, for example) the standard by which one might measure the worth of his Christian successors; and it kept alive the hope that a similar figure might reverse again those subsequent emperors' still recent reactions. For both parties, in other words, Julian raised afresh the question of who should control the future and of whether an emperor of Constantine's stamp had interpreted correctly the best relation between piety and power.

Converting the Roman family

High politics were not the only instruments of dialogue and change. Both households and cities became arenas of debate. The gradual wooing of the empire's élite to the Christian cause (for other sectors of the population were slower in making the move) represented a series of small victories rather than one great one. It was not a matter of extracting converts from their old milieux and gathering them into a new and distinct society. Adhesion to Christianity was achieved in discussion with one's family and friends. A convert's eventual willingness to be known as a Christian was often given a character quite its own, thanks to the variety of bargains that were struck between the hesitant convictions of various acquaintances. Such had been the pattern for centuries. The difference now lay in a bishop's ability to insist that a declaration of faith should be made public – by, on the one hand, participation in the new splendours of Christian worship and, on the other, by the generous patronage upon which that style of worship (among other commitments) was coming to depend.

Submission in such a style may have been easier (or sooner enforced) in the East than in the West – or at least in the East's new capital, Constantinople, and among members of Constantine's 'aristocracy of service'. In the West, those longer accustomed by birth and lineage to political influence and great wealth were slower to relinquish a religious loyalty that seemed entirely bound up with their public status. Augustine, in his *Confessions*, described the wry inquiry of Marius Victorinus (which would have been voiced, if genuine, in the late 350s), 'Is it walls, then, that make a Christian?', together with his subsequent admission that they did – that intellectual assent had to be capped by baptism and attendance at the eucharist. Victorinus was not, however, a high-flying senator but, like Augustine himself, a provincial teacher of rhetoric from North Africa, whose brilliance had gained him a career in Italy.

The circle of aristocratic converts described by Jerome, in his letters of the 380s and 390s, seems to have been dominated by women (he was another provincial *arriviste*, from what is now Croatia); but, quite apart from the issue of whether that circle formed a representative sample of prominent Christians (which it certainly did not), Jerome's engagement with women may have been itself unusual, and the families he allows us to discern in the background of his correspondence included a comparable number of Christian men.

We have outgrown, therefore, the simplistic notion that most men of standing in the West remained faithful for a long time to traditional religion. Historians in the past were too ready to suppose that a staunch cadre of conservatives had provided a natural constituency for the prefect Symmachus, when, during a confrontation with the emperor Valentinian II in 384, he had demanded the restoration of an altar to Victory in the senate house. Symmachus, famous for his plea that, in matters of religion, 'there is more than one path to so great a mystery', was instrumental in securing, in the same year, a Milanese teaching post for the rising star Augustine (as yet unbaptized). Symmachus's specifically religious aspirations were frustrated, however, by the political skill of Ambrose (who baptized Augustine less than three years later). Similar proof of entrenched sentiment has been found in the supposed 'pagan revival' that surrounded the usurpation of Eugenius after 393; but political interest counted for more in that endeavour, in spite of the régime's dependence on (among others) the distinguished traditionalist Nicomachus Flavianus the elder. The battle at the river Frigidus (394) – Theodosius I's brisk reassertion of authority – has been allowed to cast a false light over the greater part of that emperor's reign; but the battle's significance as a victory of Christians over their foes was the product of tendentious and heavily mythologized hindsight. (Eugenius was executed and Flavianus committed suicide; but the latter's son, already learned and later converted, was allowed to enjoy a distinguished career for over thirty years. Theodosius died less than five months after his own triumph.) What has to be unmasked in those high-level conflicts is the interest each party had in presenting their opponents as doomed minorities. A more modest and by no means partisan estimate would lead us to admit that, even in Rome and certainly in Milan and other major cities of northern Italy, Christians were beginning, by the late 370s, to constitute the majority. (Ambrose had been quick to make that point, which might arouse one's suspicions; but his exaggeration of actual numbers in the 380s was more an embellishment than a serious misrepresentation.)

Behind the gradual accretion of public support, individual changes of heart encompassed a variety of associations. In few instances do we find evidence of a convert abandoning the company of family members less convinced. The traditional inclusiveness of the Roman household exerted a contrary pressure. As soon as one person of significance became a Christian, younger relatives as yet unmarried, and certainly servants, were often expected to follow suit. Traditional Christian respect for widows gave them special opportunities to encourage religious change in those who lived with them. But it was not as if women succumbed, while men lagged behind. (Enemies had often suggested as much: Julian, in his tirade against Antioch, the *Misopōgōn*, berated husbands for allowing their wives to 'carry everything out [of their homes] and give it to the Galilaeans'.) Such a notion renders almost inexplicable the expansion of the clergy, for example. Many of them maintained close contact with the families who had reared them or granted them patronage; some continued to live with their wives. New liberties made it comparably easy for prominent officials and other lay figures, from an early stage of Constantine's revolution, to declare openly their allegiance to his faith. Those who spoke publicly for the Christian faith, or presided as secular officials over its material affairs, no longer fulfilled their duties hidden in modest houses; but they faced, in the cities of the empire, even amid the growing evidence of their own success, a range of conflicting and ambitious declamations: not only of Christians against Christians – a sufficient cause of confusion – but also of Christians against the philosophic rhetor in his school, the rabbi in his synagogue, or (for a while, at least) the priest in his temple. The domestic, political and religious settings within which citizens had for centuries argued over policy and belief still formed, in other words, a series of shared environments, within which any claimant to truth had to defend and at times modify that claim, unable to escape the constant company of those persuaded otherwise.

The Manichees

One conflict lacked that character of interactive debate on common ground: Christian fear and repudiation of the Manichees. Manichaeism presented a greater threat than traditional Roman religion of any sort; and the response of Christians was accordingly different. Their anxiety was justified for several reasons. First, Manichaeism, like their own faith, sprang from Jewish roots, or at least from a sect that combined Christian with other Jewish elements, practised baptism, questioned (eventually) the validity of the Old Testament, had a high regard for Jesus and carried to new limits Paul's suspicion of the 'flesh'. Mani (d. *c.* 276) was happy to link his cause with both Jesus and the Holy Spirit. Second, Manichaeism displayed, as I mentioned earlier, a strong and efficient missionary fervour, intent upon converting 'on the ground' (instead of by decree from above). Finally, it questioned not just the mechanics but the rationale of salvation, since it set up great obstacles to both human freedom and providential control. Nothing in ancient Greco-Roman religion came close to being so dangerous an inversion of Christian belief.

Mani benefited at first from Sassanian success (he was born near the Persian capital some ten years before the establishment of the new dynasty). Shapur I had been willing to offer him patronage, and Persian expansion may have aided his missionary endeavours. The guardians of traditional Zoroastrianism eventually reasserted their dominance within Persian territory, and Mani died at the hands of the Persian king Bahram; but that only encouraged an even more spectacular dispersal of Manichaean missionaries to other areas. Within twenty years of his death, his followers were widely established in Egypt (where extensive literary remains have been found) and had rapidly spread to the western provinces of the empire by the early decades of the following century. Augustine, before his definitive acceptance of Christianity, had been a devotee of the movement, and left several vivid accounts of both its practices and its North African leaders. The Manichees enjoyed equal success in regions to the east of their original Persian heartland – another rich source of evidence for their beliefs. Mani's frustrated alliance with the rulers of his country forms an ironic contrast with Christianity's bargain under Constantine. The 'Persian connection', however, reinforced suspicions in the minds of Roman authorities, even under Diocletian, and made it easier to cast Manichees as subversive infiltrators and supposed exemplars of Persian vice.

Manichaeism was dualist and rigorist to a high degree – far more so than any 'gnostic' tendency before it (for there were gnostic qualities to both its doctrine and its social structure). Mani imagined the cosmos as a battleground for the forces of darkness and light, in which light's fortunes were currently under grave threat, and in which the outcome of the conflict, although potentially weighted in light's favour, would be no more than the restoration of a fine and obscure balance. Believers were obliged to improve light's chances of victory by releasing trapped particles of light within themselves and within their food (melons were especially favoured). The notion reinforced a 'scientific' component in Manichaean thought, since its morality and metaphysics were wholly intertwined with a detailed description of the physical world, which included a negative assessment of the body, seen as the prison of the soul. Light would be released through strict asceticism, at least among the 'elect'. That ascetic element, when combined with evidence of Manichaean success in Egypt, invites inquiry about its links with early monasticism in that province. Certainly, any radical proponent of bodily asceticism in the decades that followed ran the risk of being tarred with a Manichaean brush.

But the Manichees were more than a rigorist sect. They developed a clear and detailed sense of their history, based on biographies and letters, and linking Mani with a 'prophetic' tradition that was equally honoured among Christians. They did not celebrate a eucharist; but they formed ordered communities that catered for both 'hearers' and 'elect', placed as much emphasis on visible observance and display as on inner devotion, valued books and learning, and developed a rich and intense liturgical cycle of hymns and prayers – the chief vehicle for their theological reflection. (There are suggestive parallels with the Syriac tradition of hymnography that runs from Bardaisan to Ephraem.) Those traits, reinforced by strategic anxieties and ethnic prejudices (against an enduring background of Persian threat), made Manichaeism at once a dangerous and an attractive alternative to Christianity in a range of centres within the Roman world, and caused its rivals to fear the ease with which their own convictions could be 'perverted' in a Manichaean direction. From the time of Theodosius I onwards, the tone of legal condemnation directed against them was coloured by a species of frantic repulsion less evident in measures against traditional Roman religion.

THE SPECTACLE OF CULT

To anyone walking the streets of the fourth-century empire, the chief difference attributable to the public toleration of Christianity would have been a striking alteration of the urban landscape. A building boom was under way, focused on new Christian churches. In addition to the adaptation of the 'basilica' – the long audience hall, sometimes with side aisles, and with an apse and elevated platform at one end – there were associated colonnades and courtyards, and hostelries devoted to the needs of the sick, the poor and (in some places) those on pilgrimage. Churchmen developed a liturgy, with theological implications, that supported more expansive tastes, and were delighted to welcome the financial patronage of the emperor and the aristocracy. Conversely, the new Christian rulers gained both kudos and influence from their association with public drama and display. The grand constructions that followed upon that alliance were often incompatible with the congested centres of cities, and rose on marginal or suburban sites, away from the temples, baths and *fora* of the older order. Thus, there came about a shift in the spatial balance of late Roman communities.

Inside the basilicas themselves, the extended surfaces of walls and floors allowed Christians to display a more abundant art: frescoes, reliefs and mosaics comparable in quality and style to those in traditional temples and grand domestic buildings. In the open areas of the new churches, ostentatious ceremonial could unfold, with processions, music, lights and perfume. Here lay the origins of much that Christians now associate with the word 'liturgy'. The orders of service preserved in the *Didachē* or the *Apostolic Tradition* were now overlaid by Egyptian and Syrian forms – such as those attributed to Serapion of Thmuis or found in the *Apostolic Constitutions* – and in the practices of the great cities of the later fourth century – the Rome of Damasus, the Milan of Ambrose and the Constantinople of John Chrysostom. Both surface and space fostered and sustained, therefore, a heightened emotional impact, an expanded set of symbols (many borrowed from traditional genres) and a more elevated sense of the 'holy place'. Worshippers could at once acknowledge more intensely and endow with fuller meaning the 'presence of God', and everything around them conspired to carry them away from mundane circumstance into the company of prophets, saints and angels.

And the sacred concourse could be broken into parts, each of which highlighted different sectors of religious experience. A separate baptistery, with its deep pool and circle of columns, would have emphasized the awesome mystery of initiation, creating an air of both intimacy and grandeur within its more limited compass. Shrines to the martyrs – some incorporated into churches, some independent; often housing the bones of the heroes – induced reflection on history, courage, miracles and intercession. Cemeteries (sometimes the scenes of extended and even scandalous parties, ostensibly in memory of the dead) cemented both links with the past and relations among survivors. Visibly distinct places set aside for catechumens and penitents gave further physical expression to the changing dynamics of church membership and spiritual progress. The basilica and its environs, therefore, applied a range of social labels. It framed the authority of the bishop; it provided an arena that he could claim uniquely as his own, in which to celebrate the eucharist, interpret the Scriptures and exercise his charge to discipline, mediate and forgive.

The patronage behind such enterprises was the chief symptom of an irreversible redeployment of wealth in Roman society. Among the causes of decline in traditional religion, the withdrawal of funds must rank highly: for public worship of any sort is expensive; and ancient temples in need of constant restoration, coupled with a demand for animal sacrifice, elaborate parades and community games, made the cults of the empire heavily dependent on the generosity of its leading citizens. When those citizens deflected their wealth into Christian circles, older religious practices were suddenly strangled by widespread penury – more lethal than occasional demolition and punitive law. The emperor Julian preserved a memorable image in his *Misopōgōn* (dating, therefore, from the early 360s): a priest in the virtually deserted shrine at Daphne, outside Antioch, reduced to sacrificing his own goose. Christian endowment had another effect: it created an enlarged context for the corresponding expansion of the clergy. There was simply more for church officials to do, in terms both of ceremonial and of maintenance and administration; and, like any other bureaucrats, Christian clerics soon developed a keen sense of their diverse ranks and appropriate recompense. The buildings and enterprises they serviced and the ceremonies they helped to perform catered in turn to larger numbers than had been the case in a more restrained era. Not all those in that larger assembly were as committed as the believers of the third century; but their presence created an impression in the city, even if they had come only to wonder at the architecture and the ritual, or to applaud the verbal sallies of a famous homilist or bishop. Finally, as we shall see further, there were those who could find in such display fresh grounds for suspecting the value of the new dispensation, lamenting the loss not only of moral integrity but also of the material simplicity that had marked an earlier age.

Once those grand settings had begun to take shape, the bishops who presided over them were able to take a competitive pride in the taste and liberality of their people. The rules governing the consecration of bishops, especially after the Council of Serdica (modern Sofia) in 343, demanded the attendance of other bishops on such occasions. They engaged increasingly in more prolonged synods, especially under the impulse of theological controversy. To some disenchanted observers, bishops and their numerous attendants seemed constantly on the move from meeting to meeting, as expensive and burdensome as the entourage of any prefect. Churchmen of all ranks were invited from elsewhere to attend major festivals, especially those associated with martyr-shrines, and (in later decades) to share in the exchange of relics. All such occasions demanded ceremonial. A visiting bishop would be met on the city's outskirts and led in flamboyant procession to the basilica, just like any civic dignitary. It was a moment to assess the achievements of someone else's church, compared with one's own. Neighbouring churches were thus more visibly enfolded within the constellation of cities that made up the empire, giving a new religious colour to already existing rivalries. As a corollary, with similarly wider significance, the bishop's church in town invited him to reflect on what a 'country' church might look like, always supposing that such a structure was appropriate or imaginable. The remains of such places of worship, albeit smaller in scale, can be found scattered in outlying areas, especially on what were probably the estates of landowners. They symbolized in cultic form the broader tension I have already noted between a desire to reach out to the peasant population and a need to preserve the city's centrality and dominance over rural life.

All those developments – the buildings, the wealth and the sheer pageantry of church life – were new, directly born of the opportunities Constantine created. Yet, in spite of the novelties, the bishop was still a bishop, and the understanding of *ekklēsia*, of a Christian community called into being by God, was only gradually modified. Remarkably, the core of the Christian cult remained unchanged. Although more removed from a domestic setting (a process that was, in a minor way, already evident in the 'house-church' at Dura-Europos), the eucharist remained a meal. The basilica form and the presence of large numbers of only partially committed worshippers might have made that fact more difficult to recognize; but the ineradicable images of the gospel accounts and the well developed theology of sacrifice and redemption made it impossible to turn the eucharist into any other kind of ritual. The basilica, as a traditional form, was not a specifically religious building: on the contrary, it bore more relation to secular ceremony. There was never any risk that strangers to the Christian liturgy might think that they had stumbled into some alternative form of temple. A desire to compete with Jews and non-believers – always a component of the exercise – was never reduced to mere imitation. For all the elaboration involved, all the drama, all the wealth and brilliance of architecture and art, the Christian understanding of priesthood, sacrifice and redemption – that is to say, of Jesus as priest, sacrifice and redeemer – was to a surprising degree unaffected by new styles of recollection and re-enactment. The forces that were let loose by new money, new dignity and a new aesthetic sense changed, rather, the roles and authority of the men who presided over what were now grander celebrations.

LACTANTIUS AND EUSEBIUS: A NEW SENSE OF THE FUTURE?

People and nation

I mentioned in the previous chapter the impact of *Revelation*, with its reference to a thousand-year reign, an intermediate period before the final judgment, to be enjoyed in the company of Jesus by those who had borne him witness in death, and to be followed by the establishment of the new Jerusalem. It seems from the testimony of early writers that many Christians, down to the time of Tertullian, believed in such a 'reign'. As, with increasing refinement, they absorbed into the account of their own destiny the full bulk of the Jewish past (a process that depended heavily on techniques of typological interpretation), their view of the future became coloured less by high drama and more by gradual fulfilment. Origen, as an exegete, had an important hand in that transition, and his specific treatment of *Revelation* signalled a shift from a literal to a metaphorical understanding. Not everyone followed his example, but an increasing number of believers in the third century (Origen's admirer Eusebius among them) adapted their expectations accordingly. The adaptation operated precisely in relation to history. It may seem that Origen's personal judgement on *Revelation* reflected his more general interest in states of soul and cosmic structure; but he was never timeless in his spiritual emphases. In assessing the character of the 'last days', he wrote not only of the soul's union with God but also of a time when all humanity would recognize the truth of the gospel. Individual destiny coincided with or depended upon that universal achievement. Such an ability to combine an almost territorial triumph with the temporal arcs of both personal and collective fulfilment provided an important basis for the type of history that Eusebius came to represent.

Another change to recall in this context of historical self-expression is the understanding of the Christian community as a 'people'. A familiar (although not necessarily representative) view is that provided in *1 Peter*, where believers are described as 'chosen' and 'holy', a 'kingly priesthood' and 'a people protected' or 'reserved' by God. The vocabulary borrows heavily from *Exodus* and *Deuteronomy*. It is not entirely clear, however, what the author of *1 Peter* meant by 'people', since he used a number of Greek terms – *genos, ethnos* and *laos* – that leave open the issue of whether he was talking about races, tribes or nations. While echoing the usage of the Jewish Scriptures, he would nevertheless have wanted to distance himself from any 'racial' or 'ethnic' implications, as we might understand those words. The Christian community was not, in his eyes, built upon biological descent, but displayed a more 'political' quality (such as we might now associate with the word 'nation'). That may be why he ended with a preference for *laos*, and used persistently the language of collaborative responsibility. In spite of a stress on suffering and imminent release, *1 Peter* is essentially a social catechism, describing the internal order of the group it addresses, and recommending a quiet submission to traditional authorities.

The combination of self-possessed identity and cautious engagement with broader categories of association not only governed the process of Christian integration but also affected the perceived relation between Christian history and the history of the surrounding society. The success of Constantine's policies would depend on the willingness of Christians not only to see themselves as citizens but also to accept their place within the *history* of the city, the governing framework of traditional political discourse. Having appropriated (and transformed) the history of the Jews, Christians were now poised to appropriate and transform the history of Rome. As long as the boundaries of a church community were seen to fall differently from the boundaries of city or state, the past of the Christian 'people' could remain equally distinct. Once a closer match was achieved, however, between 'church space' and 'city space', once it was admitted that Christian and non-Christian occupied a shared social arena, then the past also became a shared concern, and the way was opened towards arguing that Christian destiny was bound up, under providence, with the destiny of the empire.

A beginning had been made in that direction by the notion of a 'new race' or a 'different race' that we find in the *Letter to Diognetus* (again, *genos*, but also the more 'institutional' *epitēdeuma*) and in Justin's *Dialogue with Trypho* (*genos*, but also *laos* – there qualified as 'faithful'). Such texts still had in mind, for the most part, the distinction between Christians and Jews. Tertullian – for all his rhetoric about the separation of Athens and Jerusalem – was the first writer (in his *Ad nationes* and *Ad Scapulam*) to allow Christians without hesitation to walk, as it were, along the axis of Roman civil and religious development; to admit that their own views on such matters were logically part of a wider debate. He probably caught a hint of such possibilities in the work of Melito of Sardis. Augustine, after Constantine, was able to explore them (in his *City of God*) with even greater confidence, as he debated, with the dead Varro and Cicero, Christianity's place in the history of cult and of the state.

Lactantius and Eusebius lay midway between those poles of reflection. They dealt with notions of time and destiny that had been broached well before them and would be discussed long afterwards. They were, in that sense, conservative in their preoccupations. Their learning (which was in each case considerable) had made conservatism inevitable, since it was dependent on extended genealogies and prolonged reading. Crucially, they began to reflect upon them before Constantine achieved dominance in the West, heirs as they were to a tradition that did not, as I have said, depend on such a champion, and could not have foreseen his coming. Both men were laying down the foundations of their work before the end of Diocletian's reign. We have to imagine, therefore, how we might have assessed their importance, if Constantine had never accepted Christianity, had never defeated Licinius and gained control of a single empire. It is likely, as I suggested in the last chapter, that they were, at first, more surprised than delighted by the turn of events. They were compelled to rethink, rather faster than they might have expected, the theories they had based on a more leisured view of providence. Eusebius modified and extended his *Ecclesiastical History* (rather clumsily) after Constantine's triumph, and Lactantius is notorious for the venom of his (nevertheless informative) diatribe (written after 312), *On the Death of the Persecutors*. There was nothing essential, however, to either man's cast of mind that was not already set in place before they found such adaptations necessary.

Lactantius

In the case of Lactantius, the matter is clear: his greatness resides in his earlier *Divine Institutions*, in which his argument depends on a gradual and partially unpredictable increase of Christian liberty. It is tempting to think of him as the lesser man. Many have shared Jerome's view, expressed to Paulinus of Nola: 'If only he had been able to strengthen our own position as easily as he destroyed that of our opponents.' Yet he constructed a coherent system of ideas that inspired later writers by its humanity and optimism. Instead of dwelling on the origins and structure of the cosmos, he made a sense of movement through time essential to his main argument, as the human race passed from a lost golden age to a period of final dissolution. He constructed that gloomy narrative only to provide a basis for individual reassurance. He gave priority to moral development and believed that the world, under God's providence, could nourish justice and be transformed accordingly.

In the golden age, human worship had been focused on a single God. The collapse of that idyll had been marked, if not caused, by violence and error – both symptomatic of division. Lactantius did not make it entirely clear whether the violence and error were the work of outside forces, but he tended to the view that human beings were the immediate agents of both

The Christian empire

their failure and their restoration. He succeeded in making potentially chaotic and destructive circumstances the sphere within which each person could discover and fulfil their true nature. His anthropology was itself marked by momentum, in this instance logical. He focused first on the mind as the instrument by which one recognized, acquired and exercised virtue. Aware, however, that one could be rational without being virtuous, he developed his particular interpretation of justice — the ability to recognize the obligations of a child in relation to God and the obligations of a sibling in relation to one's fellow humans. Justice was not only the hallmark of human understanding (for no animal possessed a sense of justice): it also constituted the core of religion. Only religion made sense of rationality (by fostering justice), because the inevitably upward-looking posture of a rational being (again, a character lacking in animals) implied a gaze away from the mundane and towards the immortal. Given the divisive pressure of violence and error, it was inevitable that a religious sense of justice would be put to the test; and immortality was in turn the only just recompense for those who survived. There was the added implication that religious acts had to be free, since freedom was a feature of rationality. The sequence of the argument was clearly posted: understanding and virtue, justice and religion, trial and reward, immortality and freedom.

Success in achieving those transitions depended on self-discipline. Here, Lactantius was traditional: one eradicated vices and implanted virtues; one mastered one's passions; one gained self-knowledge under the guidance of God. However, a key mechanism in assuring those victories, peculiar to Lactantius, was an awareness of God's anger (about which he wrote a separate book). Providence by itself was too vague an assurance: a belief that God could show favour was inseparable from a fear that he might not. Human law, for example, would simply have no effect, unless the citizen felt in addition that a relatively unpredictable God (sympathetic to the legislation) was watching from above the workings of one's conscience. Such a belief implied that law (even law governed by Christian principles) was inadequate and passing, compared with the relationship of the individual to God. So, in the divided world that enveloped such moral athletes, where the polar opposite of rationality was violence, there could be nothing violent, nothing oppressive to humanity, in the just and balanced interplay between reason, law and divine anger.

The other symptom of division was error (and Lactantius was addressing chiefly the error that he detected at the heart of traditional Roman religion). Adopting a ploy that was common in contests between philosophical opponents, he explained current obscurities and disagreements as the outcome of trusting overmuch in the practices of ancestors. He recommended instead a more responsible dependence on one's own capacity for judgement (inherent to rationality). He also insisted, however, that judgements should be made in the light of tradition. The distinction between the two points of view rested on Lactantius's understanding of historical development. Those whom he criticized had, in his view, relegated to a remote past any obligation to justify their present practices. Christians, on the other hand, instead of cutting themselves off in that way, exercised their God-given rationality by envisaging a path through time that made their personal decisions part of a greater and unbroken narrative. They were guided by precedent but capable of discovery. They also agreed among themselves, and attracted increasing numbers of people by their social harmony and ideological coherence. They exemplified and maintained unity rather than division – a unity reflected in their cultic practice, for they made no distinction between priests and teachers. Jesus had been par excellence a teacher and guide, and Christian priests had to play the same role. The contrast was with those who had projected outwards the virtues of the mind and heart, symbolizing them as idols. The thrust of history was, for Lactantius, away from such a trend. The choreography of religion was acted out within the individual, and priests had to preside over that more hidden liturgy.

As for the end of time, Lactantius, in his *Divine Institutes*, had yet to be distracted by the triumphs of a Christian emperor. He anticipated more simply a collapse of ordered government and of the armies designed to protect the state. Even greater division would result, throwing society open to the plunderer and (characteristic emblem of Roman anxiety) to the rule of kings. The schooling that Lactantius recommended was designed to help one weather that escalating disintegration. It catered more for persecution (which he had witnessed at first hand) than for a Constantinian future (which he was in no position to anticipate). There would be a final victory, but his hope consisted in a calm and loosely expressed conviction that meekness (the appropriate response) would be followed by retribution. At present, the people of God lived among the nations and were oppressed by them. In the period of final disorder, those nations would simply disintegrate and the people who worshipped the one God would thus gain their freedom. What that might mean in 'political' terms was scarcely stated, but Lactantius was sure it would include the end of the Roman empire. It would be natural to pray, therefore, that the fall might be postponed. Constantine's conversion would demand a considerable readjustment of that scenario.

Eusebius

Eusebius, for his part, is referred to constantly as the 'father of church history'. The label has denied him full justice. He placed his analysis of the past within a broad exegetical and theological setting. 'Ecclesiastical history' meant, in the title of his most famous work, history (i.e. all history) viewed in a Christian light. The ten historical books that he produced or revised over a period of more than twenty years allude constantly to deeper principles, without which their full meaning is lost. Authentic human nature – the human nature revealed and assured in the person of Jesus – was marked not only by a sense of dependence on the past but also by an attachment to justice, an ability to utter and interpret prophecy, and a willingness to bear witness to the truth. In his *Demonstration of the Gospel*, written between Constantine's victories over Maxentius in 312 and over Licinius in 324, Eusebius explored the relation between law and individual responsibility, and stressed how the understanding required to balance them would depend on a keen sense of community. 'Salvation' – the salvation that Jesus represented – overcame a contrary ignorance or obtuseness. Writing at the same time *Against Hierocles* (chiefly an attack on Philostratus's life of Apollonius of Tyana), Eusebius criticized the fruitless aspirations of the revered sage. He agreed that everyone needed a 'fellow worker from above', a 'teacher' who would reveal 'the salvation that resides in heaven'. The notion would have been widely accepted, but only Jesus could, in his eyes, fill the role. Like Lactantius and like Hippolytus before him, he considered that mere attachment to a philosopher – a quite different relationship – was only a recipe for division and error. Eusebius also denied the reality of fate and defended human freedom – again, aspirations dear to Apollonius but beyond his capacity. In Eusebius's eyes, an individual's inner power was guaranteed by a shared experience of God's providence. One overcame debilitating fear by harnessing and applying within oneself the principles that governed the cosmos as a whole.

His philosophical breadth of view makes Eusebius more akin to Lactantius than one might have expected. One can detect at once a moral, salvific and teleological framework, within which the individual – endowed with freedom, enlightened with understanding and charged with responsibility – was invited to acknowledge the enveloping force of history and society, both under God's governance. Yet he was a historian. He described himself, in the opening sections of the *Ecclesiastical History*, as a pioneer, venturing upon a path hitherto untrodden. And he did so before the close of Diocletian's persecution: the first version of the first seven books was complete by 303. In the books he added later, and revised again, he had to change his emphasis twice: first to explain why persecution had begun and then to explain why it had ended.

His breadth of view continued to make his efforts more than a facile or self-serving adjustment to an unforeseen political triumph. We can learn a lot from what happened to the supposedly new tradition of 'ecclesiastical history' after Constantine's reign. Socrates of Constantinople, for example, writing in the 440s a work with the same title, placed political and other 'secular' affairs of his time (especially during the reign of Theodosius II) within a church-dominated framework. The progress, the enduring triumph of Christianity gave full meaning to all else. Thanks to a crucial sympathy, a stable church guaranteed and in that sense enfolded a stable state. Eusebius, however, had worked almost the other way around. Before Constantine had been proclaimed emperor at York or had crushed Maxentius on the road to Rome, Eusebius had given Christianity a wide setting. The growth of his single 'church' appears seamless and uninterrupted. As his early *Chronicle* reveals, however, that single-threaded story was part of an even more comprehensive purpose: to see the whole of humanity's past as a catalogue of coherently interrelated events. He matched existing accounts of political history against the chronology of the Old Testament, and allowed both to be coloured by their culmination in the founding and growth of Christianity. He thus robbed, to some degree, all other religions of their specificity. They were defined by their relation to another narrative, and were enveloped by that which they challenged. Christianity remained meanwhile, even after Constantine's conversion, borne on the older and deeper currents of God's providence. Augustine a century later in his *City of God*, influenced by Eusebius's Latin translator Rufinus of Aquileia, would adopt a comparable approach. He was equally willing to see all historical events as part of a single divine plan. However, he lived in circumstances where the power of emperors was considerably less assured; and his church was correspondingly cast in the role of a pilgrim, still falling short of fulfilment. In other words, the 'Constantinian event' did not inaugurate a single view either of the Christian past or of the Christian future.

That variety invites us to identify a deeper structure in Eusebius's endeavour. If we take first his notorious preoccupation with the heritage of bishops, we can see how skilfully (and again, how characteristically) he depicted his individual churches as instances of a more general pattern. He combined, in greater detail and with greater assurance than any predecessor, the elements of space and time, of the bounded community and the Christian tradition.

The Christian empire

His churches were bishops' churches, and he was careful to describe the reach and effectiveness of each bishop's authority. At the same time, the bishop was placed within an 'apostolic succession' – a phrase that Eusebius neither invented nor used, but that sums up his approach to history. Although the notion had been adumbrated as early as Clement of Rome, Eusebius was the first writer to achieve so complex and so consistent an integration of current authority and antecedent empowerment, charging the *territorium* of each *ekklēsia* through the *paradosis*, the handing down, of the Spirit of Jesus.

What, more generally, gave such a habit of mind its originality? As befitted an admirer of Origen, Eusebius appreciated the importance of Christianity's attachment to the Hebrew tradition. His genius resided in his ability to include Scripture within his account, and to give that account its full weight without resorting to allegory. He did not rob Scripture of its temporality or suspend it before a contemporary reader as a text full of hidden meaning. (His *Commentary on Isaiah*, for example, although not up to Jerome's later standards, displayed a constant desire to treat the text as a historical account; and he was more interested than Origen had been in the geography of Jesus's life.) The momentum that was so marked a feature of his work, and the understanding of fulfilment it implied, were sustained by more than typology. One immediate result was to make the present subsequent to Scripture, instead of illuminated by it: recent history was genuinely post-biblical. He asserted against Hierocles that ancient prophecies may have been fulfilled, but that the impact of Jesus was distinct – the impact of a teacher who was able to transform people's behaviour here and now. Because Eusebius had built so large a historical arch, the sequence of events, from the remote past down to his own day, could be seen as a single stream. As far as the scriptural tradition was concerned, that arch reached back to Abraham. The motives behind that construction are revealed both in the *Demonstration* and in its partner, the *Preparation for the Gospel*. Abraham had been the father of a people. Their universality – vital to Eusebius's thesis – was heralded in the first promises made by God, before the covenant of circumcision. Thus, Moses and the Law were bypassed – like Origen his hero, Eusebius parried with Jews as well as non-believers. Second, Abraham had led a 'natural' rather than a 'legal' life, and illustrated the priority of understanding over obedience. Moreover, the prophets had managed to maintain that more natural temper. Constantine (and Eusebius expressed the idea with caution) could be seen as another Abraham, therefore, gathering a single people under his rational rule. He had not fulfilled some promise: rather, bringing Abraham to mind would help one to define Constantine's current significance. What Eusebius wished to stress was that Constantine had the potential to restore a shared human experience that, since Abraham's time, had been allowed to diminish.

A NEW VISION: GOD'S EMPEROR AND GOD'S EMPIRE

Constantine's conversion

I have concentrated so far on four issues: urban Christianity, its relations with non-Christians, the growing visibility and opulence of its worship, and its sense of destiny. In all four areas, I have acknowledged growth but have emphasized continuity – that is, the longstanding basis of post-Constantinian developments. I have deliberately implied, therefore, as in the previous chapter, that 'the conversion of Constantine to Christianity' cannot have signalled a major break in the religion's history. What *should* we think, therefore, of that famous and undoubtedly genuine change of heart? Two processes were interwoven, both in the career of Constantine himself and in the portrayal of that career after his death. One was his unrelenting thirst for world domination; the other was the Christian interpretation placed upon that ambition, both by himself and by others.

Two events are constantly associated with Constantine's conversion: the 'Battle of the Milvian Bridge' in 312 (which did not take place at the Milvian Bridge) and the 'Edict of Milan' in 313 (which was not issued at Milan). On the first occasion, so the received version runs, Constantine saw a cross in the sky, associated with the words, 'This is the sign of your victory'; on the second, he ended persecution and 'established' Christianity. Of all the points to be made about those accounts, the first concerns their association with imperial politics. At the battle of Saxa Rubra, after a long series of campaigns through Gaul, Constantine defeated his last western rival, Maxentius (subsequently drowned in the Tiber near the Milvian Bridge, while fleeing from the scene), and 'liberated' the city of Rome. At Milan, in the following year, he accepted a carefully worked out division of authority with his eastern fellow emperor Licinius, a man whom he clearly distrusted and whom he would eventually drive from power in 324. Among the policies agreed upon was the toleration of all religious beliefs – already suggested by the persecutor Galerius in 311 and confirmed by Licinius at Nicomedia later in 313. In the context of Constantine's imperial career, therefore, dedicated to single-handed mastery of the Roman world and (in the 330s) to the extension of his power beyond the frontiers with Persia, the battle and the edict

The Christian empire

marked stages in his struggle against rivals still lodged within the older 'tetrarchic' system of government put in place by Diocletian.

As soon as Christian leaders observed Constantine's growing inclination towards their faith, they eagerly endowed it with a meaning that reached beyond politics. Their enthusiasm was quickly echoed in the East. It was not difficult to interpret the defeat of Maxentius and (eventually) Licinius as specifically Christian victories. While it is unlikely that Constantine thought in those terms in 312 or 313, there is every reason to suppose that he did so with time. Thus were our two processes interwoven; and the past was constantly embellished, not least by Eusebius, so that the details of victory and toleration could carry the weight expected of them. The cross in the sky, with its explicit inscription, made its full-blown appearance only in Eusebius's late *Life of Constantine*. We need not doubt that Constantine saw something, probably associated with a solar halo. An earlier account suggests that he had already made dedications to Apollo, the god of the sun, to whom he and his family had long been devoted. That older monotheism may have continued for some time to colour his nevertheless genuine acceptance of the single Christian deity; and success in a risky confrontation, albeit broader in its implications, could naturally be attributed to divine intervention (vaguely alluded to on a statue raised for him by the grateful citizens of Rome).

If we look at the politics of the age from the emperor's point of view (shared to some extent by the panegyrists who praised him), we quickly detect a theme of restoration, inherited from the reign of Diocletian. No doubt with some calculated simplicity, Constantine wished to be seen as a defender of ancient liberties and a guarantor of unity. The Roman statue commemorating the defeat of Maxentius referred pointedly to the death of a 'tyrant'. Even in the last revision of his *Ecclesiastical History*, Eusebius presented the downfall of Licinius, not as a promise of novel government, but as the recovery of a unity only recently lost. In his drive to achieve that unity, however mythologized, Constantine inevitably came to see his new religion as a useful instrument. (The more negative aspects of such a vision I shall examine shortly.) A crucial element in an emperor's exercise of power was his 'presence', displayed in a variety of ways: his legal decrees, which took the form of personal letters to his prefects and governors, rendered ominous by their language and their fearful seals; his statues, towering over the public spaces of the empire; and his mobility, enhanced by reforms of both army and court, bringing him, with brilliant and oppressive display, to the gates of city after city. Those instruments of government, coupled with characteristics traditional in any emperor, were now overlaid with Christian emphases

– moralistic and hieratic; hinting at intimacy with the divine; demonstrating an almost miraculous alliance with the forces of nature.

The rewards of patronage

Christian communities soon gained from the policies of unification and renewal. The advantages were not immediate, since the path from toleration to privilege had to be trodden with care. Constantine had to woo Christians, as well as curtail the influence of their opponents; but he could not afford to startle or antagonize the traditional élites of the empire, especially while he still faced an unpredictable eastern colleague. (That probably explains why old emblems of authority – references on coins to the 'unconquered sun', for example – were not instantly dispensed with.) Constantine did not subvert the laws of the empire in the name of Christianity. There were reversals and modifications in some of his legislation, especially after 324. Favour shown to the clergy, respect for virginity, opposition to the branding of slaves (although not to the institution of slavery): one might expect such adjustments under a Christian emperor. But the general temper of Constantine's prescriptions – both his moral earnestness and his brutal sanctions – would not have seemed out of place under Augustus. Significant changes would have to wait two more centuries, until the reign of Justinian; and even then, as we shall see, the changes were not always radical.

Constantine's major gestures in favour of Christianity seem to have been made outside the spheres of litigation and formal judgment. In 313, he exempted Christian clergy from public duties towards the state and the *municipium*; but that simply gave them parity with the priests of other cults. All religious leaders were given the liberty to pray for the public welfare, whatever their particular beliefs. In 318, more significantly, he allowed bishops to settle certain legal disputes, if the parties involved (Christian or otherwise) agreed to divert their pleas away from the courts. This *audientia episcopalis*, as it came to be called, was not a rival legal system; but it gave bishops both honour and power, and enhanced in theory their reputation as peacemakers. In 321, individual churches were recognized as legal corporations, with the right, therefore, to inherit property and to endow, for example, charitable institutions. That may have been the emperor's most significant gesture, especially when combined with his own willingness to finance religious buildings and public enterprises. It provided a sure channel through which wealth could be redeployed at the expense of traditional religion and in favour of new networks of patronage and dependence at the local level. The public profile of bishops was now irrevocably magnified. In 355, it was decreed that bishops should no longer be subject to secular jurisdiction. Julian cancelled the concession, naturally, and Valentinian restored it in cases of civil jurisdiction only; but exemption even from criminal jurisdiction soon crept back, and was fully re-established by Honorius in 411.

Somewhat less tangible was the impact of Constantine's patronage on the laity. Even after the founding of the new capital on the Bosphorus, dedicated in 330, a surprisingly large number of public offices were bestowed on non-Christians, right down to the end of the century. Constantinople, however, having had little significance (as Byzantium) beyond its immediate territory, now attracted ambitious men who had previously little to do with the traditional aristocracy that had for so long preserved older values. Constantine and his Christian successors used a new eastern senate – the senate of the 'New Rome' – and a burgeoning bureaucracy to reward men who shared their faith and were prepared to leave behind the recompense (and not infrequently the burden) of municipal leadership and prestige. Even when honoured with senatorial rank, the loyalty of the new élite was focused more on the person of the emperor, creating an 'aristocracy of service'. The combination of new opportunities and a favoured religion did much to further the Christian cause in the political sphere, and many of those who seized that chance were related to members of the clergy in their home towns. Gradually, therefore, the opportunities and social relations symbolized by Constantinople were mimicked in other centres: a culture of shared interest reflected back upon local churches, although a certain rival pride was also at work. The web of alliances thus set in place provided the essential context for religious disputes, which reached beyond ideas and tested the political resources and loyalties of the new governing class.

The good fortune that came with patronage demanded a theoretical as well as an opportunistic response. Eusebius has traditionally been taken as the epitome of the change required – not without justice, given his subsequent influence. The essence of his adaptation after 312 was to bind church and empire within God's cosmos, gradually making Constantine not only a new Abraham but also a virtual Messiah, or at least the agent of the coming of God's kingdom. Yet he was more than a 'political bishop'. One can still trace in his work, as we have seen, the preoccupations of Paul: a single humanity, saved by the providence of God; a cosmic economy that gave 'people' and 'power' their deepest meaning. And his adaptations were effected gradually. There was much to dissuade a man from too rosy a view, even after the defeat of Maxentius. The *Demonstration of the Gospel* linked the unity, or at least the stability, of the empire with the unity and stability of the church. But Eusebius, even in the revised books of his *Ecclesiastical History*, continued to react to events after 312 as he had done before 303. Faced with the harshness of Maximin Daia, he continued to see persecution as a punishment; continued to lament that he (and his readers) had not been found worthy to shed their blood; continued to show a confidence based on history rather than on anticipated benefits. The menace of the last great persecutor – his destruction of cultural resources, his attempted control over the instruction of the young, his encouragement of a unified theology – only went to show how a convergence of Christian and non-Christian ideals in an increasingly monotheistic society could disrupt as well as encourage the course of true piety. Eusebius was certain that persecution would end; but toleration remained for some time only a partial comfort. His most famous essay in optimism, during those earlier years, was his so-called panegyric in honour of the church at Tyre, recorded in the tenth book of his *Ecclesiastical History*. The chief purpose of the address was to exult over so public and aesthetically splendid a challenge to local cults. Constantine is praised – not least as one who crushed barbarism and tyranny – and the text as we now have it was ready to extend his reach beyond the West. But Eusebius emphasized most the analogy between the earthly and local 'temple', as he tellingly called it, and the great temple of the created universe. The church at Tyre was a 'spiritual image' of the heavens. We are nowhere near the grandiose imagery of the *Life of Constantine*, or even of the cautiously tailored orations delivered by Eusebius on the thirtieth anniversary of Constantine's accession to power. The enduring consciousness of persecution – of toleration's fragility – and the central place given to worship – not least as a challenge to other practices – provided a more lasting basis for a Christian understanding of the secular world.

Suppressing opponents

There was one new element in that vision of unity between earth and heaven: even as a strictly ecclesial and liturgical ideal, it demanded the defeat of all other religious practices. An authority that claimed to be imperial, universal and divinely ratified could brook no rival. Here we begin to touch upon the ruthlessness of righteous triumph, which would remain so prominent a feature of Christian power. Constantine himself was slow to make any legislative move. He avoided taking part in several traditional ceremonies (a novel and shocking departure for an emperor), but he did not suppress them. His prohibition, in 319, of domestic sacrifices and augury was directed against the practice of magic and the politically subversive plots that magic was believed to encourage. The first emperor to prohibit all sacrifice and all veneration of idols was Constantine's son Constantius, in 346. His sweeping gesture fomented local violence, but proved generally ineffective. He tried again in 356, threatening the death penalty; but it was still too soon for such harsh policies to carry the day, although he did succeed in having the so-called 'altar of Victory' removed from the senate house in Rome in 357. After the brief but dramatic intervention of Julian (361–63), it seems as if everyone had to start again. The altar of Victory had been restored. Valens was able to prohibit nocturnal (and therefore largely domestic) sacrifice in 364, but his brother Valentinian I was persuaded to make exceptions. A new note was struck in 371, when politically focused pogroms and trials in Antioch developed into a broader campaign. Books were burnt, blood-sacrifice and divination forbidden. But the crucial steps that signalled a strenuous and dangerous effort on the part of the Christian régime were Gratian's rejection of the title *Pontifex Maximus* in 382 and his withdrawal of state funds from traditional cults (which forced their devotees into an expensive programme of private endowment). The altar of Victory was once again removed, leading to the famous but largely symbolic confrontation I mentioned earlier, between Ambrose of Milan and the prefect Symmachus in 384. From that time forward, Christian antagonism seems to have gained a more menacing momentum, associated with the name of Theodosius I. In 391, temples (already showing signs of neglect) were actually closed – or even, as in the case of the famous Serapaeum in Egypt, violently destroyed. 'Apostates' – those reverting to their pre-Christian beliefs – were categorized as criminals. In the following year, all traditional cult was condemned, with greater effect than under Constantius, nearly fifty years before.

That catalogue of forcefulness obscures, however, a more confused situation. The usurpation of Eugenius in the West in 392 has often been associated with a 'pagan revival'; but Eugenius was a Christian – he even reiterated the prohibition of ancient cult, at least within the city of Rome. A chance to assert themselves against Theodosius (for the second time in a decade) may have encouraged certain hopes among aristocrats in the West like Nicomachus Flavianus (although, immediately following his earlier defeat of the usurper Maximus in 388, the emperor had actually honoured such champions of tradition). Eugenius's purposes, however, and those of supporters like the barbarian general Arbogast, were not limited to religion. It is true that, down to and beyond the sack of Rome by the Gothic king Alaric in 410, there was persistent competition between conservative and innovative views of the relation between religion and political stability. As I shall describe in the next chapter, the success of the barbarians became an excuse for further religious antagonism. But the competition had already been evident, even among Theodosius's chief ministers and commanders, before Eugenius's bid for power. So the belief, albeit soon entrenched, that the emperor had dealt a final blow to the pagan cause was largely a literary myth. (In his victory over the forces of Eugenius, during a decisive battle at the river Frigidus in 394, Theodosius had been aided, according to some, by armies of angels.) Perhaps it does not deserve to be called so much a 'belief' as a species of hopeful propaganda. The eastern historian Socrates was able to imagine that Christianity had come to dominate the former bastions of paganism – namely, literary refinement and philosophical debate. Two decades earlier, in 423, Theodosius II had felt sufficiently confident to express the belief that there were no more pagans anywhere – they scarcely merited further legal condemnation. Yet he felt obliged to condemn them in the same year and again in 435 and 438. The truth was that neither the cultural refinement of Theodosius II's court nor the erudition of Socrates himself was conceivable without the preservation of much that 'paganism' stood for. The assurance of its partisans in the last decade of the previous century continued to inspire the taste of the generation that followed and the imaginary landscape of their moral principle and religious devotion. The public and specifically religious celebration of older festivals may appear to have ceased by the middle of the fifth century; but intermittent demonstrations of nostalgia (some of them violent) test that assumption. It is less justified in relation to urban communities beyond the major cities of the empire, and totally awry in relation to rural areas.

THE VISION FLAWED: THE SCANDAL OF ERROR

A fragile unity

The notion that there was a single empire (a notion that Constantine did not, of course, invent, and which was not dependent entirely on any religious ideology) was maintained in the face of considerable difficulty and contradiction. Limiting ourselves to the fourth century, we can admit that there was little full-scale civil conflict. Constantine's own path to power, down to the defeat of Licinius in 324, was the only major example. Julian had been prepared to challenge Constantius in 361, but Constantius died before major hostilities were engaged. Otherwise, disruption took the form of usurpations, predominantly in the West: of Magnentius in 353 (which conveniently robbed Constantius of a brotherly rival); of Procopius in 366; of Maximus between 383 and 388 (the major disturbance); and of Eugenius in 392. The handling of succession was the key to the continuity. Constantine set some dangerous precedents, challenging the tetrarchic system and resolving the problem of his double marriage by murdering members of his own family; but the succession of his surviving sons was assured when he died in 337. Constantius was similarly ruthless with his brothers, murdered his cousin Gallus, and kept a tight if not threatening rein on Gallus's half-brother Julian. Harsh though it may seem to say, those were only predictable dynastic tensions. When Julian was killed in battle in 363, bringing the dynasty to an end, there was a relatively smooth transition to Jovian and then to Valentinian I, thanks to the influence of calm and experienced army officers. When Valentinian's brother Valens was killed in battle in 378, Gratian, Valentinian's successor in the West, was able to install in the East the trusted army officer Theodosius. A genuine sense of unity was thus maintained, even during periods of joint rule, as under Valentinian and Valens. The significant moment of weakness came when Gratian was left to himself in the West, from 379, while Theodosius was busy pacifying barbarian intruders, securing frontiers and breaking himself in politically in the East: Gratian was murdered in 383; Valentinian II suffered from the political weakness of youth and was also murdered (in 392); and the usurper Maximus was able to exercise virtually independent power in much of the West, until his defeat by Theodosius in 388. The 'lost decade' (from Constantinople's point of view), 383–94, reinforced a confident self-identity among westerners (already under way during the reign of Valentinian I).

Having argued for unity, however, it is possible to run through the same events, marking how precarious the system of government remained. Constantine's success demonstrated Diocletian's failure: he was able to work his way across the empire over a twenty-year period precisely because it had been divided into relatively independent units. Once established in the East, however, he left the West to its own devices. Constantius and his brother Constans maintained that divorce, and the usurpation of Magnentius in the 350s reflected the West's attachment to the relative independence it had become accustomed to enjoy. Julian's initial source of power also lay in the West. He issued his final challenge to Constantius while serving as Caesar in Gaul; and his popularity there depended on his skilful assessment of military needs on the Rhine frontier. Those who supported his claims were not particularly eastern in their outlook; and he was less successful in winning over eastern élites, either in Constantinople or in Antioch. Valentinian I followed in Julian's footsteps, setting up his court in Trier rather than in Italy; and his son Gratian was reared in a Gallic world. Meanwhile in the East, Valens was reluctant to seek western support and guidance, either from his brother or from his nephew, investing great effort in anti-Persian strategies, and being carelessly aggressive against the Goths on the Danube. During the generation following upon the Gothic victory at Hadrianople in 378 – the generation of Theodosius I – the Goths remained an eastern problem, which Maximus and others were prepared (and able) to ignore. Africa had a mind of its own in the fourth and fifth centuries, and that independence (which even Augustine shared in) was inherited and reinforced by the Arian Vandals.

We have to take such developments into account, because we are trying to understand the accompanying preoccupations of religiously motivated emperors. The maintenance of imperial unity, even in the case of Julian, naturally included a policy of religious unity. Conversely, a tendency to independence within the West, for example, was not easy to reconcile with a uniformity of theological opinion throughout the empire. That was partly a matter of cultural and linguistic differences, and affected large parts of the eastern empire as well. Many officials, aristocrats and army officers, however, needed convincing on other grounds that political unity was necessary or desirable. And faced with such strains upon loyalty and security, it was tempting for churchmen, after the event, to blame political or strategic weakness on religious disunity. That is an assumption we have to avoid. If we look, for example, at the efforts of pope Leo to impose upon his eastern episcopal colleagues his own interpretation of the Council of Chalcedon after 451, or at the tensions aroused between eastern and Western Christians a hundred years later, during the 'Three Chapters' controversy, we can recognize a number of forces at work that were deeply rooted in more than religious antagonisms. That is not to suggest that the religious issues were illusory, a cover for some other concern – a matter I shall deal with later. It does mean, however, that the stability of the empire cannot be interpreted in exclusively theological terms. We must be careful not to canonize 'East' and 'West' as theological categories, bandying labels like 'the Latin West', 'the Chalcedonian East' and 'the Monophysite provinces'. While the search for unity, especially after the conversion of Constantine, may have been justified in religious terms, the fragility of that unity cannot be laid entirely at religion's door.

Donatists and Melitians

After the collapse of an oppressive system, two reactions will commonly set in: on the one side, a desire to restore an interrupted way of life; on the other, a readiness to take revenge upon those who have collaborated with the oppressor. Lactantius rejoiced in the 'death of the persecutors'; but of

The Christian empire

longer-term importance were the divisions now fomented among Christians themselves, as the courageous turned upon the compromised. Toleration heralded new difficulties rather than new solutions. The Donatist schism in Africa and the Melitian schism in Egypt were the most famous examples of such a reaction. Caecilian, bishop of Carthage from 311, was repudiated by other bishops in North Africa (Numidia especially), because, they said, his consecrator had been a *traditor* – one who had surrendered books and sacred vessels to the persecutors. They soon rallied around a rival, one Donatus, and more than a century of schism resulted. The fate of the Donatists was ominous in many respects. His handling of the issue was Constantine's first foray into church politics; and his solution proved not only short-lived but also brutally intolerant. Perhaps even more ominously, it was soon taken to suggest that local differences of practice and opinion were unacceptable in a Christian empire. As their intransigence lengthened into two or more centuries of proud self-reliance, Donatists came to represent not only outrage at weakness under pressure but also a long tradition of African Christianity, stretching at least back to Tertullian, of which they felt themselves to be the most authentic representatives and guardians.

Similarly in Egypt, Melitius of Lycopolis had disagreed with Peter of Alexandria, as early as 306, over the best way to deal with the *lapsi* – those who had buckled under pressure of persecution. Both men suffered subsequently. Peter was executed, and Melitius (who lived into the 330s) was further antagonized by the intransigence of Athanasius and maintained a dogged resistance, especially among some of the ascetic communities in the south of the country. The conflict between two rigorist systems had its importance within the history of monasticism; but the driving force behind the condemnation of the Melitians was Athanasius's desire to bring not only asceticism but also every other aspect of church life in Egypt under his personal control as bishop of Alexandria. Here was another form of interfering and by no means gentle hegemony, which undoubtedly encouraged manifold senses of grievance in the more southern regions of the province, and are likely to have played their part in fomenting later tensions, during the fifth century, between the metropolitan and more distant sectors of his flock.

It was ironic that those who continued to cherish the memory of heroic resistance now found themselves an outraged minority, while the greater and more influential number of Christians were ready to forgive those who had weakened in the face of state power. Both reactions were conservative – the longing for a lost tranquillity, but also arguments over forgiveness. Routines of repentance and reconciliation had become more institutional in character since the early third century, and the problem of the *lapsi* had been particularly pressing after Decius's reign (awakening cautious sympathy in Cyprian, prior to his own death under Valerian, and contributing to the intransigence of Novatian). The principles that fuelled the Donatist and Melitian controversies were not, in other words, new. And Constantine's interference, especially in the Donatist affair, could not have been, as I say, immediately reassuring to those who thought they had survived oppression by the state in matters of religion. The Melitians would be swept up generally in the turmoil over Arius; but the Donatists provided Constantine with an early opportunity to browbeat reluctant bishops, not least by forcing them (with some help from Miltiades, bishop of Rome) to create and then abide by conciliar decisions, which he was not ashamed to influence and was eventually required to enforce. He showed in the process a hasty desire for agreement rather than a well-judged assessment of religious principle. To make matters worse for the Donatists' opponents, the rigorism of the dissenters showed every sign of flourishing, even when the pressures that had first encouraged it were released; and they were able to translate their unbending morality into a potentially more permanent theology of the church. One could argue, indeed, that supporting Constantine in his new engagement with the practicalities of Christian order represented a considerable gamble. What might be taken later as a 'triumph' for Christianity was at the time (around 316) simply another phase in the symbiosis between heroic witness and judicious conformity. The more forgiving among the bishops had now invested in a way of relating belief and power that they had previously resisted. The power was still the empire's power – the power of Diocletian's empire, which had fathered Constantine and was still the only power that believers could look to.

The Arian controversy

There is a simple way of describing the Arian conflict, in which Arius is all villain and Athanasius all hero; but such simplicity is unproductive. It has been encouraged, perhaps, by the fact that Arius's mentors and achievements are hard to uncover. He may have been influenced, like his later patron Eusebius of Nicomedia, by Lucian of Antioch (of whom more shortly). Peter of Alexandria seems to have identified him with the Melitians (and he was certainly an ascetic), but he was able to re-establish himself in Alexandria under Peter's successor, gain ordination as a priest, and acquire a reputation as a preacher in the city. He developed what was technically a 'subordinationist' view of the Trinity – placing Jesus below the Father in rank, on the grounds, as he seems to have put it, that 'there was a time when he was not';

The Christian empire

the existence of the second person of the Trinity was in some sense subsequent to that of the Father. Some have seen in that argument a connection with the Platonist triad, as interpreted by the school of Plotinus: the One, Mind and the World Soul (the last being the equivalent, therefore, of the Holy Spirit). Alarmed by Arius's views — or rather, perhaps, by the unrest they were fomenting among churchmen — Constantine convened a great meeting of bishops in 325, which he intended to draw from the whole Roman world (the *oikoumenē* — whence our term 'ecumenical'), and which met at Nicaea (modern Iznik), a hundred or so kilometres from the later site of Constantinople. Thanks to the loss of the relevant documents, it is difficult to know exactly what the assembled bishops subscribed to, at least in relation to the Trinity. They certainly condemned Arius. They seem to have thrown themselves behind an existing creed; but they also introduced the unbiblical term *homoousios* ('consubstantial', as westerners traditionally put it, although the modern phrase 'one in being' — literally, 'the same in being' — is probably closer to the Greek). The implication was that the Father and the Son partook of one divine *ousia*. Several problems were thus left unresolved, with fatal results, as we shall see. First, there was the problem of how to describe the *distinct* qualities (if that was the right term) of Father and Son; and second, the Council remained vague about the Holy Spirit. Resort to the term *hupostaseis* (which we now translate as 'persons'), and unequivocal acceptance of the equal divinity of the Holy Spirit, were left to the next generation. The Council, in other words, created as many opportunities for argument as it resolved.

Athanasius spent the rest of his career, until his death in 373, fighting to see Nicaea upheld and suffering exile in that cause five times for a total of over twelve years — in 336, 339 (when he went to the West), 356, 362 and 365. From 330 onwards, there followed a sorry tale of dispute, not helped by the fact that Constantine remained ambivalent about the theological issues involved (he allowed himself, when close to death, to be baptized by an Arian). Historians have often deplored the ferocity, and therefore doubted the sincerity, of the antagonists, who fought among themselves as well as against the state. Virulent rhetoric; riotous destruction; refusal of obedience; falsehood, intrigue and murder: these became the norm as the century progressed. Imperial agents were not shy to impose their own sanctions: the eminent were constantly exposed to exile — a deprivation that could break and even kill — and their subordinates were subjected to casual torture. The controversy also seems, in many eyes, to have been marred by futile argument over terminology. Supporters of Arius insisted eventually that the Son was 'entirely unlike' the Father, *anomoios*. Supporters of Nicaea were happy to remain faithful to the view that the Father was 'the same in being' as the Son, *homoousios*. Various other parties suggested, amid bewildering refinements, that he was 'similar in being', *homoiousios*, or just 'similar' *homoios*.

Those arguments generated a long series of mutually abusive councils. The significant opening salvo was the deposition of Eustathius of Antioch and Marcellus of Ancyra in 330. (The recurrence of Antioch in the story was not, as we shall see, accidental.) Marcellus lived until 374 (longer than Athanasius) and provided a constant rallying-point for malcontents. His condemnation reflected animosity towards so-called Sabellianism, which, although at odds with the Arian position, obscured the distinction between the Father and the Son that Nicaea had been careful to preserve. Two councils – one at Antioch in 341, the other at Serdica in 343 – set the agenda for much that followed. While Antioch accepted the moderate and shifting adjustments of Eusebius of Nicomedia, Serdica came to symbolize an intransigence that supported Marcellus and the exiled Athanasius. A more centrist position, espoused by the emperor Constantius, was outlined at Sirmium in 351 but rejected by western bishops at Arles in 353 and Milan in 355. A further compromise, built around the simple *homoios* formula, was hammered out at Seleucia and Ariminum in 359. Much of the momentum of the debate was disturbed by the brief reign of Julian, who had little interest in resolving it. Valentinian I was lukewarm in his commitments. Only Valens continued to adopt an unrelenting Arian policy, which failed to satisfy, however, a new generation of combatants. Theodosius was determined, from the time of his accession in 379, to put an end to the matter, which the Council of Constantinople appears to have done in 381, although the Gothic settlers, now active within the empire and embroiled in Roman politics, had been converted by Arian missionaries, had identified with the faith of Valens (who first brought them across the Danube), and remained faithful to those traditions for some two hundred years.

What one can too easily forget is that there were antecedents to the whole debate. In the first place, opponents of both the Arian and the Sabellianist positions sharpened their theology precisely because they felt that theological reflections in earlier centuries had been too imprecise to meet current requirements; were no longer adequate to express truth and expunge error. It may have seemed in particular that Clement and Origen, concerned with other matters, had given too little attention to the theology of the Trinity. The received wisdom among many Christians in the fourth century was that too much philosophy, too much emphasis on the 'spiritual', had impeded a full understanding of Jesus's humanity; and, as we shall see in the next chapter, it was Origen's reputation that suffered most as a result. Nevertheless, one is struck by the strength of the Alexandrian theological tradition, which weathered the contest well. The major defenders of the anti-Arian position – Athanasius of Alexandria, Hilary of Poitiers and Basil of Caesarea – were, each in a different way, students of Origen.

The issue at stake had already been identified by Tertullian, in his treatise *Against Praxeas*. Praxeas, an easterner who had suffered persecution and had established himself in Rome (like his contemporary Sabellius), was a vigorous opponent of Montanism. In his anxiety to safeguard the unity of God, he had, as Tertullian put it, 'crucified the Father' – a position attributed by Hippolytus, only shortly afterwards, to the theologian Noetus. There lay at the core of Praxeas's theology a deep unwillingness to limit incarnation to the *Logos*, for not only was the godhead thus threatened with division but God's willingness to identify with, and thereby redeem, humanity was, in part at least, called into question. The repugnance of Tertullian and Hippolytus show, therefore, that 'Sabellianism', in one form or another, had become a major source of anxiety. In the East, matters were carried another stage further by Paul of Samosata, bishop of Antioch from roughly 260 to 268, who also leaned towards a tightly knit Trinity (Father, Wisdom and Word) – at least before the creation: he appears to have been less explicit about the situation at the end of time (none of his writings have survived). A stricter Sabellianist, like Marcellus later, would have supposed that the persons of the Trinity would become once again less distinct. In the interim era of time, the Father's power, for Paul, rested upon the human Jesus – potentially a subordinationist position, akin to that of Arius. Paul has even been thought of as a precursor of Nestorius (whom I shall discuss further in the next two chapters). He was vigorously opposed by followers of Origen – the first time that the term *homoousios* was disputed (and, by Paul's critics, rejected). The complexities and obscurities of Paul's position show that Arius's later declarations were rooted in a longer debate, and are likely to have been more subtle than they were made to appear. An uncertain series of influences linked Arius with Paul, one possible intermediary being Lucian, also from Antioch, who was martyred in 312 (laying claim, therefore, to that sacred prestige) and was perhaps the most notable biblical scholar between Origen and Jerome. His reputation for critical revision and strict interpretation provides an important context for Arius's unwearying attachment to verses of Scripture that, taken literally, supported his theology.

So, once we escape from the bitter and almost deafening polarities created by Athanasius and his admirers, we gain a more accurate impression of what the furore was really about. First, it was concerned with meaning. Biblical exegesis was subjected to new and immense pressures, since 'proof texts' were scrutinized and dissected in ways never ventured before. The result, especially later in the debate, was a fresh understanding of the limits of language; of the extent to which human words could capture aright the essence of God and the relation between God and creation. Basil's *Against Eunomius* and John Chrysostom's treatise *On the Incomprehensibility of God* exemplify the progress made. Second, therefore, the churchmen involved carried to a further stage an ancient interest in cosmology – how a world distinct from God could come into being and be held there; and the part played in that process by the *Logos*, the Son. A firm belief in God's transcendence had long been a source of moral as well as logical pain: was it possible to 'know' so distant a God? Thus, the Arian controversy provided a new and characteristically distinct opportunity to revisit the gnostic tendency. Basil's great sermons *On the Six Days of Creation* (the *Hexaēmeron*) show how much the Arian debate had refined the traditions set in place by Clement and Origen; and the 'Eusebian' view of the past, given a further twist by the policies of Constantine, continued to provide its antidote to more mythical interpretations of Genesis. Third, if both the humanity and the divinity of the *Logos* could be assured, together with his role in creation, then it would be easier to understand the mechanics of redemption – first, as something creation stood in need of; second, as something that gave creation eternal dignity. Jesus was not merely a teacher or an example, although he was both: he was an instrument of genuine divinization. Fourth, baptism and the eucharist, now visibly part of a city's life, regained a cosmic identity. They were events that brought time into the realm of the timeless and reflected on earth the inner dynamism of the Trinity itself.

Those were old preoccupations, and they serve to emphasize further the extent to which tensions at the heart of the Christian body were not created solely by Constantine, or by any other believing emperor. However, in addition to its specifically theological significance, the Arian controversy did reflect political realities. With few exceptions, the imperial authorities were intent upon compromise and consensus – typical instruments of government. Many of the churchmen involved appear to have been intransigent, sticking to irreconcilable positions; but official pressure in the cause of re-examination and adjustment meant that positions did change over time. By the end of the fourth century, some clarity had been achieved that was less obvious in the 320s (especially in relation to the role of the Holy Spirit). A capacity for growth in understanding was deeply characteristic of Christian history. Adamant formulae, whether an emperor's or a bishop's, rarely achieved the unanimity they aspired to. Argument was the rule, acquiescence in monolithic authority the exception. That meant additionally that there were more dissidents than heretics. It was in the interests of the assertive party to tar all opponents with the one brush; but the confusion of the debate shows that there were frequently more than two points of view in contention.

The great champions of the Nicene cause were all, as I say, influenced by Origen; but they were drawn away from leisured reflection on the nature of the Trinity and thrust into a maelstrom of negotiations, appeals and condemnations. Athanasius, Hilary and Basil were each marked by a species of displacement. Athanasius became almost a professional exile and Hilary was banished to the East by Constantius for some four years from 356 (he died in 367); but Basil (d. 379) was also a surprisingly isolated man, who found it constantly difficult to gain and keep allies. (John Chrysostom, priest of Antioch as well as, from 398, bishop of Constantinople, was a comparably uprooted individual.)

Athanasius had proved his ability to formulate ideas in his work *On the Incarnation*; but most of his life after his consecration in 328 was an attempt to set up a circle of likeminded bishops, who would create the cultural space within which sound ideas could be articulated and protected. He wanted to impress upon the emperor and his associates both the logical coherence of his own ideas and the emperor's obligation to be consistent in supporting Constantine's initiative at Nicaea. He was particularly successful in the West, where his presence in the 340s stiffened the resolve of Roman bishops like Julius (d. 352) and Liberius (d. 366). Hilary and Basil (like Chrysostom later) were anxious to retain that strong support, although they did not always attract complete agreement from their potential allies. The long Roman episcopate of Damasus, 366–84, represented a more intransigent but ultimately more successful resistance, which probably did much to enhance the authority of the see, especially once Ambrose of Milan had died in 397. Hilary, an ardent philosopher in the Neoplatonist tradition before his full acceptance of Christianity, marshalled that talent against the Arians in his twelve books *On the Trinity*, showed a fresh subtlety in exegesis (his *Commentary on Matthew* was a novel effort in the Latin world), took advantage of his exile in Phrygia to familiarize himself with the development of eastern asceticism and still found time for a meticulously compiled history of the Arian conflict to date. Basil's chief contribution to the dispute was a highly developed theology of the Holy Spirit – certainly, something required. While one has to acknowledge his deep concern over divisions in the church at Antioch and his abundant correspondence in the anti-Arian cause, what strikes one most about Basil is his ability to rise above vitriol and myopia (not to mention his own depression) and to create a broad, tolerant view of church life and human dignity. His sermons and his spiritual counsel count for more than his polemics.

There is a moderate but revealing irony in the fact that all three men subscribed to a novel exercise in universality, the Council of Nicaea (which had at least wished to be 'ecumenical', although only half-a-dozen westerners were present). Ever afterwards, appeal was made, in both East and West, to the '318' bishops who had attended. (That was an insecure and inflated estimate – we have no entirely reliable list of signatories – but asserted later by Athanasius in the cause of symbolism: 318 armed retainers had assisted Abraham when he avenged Lot's capture at Siddim.) The irony resided in the fact that all Nicene leaders in the following half-century attempted to isolate and denigrate the champions of what they regarded as a false, politically motivated unity. It remains true, however, that their refusal to conform allowed them to rise above local interest. Instead, they had recourse to history – particularly, in their case, the history of the debate itself and of the declarations and documents that had emanated from both church councils and the imperial court. Appealing to the past in defence of one's own opinion was by now a traditional ploy, especially effective against highly conceptual theologies; but the bandying of documents, much in the spirit of Eusebius's *Life of Constantine*, was a new inflection of the old discourse.

The understandable wish to argue on a high plane does not, however, alter the fact that the controversy was also deeply embedded in the politics of the empire's great cities. Constantine could not have anticipated that the Arian conflict would at least influence heavily, if not govern, the fourth-century agenda for working out in practice the proper relations between cities and emperors. It certainly mirrored in religious terms a range of broader problems that affected those relations. Widespread corruption among officials and endemic evasion among those whom they governed helped to expand the urban class that suffered from injustice and material hardship. That class in turn provided a new and disorderly constituency for less scrupulous Christian leaders. The tensions generated for and against the Arian position impelled many bishops to appeal as much to those below them socially as to potential allies among the imperial élite. One must add to that the rivalry between the cities themselves. The pretension and privilege represented by Constantinople after 330 signalled not just a shift in the empire's centre of gravity but also a bitter and damaging affront to what were, among other things, older centres of religious authority. Here we can return to Antioch,

The Christian empire

recalling all that I said above about developments through the third century into the age of Lucian and Eustathius. It was Leontius of Antioch, bishop from 344 to 357, who first offered succour to Eunomius, the great Arian theologian of the next generation; and Eunomius was eventually championed by Leontius's successor Eudoxius, who subsequently captured the see of Constantinople. Connections of such a sort were essential to the survival of the Arian position. And this was the Antioch dangerously divided in its episcopal loyalties, the rumbustious Antioch of Julian, the Antioch so vividly displayed in the writings of Libanius, the Antioch that rioted perilously in 387, the Antioch that housed the prefecture of the East and commanded and supplied the armies that countered Persia. On a smaller scale, many cities displayed an analogous range of tensions and engagements – one thinks easily of Alexandria in the East and of Milan and Rome in the West. Within such settings, the writing of a treatise *On the Trinity*, even if not precisely so named, was almost a sine qua non for anyone ambitious for episcopal consecration – a proof of his fitness for leadership. And where the sources are sufficiently informative – in the correspondence of Basil, Chrysostom, Ambrose and Augustine, for example – we quickly gain a full picture of a bishop's dependence on the laity of his city and region; a convergence of interests that Arianism did much to both test and foster.

The death of the persecutors?

All the tensions characteristic of the Arian conflict were compounded by the reign of the emperor Julian. He proved, as we have seen, that not only could an emperor, while cast in the image of Constantine, propagate error (as Constantius had done in the eyes of the Nicene party): he could attack Christianity itself. In less than two years, Julian set in motion a process of disenchantment. Quite apart from being a member of Constantine's dynasty, Julian aped so many of the man's ambitions: single rule and the conquest of Persia, but also a sense of intimacy with the divine and a wish to set up an all-embracing culture that echoed perversely the Christian religion – in its theology, its priesthood and its social concern. Julian's 'apostasy' put a different spin on his religious diligence, when compared with Diocletian or Galerius. Christians experienced again the fears and disciplines of the martyr's world (for he did make martyrs); and Julian's youthful familiarity with Christian belief and practice made his persecution even more horrifying. Then, by his famous ordinance forbidding Christians to hold teaching positions, he forced them to reassess in starker terms their dependence on classical forms and images. They embraced the Bible with a new enthusiasm, as the undisputed and self-sufficient basis of their piety and learning. Commentaries and homilies took on a new tone in the aftermath of Julian's assault. They gave renewed attention, in particular, to those books of the Bible that lent themselves to 'mythical' exegesis – a tendency now seen as uncomfortably akin to the literary treatment of traditional deities. The time for strict, historical interpretation had come again; and the tradition associated with Origen was, by the end of the century, viewed widely with suspicion. The archetypes of the new Christian scholar were Basil in the East and Augustine in the West – Basil the author of the *Address to Young Men* and the *Sermons on the Six Days of Creation*, Augustine of *On Christian Doctrine*, *On Genesis* and *The City of God*. Yet the two men lay on either side of the 'anti-Origenist decade', the 390s; a watershed at once defined and dominated by Jerome. The Christian genealogy thus created shows how the opposition to Arianism, the dismissal of older religions and the condemnation of Origen were stages in a single process.

That process, which I shall explore again in the next chapter, produced its own brand of oppression. The fears and principles involved explain why the Christianity that had fallen victim to Diocletian could support the ruthless enemies of 'heretics' and 'pagans', and lose a degree of humanity in the process. Theodosius I, in spite of his reputation as the 'forgiving emperor' (an epithet appreciated by more Goths than Manichees), had less talent than Constantine. He presided over a harsher world and was correspondingly more limited in his achievements. Supporters of Nicaea may have felt finally relieved, when their cause was championed unambiguously after the new emperor's accession in 379 and confirmed by the Council of Constantinople in 381; but they gained their victory at the hands of a man no less pitiless than his Arian predecessors in attacking what he took to be Christian error. He was far more concerned to support Nicaea than to undermine traditional religion. Ancient temples and cults had already been dealt a body blow by the withdrawal of funds and the toleration of popular violence. Heresy was now the greater threat to the idea of God's empire. So, looking back over the century as a whole (as the old Ambrose could have done, preaching in honour of the dead Theodosius), anyone who had thought that Constantine's conversion would inaugurate an age of harmony – even the diversity of belief apparently welcomed in the 'Edict of Milan' – would have been rudely shaken by its Theodosian outcome.

While Julian's repression gave the experience of martyrdom a new simplicity, the general tenor of the fourth century was more ambiguous. Martyrs – the martyrs of the 'persecution period' – were inevitably seen as heroes of a world now lost. Many were pleased, but many were not. For a long time after Constantine's conversion, there were Christian men and women who had been reared in that different world. They were as respectful of the martyr heritage as they were grateful for the advantages of a peaceable respectability. But the older generation soon had to contend, not only with stresses induced among its own members, but also with the easily beguiled weaknesses or increasing anxieties of its children. What had seemed at first a triumph became, before the century's end, a source of guilt and anger. In those changed and unsettled circumstances, the character of martyrdom was itself adapted. Always the choice of a few, it had, in earlier times, united rather than divided the greater body of believers. Now martyrs found themselves dying at the hands of their fellow Christians. Honour was gained only among one's own party. What could one make of the futile deaths of those tainted by theological error? A willingness to die was no longer a touchstone of authentic acceptance by God. Those among one's enemies who were open in their hearts to compromise or cowardice could seem outwardly exemplars of the purest rectitude. Conversely, it became increasingly difficult to detect in one's own company those who secretly admired the obstinacy of heretics. Hypocrisy, therefore, gained a place of greater prominence in the syllabus of theological errors. The only martyrs whom one could admire with safety were those long dead. Instead of providing an incentive to resist error, they rested in their tombs, foci for a new ritual of triumph, or (at the worst) trophies of power in a church's war against its neighbours. As bishops in the fourth century expanded a culture of veneration, with shrines, relics and special festivals, the accuracy of recollection came to count for less, and the competitive impact of fervour and miracle rather more.

It is striking that, at the end of the fourth century, so many Christians were in doubt about their destiny – their individual destiny, in the sense of their capacity to escape the inadequacies of their material and sinful circumstance; but also their destiny as a people. It is easy to blame the barbarians – genuinely, an increasing threat – for stimulating such doubts. Even among those who retained their faith in God's control and favour, the crucial question, in the face of barbarian encroachment, was whether the Roman Empire, even in its Christian form, could really be the instrument of God's providence, or the setting for his encouragement of virtue. How that question was articulated and answered will be the subject of the next chapter. What I have described here is the way in which Christians were brought to the threshold of that inquiry. The circumstances of their supposed success had carried many of them to a pitch of scepticism. The Constantinian achievement, we shall find, was not only a dubious advantage but also an uncharacteristic hiatus. The second thoughts that had become so evident a mere sixty years after Constantine's death reflected a deeper series of preoccupations, which his own ambition had been unable to stem or deflect. They had underlain the opposition of various parties to the religious policies of this emperor or that; they had reflected a broad range of other problems attaching to the governance of such an empire; and now they resurfaced, modified but with deep roots, to take up, at the expense of stable authority, older contentions about the nature of God and of his kingdom.

Further reading

On Constantine, it would be impossible to list all the studies that have appeared in recent decades. Special value attaches to Timothy D. Barnes, *Constantine and Eusebius* (Cambridge, MA: Harvard University Press, 1981), T.G. Elliott, *The Christianity of Constantine the Great* (Scranton, PA: University of Scranton Press, 1996) and H.A. Drake, *Constantine and the Bishops: the Politics of Intolerance* (Baltimore, MD: Johns Hopkins University Press, 2000); and for a survey of subsequent mythologies, see Samuel N.C. Lieu and Dominic Montserrat (eds), *Constantine: History, Historiography, and Legend* (New York, NY: Routledge, 1998). On the enduringly fascinating figure of Julian, the best accounts in English are Polymnia Athanassiadi-Fowden, *Julian and Hellenism: an Intellectual Biography* (Oxford: Clarendon Press, 1981), Glen W. Bowersock, *Julian the Apostate* (Cambridge, MA: Harvard University Press, 1978) and Robert Browning, *The Emperor Julian* (London: Weidenfeld & Nicolson, 1975).

Lactantius has not been well served in English – or indeed, recently, in any language. Much can be gained, however, from the beautiful study by R.M. Ogilvie, *The Library of Lactantius* (Oxford: Clarendon Press, 1978). On Eusebius, see (in addition to Barnes above) Glenn F. Chesnut, *The First Christian Histories: Eusebius, Socrates, Sozomen, Theodoret, and Evagrius*, 2nd edn, revised and enlarged (Macon, GA: Mercer University Press, 1986), Harold W. Attridge and Gohei Hata (eds), *Eusebius, Christianity, and Judaism* (Detroit, MI: Wayne State University Press, 1992) and Michael J. Hollerich, *Eusebius of Caesarea's Commentary on Isaiah: Christian Exegesis in the Age of Constantine* (Oxford: Oxford University Press, 1999).

On the intellectual background against which Christian controversies were pursued, see A.C. Lloyd, *The Anatomy of Neoplatonism* (Oxford: Oxford University Press, 1990), John Dillon, *The Golden Chain: Studies in the Development of Platonism and Christianity* (Aldershot: Variorum, 1990), H.J.

Blumenthal, *Soul and Intellect: Studies in Plotinus and Later Neoplatonism* (Aldershot: Variorum, 1993) and Garth Fowden, *The Egyptian Hermes: a Historical Approach to the Late Pagan Mind* (Cambridge and New York, NY: Cambridge University Press, 1986), together with special studies of Iamblichus and Eunapius – H.J. Blumenthal and E.G. Clark (eds), *The Divine Iamblichus: Philosopher and Man of the Gods* (London: Bristol Classical Press, 1993), Gregory Shaw, *Theurgy and the Soul: the Neoplatonism of Iamblichus* (University Park, PA: Pennsylvania State University Press, 1995) and Robert J. Penella, *Greek Philosophers and Sophists in the Fourth Century AD: Studies in Eunapius of Sardis* (Leeds: Francis Cairns, 1990).

For the Arian controversy, see Peter Widdicombe, *The Fatherhood of God from Origen to Athanasius* (Oxford: Clarendon Press, 1994), Robert C. Gregg and Dennis E. Groh, *Early Arianism: a View of Salvation* (Philadelphia, PA: Fortress Press, 1981), Charles Kannengiesser, *Arius and Athanasius: Two Alexandrian Theologians* (Aldershot: Variorum, 1991), Timothy D. Barnes, *Athanasius and Constantius: Theology and Politics in the Constantinian Empire* (Cambridge, MA: Harvard University Press, 1992), Michael R. Barnes and Daniel H. Williams (eds), *Arianism after Arius: Essays on the Development of the Fourth Century Trinitarian Conflicts* (Edinburgh: T. & T. Clark, 1993) and Richard Paul Vaggione, *Eunomius of Cyzicus and the Nicene Revolution* (Oxford: Oxford University Press, 2001).

For an understanding of Egypt – the Egypt of Athanasius – see Roger S. Bagnall, *Egypt in Late Antiquity* (Princeton, NJ: Princeton University Press, 1993), together with his *Reading Papyri, Writing Ancient History* (London and New York, NY: Routledge, 1995) and David Frankfurter, *Religion in Roman Egypt: Assimilation and Resistance* (Princeton, NJ: Princeton University Press, 1998).

Other major figures of the period will be noted at the end of the next chapter; but the specifically Cappadocian response to Arianism can be studied in Anthony Meredith, *The Cappadocians* (Crestwood, NY: St Vladimir's Seminary Press, 1995) and Philip Rousseau, *Basil of Caesarea* (Berkeley, CA: University of California Press, 1994).

On the predominantly biblical and homiletic character of the new Christian culture, see Erich Auerbach, *Literary Language and its Public in Late Antiquity and in the Middle Ages* (1958), translated by R. Manheim (New York, NY: Pantheon Books/London: Routledge & Kegan Paul, 1965) and Averil Cameron, *Christianity and the Rhetoric of Empire: the Development of Christian Discourse* (Berkeley, CA: University of California Press, 1991). The episcopal context is illustrated by Peter Brown, *Power and Persuasion in Late Antiquity: towards a Christian Empire* (Madison, WI: University of Wisconsin Press, 1992) and M.B. Cunningham and Pauline Allen (eds), *Preacher and Audience: Studies in Early Christian and Byzantine Homiletics* (Leiden: Brill, 1998). Broader issues are raised by Robert A. Kaster, *Guardians of Language: the Grammarian and Society in Late Antiquity* (Berkeley, CA: University of California Press, 1988) and Glen W. Bowersock, *Hellenism in Late Antiquity* (Ann Arbor, MI: University of Michigan Press, 1990).

New styles of imperial patronage were lavished on the cities of empire: see John Curran, *Pagan City and Christian Capital: Rome in the Fourth Century* (Oxford: Oxford University Press, 2000) and Richard Krautheimer, *Three Christian Capitals: Topography and Politics – Rome, Constantinople, Milan* (Berkeley, CA: University of California Press, 1983). Imperial endowment of the Holy Land and the rising popularity of pilgrimage is covered by E.D. Hunt, *Holy Land Pilgrimage in the Later Roman Empire (AD 312–460)* (Oxford: Clarendon Press, 1982), Peter W. Walker, *Holy City, Holy Places: Christian Attitudes to Jerusalem and the Holy Land in the Fourth Century* (Oxford: Clarendon Press, 1990), Robert L. Wilken, *The Land Called Holy: Palestine in Christian History and Thought* (New Haven, CT and London: Yale University Press, 1992), David Frankfurter (ed.), *Pilgrimage and Holy Space in Late Antique Egypt* (Leiden: Brill, 1998) and Günter Stemberger, *Jews and Christians in the Holy Land: Palestine in the Fourth Century*, translated by Ruth Tuschling (Edinburgh: T. & T. Clark, 2000). On artistic developments generally, see two works by Jaś Elsner, *Art and the Roman Viewer: the Transformation of Art from the Pagan World to Christianity* (Cambridge and New York, NY: Cambridge University Press, 1995) and *Imperial Rome and Christian Triumph: the Art of the Roman Empire, AD 100–450* (Oxford: Oxford University Press, 1998), together with Thomas F. Mathews, *The Clash of Gods: a Reinterpretation of Early Christian Art* (Princeton, NJ: Princeton University Press, 1993; revised and expanded, 1999) and Paul Corby Finney, *The Invisible God: the Earliest Christians on Art* (Oxford: Oxford University Press, 1994).

On Manichaeism, consult Geo Widengren, *Mani and Manichaeism* (1961), translated by Charles Kessler (New York, NY: Holt, Rinehart & Winston, 1965), Samuel N.C. Lieu, *Manichaeism in the Later Roman Empire and Medieval China: a Historical Survey* (Manchester: Manchester University Press, 1985; 2nd edn revised & expanded, Tübingen: J.C.B. Mohr, 1992) and Manfred Heuser with Hans-Joachim Klimkeit, *Studies in Manichaean Literature and Art* (Leiden: Brill, 1998).

Where to begin?
Peter Brown, *Power and Persuasion in Late Antiquity*.

Chapter 8

A CRISIS OF AUTHORITY

Our task now is to assess the character of those 'second thoughts'. Christians, for all their renewed anxiety, avoided despair; and their attempts to adapt were practical, creative and optimistic. In the previous chapter, I described a tension between two policies, two attitudes, two habits of mind. One was prepared to ask what might happen, if the empire became a Christian empire. As it appeared to become exactly that, doubts arose – not just because of the character of the emperors themselves, but because either Christianity seemed incompatible with secular autocracy or the Christian emperors continued to function too much like their predecessors. For the traditional imperial system, which early Christian emperors kept in place, represented a fundamentally different attitude – different, that is, from Christianity's – towards the relation between the human and the divine. The other train of thought maintained a pre-Constantinian tradition. It was prepared to welcome some form of integration with the wider Roman world, but without any clear expectation that the institutions of the empire would (or, indeed, could) be fully Christianized. Once those two policies or attitudes began to interact, as the fourth century progressed, and once those inclined to the second point of view became fully committed in their opposition to the first, and once the machinery of government found itself threatened in other ways – by usurpation, division and barbarian encroachment – then third-century traditions, modified by the shortcomings of fourth-century experience, acquired a new force, and induced what I have called here a 'crisis of authority'. In the period roughly from 380 to 450, Christians debated in new terms the relation of religion to public life, and the nature of religious leadership.

The Early Christian Centuries

AN EMPIRE UNDER STRESS

While authorities in the Christian empire had concerned themselves, in the first half of the fourth century, with the implementation of Constantine's vision of unity, those who lived through the second half had to contend with that vision's failure. We can avoid here a general history of the later empire, but it is worth recalling the effect of larger-scale events on religious affairs. We are accustomed, from a western perspective, to focus in this period on the barbarian 'invasions' of what was later Europe. The barbarians, as I shall illustrate later, were indeed a serious threat, and their incursions acquired religious significance; but looming with no less a force was the aggressive proximity of Persia. As I mentioned previously, the new Sassanian dynasty, established in the 220s, exerted more pressure than its immediate predecessors upon Rome's eastern frontier. For the next four hundred years, major campaigns were fought at regular intervals between the two powers. They involved some humiliating reversals for Rome and, more frequently, losses of strategic advantage on the borders of both Syria and Armenia. Diocletian's reforms in the 280s and 290s were in no small part directed against that eastern challenge. Constantine and Julian had exalted ambitions to advance well beyond Rome's eastern frontier; but their immediate successors, Constantius and Valens, were compelled to adjust those hopes in the face of skilful intrusions by the opposing forces. The following century was more peaceful, partly because both empires had to contend with a common foe, the Huns. In the sixth and early seventh centuries, however, during the reigns of Justinian and Heraclius respectively, Persian armies penetrated deep into Roman territory. And no sooner had Heraclius recaptured lost provinces, in the late 620s and early 630s, than the same areas fell before the armies of Islam.

Beneath those preoccupations lay a deeper and longer-term trend: the shift of the empire's centre of gravity towards the East. The establishment of Constantinople as something approaching the empire's capital, and the subsequent loss of the western provinces to barbarian suzerainty, were not the only symptoms of that trend: for the inclination had been evident since at least the first century BC. Rome, in the days of the late republic and early empire, had gradually extended its power at the expense of the Hellenistic polities and alliances built upon the triumphs of Alexander. In an ironic inversion of influences, however, the resulting openness of the Latin world to the language, literature and philosophies of the Greeks had made Rome an increasingly Greek-thinking society. It also made more accessible the history and ideology of the Jews. So Christianity's success within the Roman world was wholly wrapped about by Rome's interest in 'things eastern'.

Once one acknowledges that eastward movement, one becomes more alert to the extent of Rome's reach. The specifically Greek areas of the empire occupied in many ways its centre. To the west lay the old Latin heartlands, with their Gallic acquisitions and the remnants of Carthage's humiliation; but to the east lay Syria and other regions of Semitic culture. In spite of the patterns of Diocletian's defences, there was no sharp line between Greek and Persian: rather, the whole of Mesopotamia, and often parts of Syria as well, from the mountains of Armenia down to the Persian Gulf, represented a region of debated loyalties; a region within which both Rome and Persia made diplomatic and occasionally military mischief, but which remained in many ways master of its own identity. Syria held the two great powers apart. Not until the encroachment of Islamic Arabs from south to north was the axis of power and resistance radically altered. During the fifth century, by contrast, when both Romans and Persians were conscious of threats from the Huns, Syria was able to acquire a new degree of cultural confidence at the expense of both. The seeds of that success had already been sown in the fourth century. The great Ephraem, for example, so crucial a model for his Syrian successors, had mastered on his own terms – linguistic, doctrinal and spiritual – the stimulating turbulence of his homeland, a seismic trench between two tectonic plates.

And what of the West? It is still common to argue that the old Latin-speaking provinces took on a life of their own, distinct from what would become Byzantium – either at the time of Theodosius I's death in 395 (when the empire was divided between his two sons), or at the time of the sack of Rome by the Goths in 410, or when the Vandals conquered Africa in the 430s or when the last western emperor died in 476. However, a distinctive sense of being 'western' had already begun to develop after the accession of Valentinian I in 364 (prior, in other words, to the intrusions of the Goths in the 370s, and to the heyday of Ambrose, Jerome and Augustine, whose central years were played out in the shadow of those later events). A freshly confident governing élite and a cluster of generals and aspiring usurpers, most of whom had cut their teeth on the northern frontiers and in Africa, felt able to dismiss or circumvent the East and its authority, focusing their admiration on the Latin tradition and investing their political loyalty in a western dynasty. Theodosius I, although himself a westerner, tried hard to overcome that drift, both militarily and diplomatically, and might have done so more effectively, had he lived longer. A more ambiguous spirit, however, survived him in the West, part self-reliant, part dependent on occasional support from the East; a spirit symbolized by Galla Placidia – Valentinian I's grand-daughter, Theodosius I's daughter by his second marriage, herself married first to a barbarian king and then to a western emperor. She retained a dominant influence in western politics during the first half of the fifth century, dying in 450 (her son Valentinian III was murdered in 455). Her régime's relationship with Constantinople – vital to her survival – continued to affect western affairs, right through into the Ostrogothic period (after 488); but she did little to relieve a more local tension between the provincial élites of Italy and Gaul, often fostered through collaboration with barbarian settlers. In that sense, the intrusion of Gallic usurpers into Italy, during and after the reign of Theodosius I, formed a distant antecedent to the rivalry between Ostrogoths and Franks a century later.

All such strains, as one might imagine, strengthened partisan forces at the level of religion, because they invited churchmen to question Constantine's hopeful legacy, the quest for political unity under the patronage of the Christian God. However, those same churchmen, in both halves of the empire, continued to feel the effects of more systemic and long-standing failures. Chief among these were the minorities and weaknesses of the emperors themselves (some never achieving, even in more adult years, a firmness of policy or leadership). The military and economic impact of usurpations, as of barbarian raids, disrupted the stability of urban life and local alliances – the world essential to a corporate episcopate. They also fostered religious divisions, not least thanks to the enduring attachment of many barbarians, including those in the Roman army, to the Arian faith by which they had first been persuaded to Christianity (already in the generation prior to the 'crossing of the Danube' in 376). The corruption and ineffectiveness of both the civil administration and the army had a similar impact at local levels, as well as in high politics. The revival of aristocratic pretensions and provincial self-interest did not automatically encourage spiritual virtue or pastoral success. A weakened central authority and a threatened or ill-defined frontier offered a new and often independent status to army officers (a development not limited to the West), which encouraged in turn a reconfiguration of polities. That included the establishment of barbarian 'kingdoms' within the empire – many of them created and led by men who were in essence generals in Roman service. The result was a crisis not only of loyalty but also of identity; a vigorous debate, lasting two or three generations, about what it meant to be 'Roman', and whether Rome (or Constantinople) was necessary to that identity. So it was not just churchmen who were cut loose from the imperial system, but a whole social echelon, which meant that Christian leaders had to strike a new set of bargains with those in power. Élite laymen, whatever their 'ethnic' origin, did not simply sit back and watch a new religious polity in the making. They placed their stakes in the game, and many took on religious leadership or controlled by their patronage their clerical relatives, friends and dependents. Christianity began to gain a new and in some respects greater prominence in a less loyal empire.

THEODOSIUS I AS RESTORER: HIS ACHIEVEMENT AND HIS REPUTATION

Wise after the event, there were those prepared to blame Theodosius I for such a situation – even though it was a situation that he foresaw or feared and undoubtedly hoped to prevent. Much had come to militate against that hope; but Theodosius's yearning for religious accord, secure defences, and a united empire were sufficiently like those of his predecessors to make him seem a natural and faithful heir to Constantine the Great. Others presented him, therefore, with equal ease, as a further agent of Christianization within the imperial system. Particularly in his vigorous legislation of the early 390s, he was indeed an unrelenting opponent of both heretics and 'pagans' (the latter word accepted by this time as a convenient and denigrating label). He seems also to lead us further along the path from Constantine to Justinian, to a view of religious and secular affairs more recognizably 'Byzantine' – a notion in which there is some truth, although, as we shall see, Justinian's world was not the placid conclusion of a long process.

But religious policies were not at the root of Theodosius's rule. He was overwhelmingly concerned with barbarian threats and with maintaining the loyalty of the West to his own régime. The catastrophe of Gothic victory, and the death of Valens, at the battle of Hadrianople in 378 – the circumstances in which Theodosius came to power – meant that ten long years had to be devoted to the taming of barbarian ambitions. Land grants and army careers mollified a new generation of settlers within the eastern provinces, and allowed Theodosius to harness them against those who had brought down Gratian in 383 and Valentinian II in 392. His loyalty to his imperial patron, who had raised him to the purple, underpinned (in 388) not only his military reaction but also his cautious marriage to Valentinian I's daughter. Following the second usurpation in a decade, the elevation of his first wife's sons, Arcadius and Honorius, was a testing affront to those who had benefited from his earlier lenience. So, whatever continuity his reign may have represented, it was achieved in circumstances very different from those of Constantine.

The apparent contradiction between reputation and reality is at once explained and resolved by a closer look at the 'Theodosian myth'. A reconstruction of the past was already under way, when Ambrose of Milan preached a panegyric in honour of the emperor, less than a month after his death. The speech was skilful in a variety of ways: in its novel deployment of scriptural typology and its calculated remedy of political anxieties, but most strikingly in its evocation of the Constantinian legacy – the profitable piety of Helena, the great emperor's homiletic mastery, and the glories of Constantinople. Theodosius's de facto successor in the West, the general Stilicho, proceeded to make good the promises thus afforded, using the poet Claudian to persuade westerners that a dangerously curtailed career had preserved the foundations of unity and lasting power. Their hopes foundered, it is true, on a Gothic invasion of Italy in 401 (encouraged from Constantinople) and on Rome's shocking sack by the Gothic king, Alaric, in 410. In the East, however, Arcadius's stable régime and the carefully guarded accession of his young son in 408 (whose reign would last until 450) allowed a more sanguine acceptance of the dead dynast's achievements. Theodosius I was increasingly presented as the restorer of threatened order; not the final exemplar of a doomed polity, but the harbinger of fresh promise for both Christianity and Rome. Even the non-Christian Olympiodorus of Thebes, writing in the mid-420s, was willing to present the previous quarter-century as the story of a challenge well met, with Theodosius II an effective ruler in the East and Valentinian III, after years of distressing turmoil for his mother's generation, safely restored to his rights (since 425) in the West. Gothic violence and an insecure succession may seem to us the outcome of Theodosius I's failures, even if not all of them were avoidable. Those who came to maturity with his grandsons, however, felt that both halves of empire had come close to destruction in recent decades; and its resilience, as they saw it, seemed only the vindication of an alliance between God's favour and the emperor's piety, which Theodosius I was taken to have symbolized and guaranteed.

The cap was put upon that interpretation by Socrates of Constantinople, a worthy (and self-conscious) successor to Eusebius in his own age (he wrote in the 440s). For Socrates, in his *Ecclesiastical History*, an unbroken tradition now reached back to Constantine, disturbed only by the Arianism of Constantius and Valens (he overlooked the important differences between them) and by the 'apostasy' of Julian. The futility of those emperors' deviance served only to enhance the value of Theodosius I's restorative and unshakable orthodoxy. Such blithe indifference (or ignorance) was fostered by simplicity of argument. Socrates placed the emperor at the heart of affairs, both secular and religious. He could not imagine, nearly half a century later, that Theodosius I had not been fully in control of both; that the survival of traditional belief, the contests for influence at the highest levels of government, the restless demands of barbarians within the empire and the enduring pressure from those without, and the fragile loyalty of several vital provinces, had conspired not only to undermine the earlier emperor's policies but also to rob him of effective significance.

Not everyone subscribed to such optimism. The eastern historian Sozomen (a little younger than Socrates) and his contemporary Salvian of Marseille in the West (monk, social critic and theorist of divine providence) show us that hard-headed satire was still a feasible reaction. The increasing strength of the Huns and the Vandals in the early 440s had begun to give everyone pause. Yet one should not be too hard on Socrates. In the 430s, before Gaiseric the Vandal and Attila the Hun had achieved their greatest victories, the increasing harmony of the empire – symbolized by the completion of the Theodosian Code and by the marriage of Valentinian III to the daughter of Theodosius II – coupled with the apparent quiescence of many earlier barbarian settlers, created a not altogether surprising atmosphere of relief. In religious affairs also, at least for a time, argument appeared to have been dampened down, following the Council of Ephesus in 431. However, only leaders increasingly distanced from what was going on in Gaul and Africa could think that way.

The combination of piety and aggrandizement that characterized the Theodosian régime in those years disguises, therefore, a certain wishful desperation. Socrates was explicit in recommending that his readers transcend the factionalism that had marked relations among Christians for so long – thus acknowledging the persistent problem that in other ways he wished to dismiss. For factionalism was now exacerbated by the passionate rivalry between the emperor's wife and sister and between their political and religious allies. Of all this I shall have more to say below. And Socrates's argument was undercut by more than conflict in Constantinople. Whatever went on in the heads of emperors, the self-identity of Christian communities continued to be local in character. Faced with doctrinal variety or overbearing *potentes* in their own bailiwick, most Christians still thought in terms of loyalty to their *municipium* and to its priests and patrons. Even of those with a broader view – the writers later venerated as 'fathers of the church' – many were beset by the practical demands of the episcopate. A keen eye soon detects how their 'timeless' thought was shaped by shifting danger and opportunity, and by the fresh agenda of a more fractured world.

THE REDEFINITION OF EARTHLY POWER

The great paradox, therefore, was that the sharpest minds of the age, from a Christian point of view, were beginning to call it into question. The 'patristic' literature of the later fourth century was marked more by hesitation than by complacency. With few exceptions, the Christian classics of those decades were based on a new understanding of what the *saeculum*, the *kosmos*, the 'world' was for. They did not attempt to justify a confident seizure of power, but rather struggled to identify an alternative arena of social engagement. *Saeculum* ceased to signify 'the other', a doomed arena of vice and despair peopled by 'outsiders', *hoi exōthen*, and became a common ground, a transient state, in which humanity journeyed towards the distant fulfilment of the divine plan. Such was the enduring result of Christian reflection in what Jerome called the *tempora cadentia*, a time when familiar landmarks, even those now Christianized, were 'slipping away'.

The archetype of that adjustment was Augustine of Hippo's *City of God*, of which I shall provide a fuller account below. What tends to be forgotten is that, while the *City of God* was written in the aftermath of the sack of Rome in 410 and was not completed until the 420s, Augustine reached his adult years in the late 370s. It is fascinating to observe the extent to which older men were then already beginning to think in terms of 'another city'. Ambrose was one – which is not surprising, given his famous influence on Augustine – and Jerome was another. Their explorations were more fragmentary, and Jerome (who also lived to see the sack of Rome) produced in those later years a less optimistic and less subtle analysis (his *Commentary on Ezekiel*). Although he and Augustine can be regarded, with Gregory the Great, as the architects of later western Christianity, the same tentative delineation of an alternative future can be detected in the work of their eastern contemporaries, Chrysostom and the Cappadocian Fathers (Basil especially). It becomes clear that Augustine's famous summation was not without deep roots in other minds.

It is reasonable to think of Ambrose as the chief among them – and salutary as well, since his attitude to 'church–state relations' is frequently misunderstood. He is famous for having criticized Theodosius I – first in 388, when the emperor had insisted on the restoration of a Jewish synagogue at

Callinicum, destroyed by (among others) a gang of local monks; and again in 390, when the emperor agreed to appear in church as a penitent, following a punitive massacre at Thessalonica. Ambrose's understanding of those victories may not have matched the emperor's, however. It is doubtful whether Theodosius saw himself as weakened or humiliated by his acquiescence, and there was no reason why he should have done so. Neither occasion initiated any significant change of policy or disposition. In any case, Ambrose's mind on such matters had been shaped in earlier circumstances. He became bishop of Milan in 374 (some ten years before he began to impress Augustine), in response to a long period of Arian influence in the city, not least at court (Milan was at that time an imperial capital). The emperors with whom he had first to deal – either insecure or inexperienced – were Gratian, Valentinian II and the usurper Maximus. His energies were devoted to building up a powerful network of episcopal allies, both in Italy and in the Balkans, who would aid him in driving out finally the remaining Arian bishops of the West. Once we read his correspondence more closely and plot his strategies on a map, we uncover the central preoccupation of any bishop at that time – the exposure of doctrinal error, made possible chiefly by political interference and clerical ambition. The parallel with his contemporary Basil becomes immediately clear. Basil amazed the emperor Valens by his authority; an amazement that evoked the reported response, 'Perhaps you have never seen a bishop before.' Ambrose would have been gratified by Theodosius's distant efforts in the same cause, reflected in the Council of Constantinople in 381, but he may have been as unnerved as his secular peers – and, as a bishop, inconvenienced – by the emperor's assertive arrival in Italy in 388. His loyalty to Valentinian II no doubt compensated for his relations with the defeated Maximus; but his hold over a younger man provided no reliable guarantee that he could dominate in the same way a subtle diplomat like Theodosius, or that domination would achieve comparable ends. Both his demonstrations of righteousness in 388 and 390 and his funeral oration in 397 were an old man's negotiation with a new and puzzling kind of authority.

Ambrose had already developed a sense, in other words, that a churchman's chief task lay to the side of secular ambitions, making the power of emperors and other civil and military leaders a distraction rather than a solution. A distancing had begun well before Theodosius I appeared on the scene, and outlasted his brief assertion of universal power. The attitude was, however, more myopic than independent, which may explain why it never became genuinely anarchic. New forms of collaboration would become increasingly necessary, and Ambrose's limitations (like Basil's) – his evident dependence on habits of mind entirely characteristic of the ruling élite – define precisely his inability to achieve the clarity of view we associate with Augustine. There was much ground to be covered between the death of Ambrose and the writing of the *City of God*; and the gradual character of the changes involved helps to explain why bishops did not disengage entirely from lay leaders. Paulinus of Nola provides a good example. Born in 354, made bishop in 409 and dying in 431, he was almost an exact contemporary of Augustine. His spectacular renunciation of wealth and station shocked many who knew him and coloured his reputation thereafter, but he never lost his touch as an aristocratic patron, and claimed old privileges of local leadership in his new guise as man of letters and builder of shrines. Augustine and Jerome admired him immensely.

We need to keep in mind the complexity of the opportunities thus seized. The redefinition of earthly power was effected within the world of Constantine rather than outside it, but only because it could also draw upon traditions that preceded him. A vision of what Christian society could become, even within an imperial system, was developed well before the first Christian emperor, together with an appropriate moral code; but inclusion did not have to be confused with identification. That was why Basil, Ambrose, and Chrysostom could pursue their goals within a society they criticized and remodelled. They already possessed third-century guides, as crucial to their politics as to their theology. A radical like Jerome might seem, as an ascetic, more of an outsider (a view I would question), but churchmen of his type (Pelagius was another) were no less embedded within the world of power, wealth and respectability. What made them distinctive and admirable was their different dependence upon or manipulation of lay patronage. Novel use of that traditional resource did most to help Christians into a post-Constantinian world.

FALLIBLE LEADERS, RESPONSIBLE INDIVIDUALS

A more immediate spur to redefinition was, as I suggested in the previous chapter, the sight of Christian leaders who failed to live up to their declared ideals or to sustain acceptable policies in the public and political sphere. Anxiety about the outward show of wealth and power may have counted for less, although wealth and power were often the fruits of moral weakness and intellectual compromise – Hilary of Poitiers was particularly handy with that accusation. Authority was being called into question, therefore; but what authority precisely? I have already described how rulers like Constantius and

Julian had 'taken off' theologically, accepting and enforcing what others regarded as error. But were not bishops just as bad? Ephraem – never a bishop himself – thought they were more to blame for their churches' woes. He still wished, even after Julian, to place his faith in secular leaders as potential guardians of right doctrine. That was equally the policy of Athanasius and Basil. Certainly, there was some irony in their using an emperor's generosity – his endowment of their buildings, his respect for their legal judgement, his provision of transport and hospitality – as a base from which to oppose him. But the rigorous reasoning of such men immediately dissolves the paradox of their dependence. To defend doctrine was not to define it. They were prepared to negotiate with legal and military power (just as were the traditional aristocracy of the empire). In the same breath, however, they loudly deplored a different species of collaboration – a submission in the interest of privilege; the substitution of servility for counsel. Whether their criticism was justified is not immediately the point. Their intransigence made clear a distinction that undermined in turn much of the theory upon which Constantine's claim to divine patronage had been based. As Ambrose had insisted in his relations with Gratian, the piety that brought victory had to be learned from bishops. It is doubtful whether Eusebius or the bishops at Nicaea were as clearsighted; and the tumultuous conflicts that followed upon their deliberations only deepened the suspicion that the new imperial Christianity was largely a symptom of misplaced opportunism. Opportunism is the stuff of politics, admittedly; but the tireless opponents of Arian emperors defined their opportunities in specifically religious terms, thus subverting among their enemies the strategies of appeal and propaganda upon which they themselves depended.

We are not facing, therefore, a simple scenario in which bishops triumphed while emperors surrendered the field. Both emperors and bishops had to prove their rights over again; both were forced to abandon the cosy expectations of their immediate forebears. Equally challenging was the fresh scope offered for individual judgement – always a sign of a weakened claim to control. Where virtue and coherence were at once variable and defensive, reflective people were able to ask themselves whom best to follow. Criteria could be articulated and applied person by person. We find, as a result, a new degree of self-awareness among Christians, a readiness to disclose at least a carefully constructed 'subject' for others to interpret and admire, a fascinated exploration of the 'inner' life. Augustine's *Confessions* may leap to mind, although their candour is at once unique and misleading; but there were many ways of constructing and projecting a self, especially in literary form.

The poems of Gregory of Nazianzus and Paulinus of Nola are perfect instances, as is the *Religious History* of Theodoret, bishop of Cyrrhus (d. mid-460s); many letters were designed to achieve a similar effect; and the proliferation of religious biography in this period, including 'lives of the saints', was nothing other than a shared exploration of subjective experience. Here was another species of redefinition, undertaken almost exclusively by clerics: for the 'selves' thus displayed were presented, among other things, as fellow believers in a new kind of society – selfhood and citizenship were still to that extent combined, in traditional style. There was nothing lonely about such images. The eye of the friend or admirer deflected the subject from any pretended isolation, any remote intimacy with God. To read, to gaze, to visit was to participate in a community of exemplars and acolytes. What we do find, however, is a fear of pretence, a fear that the mouth might not declare accurately the heart, that virtue and belief might be feigned, that hypocrisy might corrupt all human association. The fear was expressed in traditional terms (for it was a traditional fear), but encouraged a surprising intrusion into people's minds. Bishops wanted to know whether people *really* believed, *really* took conversion seriously, *really* repudiated vice and purified their thoughts. Much ascetic discipline was directed against dishonesty, wilfulness and delusion. Legal attacks on doctrinal deviance, meanwhile, demanded a standard of declaration that would have seemed unattainable to Diocletian. Yet it proved frustratingly difficult for the agents of the state to chase people into their hidden selves, and the problem of fictitious conformity became thereby another threat to older styles of government. The new society had to develop different notions of repentance and judgement, wholly foreign to non-believers and much argued over by those who did believe.

A NEW UNDERSTANDING OF HERESY

Here, then, is a context for the understanding of heresy after the defeat of Arianism. Heresy became an 'internal' enemy in more senses than one; a malfunction within the community but also a disease of the mind. Ephraem and Basil had already depended on such assertions. The brutal repression we witness as the century proceeds, especially after 379, was scarcely a symptom of security. Error was frightening as well as dangerous, and the vigour and brutality of those who opposed it betrayed their awareness of its attraction and elusive survival. It was difficult to suggest that religious dissent was a mere rejection of imperial policy, easily vanquished by torture and execution, even when the torturers and executioners were reassuringly 'orthodox'. The same could be said of traditional beliefs. Writers like Jerome and Cassian remained nervously aware of 'superstitious' habits of thought lurking in their erudite minds. One of the best-known nightmares of antiquity (Jerome's condemnation as a 'Ciceronian', described in his *Letter* 22) is testament to a beguiling danger. The apparent ease with which Basil and Augustine appropriated the treasures of ancient learning – Basil in his *Address to Young Men* and Augustine in his work *On Christian Doctrine* – barely disguises the horror and disgust with which they viewed a long-established taste for blood-letting and lust and for mythological fancy.

The condemnation of heresy, therefore, now represented a battle for minds. The word regained its root meaning of 'choice', *haerēsis* – not so much visible nonconformity as a deliberate yet potentially secret act of the will. In such circumstances, the power of the state was a dubious ally. The contest was between equals, men capable of argument and susceptible only to logic. To call in the army in such circumstances, to drum up a charge and suborn a magistrate, was to admit defeat. Doctrinal disputes, therefore, became wholly interwoven with new definitions of leadership and with competition among those who sought to acquire it. Patrons were, for that reason, indispensable. Social status was a powerful argument in itself and a welcome support to the arguer. The chances of an education, the leisure to study, access to libraries, the advertisement and staging of disputes, the intimacy with the well-placed that might follow upon victory – in other words, the whole apparatus that underpinned effective declamation – was, like any other public display, expensive.

The controversy over Origen

At the beginning of the fourth century, Origen was held in high esteem. He was greatly honoured by Eusebius and, in the early phases of the Arian controversy, proved more popular among adherents of Nicaea than among their opponents. In the Greek East, his reputation reached a peak at the hands of the Cappadocian Fathers. They opposed Arius in part with the weapons of Plato, but a Plato they had learned about from Origen, who mediated for them the 'middle Platonism' that predated Plotinus. In the West, commentators like Hilary, Ambrose, Jerome and Rufinus betrayed their debt to the great scholar and shamelessly plagiarized his exegesis. His reputation would endure in more reticent forms among the followers of Evagrius of Pontus (d. 399) and of Cassian his disciple (d. *c*. 435).

At the end of the century, however, such loyalty and admiration had been either disguised or repudiated. Explicit condemnation in 399, abetted by a powerful faction among local monks, and pronounced by Theophilus of Alexandria for reasons not least of self-interest, heralded a new aggressiveness on the part of that see, and contributed substantially to the exile of Chrysostom from Constantinople in 404. How are we to explain such a reversal, which exposed Origen ever afterwards to suspicions of doctrinal weakness? Was it simply the result of fanatical prejudice on the part of Epiphanius of Salamis, who seems to have set the condemnations in train, aided by the cowardice and vitriol of Jerome and by the theological naivety of Egyptian monks?

There were, of course, doctrinal issues at stake (although the way they were expressed may not have been fair to Origen himself). Two anxieties predominated in the controversy. The first focused on a supposed exaggeration of what Latin speakers called the 'spiritual' and Greeks the 'pneumatic'; a fear that Origen had made transcendence beyond the material too easy. He was held by his most forceful opponents to have denied or undermined the reality of the resurrection – not only the resurrection of Jesus (since some doubted whether Origen would have thought of it as 'bodily') but also the resurrection of each human being. He had glossed over, they suggested, the crucial divide in human experience, the scandal of corruption and death, which resulted, they believed, from the sinfulness that attracted God's act of redemption. If, moreover, every human creature would regain eventually a spiritual state (although Origen himself did not press in quite such terms), then moral efforts that were driven by a fear of eternal loss seemed dangerously pointless. And bodily existence deserved respect, since the body was promised redemption and eternal bliss just as much as the soul. We can detect here a new phase in the Christological debate; an inquiry into the embodiment of the divine Son of God, which had been given a special urgency after the elevated declarations of the Nicene parties in 325 and 381. How could the second person of the Trinity be also the human being Jesus? How real were his flesh, suffering and death? The fourth-century opponents of Origen were also conscious of the threat from Manichaeism, which had made substantial inroads within the empire as the century progressed – on the one hand, affecting the ascetic philosophy of many monks; and, on the other, attracting (famously) the temporary adhesion of Augustine. Selective exaggeration could easily establish a connection between the Manichees' optimistic disdain of matter and Origen's supposed glissade to glory.

The second major anxiety focused on exegesis. As I suggested in the previous chapter, a variety of developments – not least Julian's moves against

A crisis of authority

Christian teachers – had encouraged Christians to emphasize afresh their dependence on the Bible as a cultural source in its own right. Its wording was to be taken seriously, interpreted with *akribeia* – meaning 'precisely' or 'exactly' more than 'literally' in our modern sense. (It would be hasty to suppose that such exactitude ruled out symbolic interpretation altogether: the notion that there were 'Antiochene' and 'Alexandrian' modes of exegesis – the first literal, the second not – is misleadingly simple.) Origen himself, of course, had lived both inside and outside Egypt. Theophilus of Alexandria had found it possible to abandon his natural viewpoint and condemn the greatest theologian in his city's past, and the monks of the Nile valley were comparably divided in their opinions – some clinging to an anthropomorphic view of God, others flirting with gnostic speculations. The more fundamental concept, as so often in those early centuries, was history. The Bible recorded the Christian past, even when Jewish in its reference; and the reading of the Bible was also a historical act, repeated constantly by succeeding generations. That sense of continuous interpretation made novelty seem dangerously contradictory. The exegete was not expected to bring to the task of analysis anything of himself. His task was to clarify rather than add to the ancient text and the former readings of the text.

In that respect Origen had failed – at least according to Jerome, who turned upon his previously admired model well before the bishop of Alexandria. Emphasis on loyalty to tradition, on the primacy of clarification, on the avoidance of imaginative speculation, exposed any use of allegory to the suspicion of so harsh a critic. Matters were made worse by Jerome's anguished engagement with his former friend Rufinus of Aquileia, who had been translating much of Origen into Latin, including the *Peri Archōn*. Rufinus, according to Jerome, had been indulging in some creativity of his own, obscuring the extent of Origen's gloss upon the past and introducing novel notions under the cover of an ostensible translation. Jerome's change of heart should not have been a surprise, for all the self-interest and bitterness he now displayed. Since first returning to the East in 384, after an eventful but frustrating spell in Rome, he had set out on a path of scholarship that would dislodge Latin Christian culture not only from Origen but also from the Greek Septuagint (much to the later unease of Augustine). His growing attachment to *hebraica veritas* implied a concern for the 'exact' meaning of the Hebrew original and for the light that biblical history could throw upon its interpretation. (The 'Hebrew original' he struggled to understand was close to what later Jewish scholars called the 'Massoretic text'.) Both ambitions made symbolic analysis distracting. The irony in his thereby riding roughshod over hallowed reflections in the Christian past – Augustine's chief criticism – appeared to escape him.

Jerome's falling out with Rufinus, a notorious component of the controversy, was more than a sideshow. Bishops in particular had been brought into conflict. Theophilus's condemnation of Origen, the flight of 'Origenists' to Constantinople, their appeal to and protection by John Chrysostom, and the skill with which Theophilus and his supporters then brought Chrysostom down, help us to see the affair as part of a drawn-out antagonism between one of the oldest sees in the Christian world and one of the newest. A central part was played also by John, bishop of Jerusalem – the first to be roused to action by Epiphanius of Salamis. (That meddlesome and intellectually limited individual, metropolitan of Cyprus but originally from Palestine, had motives of his own – among them, a desire to establish himself as a writer and a sniffer-out of heresies. However, his *Panarion* – meaning originally a 'basket' – bundled together every perceived error, and provides a priceless account of Christian variety. He also had the generosity of spirit to distance himself from Theophilus's schemes against Chrysostom.) John of Jerusalem was bishop to both Jerome (in Bethlehem) and Rufinus (on the Mount of Olives), and more conveniently available to the latter. Chrysostom came originally from Antioch, where he had studied under the great rhetor Libanius and had been for many years a priest. Rufinus, when he abandoned Palestine, drummed up support in Italy, gaining the sympathy of the bishop of Rome and undermining Jerome's old and distant patrons in the West. So every major bishopric in the empire had been drawn into the dispute. The rivalry of prestigious sees was sharpened further by the fundamental nature of the issues at stake (the theology of redemption and the sanctity of the Bible) and by the involvement of the eastern court (already antagonized by their bishop's moral rigour and made nervous by his popular standing). Tension between Latin and Greek partisans was heightened by the political estrangement of East and West in the years following the death of Theodosius I.

The implications are revealing. First, we are reminded of Alexandria's antiquity, Constantinople's precarious claim to church leadership, Antioch's vibrant culture and strategic importance, Jerusalem's growing status as a new centre of pilgrimage (itself a support to historical interest in the human Jesus), and Rome's continued readiness to adjudicate in the widest disputes of the age (a factor of particular poignancy for Jerome, who had seen his earlier ambitions thwarted in the city, but who respected deeply the eminence of its bishop). Second, an alliance was confirmed between bishops and ascetics, or its dangerous possibility and danger made more evident. Third, each antagonist was backed by lay patrons (female as well as male), who furthered in the process ambitions of their own. Fourth, the emperor Arcadius and his family played their part in encouraging and facilitating the trials, exiles and eventual death of Chrysostom. A comparison, however, with Athanasius and Constantius or Ambrose and Gratian suggests how the balance between secular and religious authority had changed. In former times, rivals had attempted first to provoke the calling of councils under imperial patronage and second to secure the enforcement of their doctrinal decrees. Now the authorities colluded for reasons of their own in the pursuit of causes they had done nothing to initiate. It is safe to say that Arcadius had no serious religious agenda; and it was left to his son to develop new ways of yoking piety with politics.

Pelagius

The 'Pelagian' controversy is normally understood as an argument about 'grace' on the one hand and 'free will' or 'nature' on the other – and I place the terms in inverted commas, because *gratia*, *natura* and *liberum arbitrium* did not necessarily mean then what they came to mean later. Pelagius supposedly insisted that human nature, as created by God, had an inherent capacity to choose goodness, and was obliged to do so. Augustine, Pelagius's chief opponent, believed on the contrary that 'nature' was fundamentally flawed by sin, most importantly by the sin of Adam in paradise, that 'free will' was thereby deeply impaired and that the power to choose good depended entirely on the 'grace' – that is, the favour – of God. 'Grace', therefore, by definition, could be withheld. It could not be claimed on the basis of virtue, since virtue was its consequence.

There is some truth in that account, but it overlooks important factors and exaggerates the simplicity of its more familiar elements. Pelagius was a stern moralist. A natural capacity for virtue was, for him, a reflection of divine favour anyway, and failure to realize that capacity invited a harsh judgement on God's part. Augustine was driven to an extreme position in the 420s, verging on the view that God could arbitrarily condemn some and redeem others, regardless of their moral efforts; but he was encouraged by the equally extreme assertions of some of his western opponents, with whom Pelagius (who by then had left the West) would undoubtedly have disagreed. Even in the previous decade, Augustine had been more concerned with Pelagius's over-enthusiastic disciples, with his own need for support in Italy, and with the apparent inadequacy of understanding and judgement displayed by eastern bishops who had taken Pelagius's side.

Pelagius (originally from Britain) had already enjoyed a long career in Italy, and had been brought to Augustine's notice by Jerome, in terms of Jerome's own making. Once we acknowledge those connections, together with the man's success as a religious adviser in the early 390s, the question arises, can we separate Jerome's reaction from the fracas over Origen? Clearly not. Jerome had met Pelagius during his own stay in Rome a decade earlier; and Pelagius had soon begun to question his exaggerated defence of virginity – not because Pelagius himself was against virginity, but because he felt that Jerome's arguments did little service to the cause of ascetic rigour. So, on the one hand, we have the theoretical issue of a theology of the body and, on the other hand, the personal element of friendship and patronage: for Pelagius had succeeded in claiming the status of spiritual guide to fervent Christian aristocrats – a status that Jerome had lost when his patron Damasus died in 384, and that Rufinus later attempted to gain on his return to the West in 397.

The theological aspects of the matter were additionally complicated by the fact that all those men were pitted against other equally well-patronized figures, especially the ascetic Jovinianus, who not only supported the married state more unashamedly than Jerome, but also insisted that baptism was the only necessary gateway to the practice of virtue and the assurance of salvation. That emphasis, while imparting its own value to the life of the body, drew attention also to the ways in which God was supposed to foster the human capacity for goodness: for the effect of baptism was to lie at the heart of Augustine's characteristic interpretation of 'grace'. Also at stake was the question of how 'genuine' submission to baptism could be measured. Surely, Jerome and his friends would insist, a radical change of lifestyle was demanded. And was the redeemed status of a baptized person an individual achievement, or the result of incorporation within a community?

Jerome's willingness to connect such issues with those arising in relation to Origen is most clearly displayed in his accusation that Pelagius thought of a human being as *similis deo*, 'like God'. It was a clever ploy, rather than an accurate reflection of what Pelagius taught; but the 'likeness' involved was undoubtedly connected in Jerome's mind with the concept of *homoiōsis* espoused by the Cappadocian Fathers (Gregory of Nyssa especially) in the spirit of Origen. *Homoiōsis* also means 'likeness', but was rooted in the notion that human beings were *eikones* or 'images' of God. So Jerome was being far from fair; but the restoration of the image of God was crucially involved in the theology of baptism, the assessment of the effect of Adam's sin, and the nature of human beings, once they had attained their eternal reward. Origen's supposedly facile promotion of virtuous humanity to a spiritual level akin to divinity would have been easy to twin with the moral optimism attributed to Pelagius. And once one began to explore again the meaning of 'likeness', a question loomed up from the past – the question of how the Son was 'like' the Father.

Jerome was also quick to accuse Pelagius of intellectual arrogance, of an unhealthy trust in logical brilliance (which was clearly one of the secrets to the man's success, then and later). He worried particularly about Pelagius's claims as an exegete, and he was able to weave his particular charges into the general unease that marked his discussion of the topic throughout the anti-Origenist debate. Certainly, Pelagius had drawn deeply upon his understanding of Paul's *Letter to the Romans*, a text that the Augustine reread in the early 390s with less ensuing confidence. Jerome made hay of the outcome – a dismal fusion (as he saw it) of rhetorical conceit, moral laxity and a shallow understanding of the biblical tradition – exactly the sticks used to beat the Arians of the century's middle years. How that beguiling carelessness was to be countered shows once again how times had changed. The marshalling of lay patrons on this side and that was the feverish preoccupation of most combatants. There were also loud appeals to the authority of individual bishops – especially of Rome, but also of Milan. Less evident was the intervention of the state in the style of Constantine, Constantius or Theodosius I. Not until 418 did Augustine succeed in gaining the modified support of Honorius against Pelagians; and it is doubtful whether such an effort would have paid off, had it not been for eventual backing by the Pope. Augustine himself continued to agonize over the value of coercion, as opposed to the free adhesion of a persuaded mind.

LEADERSHIP AND ASCETIC VIRTUE: THE DESERT COMES TO TOWN

A common feature of the new approach to heresy was its concern with ascetic issues – the salvific value of human effort and the transcendence of the spirit over the body. Origen himself had secured the foundations of Christian ascetic theory; his later followers were keenly interested in ascetic practice (Evagrius pre-eminently); and his critics were no less conspicuous for their dedication to a devout rigour. Pelagius had provoked, in addition, a bitter dispute about the capacity of the human will, and others were calling into question the sufficiency of baptism as a sign and instrument of virtue.

Historians have long been fascinated by the development of the ascetic movement. Many have been inclined to see in it not only a hatred of the world in general but also a destructive criticism of the Roman political system, even in its Christian guise. The challenge it appeared to present to the Christian priesthood has also seemed important. That challenge, however, whatever its precise nature, was mounted not from the periphery but at the centre of both religious and civil society. Ascetics competed with one another and with both churchmen and secular authorities for a specific prize – the authority to define, teach and exemplify in definitive form the virtues of the Christian religion, and to guarantee their observance and preservation.

We have to dispel first, therefore, the illusory image of desert solitaries or extended communities remote from ordinary human habitation. Even those who embraced a more secluded life were engaged in the prolonged instruction of immediate followers. They were rarely distant from villages and towns or from well-frequented routes, at least intermittently dependent on the material support of less devoted neighbours, and besieged by admirers from distant provinces. The 'desert' presented to us in so many surviving texts (and reinforced in so much art and history) was originally heightened and stylized in a literary cause. Those who wrote and read those texts were overwhelmingly urban, and by definition members of the educated élite. The defenders of asceticism were anxious to propagate among that class their definition of human nature and human society. The exotic settings they provided for their ascetic heroes served, paradoxically, to make them more accessible to readers in a different situation. The distance thus achieved made the message of the text less limited by circumstance. The reading habits of the governing class – deeply attached to political history and novelistic romance – meant that they could find in hagiography a resting-place for their minds, from which they could gain a calmer view of their cultural past and better assess their chances of moral freedom. There is nothing odd about such technique, which has more recently inspired the idyllic and the Romantic, the Gothic and the picaresque.

Such an understanding of how texts were created and how they achieved their effect has transformed our view of the period's ascetic exemplars – Antony of Egypt, for example, and Pachomius, the supposed father of 'monasticism' (the communal practice of the ascetic life), who was imitated (according to the traditional account) by Basil, Cassian and Benedict. I am not suggesting that they did not exist, did not exert direct influence on the pattern and spread of the ascetic life. But, once we recognize the tendentiousness that drives their biographies and the displacement achieved within them, they stand out less sharply. We quickly detect a more crowded and competitive environment. The ascetics were displayed as competing among themselves, and the texts were deployed in a comparable war of words. Antony, therefore, as described in the famous *Life*, is far from having been a total recluse, while Pachomius the 'coenobite' spent long years in less formal associations, and mixed throughout his life with clerics, officials and local townsfolk. When we turn to sources less calculated and biographical – the abundant papyri of late Roman Egypt, for example – we discover that most of the ascetics mentioned lived alone or in small groups in towns and villages. Since that was a pattern of commitment deplored loudly by a succession of writers, particularly by westerners like Jerome and Cassian, we may suspect it was more common than they would have liked.

It is not surprising, therefore, that the great cities of the East, for which our evidence is more abundant, soon became accustomed to the clamorous presence of extreme devotees. (Even Jerome illustrated the trend. After early experience in Trier and Aquileia, he visited Antioch, Constantinople and Rome and settled in Bethlehem only after a visit to Alexandria – an itinerary scarcely governed by a taste for contemplative solitude.) I have already mentioned how monks supported Theophilus of Alexandria in his condemnation of the Origenist party. They also helped to demolish temples (most famously the Serapaeum in 391) and were involved in the shameful murder of the Neoplatonist philosopher and mathematician Hypatia in 418. We know from John Chrysostom's Antiochene addresses (before his transfer to Constantinople in 398) that there was a constant interplay between Christians in the city and ascetics in the surrounding hills, which underpinned his own interpretation of asceticism and endured in such later accounts as the *Religious History* of Theodoret and the correspondence of Severus, bishop in the city from 512 to 518. In Jerusalem, Rufinus and his associates had (since 381) established ascetic communities on the Mount of Olives, while Jerome's Bethlehem was not far away. (Cassian had also lodged there for a while). The increasing popularity of the city as a natural focus of pilgrimage attracted many ascetics, both from Egypt and from Asia Minor, as well as stellar and pious patronesses like Melania (d. *c.* 410), her granddaughter Melania the Younger (d. 438), and the empress Eudocia (d. 460). The long monastic career of the Cappadocian Sabas between the late 470s and his death in 532 highlighted the enduring alliance between Palestinian monks and the bishop of the city, harnessed in particular to the Chalcedonian cause (in the Christological conflicts to which I shall turn below).

The clearest evidence of a new wind blowing in religious affairs was the presence of ascetics in Constantinople. All those who flocked to the empire's new metropolis were by definition *arrivistes*. Like others in search of careerist adventure, those dedicated to ascetic self-discipline were able to find advantage in the capital city, which was steadily expanding, both physically and in its empire-wide prestige. The presence of the emperor, now increasingly enclosed within the city; the growing status of its bishop, even vis-à-vis his counterpart in Rome; and the ready generosity and patronage of its heavily Christianized aristocracy: all ensured that Constantinople was as much a magnet for the devout as it was for the ambitious. Asceticism may seem to represent a stark criticism of worldly power, oddly placed in an empire's metropolis; but the success of that criticism depended on the visible and immediate vulnerability of the powerful and the availability of resources that only the respectable and the influential could supply. ('Vulnerability' here refers not only to moral failings but also to nervousness about the security of political and cultural values.) The same formula had been working in Rome, to at least the temporary benefit of Jerome and Pelagius.

One can detect thenceforward an ascending curve of ascetic fortune. From 380 onwards, increasing numbers of religious enthusiasts began to settle permanently in Constantinople. Some, as in Rome, were society gurus; others resided in well-endowed communities, like the famous *Acoemitae*, the 'Sleepless Ones', with their ordered and uninterrupted liturgy; others shifted from chance to chance, freed from the control of superiors and brethren. Such were the men and women who helped to create the atmosphere in which John Chrysostom at once flourished and aroused resentment (among his clergy as much as among the well-heeled he so brilliantly castigated). The same atmosphere later sustained Melania the Younger. The laity's admiration for a life they found difficult to imitate and for a level of criticism they were yet ready to endure inspired the *Lausiac History* of Palladius, written in the early 420s and dedicated to a high official of the court. A substantial proportion of its vignettes describe an urban milieu.

As the 430s and 440s progressed, Theodosius II's sister Pulcheria, unrelentingly fervent and virginal, achieved increasing political dominance, with ascetic support and at the expense of Theodosius's more cultivated wife, Eudocia. Ever since the imperial marriage in 421, the two women (and their supporters) had presided over a struggle between two notions of how an empire should be ruled – by intransigent principle, or by political adaptability; by the ardent implementation of religious ideals, or by skilful compromise and careful adherence to well-tried styles of government and administration. The first inspired antagonism to the ancient cults, to perceived errors of doctrine and to the pretensions of barbarians; the second

A crisis of authority

was more accommodating and realistic on all three counts. Theodosius II had been schooled for the most part in the latter approach, and his marriage appeared to cap the tendency and promise its endurance. Pulcheria, however, resented having to surrender her hold over her brother to a woman but recently persuaded to Christian observance. Socrates, in his *Ecclesiastical History*, was silent about the emperor's sister (unlike Sozomen), recognizing the danger that religious fervour might be considered too 'domestic', too characteristically feminine. Describing the context of her manoeuvres, he had to balance the use of imperial piety, as a symbolic repudiation of the empress's only recently abandoned paganism, against accusations that such piety was inappropriate in a political leader (accusations that one suspects had been levelled).

Undaunted, Pulcheria encouraged radical parties, who then embroiled themselves increasingly in the factions spawned or nourished by the Council of Ephesus in 431. The best known ascetic of prominence in those troubled years was the archimandrite Eutyches, whose intense and active hostility towards the deposed bishop Nestorius exposed him to the charge of dangerous exaggeration on his own part. Pulcheria was able to take particular advantage of the fray – her piety was matched only by her strict adherence to the Council's cautious formulae – and she brought down in the process Eutyches's patron, the eunuch Chrysaphius, who had already abandoned Eudocia, his own original supporter at court. So twisted a tale shows perfectly the almost anarchic power that more extreme devotees could exert. As I shall explain shortly, the reaction of churchmen was soon to be forceful.

What encouraged so much apparent opportunism and compromise? Behind the spectacular pogroms and political intrigues, less famous ascetics pursued a more measured but ultimately more fateful agenda. They had no wish to control traditional levers of imperial power but rather to create new patterns of order and authority, new senses of social obligation, and new instruments of formation. In some ways, they wanted to make the state a monastery. Although it would be long disputed what 'monastery' might mean, their novel convictions coincided conveniently with the doubts and weaknesses of the imperial system. They were not, of course, the only ones intent upon visionary subversion. Men of less religious stamp – army officers, provincial aristocrats – were equally capable of abandoning political commitments that now seemed less legitimate or productive. The ascetic impulse, however, cut a deeper furrow. Ascetics were dealing with human destiny, with the sources of moral freedom, with bringing into being a future that matched their sense of dignity and worth. Both their capacity for disdain and their alternative disciplines, undercutting current understandings of status and power, awakened the respect of a wider audience, who had found themselves as much oppressed and frightened by civil society as inspired or elevated, whether spiritually or materially.

The security of that alliance – between rigorists and lay admirers – was crucial to the future of Christianity. The society that Christians had first feared (often with good reason), then courted (with no sense of loss or compromise), and finally captured (at least at the top) was now seen as inadequate to the longer-term purposes of God. The ascetic inclination sharpened vague senses of dissatisfaction. Other sectors of society then clamoured to share in a revised expectation of human experience. The exemplars of more precise commitment – abstemious, impoverished and self-effacing – were surrounded not only by lay supporters but also by churchmen (who imitated their abnegation and envied their appeal), by aristocrats and officials, and by the emperors themselves, all of them prepared to admit the attraction of a different type of glory. The Roman world did not, in short, adopt virginity, embrace hunger, pain and early death, and promptly perish; but it did propose to itself a new sense of purpose, at both the individual and the corporate level.

Competition quickly followed. Developments in the fourth century had already mapped the field. The interpretation of Scripture, at issue in the conflict with Arius and deeply enfolded within the debate over Origen, had given new urgency to an old question: how should a Christian teacher engage with or submit to the clergy? Among their own, ascetics were teachers, eager for spiritual experience and understanding and ready to pass them on to pupils. That continuity between master and disciple, buttressed within community life, created institutions more likely to survive the death of their virginal founders. Lay admiration, meanwhile, offered them control over the young, who were recommended to seek and follow their advice, even if they did not join their communities. Ascetic culture began to colour the rhythms of the ordinary household. On a broader stage, ascetics' mastery in spiritual direction, their successful deployment of inspiring literature, even their power to draw pilgrims, stood in potential contrast to clerics now preaching homilies in ostentatious basilicas. The spectacle of the liturgy found its rival not only in Jewish synagogues but also in the ceremony of adulation and inquiry that surrounded a 'holy man'. Baptism, as an experience carefully controlled by bishops and as theoretically the all-sufficient instrument of salvation, had its honesty called into question by both the sumptuousness of its setting and the alternative earnestness of lifelong self-denial. A bishop's care for the urban poor had to be exercised in the face of their readiness to flock elsewhere for interpretations of their penury or hunger.

While emperors, therefore, attempted to present themselves as models of Christian piety and renunciation, bishops and ascetics entered a new phase of tense coexistence. This was no simple tussle between sacrament and self-denial, for ascetics frequented the sacraments and sacramental worship demanded discipline. It was a debate over the meaning of homily and catechesis, over the basis of its content and over the authority of its deliverer. Nor can one argue that imperial or episcopal enthusiasm for a more rigorous piety meant that civil and religious leaders were following ascetics into a non-secular desert. All shared the one public arena of the late Roman city; an arena that remained 'secular', in the sense that its elements were amenable to or supportive of a number of emphases but necessary to the articulation and exercise of any one of them. One did not practise virginity or obedience or instruct disciples in the spiritual life within a social vacuum. Those commitments represented not the abandonment but the realignment of a familiar setting and of a familiar vocabulary. Only a sense of crisis made clear both the possibility and the necessity of realignment; but weakened security and weakened systems of government still provided the only available context within which to maintain order, instruct ignorance, heal disease and alleviate hunger.

KINGDOM AND CITY

Barbarians as threats and as models

I have already described how the West had to cope in those years with its special form of realignment, the settlement of barbarians. Popular fancies need to be curtailed. We are not talking about savages in studded leather with horns on their helmets. Most barbarian armies were small, assembled with haste, intermittently engaged and manned by migrant farmers, who were frequently in flight from more remote oppressors and made temporarily desperate by hunger and deprivation. Their leaders were as much politicians as conquerors, as keen on diplomacy as on destruction, and anxious to acquire both land for their people and status for themselves within the Roman system. What could seem in the short term fearful and destructive – a pillaged *territorium* is inescapably pillaged – became in the longer term symptomatic of an acceptable alternative. Different regions of the western empire experienced the transition at different times. Visigoths inflicted considerable damage on parts of Italy in the decade following 401, but became a fixture in southern Gaul after 418. Vandals terrorized Spain and North Africa down to the late 420s, but were irremovable players in Mediterranean politics from the mid-440s. Franks disturbed the political balance in Gaul after 480, but dominated the province from the early 500s. Lombards disrupted an already weakened economy and social structure in Italy from the mid-550s, but presented a more coherent threat to Frankish pretensions within a century. (The Ostrogoths, who governed Italy from the early 490s to the mid-550s, were different – agents, in theory, of the eastern government.) The fact that local disruption was staggered regionally over more than two centuries gave the *Völkerwanderung* great prominence in Europe's later imagination; but, within any one province, the shift to acceptance and relative tranquillity was quicker and predictable.

Several factors conspired to make it so. Chief among them I have mentioned already: a barbarian leader's desire to be 'Roman'. The confederations of land-hungry migrants over whom they presided were cut off not only from their old sustaining homelands but also from ancestral patterns of organization and leadership. The 'kingship' to which their leaders now aspired (learning sequentially from one another over long periods) was invented or radically redefined after their entry into the empire. Their incursions often began and were as often confirmed by negotiation, in which the 'kings' demanded a degree of autonomy over distinct tracts of Roman territory. The negotiation was sometimes conducted with imperial authorities but increasingly with local officials and landowners. The 'royal' status that men like Alaric and Clovis captured and bequeathed was made both stable and acceptable beyond their immediate henchmen because they were able to claim also titles of Roman rank, which made them seem more useful than exotic. They benefited, therefore, not only from the helplessness of their own people but also from the increasing prominence of senior army personnel, many of whom were already barbarian in origin. *Magistri*, as they were called, 'masters' of infantry or cavalry (or both), could aspire not only to the control of rich and distant frontier regions (where, by definition, barbarians first made their presence felt) but also to alliance with the imperial family and perhaps to imperial rank itself. Just as Stilicho, half-Vandal, had married Serena, the adopted daughter of Theodosius I, so Athaulf the Visigoth would marry Galla Placidia (and leave her, for a while, a childless widow) and Gaiseric the Vandal would betroth his sons to the daughters of Valentinian III (thus ensuring that at least one future Vandal king would be the descendant of emperors). Theodoric the Ostrogoth and Clovis the Frank adopted without effort or serious challenge a variety of imperial attributes.

A crisis of authority

The other major factor was less tangible, but in the longer term more significant. At least since the time of Tacitus, Romans had been prepared to attribute to the alien peoples of the north virtues they themselves admired but did not always practise. Courage was one, exercised in defence of another, liberty; and barbarians were considered loyal and affectionate to their wives and children. The Latin word *virtus*, which we habitually translate 'virtue', was ambiguous, since it carried also the sense of 'manliness'. (The prejudiced view in antiquity was that only males could be truly virtuous in our sense. Women became virtuous by adopting male characteristics.) Similarly, a martial allusion lurked behind the Greek word *aretē*, Ares being the Greek equivalent of Mars. The arrival of barbarian refugees and settlers in larger numbers stimulated doubts about Roman vigour, but at the same time made the vigour of barbarians not only a condemnation of Roman ineptitude and dissolution but also an attractive alternative for those who suffered most from the corruption and injustice of imperial rule. There were certainly cases, in the fourth century as well as in the sixth, where Roman citizens – both restless peasants and opportunistic aristocrats – welcomed the intruders. Eunapius of Sardis had already noted the inclination in the 380s, and later Gallic writers like Salvian of Marseille and Sidonius Apollinaris, for all their enduring fidelity to many Roman ideals, verged on rejoicing that Visigoths and Burgundians might restore dignity and security to a world that Rome had lost the right to rule. 'Virtue', therefore, became a quality entirely proper to a post-Roman mentality and ethic; and some prejudiced eyes would see in the empire of East Rome characteristics of dissolute tyranny formerly attributed only to Persians.

However, the establishment of 'kingdoms' on Roman soil was a shocking challenge to the notion of Rome's eternity. Constantine and his immediate successors had succeeded in making the eternity of Rome a sign of the Christian God's favour, albeit modified within a broader view of creation and time. While some (including Salvian) were ready to see invasion as a punishment for moral and theological laxity (somewhat as Eusebius had regarded persecution), others were led to question whether God's providence could be trusted at all. Treatises on providence began to proliferate – one of Salvian's major works was entitled *De gubernatione dei*, which was less about 'government' than about effective 'control'. The concern dovetailed naturally with the concurrent theological debates about 'natural virtue', predestination and final judgement. Once the effective authority of God had been called into doubt, people started to wonder whether *any* authority could claim legitimacy.

Such was the atmosphere within which barbarian leaders struggled to achieve eminence – to restore order within a system they themselves had driven to a pitch of chaos and uncertainty. It is true that the notions of 'kingdom' and 'kingship' did not at first appeal easily to western Romans: those prepared to distance themselves from the authority of emperors, or to acknowledge the distance imposed upon them, might have thought more naturally in terms of a 'republic'. Greeks were in a sense more fortunate: their use of the term *basileus*, 'king', with its Hellenistic overtones, would not have called to mind the *reges* of pre-republican days. However, although the connection was recognized only slowly – Theodoric the Ostrogoth, for example, was thought of in his time as another Trajan or Valentinian – the 'kings' of the Old Testament came to symbolize a natural alliance between post-imperial and barbarian polities. Even Justinian, no lover of barbarians, appropriated to himself the mantle of Solomon.

'Political' incompatibility was to some extent prolonged by barbarian religion. The majority of the new settlers were nominally Christian. Conversion to Christianity had been one of the conditions on which Valens had let the first major body of Goths cross the Danube in 376. Christian missionaries had been at work among small sections of the Gothic peoples beyond the frontier for several decades before. That meant, however, that Arianism was the dominant faith among the new settlers, and remained so until the expansion of the Franks beyond modern Belgium in the middle years of the fifth century. Enduring fidelity to what most Romans by then regarded as heresy erected something of a barrier between the settlers and their imperial hosts: it made them outcasts within the very system they had adopted. The Franks, however, at the time of their expansion, were still predominantly unconverted to Christianity, which may explain why significant numbers of Romans in Gaul, including bishops, were ready to encourage their ambitions against Arian rivals like the Visigoths: for the Franks quickly perceived either the validity or the convenience of an orthodox baptism. Fortune, in northern Gaul, was on the side of Nicaea. The Franks went on to achieve a towering presence in the province; and the forms of their new belief reinforced the threat they presented to the Arian Ostrogoths in Italy. Yet the effective wooing of barbarian kingdoms away from Arianism was not assured until the seventh century, the most notable landmark on the route being the shift of allegiance among the Visigoths in Spain under King Reccared in 589. No wonder that so many homilies in the early barbarian West, centuries after Nicaea and the first Council of Constantinople, continued to fulminate, often nervously, against Arian error.

While we may not subscribe, therefore, to the popular image of pillage and slaughter, the barbarians' attempt to gain Roman status and standards of living increased the potential for tension or despair. It was not just the crossing of a river, the sacking of a city, the theft or destruction of a harvest, although they were sudden enough and catastrophic on the ground. Those were the preliminaries to a mass settlement that encouraged further the more fundamental processes of realignment already in train. Take, for example, what I said above about the 'secular' arena of the late Roman city. If any fourth-century Christians had toyed with the idea that they could dispense with the secular, the arrival of the barbarians would have brought it home to them that something had to be rescued or restored at the practical level of peace and order. Barbarians were not God's gift to the reclusive or the anarchic. Bishops had to adapt to warrior rule, while preserving patterns of Roman law and administration. Monks had to function in a world less amenable to pilgrimage, with new patrons and different economic pressures. And the process of displacement I discussed above was also carried a stage further. The sleight of hand to which Christian literature lent itself – a text's ability to carry a reader 'somewhere else', while leaving him or her in their familiar place – was put to new use. In earlier instances, admirable holiness was cut free from the 'desert' context that appeared to make it so, and became available in a new and predominantly urban setting. Now, in addition to demonstrating that holiness was possible beyond Rome's mental frontiers, Christian literature of many sorts, histories and homilies especially, began to make the apparent void of barbarian politics and culture an acceptable arena for the redeployment of ancient Roman values. It was now the barbarian that had 'come to town'.

Augustine: God's new community

Few people saw this as clearly as Augustine of Hippo. His *City of God* was penned between the sack of Rome by the Visigoths in 410 and the siege of his own city by the Vandals in 430. The threat of the Visigoths had been mitigated by their settlement in Gaul; but the approach of the Vandals formed a dark cloud on Augustine's horizon, long before their arrival at Hippo. He began writing the twenty-two books – what he eventually called his 'huge work' – in response to the physical assault on the empire's old capital; but, as the instalments emerged, their focus changed. He had recognized, immediately after the events of 410, that it was both necessary and possible to separate in people's minds the visible remnants of ancient power from the firm bases of political culture. As its eventual subtitle implies, however, the work was directed 'against the pagans'; and, as his argument expanded, he called into question almost every tenet upon which Rome's claim to righteous domination had been grounded. Cicero and Varro, archetypes of political and religious commentary in the late Republic, were subjected to a particularly exhaustive criticism. From a strictly theological point of view, the *City of God* may not rank as Augustine's major work. Had it been all that survived of his writing, the religious cast of mind in the medieval West would have been different. Yet he would still have exerted a towering influence on Christianity's development.

The sheer weight of that influence, which is impossible to summarize in a book of this compass, can give a false impression of Augustine's circumstance and status in his own lifetime. He had important contacts in Italy, religious and lay. His earlier experience and success in Rome and Milan had depended on a patronage that continued to serve him well after his return to Africa in 388; and his engagement with Pelagius in particular helped him maintain his connections with authorities in the peninsula. More generally, however, he was restricted by his provincial setting and by the controversial nature of his views. One should remember also that his major theological and exegetical works were either completed or well under way before 410 – works on *Genesis*, the Trinity, baptism and 'Christian doctrine', as well as the *Confessions*. By 410, he was heading for sixty – a good age for that period. His last twenty years, apart from the *City of God*, were devoted to less creative preoccupations, governed by the concerns of his opponents – the nature and effect of sin, and the centrality of baptism in the redemptive economy.

Nor should we see him as the dominant figure in a distinct 'Latin' tradition, eclipsing all but Jerome. From a fifth-century viewpoint, the future that Augustine came to dominate was still unimaginable. Compared with Jerome or his own mentor Ambrose, his theological and linguistic resources would have seemed limited. Perhaps that gave greater liberty to his imaginative genius; but a contemporary could have noted in particular how conservative he was in relation to Hebrew, and how narrow he was in his knowledge of Greek. Exile and pilgrimage, the fruit of Arian rule and Holy Land endowment, had ensured in the fourth century a constant traffic of ideas from East to West (by no means all of them religious). As the fifth century progressed and western horizons shrank, the smaller numbers of those who did travel to the East (not least as refugees from barbarian disturbance) were more likely to stay (including Pelagius). Melania the Younger, accompanied at first by her husband Pinianus, fled the Goths in Italy, lodged for a while in

Augustine's North Africa and settled finally in Jerusalem (with visits to Egypt and Constantinople). She was an archetype of the trend.

A protégée of her grandmother and inspired by the generation of Jerome and Palladius, Melania still carried within her the traditions of Origen that would dominate east Roman Christianity, mediated (as they had been to Ambrose) through the reflective syntheses of Basil and the two Gregorys. An ever-deepening appreciation of 'spirit', both human and divine, and a rigorous but optimistic acceptance of humanity made in the image of God, would have been to a discerning eye rather different from the central elements of Augustine's theology. The two strands of thought, which would increasingly diverge, were not incompatible, and Augustine would not have seemed a belligerent proponent of some radical alternative. Nor did access to Greek religious ideas expire completely. Boethius in the early sixth century, and even Gregory the Great at its close, were well informed for their times. Augustine might have been regarded, however, by someone outside the African sphere, as a man with less of a future, intellectually, compared with a Greek tradition that would be little modified until the apogee of the eighth-century iconoclasts. It would assert itself in a long line of thinkers, reaching from John Climachus (d. 649), through Maximus the Confessor (d. 662), John of Damascus (d. *c.* 750), and Simeon the 'new theologian' (d. 1022), down to Gregory Palamas (d. 1359). In a period when western monasticism was still in its infancy, with a century yet to pass before Benedict defined its most enduring forms, Greek Christianity already possessed its master in Basil, whose prescriptions would command respect until and beyond the reforms of Theodore of Studios (d. 826).

Nevertheless, Augustine was to be a founding father of Latin Christianity. The implications of his theology remain inescapable. Major components of that theology I have already touched upon when discussing Pelagius. The intimacies of the *Confessions* – their understanding of desire, temptation, time, memory, aspiration and prayer – have coloured the devotion of the Christian West. His understanding of the Trinity, developed away from the centres of dispute, has a calm and singular quality (although, via Leo, it had some influence at Chalcedon). His conception of the Son as the Father's thought and of the Spirit as the love between them matched brilliantly his skill in dissecting the mechanisms of the individual mind and heart. He did more than any church council to bring human experience close to the workings of divinity. It would be artificial, therefore, to isolate a single theme in the writings of so versatile and long-lived a thinker; but it does not seem risky to suggest that the motive and capacity of human affection lay close to the centre of Augustine's religious understanding. He longed for an assured and encompassing love of God; and that longing compelled him to a prolonged reflection on the character and purpose of material creation, and on the human spirit's chances of breaking through it. Matter itself was problem enough; but humanity's interior aspirations were also obscure and fragile. Augustine worried constantly about the impediments thrown up against the spirit, often by human beings themselves – ignorance, habit and desire. How was one to distinguish between the strong forces that pulled one away from God and the equally strong forces that would pull one towards him? How was one to instruct and encourage even those already baptized? What social setting would guarantee insight and discipline? How was one to explain the contradiction of sin, the willingness to reject what should be irresistible – the goodness of God?

The same concerns colour the *City of God*, which is famously a study of 'two loves', one of God and one of self. The 'heavenly' city, God's city, is inspired by the former, while a city inspired by love of self was doomed to share the fate of the devil in hell. The *libido*, the motive power that characterizes self-love, is a *libido dominandi*, a desire for mastery over others. Augustine did not embark, therefore, on a species of political theory: rather, he dissected the history of Roman dominion as if he were analyzing an individual heart. To build a *civitas*, a civil society, that would reflect and sustain a focus on the divine required more than law and conquest (which was, for the most part, what the Roman past had depended upon). Augustine based his society on consent – a harmony of inclinations, a sense of shared humanity and an agreement about appropriate goals. Consent implied also recognition of the authority required to stabilize relations and to maintain society's momentum; an authority that mirrored the fatherly justice of God. The expansion of Rome, and the religious cults that supposedly justified and explained it, had now been radically curtailed and found wanting. The effective consent Augustine wished to put in their place called for a more realistic understanding of the human will and the scope of its ambitions.

So he embarked, in the face of doubt and panic, on the practical task of giving meaning to what was by definition impermanent. The now obviously threatened character of *romanitas* – the splendour, power and refinement of Rome and its empire – could not be allowed to rob human association of lasting significance. The impermanence that aroused anxiety would now become the key to Augustine's alternative. Longing would replace self-satisfaction, and the obscurities of the future would count for more than the certainties of the past. The society of current experience was not the antithesis of the 'city of God', but a society in transition, impelled by hope. Its characteristic members were *peregrini*, pilgrims (meaning wanderers or travellers). The 'citizens of the earth' were, by contrast, content to make their home in the here and now. The 'heavenly citizen' 'used', in Augustine's crucial phrase, the resources of earthly existence, but only as the means to a postponed and more worthy achievement. Those resources were the familiar components of civil society – family, commerce, law and security – subsumed under a religious awareness of God's presence, majesty and beckoning hand.

For Augustine's city was not barbarian in form. He valued the best insights of his own culture, and wished only to make their survival more secure and their exercise more perceptively based. He gave a new twist, therefore, to both disillusionment and realignment. He was worried not only by the inadequacy of Constantine's legacy but also by the inadequacy of human experience. He genuinely believed that the entire history of his species had been a mistake; that men and women should now take to a path scarcely ventured upon since the days of Cain and Abel – the city-building farmer and the nomad herdsman. Much of Augustine's personal past, as he recognized himself, had led him to that view. He had aimed at a career natural to a new class of ambitious Christian laymen; still eager for patrons, wealth, the advantages of rank and a 'good marriage', the possibility of imperial favour and political influence. But a breakdown in his health and the resignation of his teaching post in Milan provided him with greater opportunities for philosophical reflection – preserved for us in the treatises he wrote, while enjoying the more tranquil atmosphere of a friend's villa at Cassiciacum. He then went back to Africa and took up a life of shared asceticism similar to that he had found in Milan and Rome. Whether he intended thereby to reject society completely is hard to tell, but, given what I have said already about the proximity of ascetics to urban life, it seems unlikely. He was apparently hijacked by his ordination to the priesthood in 391 (he became a bishop in 395). He had studiously avoided churches where a vacancy was obvious, and Hippo had seemed a safe place to worship. One suspects, nevertheless, that he had anticipated consecration somewhere; and his initial hesitation in the face of popular clamour at Hippo may have signified disappointment at a less elevated promotion, or was at most a formal display of humility. What his ordination and eventual consecration meant in practice was that his asceticism was interwoven thereafter with a sense of clerical responsibility, as had been and would remain for centuries a characteristic pattern in western Christendom. When one caps that with the Roman character of the *City of*

God, Augustine exemplifies perfectly, in his later and different setting, the shifts of definition already apparent among the contemporaries of Ambrose.

EPHESUS AND CHALCEDON

The vulnerability of the eastern empire

I have already given some impression of the comparable strains induced within the eastern empire, after the death of Theodosius I in 395. The discontents of the Goths under Alaric in the Balkans, rebellion in provinces further east and far from friendly challenges from the government of Honorius in the West, all exacerbated the comparative ineptitude of his son Arcadius. When the latter died in 408, the East had to cope with the long minority of his own son Theodosius II (born in 401), which inevitably fomented rivalries at court.

It is, moreover, an illusion to suppose that the East was spared barbarian pressure. In a remarkably short-sighted gesture, Arcadius and his ministers had attempted to shake off Alaric's Visigoths, who constantly demanded territory and, for their leaders, rank, by turning them against Italy in 401 – a decision that led ultimately to the symbolic tragedy of 410, although also to the subsequent removal of the invaders to even remoter provinces in Gaul. The government of Zeno was to follow the same policy in 488, sending Theodoric's troublesome Ostrogoths into Italy – ostensibly to restore the authority of the empire, but in truth to be rid of violent demands for territory and of dangerous interference in high-level politics.

However, there were greater threats to worry about. The pressure of the Gothic peoples upon the empire at the close of the fourth century had been due to massive aggression by the nomadic Huns beyond them. From the 390s through to the 460s, we have enough evidence to sketch the formation of a powerful system of dominant leadership and satellite peoples – the central figure being, of course, Attila. The 'Huns' were in fact a fragmented entity. Small groups of them crop up as mercenaries or petty raiders throughout the period. Attila and his family had been able to create, however, a more formidable federation, held together by the rewards of plunder and tribute. During the 430s and 440s, he battened himself upon Theodosius's territories, demanding enormous sums of money. Theodosius was willing to pay for peace, although the policy was not always effective, since his willingness had to be pricked at intervals to ensure the northward flow of wealth. The policy provoked disagreement among the east Romans – a further instance of the clash of philosophies I mentioned above. Cultivation and appeasement were increasingly resisted, bringing about the eventual fall of both Eudocia and Chrysaphius. It was forcefully reversed by the new emperor Marcian in 450 – an emperor whose legitimacy depended on his symbolic marriage to the chaste Pulcheria – and Attila promptly turned to inflict himself on the West. There he acquired his reputation as 'the scourge of God' (the instrument of a harsh but enduring providence) and, in a heavily mythologized confrontation, was turned from the gates of Rome by the pleas of Pope Leo. His ultimate withdrawal from Roman territory was more the result of an earlier defeat in battle, overstretched supply lines and the sickness induced by a strange and warmer climate.

To the Huns we must add the Vandals. Once they had captured Carthage in 439, they were able to set up a powerful kingdom that lasted until it was destroyed by the armies of Justinian in the early 530s. The architect of that success was Gaiseric, who, like every other barbarian leader, had strengthened his hold over a displaced people by promising them land. He did not die until 477. His ability to carry his success further than the Visigoths and other contemporary settlers rested on two unusual factors: the strategic position of his new domains and his successful alliance with the western imperial family, which reached further than the winning of high military rank. He was also more brutal in enforcing his authority as an Arian over the Catholics of North Africa, many of whom suffered great privations or were forced into exile. The eastern government viewed the new polity with aggressive alarm and mounted several expeditions against it. Valentinian III accepted, meanwhile, the unforeseeable implications of betrothal between Gaiseric's son Huneric and his own child-daughter Eudocia. The arrangement underwrote a humiliating guarantee of corn supplies. Gaiseric proved his attachment to the bargain by carrying off not only Eudocia but her mother and sister as well, when Valentinian was murdered in 455. As for strategy, that foray into Italy proved how easily Gaiseric could command the sea. A Carthaginian fleet reached dangerously into the eastern waters of the Mediterranean, crowning orthodox outrage at Constantinople with economic peril.

Jesus human and divine

That catalogue of threats and misfortunes cannot by itself explain the religious developments of the period; but dangerous military and naval engagements, humiliating diplomacy, and consequent political tensions among the Romans themselves constituted a vital element in religious history. The justification of a 'Christian empire', as Augustine had recognized, depended either on a firm belief that God intended it to survive – a belief that implied some enduring confidence in *romanitas* and echoed the basic constituents of pre-Christian confidence – or on a sense that God was punishing Romans for failures, which did not rule out, however, his willingness to heal and restore. So it counted for something that the East should have been beset by such problems – a less secure régime in the West, aggravated by increasing disruption and fragmentation in Gaul and beyond; the effective loss of Africa; and fearful pressure from Attila's Huns. It is true that, in seeking to explain that sorry turn, the Christians of the East were more inclined to blame heretics, Manichees, Jews and recalcitrant non-Christians than they were to imagine an increasingly barbarian future; but they assumed that the condition of the empire was fundamentally the result of divine displeasure, which provoked questions of policy and command, as well as doctrine.

At the level of theological debate, therefore, we cannot imagine a smooth path from Nicaea to Chalcedon. It is true that the bishops at Chalcedon in 451 were conscious of their obligations to the '318' holy fathers of Nicaea. It is true that their debates continued to focus on the nature of the second person of the Trinity. The difference of circumstance was, however, momentous. The Arian controversy, within the Roman world, had been governed entirely by the expectations and mechanisms of Constantine's dispensation. The rivalries of churchmen and the intrusions of civil authority would have been inconceivable without that dispensation; and those with most at stake did little immediately to call it into question. After 381, however, religious disputes followed a different pattern. The Origenist and, to a lesser extent, the Pelagian controversies had explored, among other things, the further implications of humanity's potential 'likeness to God', asking how that potential was affected by the unique and total likeness of the Son to the Father – how, in other words, human beings could relate to so divine a saviour. In the later arguments about the nature of Jesus, about the relation between his humanity and his divinity, the bishops and other figures at the forefront of affairs were differently placed. They depended more on resources of their own making – on the personal loyalty of their 'people', often disaffected from the élite, and on bands of fanatics and armed retainers; less on those at the heart of the imperial system, whose ability to unify opinion and to enforce it with the power of the state was irreparably undermined by political faction, fiscal uncertainty and a tainted claim to the protection of God.

The two councils at Ephesus in 431 and Chalcedon in 451 were dominated by two concerns. The first was an enduring opposition to anything that remotely smacked of Sabellianism. That was clearly a hangover from the Arian controversy and its third-century antecedents. Any radical attack on Arius's position was inevitably exposed to the risk of exaggerating the suprahuman divinity of Jesus. The persistence of that danger had been highlighted in the teaching of Apollinarius of Laodicea, who did not die until the 390s. Apollinarius wrote more than has survived, and his influence (and obscurity) is attested not only by the reaction it provoked but also by the incorporation of his exegesis and even his theology into works attributed to writers of a more Nicene stamp. He forced theologians to recognize that the terminology of the Arian controversy needed further precision. The challenge at Nicaea had been to explain how a single *ousia* could be shared in by Father and Son. In its adherence to the term *homoousios*, the council had focused on what it saw as a single divine *phusis*, or 'nature'. Arius's subordinationism had drawn the divinity of the second person downwards, to associate it more closely with the humanity of Jesus. Apollinarius worried on that score about a loss of singleness in the godhead. He was, in a sense, more Nicene than Nicaea. A new problem was thus accentuated. Instead of worrying how a single *ousia*, the divine *phusis*, could be associated with more than one *hupostasis*, one was forced to ask how a single *hupostasis*, the second person of the Trinity, could be associated with two *phuseis*, one divine, the other human. Apollinarius himself failed to propose a lasting solution; but he had raised the crucial issue of individuality. How much of the core of any being was included under *hupostasis* and how much under *phusis*? If the being was divine, yet associated with a human *phusis*, how much of its divine identity could bear, as it were, association with a human body, soul or spirit? Debate had swung, in other words, from being to person. Such questions had not afflicted Arius and were little discussed by his opponents. Now they hung more ominously in the air.

Chief among the opponents of Apollinarius was an Antiochene friend of John Chrysostom, Theodore, who had just become bishop of Mopsuestia in Cilicia around the time Apollinarius died. In addition to displaying the *akribeia*, simplicity, and historical imagination associated with many Antiochene exegetes, Theodore concentrated further on the question of how Jesus could act as saviour of humanity. His solution was that Jesus had to experience genuine temptations and painful victories, in order to demonstrate how one could and should bring one's will into conformity with the will of God. While insisting that in Jesus the divine and the human were genuinely united in a single *prosōpon* or 'person', and that Jesus alone had made possible the virtue he represented, he was firm in his wish to safeguard

Jesus's full and genuine humanity. That complex, courageous and honest argument aroused the suspicion of Cyril of Alexandria – not helped by residual antagonism against the now dead Chrysostom. Cyril felt that Theodore had reduced Jesus to an encouraging example of human potential (a view attributed earlier to many Arians). He proceeded to create and attack a simple and unjust account of Theodore's speculations.

That brings us to the second major concern of the subsequent councils, the teaching of Nestorius (d. *c.* 451). Nestorius was also from Antioch, and had been taught for a while by Theodore of Mopsuestia. His consequent opposition to Apollinarius took a specific turn after his consecration as bishop of Constantinople in 428, when it became more widely known that he distrusted the use of 'mother of God' as an epithet for Mary. (The title *theotokos* – literally, 'God-bearer' – had been in popular use long before the fourth century. 'Mother of God' corresponds more exactly to the later Latin epithet, *dei genetrix*.) It is uncertain how matters might have proceeded, had it not been for the fact that Nestorius intervened in a dispute between Cyril and certain persons who had complained at court about his violent behaviour. Cyril's counter-ploy was to suggest that Nestorius was a heretic and therefore unauthorized to censure him. The theological charge, scurrilously propagated, revolved around the unsubtle notion that to deny the use of the title *theotokos* was to deny the divine nature of Jesus. Nestorius was linked with Paul of Samosata. Cyril was also careful to cultivate the support of Pulcheria (no lover of Nestorius) as a way of wooing Theodosius II away from his favoured bishop. In addition to thus fostering suspicions, Cyril addressed Nestorius directly, and thereby laid out the terms of debate for the coming twenty years. He recognized that it was appropriate to distinguish a divine from a human nature, but was reluctant to accept their genuine distinction in the incarnate Word, thus strengthening the 'single nature' argument – what came to be labelled 'Monophysite'. His own unifying principle was the old notion of *hupostasis*, which implied (as he explicitly insisted) that the human experiences of Jesus were properly applied to the godhead. God had been born in Bethlehem and God had suffered and died on Calvary. Finally, Cyril did what he could to attract the support of Celestine, bishop of Rome, playing on his anger that Nestorius had appeared to favour disciples of Pelagius (who by this time was probably dead).

The Council of Ephesus was summoned by the emperor; but its proceedings were dominated by violent partisans, many of them monks, and by the jealousies of eastern bishops, especially the rivalry between Antioch (a natural supporter of Nestorius) and Jerusalem (increasingly eager to capitalize on its popularity as a centre of pilgrimage). Ephesus represented also the power of popular devotion: for the theological reasonableness of Nestorius's position was successfully obscured by simpler loyalties to the notion that God had humbled himself in the Incarnation without prejudice to his divinity. However, a definitive proclamation was never forthcoming. The 'council' was in fact a fragmented affair, in which rival groups of bishops condemned one another, and the sharply reduced significance of the emperor was betrayed by the fact that he declared everyone in the right and then imprisoned most of them. Nestorius, worn down by Cyril's intrigues, simply resigned; but then Cyril found himself forced to accept a 'two-nature' formula drafted by Theodoret of Cyrrhus, which (not surprisingly, given Theodoret's associations) preserved intact much of the Antiochene position.

Within a few years, it became obvious that Ephesus had left the serious issues unresolved. By the end of the decade, Theodoret of Cyrrhus and Ibas of Edessa, another advocate of Theodore of Mopsuestia, controlled much of the theological debate. Against them, naturally, after 444, Cyril's successor at Alexandria, Dioscorus, marshalled his supporters, depending heavily on the patronage of Chrysaphius and his mentor Eutyches. Amid a fiery exchange of pamphlets, Theodosius II decided to call another council – impelled partly by a desire for unity but partly by the capacity of the dispute to confuse or undermine the politics of the court. A fateful development was the involvement of Leo, bishop of Rome, who produced for consideration at the council his so-called *Tome*, which attacked Eutyches, insisted on the distinction of two natures, and brought ironic consolation to the aging Nestorius. However, the *Tome* was ignored. Theodosius's council of 449 (the *latrocinium*, as Leo called it, 'the den of thieves') was controlled by Dioscorus and his powerful allies. Theodoret and Ibas were deposed.

Once again, imperial intervention, at least as envisaged by Theodosius, had failed. Initiative, still out of the emperor's hands, passed now to the infuriated Leo and to Pulcheria, ready to avenge herself on Chrysaphius. When Theodosius was suddenly killed in a riding accident, she had Chrysaphius executed and Eutyches exiled. She married Marcian, which symbolized a stronger military stance against the Huns but led also to the summoning of yet another council. Pulcheria was sure that this time she would dominate it, as she dominated her convenient husband. The leading churchmen of the East outside Alexandria suddenly discovered a common interest and banded against Dioscorus. Leo's *Tome* was read with reverence. The council's doctrinal formula, however, echoed (deliberately) some of the ambiguities that had immediately followed upon Ephesus in 431. Jesus, divine and human, was said to reside 'in' two 'natures' – the 'in' being Leo's conception – but to do so 'without confusion, change, division or separation' of those natures, while constituting at the same time a single *prosōpon* and *hupostasis*. The explanatory details, however, appeared to accept at least some of Cyril's earlier glosses, and Leo's Latin understanding did not, as events proved, coincide exactly with Greek interpretations. The prospect of enduring harmony was far from assured.

The label 'Chalcedonian' was soon to become, therefore, a slogan in further conflicts. Where the council had a more stable effect was in its legal and administrative prescriptions. Given the triumph involved for the Constantinopolitan élite, it is not surprising that they seized the opportunity to assert the importance of the capital at the expense of Alexandria and other major sees in the East. Warm relations with Leo may have encouraged the move, but he viewed the declaration with considerable suspicion. His surprisingly prolonged reluctance to endorse the council should have warned the easterners that they had taken too much for granted. The structures of civil government in the West were just then being further weakened; bishops throughout the Latin provinces were acquiring greater independence from imperial control; and Leo and his Roman successors became increasingly aware of their power to enforce in the region the primacy they had for a long time claimed. While Constantinople deserved respect, it could not be tolerated as an equal. The council's other crucial assertion was that bishops were to enjoy unchallenged authority over monks – at least in the foundation of monasteries (which were to be the norm for ascetic society) and in their external relations. The assembled episcopate was reacting in part to the dangerous liberties ascetics had asserted during recent decades, when they infiltrated factions and took to the streets. It was an important victory, and did much to govern relations between clerics and ascetics thereafter.

Many histories of early Christianity are content to close at this point. By the middle of the fifth century, the so-called 'fall of the western empire', coupled with increasing barbarian encroachment, seems to herald a period recognizably 'medieval'. In the East, the unrelenting estrangement of so much of Syria and Egypt, bound together by opposition to Chalcedon, creates a world more apparently 'Byzantine', especially when augmented by the reciprocal suspicions of Constantinople and Rome. The imperial aspirations of Ostrogothic rule in Italy and Justinian's grand schemes for Mediterranean unification proved hollow, not least because of their mutual incompatibility. I have tried, however, to suggest in this chapter a different interpretation.

Having embarked on one experiment under Constantine, Christian leaders in the old Roman world were now embarking on another. The fresh adventure was prompted in part by unease at what 'Christian empire' had begun to imply, and in part by the disturbing though genuine opportunities presented by weak government and alien settlement; but it depended also on a reversion to long-standing ideals. The 'crisis' I have described generated novel conceptions of destiny and order, but drew upon long-standing customs and habits. While it is proper, therefore, to keep 'late antiquity' in play for longer than used to be thought possible, we should not forget the implication: namely, that the Christian past, like the Roman past, was a storehouse from which one could draw forth both old things and new.

Further reading

I omit general studies of the Roman empire in this period; but, on some of the issues covered in this chapter, see Richard Lim, *Public Disputation, Power, and Social Order in Late Antiquity* (Berkeley, CA: University of California Press, 1995), Jill Harries, *Law and Empire in Late Antiquity* (Cambridge and New York, NY: Cambridge University Press, 1999) and Clifford Ando, *Imperial Ideology and Provincial Loyalty in the Roman Empire* (Berkeley, CA: University of California Press, 2000). One of the most stimulating reinterpretations of barbarian settlement is C.R. Whittaker, *Frontiers of the Roman Empire: a Social and Economic Study* (Baltimore, MD: Johns Hopkins University Press, 1994).

On the major controversies covered in this chapter, see (on 'Origenism') Elizabeth A. Clark, *The Origenist Controversy: the Cultural Construction of an Early Christian Debate* (Princeton, NJ: Princeton University Press, 1992) – a topic covered also in biographies of Jerome and Chrysostom (see below) – and (on Pelagius, the most authoritative work being in other languages) older studies that include John Ferguson, *Pelagius: a Historical and Theological Study* (Cambridge: Heffer, 1956), two books by Robert F. Evans, *Four Letters of Pelagius* (New York, NY: Seabury Press, 1968) and *Pelagius: Inquiries and Reappraisals* (New York, NY: Seabury Press, 1968) and B.R. Rees, *Pelagius: Life and Letters* (Rochester, NY: Boydell Press, 1998), which combines in revised form work first published in 1988 and 1991; and then more recent work, especially Theodore de Bruyn's introduction to *Pelagius's Commentary on St Paul's Epistle to the Romans* (Oxford: Oxford University Press, 1993). Two provoking essays by Peter Brown are reprinted in his *Religion and Society in the Age of Saint Augustine* (London: Faber, 1972): 'Pelagius and his Supporters' (1968), pp. 183–207, and 'The Patrons of Pelagius: the Roman Aristocracy between East and West' (1970), pp. 208–26. On the Councils of Ephesus and

Chalcedon, general histories of the church in that period will offer full accounts, to which one may add Timothy E. Gregory, *Vox Populi: Popular Opinion and Violence in the Religious Controversies of the Fifth Century AD* (Columbus, OH: Ohio State University Press, 1979).

For studies of major figures, see Neil B. McLynn, *Ambrose of Milan: Church and Court at a Christian Capital* (Berkeley, CA: University of California Press, 1994), J.N.D. Kelly, *Jerome: his Life, Writings, and Controversies* (London: Duckworth, 1975), Dennis E. Trout, *Paulinus of Nola: Life, Letters, and Poems* (Berkeley, CA: University of California Press, 1999), J.C. Baur, *John Chrysostom and his Time*, translated by M. Gonzaga, 2nd edn (Vaduz: Buchervertriebanstalt, 1988), J.N.D. Kelly, *Golden Mouth: the Story of John Chrysostom – Ascetic, Preacher, Bishop* (London: Duckworth, 1995), Wendy Mayer and Pauline Allen, *John Chrysostom* (London and New York, NY: Routledge, 2000), Sebastian Brock, *The Luminous Eye: the Spiritual World Vision of Saint Ephrem* (1985) (reprinted Kalamazoo, MI: Cistercian Publications, 1992) and (by the same author) *From Ephrem to Romanos: Interactions between Syriac and Greek in Late Antiquity* (Aldershot: Ashgate, 1999). On Augustine, the standard work remains Peter Brown, *Augustine of Hippo* (1967), now reissued with extensive bibliographical additions and a long and new 'Epilogue' (Berkeley, CA: University of California Press, 2000). See also, among a host of studies, R.A. Markus, *Saeculum: History and Society in the Theology of St Augustine* (Cambridge: Cambridge University Press, 1970).

The literature on asceticism is extensive. Classic studies are Derwas J. Chitty, *The Desert a City: an Introduction to the Study of Egyptian and Palestinian Monasticism under the Christian Empire* (Oxford: Blackwell, 1966), and a paper by Peter Brown, 'The Rise and Function of the Holy Man in Late Antiquity' (1971), reprinted in his *Society and the Holy in Late Antiquity* (Berkeley, CA: University of California Press, 1982), pp. 103–52. A more recent assessment: Douglas Burton-Christie, *The Word in the Desert: Scripture and the Quest for Holiness in Early Christian Monasticism* (New York, NY and Oxford: Oxford University Press, 1993). For my own views, see Philip Rousseau, *Ascetics, Authority and the Church in the Age of Jerome and Cassian* (Oxford: Oxford University Press, 1978), *Pachomius: the Making of a Community in Fourth-Century Egypt* (Berkeley, CA: University of California Press, 1985; paperback edition with a new preface, 1999) and the chapter 'Monasticism' in *The Cambridge Ancient History*, XIV, edited by Averil Cameron, Bryan Ward-Perkins and Michael Whitby (Cambridge: Cambridge University Press, 2000), pp. 745–80. Our notion of 'the desert' has been fundamentally modified by James E. Goehring: see his collected papers, *Ascetics, Society, and the Desert:*

Studies in Early Egyptian Monasticism (Harrisburg, PA: Trinity Press International, 1999). For more particular issues, see Elizabeth A. Clark, *Ascetic Piety and Women's Faith: Essays in Late Ancient Christianity* (Lewiston, NY: Edwin Mellen Press, 1986), Yizhar Hirschfeld, *The Judean Desert Monasteries in the Byzantine Period* (New Haven, CT and London: Yale University Press, 1992) and Susanna Elm, *Virgins of God: the Making of Asceticism in Late Antiquity* (Oxford: Oxford University Press, 1993). On ascetic literature, see Patricia L. Cox, *Biography in Late Antiquity: a Quest for the Holy Man* (Berkeley, CA: University of California Press, 1983). A more general emphasis is made by Vincent L. Wimbush and Richard Valantasis (eds), *Asceticism* (New York, NY: Oxford University Press, 1995) and Geoffrey Galt Harpham, *The Ascetic Imperative in Culture and Criticism* (Chicago, IL: University of Chicago Press, 1987).

Where to begin?
Richard Lim, *Public Disputation, Power, and Social Order in Late Antiquity.*

Chapter 9

AN ANCIENT LEGACY AND ITS POST-ROMAN FUTURE

The interplay between the old and the new is one of the more arresting features of the period. The notion that a species of disillusionment allowed the reassertion of old patterns of belief and social order, which then in turn had to cope with unforeseen novelties, has fundamental consequences for our understanding of what those novelties were, and of their religious character. Older notions of 'decline and fall', of a catastrophic hiatus in Mediterranean history, have been greatly modified by historical research in recent decades; and the question arises whether 'ancient Christianity', as a definable phase in time, had been brought to some kind of closure by barbarian settlement and by divisions between East and West.

There is no doubt that the bitter and complex struggles I have just described delivered a great shock to the Roman system. By the end of the sixth century, imperial authority and control had been drained from many areas. Leadership in the western provinces had passed into the hands of barbarian kings, who dealt rather differently with provincial élites and Christian bishops (many of whom welcomed, or at least turned to advantage, their dominance). Scarcely less in the East, the power of the emperor and his associates had been gravely challenged – by political instability, economic weakness, Persian aggrandizement and further barbarian incursions in the Balkans – while doctrinal division was no less serious a threat than the enduring Arianism of barbarians in the West.

So there seems to have been little left of a world that Constantine would have recognized. Yet Roman culture had not collapsed entirely. Nor can we rest content with supposing that it survived only in the East, in 'Byzantine' form, while disappearing in the West. That would be to underestimate the enduring *romanitas* of the western provinces, and to misinterpret the continuity in the East between the fourth century and the sixth. Both the Frankish king Clovis (d. 511) and the emperor Justinian (d. 565) appealed, and were understood by their contemporaries to have appealed, to the legacy of Constantine. Their claim — and this is where confusion can arise — was both political and religious in character, and affected in turn the conduct and self-understanding of religious leaders, in both parts of the old empire. Nevertheless, even at a political level, we see, throughout the Mediterranean world, the application of traditional principles to novel situations. We might feel today a certain thrill, as we peer, apparently, over the lip of history into a medieval or a Byzantine world. People at the time, however, were for the most part committed to the notion that much of the old order remained in place (including a surprising degree of the religious sentiment that went with it); and their readiness to adapt was entirely bound up with their desire to preserve their ancient values. The 'crisis' of the previous chapter — and this is what made it particularly dangerous — was constantly disguised by habits of mind.

THE ENDURING INFLUENCE OF AN OLDER WORLD

To what extent were Christians of the fifth and sixth centuries justified in that sense of their antiquity? It is beyond dispute that many ancient features had been inherited and fostered within the Christian empire — the episcopate, the sacraments, the biblical culture, elements of doctrine and dedication to asceticism. Bishops continued to consecrate successors, defend their dioceses, and attend synods and councils. They jealously guarded their administration of baptism and the eucharist, and their right to preach or allow others to preach. They depended upon, and often contributed to, textual scholarship, careful interpretation and the literary creation of a past that Christians could claim for themselves. The notion of orthodoxy, so crucial to their status, brought many of those strands together — office, rite, interpretation and heritage. The ascetic tradition, not yet hardened into a 'monastic' form, continued to challenge Christians generally and to protect, in the old style, virginity and widowhood, discipline and virtue. All those religious forms were as evident at the end of our period as they were at the beginning, and showed no signs of diminution.

Wherein resided the change, therefore? Let us set up three areas of inquiry, government, law and art — bearing in mind the question we want to pose: were they marked most by a shift in religious perspective? First, the emperors had obviously ceded some authority to ambitious provincials and assertive barbarians. They were increasingly restricted (at least from the time of Arcadius and Honorius, after 395) within the imperial courts at Constantinople and Ravenna. Either as a cause or as a result (an issue yet to be resolved), there raged around them a contest between political philosophies; and the contest frequently acquired religious colouring, not least because it appeared to be based on rival appeals to the religious past. Barbarian threat prompted in some a renewed loyalty to the old gods: they blamed the empire's misfortunes on what they saw as a newer faith. Christians, on the other hand, regarded traditional cults as the root cause of God's disfavour: those cults had betrayed and undermined the hallowed bargain between human morality and divine power, upon which the stability of the empire had long depended.

But did that conflict (so typical of Ambrose's generation and of the years following the death of Theodosius) constitute a genuine change at the religious level? Did it reflect simply the final demise of one religious tradition and the new-found confidence of another? The 'survival of paganism' should not be underestimated, certainly; but, more particularly, one has to be struck by the extent to which the two contesting parties were within themselves divided over method. Each asked whether one should handle Goths or Huns with military vigour or subtle diplomacy. How was any kind of religious conservatism, of fidelity to the past, supposed to bear political and strategic fruit? For all their mutual recrimination, each party came up with more than one answer. On the Christian side, for example, during the reign of Theodosius II, the piety of Pulcheria was pitted against the accommodations of Chrysaphius. Pulcheria was then content to support the unambiguous aggression of Marcian against Attila, while the energies of churchmen were deflected to the resolution of Christological conflict.

One is led to suspect, therefore, that neither insinuating eunuchs nor overzealous virgins provoked a disagreement that was exclusively religious. If Pulcheria and her minions were for a time triumphant, it did not mean that a novel form of Christianity had captured or subverted the engines of government. Plenty of pagans distrusted eunuchs, and plenty of Christians questioned the elevation of virginity. The matter is illustrated in a comparable way by the reign of Justinian. According to the contemporary historian Procopius, that emperor's effectiveness was threatened by an unhealthy confusion between the imperial family and the imperial state; a confusion symbolized (as he suggested) by the meddlesome hostility and hypocritical religiosity of the empress Theodora. Here was another woman who allowed personal principles and domestic jealousies to infect public policy. Such was the main drift of Procopius's notorious *Secret History*. But it was also a longstanding theme in Roman political literature; and one could argue that Procopius, for all his florid and embittered exaggeration, had put forward a perfectly reasonable argument. Justinian's wish to secure his authority depended as much on government reform and military adventure as on theological speculation and a mastery of religious symbolism; and it was administration and strategy that Theodora had done most to threaten.

Neither in Justinian's reign, therefore, nor in the century that preceded it, had there been a simple substitution of piety for politics. Post-Constantinian society witnessed familiar debates, brought to bear on inherited systems of government. The ostensible 'reinvention' of the Constantinian image, under Justinian especially, with all its religious overtones, was designed to address a loosening of political bonds – the disaffection of old élites, and modified definitions of loyalty towards the empire. Barbarian leaders in the West were also, for comparable reasons, keen to strike an imperial note: Athaulf the Visigoth was tempted to claim, according to Orosius, the legacy of Augustus; Theodoric the Ostrogoth, as I said, was likened in his time to Trajan; Clovis the Frank emerged from the baptismal font, according to Gregory of Tours, like a 'new Constantine'. Those were emphases carefully calculated to assuage anxiety and evoke deep memories among the self-conscious heirs of a revered polity.

Let us turn to other hallmarks of the period between Constantine and Justinian: reform of the law, and changes in artistic patronage. They have often been associated with a new era of Christian triumph; but they constantly recalled or appealed to older practice. Constantine created many legal opportunities previously withheld from Christians; but he did not, as I said earlier, subvert the laws of the empire in the name of Christianity. His principles of civic propriety – loyalty to the emperor, a sense of public duty, rights in property and marriage – were not radically different from those of Augustus. The religious complacency of the *Theodosian Code*, finally promulgated in 438, was a feature chiefly of its prologue. Its bombastic declarations against superstition and error were added as introductions to more cautious and often frustrated edicts drawn from the archives of earlier reigns. Justinian's *Corpus Iuris Civilis* of 532 – set up under the guidance of the great jurist (and non-Christian) Tribonian – made its fundamental appeal to ancient authorities, in spite of some rhetoric to the contrary. Its misleading simplicity and clarity attempted to disguise the older and sometimes conflicting liberties defended by great Roman jurists of the past. For all the forcefulness of its application, it failed in any case to destroy the customs it so haughtily attempted to erase from legal memory. Justinian's treatment of women and slaves may suggest the inspiration of Christianity; but his changes were moderate, and reflected longstanding sentiment. Frequent reference in the *Corpus* to equality, freedom and natural law reiterated old Roman principles. Indeed, the outwardly Christian setting in which accommodation was made in matters of marriage and enslavement may even have postponed any genuine relief: for it could now be argued that perfect justice was to be found only in the next world. So, in a way characteristic of Justinian, the bravura of reform was allowed to reinforce the oppression of an older culture. Nothing illustrates more clearly the divorce between rhetoric and policy. On the one hand, Justinian adopted the old mantle of Constantine in order to retain control over new circumstance. On the other hand, in his legislation, he played the role of Moses and Solomon (novel in an emperor) to enforce a Roman code of practice. Meanwhile, in the West, the legislation articulated in the canons of councils reflected the ambitions of the kings who patronized them. They focused as much on behaviour and contractual obligations as on purity of doctrine and clerical order. Bishops, for their part, looked to the power of the state to enforce their decrees.

Turning to the public patronage of art, we do seem to have vivid and tangible evidence of a new order in the Christian empire. As I described in Chapter 7, Constantine and his immediate successors had set the pace, particularly in Constantinople and Palestine. The wealthy laity was not slow to imitate them. Every modest city with a Christian community now housed its devotion in a structure modelled on the greatest basilicas. However, the inclination to civic munificence, providing one's city with public spaces beautiful and useful enough to attract a clientele and clinch an enduring reputation, had been indulged long before the establishment of Christianity. The inclination was affected, certainly, by a new species of competition between, on the one hand, mouldering temples starved of funds and, on the other hand, churches, monasteries and hospices; and the latter were in some instances placed in less favoured quarters and beyond the walls. But, where sudden expansion or fresh importance was matched by a strong Christian presence (as in Trier and Milan in the West and Constantinople and Jerusalem in the East), they could occupy the heart of the city, bold and impressive in their fresh stonework and exuberant décor.

Three other factors need to be noted. First, the new spaces thus created were designed to frame rituals – processions, hymns and more loosely structured celebrations – that had long been a feature of urban life. Christianity did not merely appropriate a calendar of older festivities, but aped the choreography of older religions. Second, Christian emperors inherited from their predecessors a shrewd understanding of public display, and were never slow to colonize the new liturgical space, endowing buildings and installing statuary, frescoes and mosaics that honoured their own authority as well as God's. In Constantinople, they even inserted their own persons into the ceremonial that now surrounded churches and attendant structures. Most of the emperors before Constantine, especially within the sacred spaces of the old Roman religion, had shown a comparable appreciation of the influence thus enhanced. Third, early Christian art — its techniques, its iconographical themes, even the very postures and gestures of its figures — was deeply indebted to non-Christian antecedents. The same was true of church buildings. Only as one moves into the later fifth century does one begin to see an inventiveness that can be described as specifically Christian: stylized images of holiness, the figures displaced from material circumstance; and churches that explored the potential of cruciform layout and domed roofs — the forms that we now think of as typically 'Byzantine'.

Styles of leadership, therefore, the force of law, even the visible fabric of public life, brought no 'ending'. Alongside the specifically Christian antiquity of bishops, sacraments, Scripture and morality, a Roman quality, older still, continued to colour the notions of authority, public order and urban life. There was a recognizable identity of emotion, of aesthetic response, in the flamboyant processions of an emperor or aristocrat and the reception of a bishop by monks and virgins: the same sense of crowded exuberance, dust and noise, singing, colour and torchlight, cautious deference and rigid protocol. Constantius II, described by Ammianus Marcellinus entering Rome in 356, and Victricius of Rouen, pictured by Paulinus of Nola receiving visitors in his Gallic 'Jerusalem' some fifty years later, occupied similar worlds. When Sulpicius Severus recounted his vision of his patron Martin of Tours, he depicted the saint with the dress and gesture of an emperor.

Instead of an end, therefore, one is faced with a gathering momentum of adjustments, rooted in a past non-Christian as well as Christian, and destined to affect the Mediterranean world long after Gregory the Great. 'Byzantine' society — the world of Constantine, Arcadius, Theodosius II, Anastasius and Justinian — was enduringly 'Roman'. The emperors symbolized a necessary liaison between past and present, between the human order and the divine. In that achievement, they were the heirs of Augustus and Hadrian, as well as vicars of Christ. The West was not so much severed from that imperial legacy as dependent upon it. Popes from Leo to Gregory (440–604) were wholly engaged with Constantinople and other sectors of eastern church life. No church council with ecumenical pretensions could content itself with a western membership until long after our period. No westerner, after 476, could make a convincing claim to the imperial title until Charlemagne. On the contrary, the emperors in Constantinople not only claimed but often exercised direct authority in parts of the old western provinces; and many who lived there continued to regard themselves as their subjects. Local church councils upheld the doctrinal decisions of Nicaea and Chalcedon, and took note of eastern ordinances: significant divergence becomes evident only in the 'Trullan' synod of 692. Largely for economic reasons, Theodoric the Ostrogoth would be the last notable builder on an imperial scale for more than two hundred years; but, throughout Italy and Gaul, churches and other religious buildings of more modest proportions were built and added to in traditional styles. Theodoric himself, 'king of the Goths and Romans in Italy', attracted the loyalty of the old aristocracy and held, for short periods, large parts of Gaul, Spain and North Africa in a single confederation of loyalties, while remaining duly deferential to Anastasius and Justin I. He and leaders like him (especially among the Franks and Visigoths), by their laws, their court culture and their religion, preserved an ideal of integrated social order and political unity that could only be described as 'Roman'.

THE TRIUMPH OF BARBARISM?

Within this context of enduring *romanitas* and the reassertion, among Christians, of traditional anxieties and social forms, we have to fit the settlement of barbarians on Roman soil and the associated or resulting estrangement of the West from the East. For they constituted the unavoidable reverse of the same coin; compatible with – indeed, sometimes instrumental in – the survival of tradition, yet (in the case of the barbarians) startlingly, even distressingly different in their appearance, conduct and political ambition. This is what I described above as the 'great shock to the Roman system'. Within the Christian setting, it appears to have been accompanied by religious novelties. This was the age in which miracle stories began to abound, 'holy men' attracted adulation, sacred bones were revered: all betokening developments in literature, pilgrimage and church architecture. Those developments have been taken by some, since the time of Gibbon, as symptoms of decay, the assertion of a less rational, more demotic religiosity. If one thinks of barbarians as alien and uncouth, it is easy to suggest a connection between their arrival and this supposed increase in credulous fantasy. Or else the barbarians are seen as heralds of a specifically 'Germanic' Christianity, different in its view of the self and the world. One claims to discover a temper to their faith, a sense of virtue, that was absent from the Roman past.

Romans themselves, continuing to write on the basis of traditional philosophical and political preoccupations, do not always help us to achieve clarity of interpretation. The presence of barbarians seems at times to have scarcely ruffled their self-assurance. They were not familiar with their social structures, and knew little of what was going on in their heads. The fourth-century historian Ammianus Marcellinus thought the intruders unpredictable and treacherous, as irrational as animals. They seemed to embody all that was contrary to well-argued policy and a sense of moral values. Writing some fifty years later, when settlement in the West was a fait accompli, and Visigoths, Burgundians and Vandals were more familiar figures, Salvian of Marseille felt able, as I said in the previous chapter, to admire their liberty and probity, which he hoped would put Romans to shame. Yet both men took for granted the values of their own ancestors. Christians might suggest, as had Lactantius and Eusebius, that misfortune was a punishment for infidelity and sin; but the world they hoped to regain by a reform of morals was still recognizably Roman. The Welshman Gildas, writing his *Ruin of Britain* a century again after Salvian, made the same point in even less settled circumstances (when Saxon raiders were causing real havoc among the Romano-Britons).

The barbarians, for their part, tell us nothing, for they were illiterate, or at least what literacy they possessed was Greek or Latin. The Bible had been translated into Gothic – sections have survived – but, after the first firm agreement with the Visigoths in 382, the settled barbarians mingled with the Roman population, and their leaders spoke the languages of their hosts. The barbarian *mentalité* was filtered to Romans themselves through those languages. Even when barbarians find their voice – in the *Gothic History* of Jordanes, for example, written in the 540s – native sentiment and culture are obscured by an adopted tongue. The *Histories* of Gregory of Tours, written in the 590s, show how relentlessly barbarian memory could be smothered by Roman supposition. When the Frankish king Clovis rehearses, in Gregory's text, his genealogy, his divine ancestors are given Roman names – Saturn, Jupiter, Mercury and Mars. By the time Isidore of Seville came to write his *History of the Goths* some two decades later, the Visigoths of Spain could be presented, in all their de facto isolation, as the last of the true Romans. The archaeological record that has revealed so much about Celtic or Near Eastern religion has virtually nothing 'German' to offer us in the actual areas of settlement. The refugee bands clamouring for entry into the Roman provinces had been tiny in relation to the populations among whom they settled – no more than tens of thousands in any one area. Intermittent plunder magnified their presence in misleading ways. Their leaders, anxious to share in the offices of the Roman military high command, allowed their followers to cluster as soldiers around specific centres – Toulouse, Carthage, Paris. It was hardly a recipe for widespread cultural impact.

The barbarians were also Christian, loyal to the Arianism of the missionaries who had first moved among them, and to the Arian emperor Valens, who had first encouraged (in the case of the Goths) their settlement. Such loyalty, as I suggested in the previous chapter, strained relations with the Roman population. Yet few of them oppressed their Nicene neighbours. They sought toleration for themselves as much as conformity in others. The Ostrogoth Theodoric, during his government of Italy (493–526), was firm but cordial in his approach to his Catholic subjects. The notable exceptions were Euric the Visigoth (466–85) and Huneric the Vandal (477–84), ready enough to maim, murder or exile, and to expropriate churches and lands. (The accounts provided by Sidonius Apollinaris in his letters and by Victor of Vita's *History of the Persecution in Africa* are embellished and partisan, but still convincing.) The Vandals were particularly persistent in persecution, and did little more than modify that policy between Huneric's death and the destruction of their kingdom in 534. Clovis, however, was baptized by a Catholic bishop in the later 490s, the Burgundian Sigismund renounced Arianism in 516, the Visigoths in Spain accepted Catholicism under Reccared in 589, and the Lombards, after their entry into Italy in 568, were at least partly inclined to a Catholic loyalty. Their rapport with Rome is less than surprising. The collapse of the Vandals and Ostrogoths before the armies of Justinian in the 530s cannot be explained simply by their religious intransigence. They were unlucky enough to lie close to the territory of an emperor intent on domination and affronted by their entrenchment in traditional centres of Mediterranean power. Franks and Visigoths in Gaul and Spain were much less seriously affected.

So, just as Romanization may have hidden, disguised or even corrupted their own culture, the relatively small numbers of the barbarians and their early Christianization make it difficult to believe that they subjected their new religion to an 'alien' influence. The apparently 'post-classical' elements discernible in the Christianity of the fifth and sixth centuries – the adaptation of non-Christian practices, the growing interest in miracles and the popularity of hagiography and the virtues it prescribed – were often developments within the provincial cultures of the Roman world, not intrusions from outside it.

Spectacular opposition to the old cults is not hard to find. The destruction of the Serapaeum and the shameful murder of Hypatia were echoed in the razing of Gaza's temple of Marnas in the middle of the fifth century. But for every prominent target of such a sort, urban and readily accessible to bishops, thousands of ordinary folk in the country areas frustrated any effort to wean them from the rituals of the past. Roman Christianity was slow to reach beyond the city. When it did, it met with a stoutly built tradition, indifferent to the queries of outsiders, less intelligible to sophisticated minds than the wearied loyalties of the old élite. City people despised peasants, and saw no charm in rusticity. Peasants for their part had long made sense of their world without the aid of Greek or Latin culture. Closer engagement between the two groups was hard for contemporaries to envisage, and promised for that reason to be startling.

A number of conditions had first to be fulfilled, before such interaction could be realized. Rural life had to stand for more than a landowner's income or the revenue of the state. The rural setting needed to suggest, if not offer, tranquillity for the spirit. One had to value for its own sake the 'simplicity' of the peasant. Wealth, bustle and sophistication, in other words, had to become dispensable. Old Romans, although highly moral and philosophically earnest, often found it difficult to define their self-denial in such terms. Eunapius's *Lives of the Sophists*, for example, written in the late 390s, depict men and women of property and learning, committed to teaching in town. When great senators took their periodic rest from public office, they carried their wealth and learning with them to their villas. Estate management and quiet reading enhanced those qualities, while correspondence and hospitality kept them in touch with the political milieu that guaranteed their status. Moral achievement in the ancient world, even for those with less obvious power, was wholly interwoven with study and rhetorical brilliance. The Christians who read Basil's *Address to Young Men* or Augustine's *On Christian Doctrine* would not have been markedly different. Even Jerome, personally abstemious though he may have been, lived in cities amid his books and under the patronage of the well born. His protestations to the contrary were only a reaction to his constantly resented exile.

Christians would have found it just as hard as their opponents, therefore, to break away from urbanity and refinement. Works like the *Life of Antony* and the *Life of Martin* may suggest that the attempt was being made. Antony spends his religious life in desolate country. Martin, even as a bishop, maintains his deprivations, flouts the sensibilities of his peers and presses fearlessly into the Gallic countryside in search of mountebanks and shrines.

They appear to abandon the urban heartland of the ancient world. Yet both biographies observe events from a cultivated viewpoint. The authors themselves are not rustic. They attack heresy and understand a churchman's anxieties and responsibilities. Their rough heroes are wrapped in polished prose. That they apologized for the fact was itself a symptom of literary erudition. Where they feared aloud how their 'simple' story might be received, they anticipated and catered for more polished expectations. The effect of such literature, with its roots in the biographical traditions of Greece and Rome, I have already touched upon in the previous chapter: a release of the reader from circumstance, which served nevertheless to sponsor a fresh impression of the self. Fewer and fewer of those thus affected ever expected to see a 'holy man' in the flesh. As for the urban heartland, those who passed through institutions of ascetic formation, like the great island monastery of Lérins in the early decades of the fifth century, could soon find themselves immersed again as bishops in the cities of southern Gaul. Honoratus, who founded Lérins, and was bishop of Arles 426–29, was only the first of a long line.

The 'desert scene' in Gaul had already been transformed into less fearful peaks and woodlands. Cassian (writing for patrons who were churchmen) deplored the associated loss of eastern vigour (which he somewhat artificially reproduced in his *Conferences*), yet happily began to cater for it. Compared with the heroes of ostensibly 'real' deserts in the East, most religious enthusiasts in the West lived in less challenging surroundings – although, as we have already seen, the same was true for the majority of their eastern counterparts. Hagiography was designed less to describe ascetics in literal terms than to reduce by calculated imagery the estrangement of distance. Eucherius of Lyon's *Praise of the Desert* provides an apposite example. He portrayed Lérins, his monastery, as at once a sanctum for the souls of his readers and the seedbed of city bishops. His companions (he became a bishop himself in 434) had withdrawn like Moses into the desert, in order that they might re-emerge as leaders – transformed from 'pastors of sheep' to 'pastors of their people'. Similar points can be made about miracle stories. Martin's destruction of a tree sacred to non-Christians, for example, was not designed to assure readers that rural evangelization was well under way, but rather that their new-found faith was not threatened by the obdurate ignorance of peasants; that they would not court disaster if they loosened a little the hold of their ancient culture; that they could welcome, as authoritative leaders of their communities, men who had gained the admiration, or at least the obedience, of more simple souls. Miracles, like the sanctity of those who worked them, did not invite readers to adopt religious novelties, but reassured them in a faith they had already begun to embrace.

Not that the reassurance was without its critics. Augustine and Cassian, for example, preferred to deflect attention away from the spectacular. 'Why, it is asked, do no miracles occur nowadays?' One might say, as Augustine replied in Book 22 of his *City of God*, that with Christianity established they were no longer required. What did persist, on the other hand, was the more modest effect of sacrament and prayer, which avoided 'the blaze of publicity' associated with the miracles of Scripture. Augustine had already declared in the previous book that any wonder, contrived or otherwise, paled before 'that miracle of miracles, the world itself'. The true marvel for Cassian was a man's ability, aided by God's grace, to overcome the lure of the flesh; and he shared Augustine's fear (in the fifteenth book of his *Conferences*) that apparent miracles might be pulled off 'by the intrigue and deceit of demons'.

The hagiographers of the sixth-century West worked, therefore, under some pressure. The archdeacon Leunast, so Gregory of Tours informs us, was afflicted by cataracts, and sought the help of doctors. They brought no relief; but a long retreat before the feast of Martin improved the man's sight. Foolishly, as a follow-up, he consulted a Jew (so Gregory developed the tale). His blindness returned, and no amount of subsequent prayer could reverse the sentence. The villains of this story – doctors and Jews – were Gregory's competitors. What horrified him was that they had been welcomed by a senior cleric. Gregory the Great, in the preface to his *Dialogues*, compared miracles with Scripture: the latter 'teaches us how to attain virtue . . . whereas a description of miracles shows us how this acquired virtue reveals itself'. But he was untiring in his distinctions: almost every one of his stories includes a hesitation, a desire to instruct and warn. Sanctulus of Nursia produced miraculous oil and bread for local workers, but his 'inner virtue' was more important. Having released a captive of the Lombards, for whom he had stood as surety, he happily surrendered himself to execution. The attempted punishment was thwarted – the executioner was unable to bring down his sword – but the real wonder was the hero's willingness to give up his life for another.

Both stories were written by bishops. Gregory of Tours wrote at least his *Histories for* bishops. He was unrelenting in his defence of his own city and church, and in his opposition to heresy. Gregory the Great was more concerned to show that bishops could aspire to a holiness of their own. The portraits in his *Dialogues* have to be measured against his rather different work, the *Pastoral Care*, which became the Middle Ages' textbook on episcopacy. It places great faith in skilful oratory, a well-maintained presence, even-handed judgement and the careful disguise of any lack of confidence. He commanded bishops, in several letters, to keep their distance from ascetics – echoing in his way cautions expressed by the Council of Chalcedon. There were, however, two sides to such a prohibition. Ascetic culture was to be protected from undesirable interference (which showed how highly Gregory regarded it); but, as the *Dialogues* make clear, monks and wandering holy men were not to imagine that they might monopolize the authority that went with virtue. There had been, in spite of Chalcedon, a real danger of their trying to do so. The bishop Castorius, in another of Gregory's anecdotes, attempted to browbeat the abbot Equitius. Their mutual suspicion was probably based on Equitius's missionary enthusiasms. He 'went a greater distance than usual from the monastery'; he 'travelled about from one place to another'; he was able 'to find time, besides, for preaching in the churches of the surrounding hamlets and villages and for visiting even private dwellings'. Clergy urged the Pope, Gregory's predecessor, 'Let an order be issued for [Equitius] to come to Rome where he will learn to understand the discipline of the church.' Gregory, while admiring great ascetics like Benedict, would not have objected to such 'discipline'. The story makes clear the conflicting authorities among which both bishops and hagiographers were compelled to manoeuvre.

So the culture of the miraculous was not a symptom of popular superstition, barbarian or otherwise. Nor can one isolate or privilege the definitions of virtue that hagiography defended: the declarations of such texts betray by their forcefulness the doubts that were voiced by others against them. Gregory the Great, in his *Dialogues*, attached chief value to miracles that brought tangible advantage – health, rural productivity – or reinforced allegiance to right belief. His other writings and his practical endeavours had more to do with those 'pastoral' concerns than with canonizing the wondrous for its own sake. Too trusting a concentration on stylized behaviour within a text can distract us from the intended thrust of the writer. Whatever was 'wondrous' about Equitius was made by Gregory to reflect an authenticating light sideways onto 'preaching in the churches' – an action scarcely wondrous at all, but a key engagement between pastor and people. The abbot Eutychius, similarly, was 'very active in converting souls to God by his holy exhortations'. His monks, by contrast, were envious of other holy men, because they themselves 'could boast of no miracle for their master' – only after his death did Eutychius oblige them. The 'true preacher', according to Gregory, in the fourth book of his *Dialogues*, 'stretches out his arms at the end of his address and calms the troubled spirits of the assembled people, calling them back to one way of thinking'. The major effect was invisible. Thus were the principles of the *Dialogues* and the *Pastoral Care* allowed to intersect.

In the story of Equitius, with its reference to 'hamlets and villages', the indignation of the clergy reflected as much their enduring urbanism as their anxiety about 'the discipline of the church'. If pastors were to go that 'greater distance', they would have to modify existing norms. A bishop would have to extend his notion of 'the assembled people' – not by choosing a different audience, but by incorporating more and more sectors of society within it. Readers of saints' lives had been encouraged to travel away from town in their imaginations. Now the country people were encouraged by homiletic discourse to join the urban crowd. I observed in the last chapter how a bishop's sermon could create in an audience's mind a different conception of the community to which they belonged. I commented also on bishops' appropriation of the urban poor as a constituency peculiar to themselves. The other two processes now impinged upon them, aided by the shrinking size of some towns and a decline in agricultural productivity. The canons of church councils legislated increasingly for rural situations. The anniversaries of holy men and women were made occasions for regional gatherings, centred on shrines and churches over which bishops claimed or exercised patronal authority. A truncated hagiography was brought into play – abbreviated lives, rich in formulae and stripped of novelistic drama, read out to the people as part of the homiletic address. This was now the context for experienced wonder. Cures and exorcisms were obtained not by the vigorous theatricality of the eccentric but 'by [Christ's] sacrament', as Augustine had put it in the *City of God*, 'by the prayers or the memorials of his saints'.

It is within those homiletic and liturgical settings that one should look for an increase of 'popular' sentiment. Reference is made in the conciliar decrees of sixth-century Gaul, for example, to a range of less than Christian attitudes and practices. They are nevertheless recognizably Roman in character, betraying no obviously barbarian novelty. Homiletic attack on superstitions – concerning the safety of crops, for example – was heavily weighted towards pre-barbarian concerns. Inappropriate behaviour in graveyards – feasting and dancing; the burial of talismans – had long been frowned upon by Roman Christians. Augustine, writing in his *Confessions*, was clearly relieved that, 'instead of her basket full of the fruits of the earth', his mother Monica 'learned to bring to the shrines of the martyrs a heart full of prayers far purer'. Spells, sorcery, auguries and astrology had been catalogued and scorned by Varro and Pliny, and it was to such authorities that Augustine, and later Isidore of Seville, felt able to appeal. Warnings addressed by their bishop Caesarius to the 'careless and lukewarm Christians' of Arles, listing a florid range of beliefs and customs obviously still widespread, were based on that ancient tradition. His alternatives were Augustine's: sacrament, prayer and blessed oil. (Caesarius, originally a monk at Lérins, was bishop for forty years, from 502.)

A number of themes converge at this point. The conservative simplicity of the bulk of the people in both town and country, and the attempts of the clergy to win their hearts, are not enough to explain developments. The surviving texts reveal a series of dialogues among the cultured themselves: novel ways of bridging the gulf between town and country; efforts by the clergy to confound competitors; and a skilful alliance forged between apparent credulity and pastoral effectiveness. The story of Equitius offers further assistance. The abbot's missionary zeal was challenged first by a well-born layman, still alive and admired by Gregory. Prominent Christians of such a sort are often unobtrusive in the evidence that survives, but indubitably influential at the time. They could be at once the rivals and the allies of churchmen. Gregory's *Dialogues* catalogue their patronage of monasteries. The Syrian ascetic Isaac attracted 'men and women of high and low station', some of whom offered him estates on which to build. There was always a danger that such persons could eclipse or obstruct the authority of a bishop, especially when they possessed the power (not least over peasants) that went with rural property. Gregory of Tours describes a related danger. Desiderius, from Bordeaux, claimed to work miracles (dependent most on a vigorous physiotherapy), and 'the country folk flocked to him in crowds'. Eventually his deceits were 'comprehended by my people'; but Gregory could only ensure that he was 'expelled from the city boundaries'. He follows this story with another about a weird Spaniard, who paraded himself with phials of oil and reputed relics. He also claimed the support of King Chilperic (not one of Gregory's favourites). Leaving Tours, he gatecrashed the Rogations ceremonies at Paris, 'gathered round him a mob of ruffians and peasant-women, formed up his own procession, and prepared to visit the holy places'. After rough treatment at the hands of local clergy, the discovery of 'magic' roots and bones in his baggage, and some interrogation before a church council, the man was eventually exposed as a runaway servant of the bishop Amelius. Those stories show us that the attempt to reach out into country areas and undermine the attraction of longstanding traditions was not simply a matter of shouting more loudly to a less sophisticated audience. While the achievement of broadly based consensus was no doubt a preacher's aim, sermons and their liturgical settings were also social occasions, during which one might have to negotiate one's own claim to leadership in the presence of rivals with attractions and skills of their own.

The Roman character of those challenges and ploys – spells, incantations and a canny grasp of nature – is reflected in other enterprises. Churchmen, busy correcting the common people, reflected just as readily on the inner, spiritual person, whose salvation they continued to have at heart. Pastoral effort was more than a struggle for power. Amid the polemic of homily, hagiography and canon, protagonists found time to pen more theoretical treatises. Here, too, they reached into a non-barbarian past and engaged in debate with their cultured peers. Barbarian religion encouraged attention to Arianism, and the Pelagian controversy sustained bitter western faction in the fifth and sixth centuries. One is struck, nevertheless, by the ease with which doctrinal concern was joined to pastoral interest. Faustus of Riez (d. *c.* 490), writing *On Grace*, addressed most of the issues made familiar by Augustine, strove to safeguard the practical 'duty of service' without which God's grace would bear little fruit, and ended with detailed reference to the doctrine of the Trinity. Julianus Pomerius (writing *c.* 500) presented his work *On the Contemplative Life* in terms that recalled Augustine and anticipated Gregory the Great. He insisted that clergy who aspired to higher insight should also teach intelligibly, and that virtue demanded social engagement. Cassiodorus (d. *c.* 580), having retired from political service under the Ostrogothic kings of Italy, based his little treatise *On the Soul* on traditional philosophical arguments, focusing first on the ancient ideal of knowing oneself, and concluding with observations about created nature, freedom and grace. Those works illustrate how doctrinal controversy related constantly to the enduring theme of soul and world, and how the hurly-burly of pastoral engagement was informed by an ancient understanding of human personality.

HOW 'DIFFERENT' WAS THE EAST?

It used to be argued that the eastern empire 'survived' because it was richer and more densely populated than the West, and free from barbarian pressure. Hand in hand went the assumption that sixth-century Byzantine Christianity was indeed a survival, enshrining a tradition of authority and devotion that reached back with scarcely a break to the time of Constantine. I have said already that Justinian's world was remarkably conservative and certainly Roman; but equally important is the novelty of the circumstances that conservatism was invited to address. What were those circumstances? Although the wealth, population density and relative stability of eastern *municipia* did make a difference, both parts of the empire witnessed an important change in the relation between town and country. Competition between religious officialdom and lay piety was now played out in rural as well as urban milieux. (The shift affected élite loyalty generally, and the cohesion of the empire.) Towns were not exclusively under the thumbs of bishops, and the countryside was not exclusively the domain of ascetics. The pattern of fourth-century asceticism – based in villages and towns – persisted in urban or suburban monasteries, while bishops fretted over distant parishes and the obstinate error of rustics. Those with status, wealth and property loomed over both spheres; and the increasing development of large estates – both in Syria and Egypt, and in North Africa and Gaul – ensured that *territoria* were no less the region of contention. Archaeology reveals innumerable chapels and mini-basilicas scattered over the more intensely cultivated countryside – most of them a landowner's provision to workers and tenants. Both bishops and ascetics were heavily dependent on lay support, just at a time when the laity itself was intent upon building up new and more localized patterns of influence and dependence. The attempt to extend the territory of an effective pastorate beyond the city walls was precisely what generated competition among the pious.

Both kings and emperors attempted to preside effectively over those local competitors, and to offer a more central focus for both their ambition and their loyalty. To that extent, the archetypal figure of the new West, the barbarian king, was not as alien as his long hair, trousers or rough warrior guard might imply. In spite of their Arianism, which certainly modified the standing of Gaiseric or Euric (although not, of course, that of Clovis), they were as assiduous as any emperor in wooing the well born and the prosperous to their grander causes. Here, as I have suggested already, another development came to their aid. The royal heroes of the Old Testament – David and Solomon, for example – provided models that may have been close to their own hearts, and were certainly close to the hearts of the bishops who attempted to influence them. Even Gregory of Tours, with his image of Clovis as the 'new Constantine', more readily sought refuge in the vigorous record of ancient Israel's royal warriors. Old Testament themes became increasingly common in the clerical exhortations of the fifth and sixth centuries, which included allusions to clerical advantage: the alliance, or at least the interaction, of royalty with priestly and prophetic exemplars. The transformation of the Chosen People from a wandering tribe to a prosperous kingdom, a people of God, might have appealed, meanwhile, to the political ambitions of Vandals and Goths.

One should not rush to suppose, however, that such emphases could underpin a sharp contrast between East and West. Attachment to the Old Testament was hardly novel among Christian exegetes; and the Greeks were the leaders in that commitment. I noted, second, in Chapter 7 that the strident objections of unconverted (or apostasizing) littérateurs – that Greek and Latin literature belonged to them, and that Christians could not claim a culture as ancient or as blessed with textual beauty – had already given added edge to Christian interest in the biblical heritage, well before the fifth century. This is also a moment to repeat my earlier point, that the political aspirations of barbarian leaders had developed within the empire, and were coloured by models of authority and leadership entirely Roman in character. Even more striking, Alaric the Visigoth and Theodoric the Ostrogoth were both schooled at first in the Roman politics of the East: their specifically 'barbarian' endeavours in pursuit of land and new kingly status were conducted in the Balkans, and were closely embroiled in the politics of the eastern court, under both Arcadius and Zeno. Finally, the eastern Roman emperors themselves, more than the last of their western colleagues, claimed the heritage of Old Testament kings. Justinian in particular was conscious of his Old Testament roots. The most famous emblems of his achievement – the *Corpus Iuris Civilis*, the church of the Hagia Sophia in Constantinople and the mosaics at San Vitale in Ravenna – are heavy with the heritage of Solomon, of Moses the lawgiver and of Melchisedech the priest.

In many other respects, the 'barbarian' distinctions were not as sharp as they might at first seem. Visigoths and Ostrogoths affected the economy and politics of the East for decades before they were skilfully deflected westwards. At significant moments in the fifth century, before the more substantial and disastrous interventions of Justinian, the eastern government had demonstrated its sense of involvement in western affairs, particularly in expeditions against the Vandals. Constantinople had to contend later with two major confrontations with Persia in the sixth and seventh centuries, the second of which involved deep and longstanding invasion of Roman territory; and it acquired in the same period a persistent and dangerous 'barbarian problem' of its own, the encroachment of the Slavs upon the Balkans. Roman culture was no less 'threatened' in the East, therefore, than in the West. And given the assertive parochialism of provincial élites and the strategic stresses brought to bear upon the Balkans, it seems natural to ask about eastern Christianity the question already raised in relation to the West

– namely, were there signs of an end to ancient practice? We find that, just as adjustments in the West failed to subvert what remained an essentially Roman religion (even with a barbarian presence and a decline in imperial authority), so also in the East, the undoubted shifts in both religious sensibility and the exercise of power left the Roman heritage substantially unaffected.

The religious literature of the period helps to make the matter clear. Turning first to hagiography, the surviving corpus is a rich one. Large collections of anecdotes were bound together and added to by later monasteries: the *Sayings of the Fathers*, which first took shape among Egyptian exiles in southern Palestine during the early fifth century, and the *Spiritual Meadow* of John Moschus (d. 619), augmented by his friend Sophronius, the later bishop of Jerusalem (d. 638). There were more extended biographies, like those of Symeon and Daniel the Stylites and of Theodore of Sykeon. Somewhere between the two genres, and comparable to the *Lausiac History* of Palladius, were the works of Theodoret of Cyrrhus, John of Ephesus (d. 586) and Cyril of Scythopolis (d. after 560), which provide more formal and calculated accounts of eastern ascetics in the fifth and sixth centuries. Their predominant reference to Syria and Palestine places them at the heart of religious controversy as instruments in the contest between clerical and lay piety. Yet they describe religious practices entirely characteristic of eastern Mediterranean culture. The chain-laden constriction of a Syrian recluse or the exposed heroism of Symeon on his column (as described by Theodoret), the cave-dwellers of a Palestinian *lavra* (in the work of Cyril of Scythopolis), the rambling monasteries of Monophysite Syria (in the account by John of Ephesus), all represented developments based upon fourth-century patterns with long local pedigrees.

They were comparable, in other words, with their western counterparts, and were equally, of course, untouched by the 'peoples of the north'. The comparability rested on their sense of purpose. Again, one could not construct a social history merely on the basis of their apparent reportage. They never intended readers to become participants in a simple sally into the countryside. Rather, they respected and reassured the traditional prejudices of the urban élite, so that readers could make better sense of a more extended arena for their influence and advancement. Drawn in their imaginations into settings less familiar in 'political' terms, they were invited, by manipulative writers, to order in new ways both their patronage and their piety. And if the hagiography appears to plunge a modern reader into a whirl of post-Roman fanaticism, one has only to relate it to the measured advice, the *Instructions for the Help of Souls*, by Dorotheus of Gaza (d. in the late sixth century). Here was a man, equally a professional ascetic, inspired by the world-view of Plato, filtered through Origen and the Cappadocian Fathers. In any case, the bulk of the eastern material, in Syriac as well as in Greek, was written by clerics, often by bishops, who reached beyond a merely monastic clientele to other members of the pious élite. Ostensibly remote holy men are consistently portrayed as hosting the visits and fielding the inquiries of priests and laymen. With few exceptions – even the *Sayings of the Fathers* and the responses of Barsanuphius betray the anxiety – hagiography presents us with ascetic figures compelled, for all their oddity and spirit, to renegotiate the boundaries of authority and responsibility between themselves and the Christians of the towns.

Homilies give an analogous impression. The homilies of the late Roman East can seem formal and derivative, when placed beside the vivid appeals of a Caesarius in the West. Collections owed an enormous debt to Chrysostom (Ambrose and Augustine exerted a similar influence in Latin); but the fact that so few original homilies have survived may reflect the tastes of later compilers. The 'Trullan' synod of 692 instructed preachers to read out revered exemplars, rather than rely on their own ineptitude. In the sixth century itself, worshippers might just as easily find themselves addressed in verse, like that of Paul the Silentiary, as he celebrated the reconsecration of the Hagia Sophia in 562, or the hymns and metrical sermons of the Syrian Romanos Melodos, working in Constantinople from the 540s onwards. The latter in particular were wonderful creations, with lasting liturgical influence, although one wonders how many would have been able to appreciate them. A few sermons were more obviously tailored to the less sophisticated ear. Those of Leontius the presbyter, delivered in the 550s, are full of anecdotes and allusions that reflect the experiences and anxieties of the ordinary Christian. The fact that he was a simple priest may explain why he stands out in the surviving material. Bishops may have delegated more accessible oratory to their subordinates; and later compilers may have thought it less worthy of preservation. The greater density of settlement in the East meant that many rural communities were already close to a town, and therefore to its liturgical celebrations; but the sermon may also have given place to other forms of popular instruction. Religious ceremony remained awesome in its complexity. Churches were decorated with ever richer and instructive mosaics. The less educated attached increasing value to icons, which were no mere portraits, but full of imagery and historical associations, carrying the symbolism of the greatest basilica into the poorest home. Those able to read were provided with simple pamphlets, containing prayers and spiritual guidance. That varied engagement with the minds of their people was no doubt sustained by the wealth of the eastern churches; but one should not exaggerate the contrast with the West. Hymns, processions, frescoes and statuary — all cast in the Roman mould — were just as available there.

AFTER CHALCEDON: NESTORIANS AND MONOPHYSITES

If one still wished to choose, in the field of religion, an eastern event that marked at this point a watershed in Christian history and an irreversible estrangement from the West, it would have to be the Council of Chalcedon. That assembly brought to a new pitch the doctrinal controversies that reached back to Nicaea. It also set a new agenda, and helped to prise open latent fissures in the Roman world. I have described its canonical disposition of the ascetic life, which later hagiography would often thereafter defend. Bishops asserted themselves (with some optimism) against the anarchic enthusiasms that had accompanied the rise of the 'political ascetic' during the turmoil of the 430s and 440s. The norm in future was to be containment in a monastery, subject to some episcopal control. Ascetics, according to the council's fourth canon, were not to wander from place to place at the risk of their reputation, but to stay in a community devoted to fasting and prayer. The stipulation was frequently confirmed, in both East and West.

But the broader effect of the Council was more dramatic. It confirmed, although it did not directly cause, intransigent loyalties to the Monophysite or 'single nature' doctrine. I provided in the previous chapter the bare outlines of Chalcedonian theology, together with that of its opponents. What concerns us here is the unfolding social and political drama that followed upon the decisions of 451. Parties had begun to form before Chalcedon, ranging themselves for or against Nestorius. Those conflicting allegiances continued to govern the response to Chalcedon itself, which was no less a compromise than other attempts at reconciliation. The emergent 'Nestorian' church was not thrust at once into 'oriental' exile, leaving the field to Chalcedonians and Monophysites. It represented a natural opposition to Monophysitism within the Syrian sphere. Chalcedonians, attempting to strike a balance, could only look on in frustrated helplessness at their original enemy thus pitted against their current foe. From 435, after the death of Rabbula of Edessa (who had firmly opposed Nestorius and whose *Life* presents an arresting saga of culture, conversion and office), the city became, under its new bishop Ibas (the admirer of Theodore of Mopsuestia and supporter of Theodoret of Cyrrhus), a centre of theological learning sympathetic to the Nestorian cause. When Ibas died (457), the tradition was maintained by his pupil Barsumas (d. *c.* 490), who subsequently became bishop of Nisibis (within Persian territory) and welcomed exiled scholars driven from Edessa in 489. We are not dealing, therefore, with a peripheral enterprise. The doctrine and the party had developed in Antioch, had followed Nestorius to Constantinople, and was only later scattered eastwards by the stratagems of the dead Cyril's allies.

The government's preoccupation with compromise can obscure its fundamental aim: to distract Monophysites from their Nestorian enemy by stressing how much they must therefore have in common with Chalcedonians. The situation bears only superficial comparison with that following Nicaea, although emperors ignored the niceties of doctrinal disagreement and churchmen pandered to their simplicity (chiefly to outwit their enemies). The emperor Zeno's *Henotikon* of 482, a formula designed to regain Monophysite allegiance, brought clearly into the open the rifts that now permanently fractured eastern Christianity. Zeno had managed to gain the cooperation of both Acacius of Constantinople (d. 489) and Peter Mongus of Alexandria (d. 490). This involved a change of heart that did him little good (he had originally opposed Peter, as also his Monophysite predecessor, Timothy Aelurus, bishop 457–77). The sop offered to Monophysites by the emperor was a renewed condemnation of Nestorius and Eutyches, and a general silence on the subject of 'natures'. As soon as Peter had accepted the new policy, more rigorous Monophysites repudiated him. Bishops of Rome, from Simplicius onwards, opposed both Peter and Acacius, provoking (until 519) the so-called 'Acacian schism'. A pattern of futility was thus established. Nestorians remained permanently estranged; Monophysites were nevertheless constantly divided, whatever gesture the eastern government might make; and the bishops of the West refused to countenance a modification of Chalcedon, insisting further that it be interpreted in the light of Leo's *Tome*.

The next phase of the tragedy was dominated by two figures, Severus of Antioch (d. 538) and Jacob Baradaeus (d. 478). After ascetic formation in circles opposed to Chalcedon (particularly under Peter the Iberian at Maiuma in Palestine), Severus was made bishop of Antioch in 512. In spite of later setbacks, he was the acknowledged leader of the Monophysites of his day. He benefited in part from the emperor Anastasius's sympathy for the Monophysite cause (Anastasius had succeeded Zeno in 491). After Anastasius's death in 518, he was forced into exile in Alexandria, and a brief attempt to regain imperial favour in 535 was quickly subverted by a synod in Constantinople the following year. But his tenure at Antioch involved two other debts: first, to the careful alliance between Peter Mongus and his namesake Peter the Fuller (d. 488), who intermittently laid successful claim to the Antiochene see against Chalcedonian rivals; and second, to the prestige and influence of the Syrian Philoxenus of Mabbug (formerly Hierapolis, north-east of Antioch), a man deeply suspicious of the *Henotikon* (and therefore of Severus's immediate predecessor, Flavian) and bishop for nearly forty years (485–523). Even in exile, Severus made his mark, taking to task fellow Monophysites like Julian of Halicarnassus (who taught that the body of Jesus was incorruptible, rendering his humanity a virtual illusion). At the other extreme, in Constantinople itself, the 'Theopaschites' were prepared to believe that God had suffered in the death of Jesus – a view designed in part to awaken sympathy in the West (a fruitless hope) and supported by the future emperor, Justinian. Once again, the chimaera of reconciliation served only to set the Monophysites one against the other.

That fracturing of the Monophysite church set the tone for Justinian's religious policy. In spite of propaganda to the contrary, at no point in his reign was he a convinced upholder of Chalcedon. In abandoning the outright persecution that had characterized the reign of his uncle Justin before him (518–27), he was swayed by the divisions in the Monophysite camp, which now made Severus seem a moderate. He was encouraged by the sympathies of his wife Theodora, whose earlier religious formation had owed much to Monophysite exiles in Alexandria. It was Theodora who invited Severus to the imperial capital in 535; and she secured the election (albeit short-lived) of sympathetic patriarchs there and in Alexandria – Anthimus, who had been won over by Severus's views, and Theodosius, a firm ally. Even when her plans came to nought (thanks to intervention by successive Popes), she continued to offer sanctuary to leading Monophysites within Constantinople itself, especially Theodosius (who, although deposed, did not die until 566) and John of Ephesus. (John himself describes her amusing subterfuges, turning parts of the imperial palace into makeshift monastic dormitories.) The emperor for his part hoped that Severus might be persuaded to accept Chalcedon; but his Theopaschite proposal was predictably rejected by the West. Justinian mentioned neither church councils nor Leo's *Tome*: so, in spite of condemning Eutyches and Nestorius – the familiar ploy – his initiative satisfied no one.

The failure, exile and death of Severus opened a new phase in Monophysite politics. Jacob Baradaeus (*c.* 500–78) had been trained as a monk near

Legacy and future

Nisibis, came to Constantinople in 528, gained the favour of Theodora, and remained in the capital until his appointment as bishop of Edessa in 542. Here was a Monophysite, therefore, who had truly penetrated the Nestorian heartland. Supported at first by Theodosius in the capital, he set out on a markedly mobile pastorate (much of it obliquely revealed in the work of John of Ephesus, his admirer), strengthening the infrastructure of a northern Monophysite church by ordaining priests, building churches and encouraging the development of monasteries. He may have gained the name Baradaeus ('Burdaya', 'the man in rags') from his frequent resort to disguise, which highlighted the underground and 'back-country' nature of his career. While he no doubt secured thereby a future for what came to be known as the 'Jacobite' church, he was less successful on the political front, losing in 564 a crucial chance to anchor his achievements in Antioch itself. The aged Theodosius was able to install his personal secretary, Paul. Jacob, like many Monophysites before him, had been thwarted by divisions he had to some degree fomented.

Events had by now become dominated, more broadly speaking, by the so-called 'Three Chapters' controversy, leading up to the second Council of Constantinople in 553. The 'three chapters' were sets of passages taken from the writings of Theodore of Mopsuestia (Cyril of Alexandria's arch-foe), Ibas of Edessa and Theodoret of Cyrrhus – all, as we have seen, key figures in discussions before and after the Council of Ephesus. They were now taken, over a century later, as usefully reprehensible examples of 'Nestorian' teaching. The Council condemned them, with the rueful and enforced support of Pope Vigilius (of whom more below). This new attempt to woo Monophysites by attacking Nestorius had more distant roots, since Flavian of Antioch had quoted the trio against Philoxenus of Mabbug in 509, while Anthimus of Constantinople, writing to Severus in 536, had condemned them as 'Antiochene'. Justinian was persuaded to the same course by the Palestinian Theodore Askidas, bishop of Cappadocian Caesarea. By engineering an attack on 'Antiochene' theology, Theodore probably hoped to defend the Alexandrian tradition, foster loyalty to Chalcedon and appease at least some Monophysites; but he wanted most (like the contemporary theologian Leontius of Byzantium) to enhance the reputation of Origen (an ambition thwarted by Justinian, who engineered Origen's condemnation at a synod in Constantinople in 543 – a condemnation conveniently endorsed by the Pope).

As with the *Henotikon* and the Theopaschite enterprise, the policy had no chance of success. The western bishops were for a short period cowed into collaboration (with war against the Ostrogoths in full swing); but their compliance marked no more than a brief hiatus in a century of prolonged resistance. Vigilius, bishop of Rome 537–55, was, in this undertaking, Justinian's hapless stooge. He owed his accession to Theodora, his predecessor Silverius having allegedly sided with the Ostrogoths (which was probably not true). It was thought he might modify, if not repudiate, Leo's *Tome*; and in 540 he accepted the emperor's manoeuvres of 535–36. Justinian, in 544, proceeded on his own initiative to condemn the three supposed Nestorians, and attempted to mollify the westerners as much by his silences as by his contentions. Since he did not condemn Chalcedon at the same time, few Monophysites were impressed. The bishops of the West, for their part, more sympathetic to the 'Antiochene' tradition, were violently opposed; but they did eventually agree, in 551, to the holding of the general Council. Vigilius, browbeaten in Constantinople over several years (547–55), at first subscribed to the condemnation – the chief preoccupation of the Council – while reiterating his support for Chalcedon. His colleagues in the West were outraged by his confused assertions. To his credit, he gradually retracted his approval, refused to preside over the Council itself, suffered imprisonment in the immediate aftermath and died two years later, while returning at last to Rome. He was the second Pope in that century to have been humiliated in such a way; and the affair provided a rough training for his successor, Pelagius I, who had to cope with a virtual schism in the West, scarcely resolved by the time of Gregory the Great.

So, controversy was far from over and, by 553, lasting divisions had been set in place. The three fundamental components of the new ecclesiastical map were the permanent alienation of the Nestorians, the constant fission of the Monophysites, and the intransigence of the church in Rome, with its severe interpretation of Chalcedon. The imperial government sought as usual for vague accommodation. Churchmen fought ruthlessly for exclusive clarity. The fathers at Chalcedon had hoped to arbitrate between two factions. The western churches, however, had boldly appropriated their formula in Latin terms, distancing themselves from both the contestants and the referee. Even more fundamental was the enduringly Roman character of the whole debate. Neither the ideas rehearsed nor the administration and organization relied upon show any signs of influence from beyond the borders of Roman culture. The novelty resided in a shift of relations within a single system. What had been brought to an end was a dream of unity barely two hundred years old.

The story teaches us a good deal about the geography of eastern Christianity. Those sympathetic to the Nestorian cause occupied a central rather than a marginal position. The briefest glance at the topography of what is now called the Middle East will reveal a north-to-south axis, from the great curve of mountains in Armenia and western Iran, down through the fertile valleys of the Tigris and Euphrates to the Persian capital Ctesiphon and out to the southern deserts and the Gulf. The Persians, pressing into the Roman world (as they did so forcefully in the third century and the sixth), moved north along the rivers and only then swung westwards towards Antioch. Justinian, like emperors before him, would have seen his frontier as lying to the south – across Turkey, through the Cilician Gates, into Antioch and then beyond to the 'great river'. He sent out other feelers in the same general direction, to Ethiopia and to the Arab principalities of the desert fringe. That area, to which Islam would soon lay claim, formed a natural unit, making Baghdad eventually a sensible capital; and it continued to harbour in its ancient cities a Christianity all its own. Viewed in that way, the Nestorians seem less 'eastern' and the Monophysites, with their safest bases in Antioch and Alexandria, less than masters of the Syrian world.

The West had already witnessed a new alliance between ascetic piety and disaffected provincial élites, especially in southern Gaul and northern Italy. Now in the East, during the first century of the Monophysite conflict, one detects the analogy: not rebellion by less sophisticated rural fanatics, but a further step in the unfinished business of struggle between province and empire. An old confrontation of interests was being given a new, religious tone. Coptic and Syriac were by this time well established literary languages, preserving complex traditions and expressing subtle ideas. The Monophysite and Nestorian positions were also fully documented in Greek. The success of each movement depended on its ability to attract educated leaders from families with histories of public service. Theological debate was possible only between those with common ground – principles and concepts, and often language itself. To be dubbed a heretic might estrange one from local peers and from the imperial government; but it did not bring exile from Mediterranean culture. The Vandals had proved that just as clearly in the West. Huneric responded to the orthodox emperors of his day, just as the orthodox had reacted to Arian emperors a century before: he thought them too prone to error to command respect. At least some Africans agreed, churchmen and laymen alike. Theological accuracy counted for more than imperial unity. Yet, while orthodox exiles sought solace at the eastern court, the Arians of Africa numbered among their allies other Arians from as far away as Thrace.

NOSTALGIA AND FORESIGHT: THE WORLD OF GREGORY THE GREAT

The greatest Christian figures of the sixth-century West were Boethius, Cassiodorus, Benedict and Gregory the Great. Each of them represents, especially for those reared within a European tradition, a central element of medieval Christendom. Boethius (d. 524) gave a Christian and Latin voice to many of the logical and technical riches of an older learning – Platonist, Aristotelian and Stoic. His *Consolation of Philosophy* (the 'consolation' residing in a true understanding of God's providence) was one of the founding documents of medieval Europe. The circumstances of its writing, however, were the tragic culmination of a career that had brought him the highest honours in the state, which Theodoric had carefully preserved. It gains a special poignancy from its having been completed just prior to his brutal execution for supposed treason. He stands, therefore, as a good example of the Janus-like quality of culture in his period: a man who, in his aristocratic birth, deep learning and political ambition, was typical of the Roman past; but a man whose historical significance rested also upon his reputation as one of the chief inspirers of medieval European philosophy.

The same quality attaches to the other three figures. Cassiodorus, like Boethius, came from a family long accustomed to high office; and he gained his own prominence at the Ostrogothic court. He was *quaestor* (in effect, political secretary) to Theodoric; he succeeded Boethius as *magister officiorum* (illustrating the rivalries induced among aristocrats by Ostrogothic favour); he was made Prefect of Italy in 533 (still in Ostrogothic service); and he later gave support to Pope Vigilius in the 'Three Chapters' affair (for, after retiring from politics in the later 530s, he established a close relationship with papal circles). Soon after returning to Italy in the 550s, after a period of voluntary 'exile' in the East, he embarked upon a monastic venture at 'Vivarium', built on his southern family estate at Squillace. There he worked to preserve, as he explained in his *Divine Institutes*, the skills of literary culture, and many of its texts. Benedict (d. *c.* 550) is widely accepted as the father figure of western medieval monasticism; but, in his *Rule*, he recommended virtues and institutional forms that had been defined, discussed and argued over by Romans for centuries. His emphasis on 'school' and 'service' are particularly striking examples. His ascetic achievement was heavily dependent on experiments in Gaul and Italy during the century and a half before his death: he admired Cassian, and was especially beholden to the traditions represented in the so-called *Rule of the Master* (written *c.* 515). Gregory the Great (d. 604) seems worthy to claim the title of the first medieval Pope; but he was also of aristocratic birth, with civil as well as religious leaders (including Popes) in his family's past. Before becoming bishop of Rome in 590, he had held high civil office in the city (being Prefect there in 573) and, after becoming a monk, he spent (like Vigilius in the 530s) several years as an *apocrisiarius* or church envoy in Constantinople (579–86). He is remembered on his tomb as 'God's consul'.

The sixth century in the West, therefore, may be called a century of paradox. It contained the seeds of a world it could scarcely foresee; but it measured its security entirely in relation to the past – 'looking back toward land', as Gregory put it in his *Dialogues*, 'and sighing as I beheld the shore'. A premium was placed on recollection. Western Christians showed no sense of having abandoned or lost an ancient heritage: rather, they held fast to what they could, in ways that met their immediate needs.

There is some justice in seeing the papacy as the most obvious example of such an attitude. That was partly because the bishops of Rome came close to exercising the central authority in the West that the emperors had lost immediate hold of in 476. Yet the path from Leo to Gregory was not only long but indirect. Leo made his mark on the broader stage because of the way his *Tome* of 449 was to govern the western interpretation of Chalcedon. More locally, however, he had considerable difficulty in imposing his authority over the episcopate of Gaul, reflecting in religious terms the longstanding rivalry between Italian and Gallic élites. The Popes who immediately followed him (particularly Gelasius I, 492–96) were distanced from the East by the Acacian schism, and were prevented from making any effective distinction between their authority and that of the emperor (in spite of the theoretical declarations that have made Gelasius famous). Theodoric the Ostrogoth in many ways restored an imperial style of government closer to home in Italy, while Clovis and his successors in Gaul at once fragmented and controlled their own episcopate. As Theodoric's government began to weaken, Hormisdas and John I (514–23 and 523–26) might have begun to congratulate themselves on better relations with Constantinople; but John met a frosty and debilitating reception in the capital, and we have seen how sadly Vigilius fared (537–55), before and during the Three Chapters affair. Gregory, born in 540, grew up in that clouded atmosphere. His family was associated with Vigilius's comparably unsuccessful predecessors, Felix IV and Agapetus (526–30 and 535–36). By 590, he had virtually to rebuild a stable and commanding papacy, inheriting from the débâcle of 553 what he called in a letter 'an old and grievously battered ship'. The burdensome legacies of Theodoric and Justinian were exacerbated by invading Lombards (after 568) and the demands of the Byzantine exarchs in Ravenna. Quite apart from ensuring his own prestige and imposing order on his subordinates, Gregory had to put into effect the expectations of Justinian's *Pragmatic Sanction* of 554 – the emperor's weary abandonment of a world he had failed (after the wars against the Ostrogoths) to control more closely, giving bishops various civil duties, including in part responsibility for appointing local governors.

Little wonder, then, that Gregory felt despondent, faced with the sorrows that 'crowded unhindered before my eyes'. In several passages of the *Dialogues*, he presents a vivid picture of Italian decline, with harrowing references to climate, disease, famine and depopulation. (He also provided, in the second book, a subsequently influential portrait of Benedict, in a social setting that gives added and at times surprising colour to the *Rule*.) The world, he wrote, was already providing a foretaste of its imminent ending. In his *Moralia*, he echoed Ezekiel's judgement on a doomed kingdom. Yet he appealed in the *Pastoral Care* to the same prophet's vision of 'supernal peace' in the Jerusalem above. Sending the *Moralia* to Leander of Seville, he stressed how a sense of the world's collapse demanded dedication to a flock's material welfare – another expression of our paradox. While fearing the judgement and seeking the mercy of a very Roman God, Italians were exhorted to redefine 'society' and 'state' in Christian terms, rather than attempt to escape from it. Thus, Gregory rallied contemporaries who had been prepared in previous decades to abandon Italy, desolated first by Justinian's long struggle against the Ostrogoths and then by the incursions of the Lombards. He showed that Lombards could be enticed to a Christian agenda (his *Dialogues*, presented to the orthodox queen Theudelinda, were part of the enticement); and for that reason, in the absence of tangible support from the emperor Maurice (582–602), he brazenly (and successfully) made treaties with the Lombard kings.

Gregory may have clenched his jaw, therefore, but remained an optimist. He peered into the future with a mental vision governed by the paradigms set in place by Augustine's *City of God*. Like Augustine, he valued peace and discipline; and he knew that its guarantees would now have to be different. His most characteristic quality was his ability to balance sorrow and compassion. He countered an instinct to flight from adversity by an unflinching commitment to the welfare of the needy and the order of the state. He valued 'contemplation', which seemed to depend on the tranquillity that came only with monastic retirement. One might, as a monk, 'see the light more keenly'. In a classic passage of the *Dialogues*, he described how Benedict saw the departing soul of Germanus, bishop of Capua: 'the whole world was gathered up before his eyes in what appeared to be a single ray of light'. Gregory reflected, 'The light of holy contemplation enlarges and expands the mind in God, until it stands above the world.' But that understanding of contemplation opened up a path to the resolution of paradox: for the elevation of spirit thus achieved enabled the contemplative to understand the world of experience more fully. Gregory reached beyond a frustrating oscillation between *otium* and *negotium*, the traditional duality of leisure and public duty. A good bishop, he told a colleague, was able to care for both 'the salvation of souls' and 'the external advantage and safety of his subjects'. Flourishing religion depended on material welfare: otherwise one might 'no longer have anyone to preach to'.

Here was the voice of the hard-headed administrator, who penned so many practical letters to the trusted officials who ran the Roman church's far-flung estates (including many in North Africa) and kept a wary eye on local bishops. The *Register* of the Pope's letters provides a fund of information on social mores and the constituents of government. Their busy attention to detail formed a local and solid basis for his grander and more famous preoccupations. We justifiably view Augustine of Canterbury's journey to evangelize the Anglo-Saxons, for example, begun in 596, as the first step in a new understanding of conversion and mission. It is doubtful, however, that Gregory saw the venture clearly as a radical reach beyond the limits of the old Roman world. Augustine, as he travelled north, was to reinforce the careful alliances already built up by Gregory's correspondence with Frankish royalty. His pastoral engagement with Æthelberht of Kent was to rest on the Christianity of his wife Bertha, daughter of the Frankish king Charibert I. Gregory's independent agreements with the Lombards were contemporary with letters to members of the imperial family in the East, extolling the Christian empire as the surest weapon against barbarians and the surest defence of the faith. There are fewer such eastern letters in the *Register*, but that may be an accident of preservation and perceived usefulness in later times. The gesture was associated with his reaction to the use, in Constantinople, of the term 'oecumenical patriarch'. The patriarch himself may have thought that the bishop of the capital deserved some precedence; but Gregory, with his broader and more detailed experience, could see that Constantinople's power was increasingly limited, as much (in his opinion) by the foolish choices of its emperors as by pressure from outside enemies. In such a world, religious authority had to operate more independently of traditional political associations; and the Pope's epistolary relations with bishops in the East, as in the West, both underpinned that judgement and provided him with further opportunities to defend it.

It is difficult to judge what species of personal courage it took to carry forward in that way habits of control traditional among the Roman nobility, while shedding any desire either for ease or for wealth and status. The outcome, however, is beyond doubt: Roman values, both philosophical and administrative, were made ready for their role in a post-Roman world. However, if (as seems the case) Christians in the West felt that an 'end' was in sight, it was not because they had chosen, or could confidently predict or discern, an alternative future. That future, for which they had in fact begun to prepare, and which was gradually taking shape around them, had yet to be impressed upon their conscious minds. Christians in the East, on the other hand, were often locked in a more dangerous oblivion. Many were simply incapable of imagining that the future might be different. Even if the possibility had been brought home to them, they would have seen no reason why it should be realized. Greek culture was still happily allied to the Platonist tradition, still wedded to the centrality of the *polis*, still habituated to the ancient formality of public ceremonial. Frontiers were manned, armies deployed, taxes collected and laws enforced. Eastern Christians were, of course, in for a ruder shock – the eruption of Islam: one must not forget that, when Gregory the Great died, Muhammad was already in his thirties. Having said that, however, Byzantine Christians, once chastened by Islam, engaged thereafter in a long and far from fruitless dialogue with the new religion. The two polities, Christian and Islamic, redefined the relation between 'Romans' and the world to their east; an amalgam of tension, respect and mutual dependence. Christians in the West, by contrast, despite the encroaching symptoms of a new order, became adamant in remaining aloof from such an essay in collaboration. As much as possible, and with increasing vigour, they drove Islam (and in the process Byzantium) from their borders. The responses seem to be the reverse of what one might have expected. Both were based, however, on an instinct to hold change in check. It is still not certain which policy was more sensible at the time, or which fortune proved in the end more rewarding.

Further reading

For a general understanding of barbarian settlement in the West, see Walter Pohl (ed.), *Kingdoms of the Empire: the Integration of Barbarians in Late Antiquity* (Leiden: Brill, 1997). Still useful is Walter Goffart, *Barbarians and Romans: the*

Techniques of Accommodation (Princeton, NJ: Princeton University Press, 1980) and there is a splendid treatment of the background in Jill Harries, *Sidonius Apollinaris and the Fall of Rome* (Oxford: Clarendon Press, 1994). For general religious considerations, see Robert A. Markus, *The End of Ancient Christianity* (Cambridge: Cambridge University Press, 1990). The story continues, of course: see Walter Pohl, Ian Wood and Helmut Reimitz (eds), *The Transformation of Frontiers from Late Antiquity to the Carolingians* (Leiden: Brill, 2001) and Judith Herrin, *The Formation of Christendom* (Oxford: Blackwell, 1987).

On issues of 'conversion', see, for an older perspective, J.N. Hillgarth (ed.), *Christianity and Paganism, 350–750: the Conversion of Western Europe* (Philadelphia, PA: University of Pennsylvania Press, 1986) and more recently Richard Fletcher, *The Barbarian Conversion: from Paganism to Christianity* (Berkeley, CA: University of California Press, 1997).

For more particular studies of the West, especially Gaul, see P.S. Barnwell, *Emperor, Prefects and Kings: the Roman West, 395–565* (Chapel Hill, NC: University of North Carolina Press, 1992), Raymond Van Dam, *Leadership and Community in Late Antique Gaul* (Berkeley, CA: University of California Press, 1985) and John Drinkwater and Hugh Elton (eds), *Fifth-Century Gaul: a Crisis of Identity?* (Cambridge: Cambridge University Press, 1992). Religious aspects are well introduced by Peter Brown, *The Cult of the Saints: its Rise and Function in Latin Christianity* (Chicago, IL: University of Chicago Press, 1981) and Ralph W. Mathisen, *Ecclesiastical Factionalism and Religious Controversy in Fifth-Century Gaul* (Washington, DC: Catholic University of America Press, 1989), together with his *Roman Aristocrats in Barbarian Gaul: Strategies for Survival in an Age of Transition* (Austin, TX: University of Texas Press, 1993). For a fine portrait of a significant Gallic bishop, see William E. Klingshirn, *Caesarius of Arles: the Making of a Christian Community in Late Antique Gaul* (Cambridge: Cambridge University Press, 1994).

Individual barbarian settlements have been studied in detail. On the Franks: Ian Wood, *The Merovingian Kingdoms, 450–751* (London and New York, NY: Longman, 1994) and Yitzhak Hen, *Culture and Religion in Merovingian Gaul, AD 481–751* (Leiden: Brill, 1995). The Goths generally: Peter Heather, *Goths and Romans, 332–489* (Oxford: Clarendon Press, 1991), together with his *The Goths* (Oxford: Blackwell, 1996). The Visigoths: Peter Heather (ed.), *The Visigoths from the Migration Period to the Seventh Century: an Ethnographic Perspective* (Woodbridge: Boydell Press, 1999). The Ostrogoths: Patrick Amory, *People and Identity in Ostrogothic Italy, 489–554* (Cambridge: Cambridge University Press, 1997) and see James J. O'Donnell, *Cassiodorus* (Berkeley, CA: University of California Press, 1979).

Turning to the East, and specifically to Syria, see H.J.W. Drijvers, *History and Religion in Late Antique Syria* (Aldershot: Variorum, 1994) and the work of Sidney H. Griffith – for example, 'Asceticism in the Church of Syria: the Hermeneutics of Early Syrian Asceticism', in *Asceticism,* edited by Vincent L. Wimbush and Richard Valantasis, with Gay L. Byron and William S. Love (New York, NY and Oxford: Oxford University Press, 1995), pp. 220–45.

On the Monophysites, we are still heavily dependent on W.H.C. Frend, *The Rise of the Monophysite Movement: Chapters in the History of the Church in the Fifth and Sixth Centuries* (London and New York, NY: Cambridge University Press, 1972). Much background can be gleaned from theological surveys: Roberta C. Chesnut, *Three Monophysite Christologies: Severus of Antioch, Philoxenus of Mabbug, and Jacob of Sarug* (Oxford: Oxford University Press, 1976) and Iain R. Torrance, *Christology after Chalcedon: Severus of Antioch and Sergius the Monophysite* (Eugene, OR: Wipf & Stock, 1998). John of Ephesus has attracted particular attention: Susan Ashbrook Harvey, *Asceticism and Society in Crisis: John of Ephesus and the Lives of the Eastern Saints* (Berkeley, CA: University of California Press, 1990) and Jan J. Van Ginkel, *John of Ephesus: a Monophysite Historian in Sixth-Century Byzantium* (Groningen: Rijksuniversiteit Groningen, 1995).

On Justinian, see Averil Cameron, *Procopius and the Sixth Century* (Berkeley, CA: University of California Press,), together with Robert Browning, *Justinian and Theodora* (London: Thames and Hudson, 1987). On law: Tony Honoré, *Tribonian* (London: Duckworth, 1978).

On Gregory the Great: Robert A. Markus, *Gregory the Great and his World* (Cambridge: Cambridge University Press, 1998), which does not supersede, however, Carole Ellen Straw, *Gregory the Great: Perfection in Imperfection* (Berkeley, CA: University of California Press, 1988). On the *Dialogues*: Joan M. Petersen, *The Dialogues of Gregory the Great in their Late Antique Cultural Background* (Toronto: Pontifical Institute of Mediaeval Studies, 1984). On the political background: Neil Christie, *The Lombards* (Oxford: Blackwell, 1995). On the mission to England: Henry Mayr-Harting, *The Coming of Christianity to Anglo-Saxon England* (1972), 3rd edn (University Park, PA: Pennsylvania State University Press, 1991) is still valuable; and see two books by N.J. Higham, *The English Conquest: Gildas and Britain in the Fifth Century* (Manchester: Manchester University Press, 1994) and *The Convert Kings: Power and Religious Affiliation in Early Anglo-Saxon England* (Manchester: Manchester University Press, 1997).

Where to begin?
Robert A. Markus, *The End of Ancient Christianity.*

Epilogue

THE PRICE OF SUCCESS

It is tempting to think of Gregory the Great as a despondent seer, faced with a dark future. He had in fact in his final years welcomed the accession of the new emperor Phocas, who he hoped would develop a fresh and effective interest in the old empire's western provinces (and strengthen his stand against the patriarch of Constantinople). As for the east Romans themselves, their immediate problems were to revolve around Persian aggression: for Persia was about to invade and conquer large tracts of Roman territory, occupying Egypt and coming fearfully close to Constantinople. To the emperor Heraclius, however, that would have seemed an old problem to be solved with old strategies, albeit difficult in that instance and dependent upon radical military reform. It was ironic that he should have mounted his offensive from a western base in Carthage and should have completed it with the help of non-Roman allies. However, when he succeeded in driving the Persians back and restoring Christian rule to Jerusalem (628–29), he could scarcely have anticipated the eruption of triumphant armies that was about to descend on his restored domains from the newly Islamicized south.

So, there are, as I said in my preface, no endings in history. Nevertheless, one of the chief challenges historians face is the need to keep in mind the total obscurity of everyone's future. In any period, the future is simply not available, even though it may be imagined. The 'dark ages' or the 'rise of Islam' were not part of anyone's thought-world at the beginning of the seventh century. The empire's prospects, for both Gregory and Heraclius, were defined by the interplay between experience and imagination. In relation to Christianity, the exercise of the imagination had particular significance. The early six centuries I have described invited Christians to constant adjustments of the future – the future of the individual, of the human race, of the cosmos. The terms in which they made and expressed those adjustments, however, were defined by their past; and the past itself, therefore, became similarly modified in their minds, in order to justify their varying expectations. Such, probably, is the history of any religion.

Christianity's greatest 'success', therefore, may have been its ability to keep itself a part of history. In the minds of many Christians, the whole of the past since the creation of the world had been designed as a prologue to their own achievement; and the whole of the future, therefore, could be correspondingly claimed in the terminology of Christian fulfilment. In practice, they argued about the nature and pathways of 'tradition' and imagined a range of futures; but some species of rootedness and continuity was required of any group that wished to lay claim to 'orthodoxy'. The perceived advantage of such antiquity, of a controlling heritage, was that the religion itself could never be cultivated in isolation or under the aegis of 'world-denial'. The price to be paid for that historical assurance was the risk of confusing God's history or Christian history or 'church history' with other histories of a more transient or political nature. The definition of the religion itself could be too heavily coloured by the character and development of beliefs, practices or institutions upon which it appeared, in its own eyes, to depend. That is what makes Augustine so towering a figure. Not everyone understood or accepted his arguments, and he was prone to hesitation and compromise; but he recognized what distinctions were required.

Christians could congratulate themselves on other successes. It may be rash to rank them; but, by any calculation, the setting of the Bible at the centre of the cultural stage must bulk large. Whereas in previous centuries the majority of cultivated men and women in the Mediterranean world had measured that cultivation by its fidelity to the legacies of Homer and Virgil, Plato and Aristotle, Demosthenes and Cicero, now the Pentateuch, the Psalms, the Prophets and the Gospels defined the virtues and insights of an equally dominant and enduring élite. As I shall recall shortly, the shift depended on the imposition of a fateful divorce between the Old Testament and the Jewish people – a divorce that Jews themselves had no reason to accept. And it did not represent a simple displacement of one culture by another (for Christians were Romans): the interpretation and proclamation of biblical texts as cultural resources depended substantially on the techniques of non-Christian literary practice. Moreover, the purely literary quality of the Scriptures – including, crucially, the Jewish Scriptures originally in Hebrew, which were rarely savoured by Christians in their original language – continued to be judged by canons of taste developed in a wholly different context.

Epilogue: the price of success

Tied in with the development of Christians' biblical culture were the theological developments concerning the meaning of Jesus of Nazareth, which implied in part a shift from messianic and prophetic paradigms to the concept of a divine saviour. By the end of the sixth century, Christians had explored the major philosophical and terminological difficulties attendant upon the notion of a human being who was also God. By no means were the formulae universally accepted; but the issues had been identified, in ways that would govern debate for the best part of a millennium. The enterprise had been inventive, taxing and brutal; but its general conclusions affected more than the intellectually curious, since they informed catechesis and inspired liturgical and devotional practice. The impresario of both discourse and cult was the bishop – at the institutional level, Christianity's most significant invention. The entanglements of religious and civil leadership can obscure from us the breadth of episcopal responsibility, which included theology, judgement, interpretation, rhetoric, ceremony, administration and guidance, all laid upon a single figure – always male, chosen for life, possibly the custodian of considerable property and wealth, and often without children or other debts to familial posterity. It was easy for such a figure to appropriate duties and rights that other persons with hopes of power could only partially match and consequently envy. The way in which episcopacy had come to be defined made it inevitable and imperative that bishops and civil leaders should negotiate over spheres of influence. It was impossible to separate those spheres completely, and bishops were able to maintain surprising initiatives at the expense of their civil peers – sometimes, of course, because the civil authorities had disappeared.

Having outlined such successes, it is sobering to observe how much had yet to be resolved. The humanity and divinity of Jesus, although for the most part accepted by all Christians, was still susceptible to a range of conflicting interpretations, which allowed believers to oscillate between awe in the presence of a transcendent saviour and identification with a wise, powerful, sympathetic and vulnerable Galilean. That variety immediately posed the question of how much freedom should be allowed believers. Some recommended the coercive application of narrow principles, which demanded a leadership endowed with a distinctive and forceful authority. The overlap between religious and civil spheres could encourage in turn a dependence on law, trial, imprisonment, torture and execution. Even the recruitment of Christians remained problematic. Should one depend on 'mission' and 'conversion'? What did such concepts imply? Or should one trust more in the cautious formation of Christian youth, of those born into Christian families?

In which case, who should undertake it? The persecutors who predated Constantine had worried about enforcement, and provided Christians with subsequent models of both tolerance and cruelty. Christians themselves had raised all the other issues in the first two centuries of their own era.

I mentioned above the fateful divorce between the Old Testament and the Jewish people. Of all the heavy prices paid by early Christianity, that was the heaviest. Almost by definition, Christians' agenda made their rejection of the Jews inevitable. Paradoxically, the impulse was strengthened by the fact that Jesus himself would not have understood it. Even Paul's letters, when compared with the much later thesis of *Acts*, reflect the slow pace of change. Rejection was bound to be a monstrously difficult task. So much that was 'Jewish' was also indispensable, and the distinction between a Jew who was a Christian and a Jew who was not remained for a long time difficult to express, let alone enforce. The reinterpretation of history that I referred to earlier was dedicated for the most part to that enforcement, which meant staking constant claims to every sector of Jewish thought and the Jewish past. Yet the habit of labelling errors as examples of *judaica superstitio*, even at the end of our period, shows how much Christians continued to feel that the frontier between themselves and Jews was perilously ill-defined. *Superstitio* created a totally unjust association, and suggests that Jews could only be held at arm's length if they were tarred with the 'pagan' brush – a telling admission. As for 'paganism' itself, Christianity had taken advantage of changes of attitude within Roman society generally. Its attachment to monotheism and its elevated ideal of human perfectibility were shared with many non-believers, and expressed in language that they would have recognized as their own. Nevertheless, the suppression of the ancient cults, not to mention the repudiation of more recent patterns of belief like those of Mithras and the Manichees, had involved the sacrifice of many noble elements and of a view of humanity and nature that can still justify admiration or respect.

What some might regard as the invention of 'heresy' signalled another irreparable weakness. I call it invention only in the sense that the theoretical 'unity' or 'orthodoxy' of the Christian community seems often to have depended on its willingness and ability to label certain people as outsiders. The need for unity created the need for heresy. One might think that a regrettable price had been paid, when this or that definition of unity could survive only by declaring certain styles of belief or behaviour beyond the pale. We are leaving Christians at the end of the sixth century as divided as we could possibly imagine them to be. If we accept the definition of catholicity proposed

Epilogue: the price of success

by Vincent of Lérins (d. *c.* 450) – *quod ubique, quod semper, quod ab omnibus*: what had been believed 'everywhere, always and by everyone' – then 'catholic' doctrine would have been a thin corpus indeed. However, many of the theological partisans abroad in the Christian world in the year 600 would have thought that they alone filled Vincent's bill. They remained for a long time almost as harsh towards one another as they were to Jews.

Together with episcopacy, the celebration of the sacraments remained the hallmark of most Christian communities. Baptism and the Eucharist (neither of them entirely original to Christianity) created and sustained the members of a church. There were two sides to that essential cultic badge. First, the notion of sacrament depended on a deeper belief, which referred in its turn to the understanding of the Incarnation and of created nature: namely, the belief that the visible world was both the arena and the instrument of God's redemptive activity. Specifically, water, bread and wine brought divine power to rest in human circumstance: cleansing and nourishment were made to imply, and effect, more than was normal. Second, submission to baptism and participation in the Eucharist were, according to one line of argument, the primary means to spiritual excellence, to the fulfilment of human destiny under God. One can see at once that disagreement about the Incarnation would immediately invade the cult of the community, radically affecting its implications. Equally ominous, if one were to think additionally that 'nature', human or otherwise, was vitiated by 'sin', then the aid to spiritual excellence represented in the sacraments was not just a matter of teaching and nurturing but of altering human nature. As I suggested in Chapter 8, Latin Christianity entertained a greater degree of pessimism about 'nature', which encouraged a 'sacramental theory' heavily weighted towards enhancing the independent power of the sacramental act itself. It also focused on its effect at the level of the individual. Among eastern Christians, however, who were more optimistic about a person's capacity to achieve 'likeness to God' on the basis of shared creation 'in God's image', the sacraments – the Eucharist especially – strengthened and advanced a trend already inherent in the worshipper's devotion. The less optimistic and more mechanistic tendency in the West (albeit misjudged or exaggerated) would sometimes provoke a rebellious misgiving (right through to the Reformation), while the difference in attitude contributed much to the continuing estrangement between West and East.

That estrangement, while a regrettable legacy, can easily be misinterpreted, however. It was not a matter of maintaining 'Constantinianism' in the East while rejecting it in the West. Challenges to the notion that the emperor, or any civil authority, was the chief mediator of divine providence were as evident under Justinian as they were in Italy and Gaul. 'Byzantine' Christianity was not based on a theocratic view of worldly power that relegated churchmen to a compliant service of the state. Theological dispute, popular piety and monastic assertiveness, inside the Chalcedonian sphere as well as outside, kept every leader under pressure. Similarly, we are forced to adjust our view of the western medieval future. We have, on the one hand, a convenient image of bishops and kings battling for control over such instruments of government as law and punishment. We picture, on the other hand, as if in a distinct world, the intensity of scholars and monks, laboriously preserving the 'classical tradition' and a less brutal and opportunistic view of humanity and intellect. The image is inadequate. Plenty of medieval kings saw themselves in imperial terms, and were conscious of that tradition. Bishops and monks did not play out their roles on two separate stages, but contended with one another in the attempt to define and control the aspirations of their rulers. The experiences of the fifth and sixth centuries were clear antecedents of much that followed throughout the Mediterranean. Barbarian nostalgia for a lost 'heroic age' contributed much more to a sense of distance from antiquity.

In the East, however, the emergence of Islam seems to constitute a more radical divide; and the change has often been blamed on the divisions of eastern Christianity, which supposedly weakened both theological clarity and political loyalty in the most crucial provinces of Syria and Egypt. The truth, no less evident than in the West, is that Muslim leaders were prepared, certainly under the Umayyads, to learn from (without merely imitating) imperial styles of government; and the Christians who continued to live under their sway negotiated with them just as westerners did with Merovingians and Lombards. And let us not exaggerate the divide between religions. Islam has always been justifiably linked with Judaism and Christianity – forms of monotheism properly distinguished from other religious ideologies. The character of the connection is especially poignant, given what I have ascribed to Christian history. In the 620s and 630s, sons and daughters of Abraham were about to launch themselves upon yet another experiment in the reinterpretation of their religious past. Muhammad was a figure whom both Jews and Christians could recognize at once – a prophet. His devotion to a single God was given a special edge by the proximity of unbelievers in the communities immediately around him; but the territories bordering on both of the Red Sea's coasts were rich in Christian and Jewish memories, many of them reflected in his own prophetic declarations. Once the citizens of the Roman

East were forced to come to terms with Islam directly, in the middle years of the seventh century, they were bound to recall the ambiguities of their own development during the hundreds of years before; their arguments about the nature of God, the humanity of Jesus, the privileges of prophecy and the morality of forceful conversion. Islam was a reminder of the possible varieties of emphasis within Christianity itself, and revealed with new urgency the extent to which choices were still open and debates still unresolved.

FURTHER BIBLIOGRAPHICAL NOTES AND ACKNOWLEDGEMENTS

◆

I have omitted basic histories of the Roman world, and all material in languages other than English. Most of the original texts are available in a number of series: the nineteenth-century collections made by J.-P. Migne, the *Patrologia graeca* (*PG*) and the *Patrologia latina* (*PL*); the *Corpus scriptorum ecclesiasticorum latinorum* (*CSEL*); the *Corpus scriptorum christianorum orientalium* (*CSCO*); the *Corpus christianorum*, in both Latin, Greek and medieval parts; and sections of the *Monumenta Germaniae historica* (*MGH*), especially the *Auctores antiquissimi*. English translations are also for the most part grouped in series: *Fathers of the Church*, the *Cistercian Studies* series, Routledge's *Early Church Fathers* series, *Translated Texts for Historians*, the discontinued *Ancient Christian Writers* series, *Eastern Christian Texts in Translation* and new ventures such as *The Library of Early Christianity* and the Australian series *Early Christian Studies*. The *Loeb Classical Library*, in both its Greek and Latin series, contains a wealth of Christian material, as to a lesser extent do the *Penguin Classics*. For those who read French, *Sources chrétiennes* is another great treasure-house of material.

Most up-to-date research appears first in article form. Those with access to good university libraries may find it enjoyable to consult some of them. The leading relevant journals publishing in English, or with a good proportion of English essays, are *Byzantion*, *Church History*, *English Historical Review*, *Greek, Roman and Byzantine Studies*, *Harvard Theological Review*, *Historia*, *Journal of Early Christian Studies*, *Journal of Ecclesiastical History*, *Journal of Roman Studies*, *Journal of Theological Studies*, *Vigiliae christianae* and *Speculum* and *Traditio* (although these two are predominantly medieval in scope). Many established scholars will have had their collected papers published in Variorum's *Collected Studies* series. A comprehensive list of authors publishing in a range of languages on all aspects of antiquity, including Christianity, is published each year in *L'Année Philologique*, which is easy to use, even if one does not read French.

Acknowledgements

To provide otherwise a full bibliography of six hundred years of Christian history would exceed the proper proportion of a book like this. In addition to the authors mentioned in the various lists of recommended reading (many of whom have produced other equally important work), the following have contributed directly to my account of the period. By consulting their names in the catalogue of any good research library, those interested will discover another layer of books and articles. In a work of this scope, based to some degree on decades of reading and reflection, it is inevitable that I should have forgotten or have overlooked the work of some scholars. I ask them to forgive me, and assure them that I lay no claim to the insights of my colleagues. I acknowledge my debts, therefore, to Dorothy Abrahamse, Luise Abramowski, Neil Adkin, Werner Affeldt (with Annette Kuhn and Sabine Reiter), Philip Alexander, A. Alföldi, Karin Alt, J. José Alviar, Julia Annas, A.H. Armstrong, David Balch, Tamsyn Barton, Richard Bauckham, Pier Franco Beatrice, John Behr, Jean Bernardi, Alan Bernstein, Ugo Bianchi, Ludwig Bieler, John Binns, Susanne Bobzien, Alexander Böhlig, Barbara Ellen Bowe, Alan Bowman, Keith Bradley, David Brakke, Jan Bremmer, Hans Christof Brennecke, Richard Burridge, René Cadiou, Alan Cameron, Paul Canivet, Claude Carozzi, Maurice Casey, G. Caspary, Richard Cassidy, Peter Charanis, Antoine Chavasse, Katherine Clarke, Gillian Cloke, John J. Collins, Franca Ela Consolino, Gail Patterson Corrington, Lellia Cracco Ruggini, Brian Croke, Agnes Cunningham, Wendy Dabourne, Gilbert Dagron, Brian Daley, David Dawson, Marinus de Jonge, Adalbert de Vogüé, Jeanne-Marie Demarolle, M. Dembinska, George T. Dennis, Donald J. Dietrich (with Michael J. Himes), Karl Paul Donfried (with Peter Richardson), F. Gerald Downing, Michèle Ducot, Dennis C. Duling, Peter Dunn, Yves-Marie Duval, Bart Ehrman, Stephen Emmel, Robert Eno, Craig A. Evans (with Donald A. Hagner), E. Eyben, Paul Fedwick, Everett Ferguson, André-Jean Festugière, Elisabeth Schüssler Fiorenza, Menachem Fisch, Jacques Fontaine, Georgia Frank, Karl Suso Frank, Eric Franklin, Peter Garnsey, Judith W. George, Dieter Georgi, Stephen Gero, W. Gessel, Elena Giannarelli, David W.J. Gill (with Conrad Gempf), Graham Gould, Patrick Gray, Henry A. Green, Jean Gribomont, Veronika Grimm, Judith Evans Grubbs, Antoine Guillaumont, H. Hagendahl, Johannes Hahn, Kim Haines-Eitzen, Carol Harrison, David J. Hawkin (with Tom Robinson), G.R. Hawting, Charles W. Hedrick, Françeois Heim, Martin Heinzelmann, Colin J. Hemer, Patrick Henry, David Hill, Julian Hills, Kenneth Holum, James Howard-Johnston (with Paul Hayward), Elaine Huber, Mark Humphries, David Hunter, Larry Hurtado, J.S. Jeffers, Georg Jenal, Chris Jones, Edwin

Judge, Walter Kaegi, Richard Kalmin, Adolf Kalsbach, Adam Kamesar, Clemens Kasper, George A. Kennedy, Philip H. Kern, Alexandr Khosroyev, Frederick W. Klawiter, Richard Klein, Ludwig Koenen, Martin Krause, Derek Krueger, D.J. Kyrtatis, Hans Peter L'Orange, Peter Lampe, Henri Lavagne, George Lawless, Bentley Layton, Alain Le Boulluec, Johannes Leipoldt, Fannie LeMoine, J.E. Lendon, Hartmut Leppin, Blake Leyerle, Conrad Leyser, J.H.W.G. Liebeschuetz, Joseph T. Lienhard, Salvatore Lilla, Vasiliki Limberis, Rita Lizzi, Sabine MacCormack, Leslie S.B. MacCoull, Dennis Ronald MacDonald, G.W. MacRae, Goulven Madec, Paul Magdalino, Jean-Pierre Mahé, Pierre Maraval, Christoph Markschies, Henri-Irénée Marrou, Michelle Marshman, Annik Martin, Michael McCormick, Bernard McGinn, Andrew McGowan, John Anthony McGuckin, J.S. McLaren, Jo Ann McNamara, Charlotte Methuen, John Meyendorff, Fergus Millar, Stephen Mitchell, Arnaldo Momigliano, Dominic Montserrat, Claudio Moreschini, Charles Munier, Robert Murray, Herbert Musurillo, Pierre Nautin, Randall Stranton Neal, Jacob Neusner, Ulrich Neymeyr, Oliver Nicholson, Steve Nimis, Alanna Emmett Nobbs, Arthur Darby Nock, Friedrich Normann, Dominic J. O'Meara, J.C. O'Neill, Steven Oberhelman, Tito Orlandi, Eric Osborn, Carolyn Osiek, Elaine Pagels, Andrew Palmer, Evelyne Patlagean, Birger Pearson, Paul Petit, Stanley E. Porter, Aline Pourkier, Kim Power, Simon Price, Friedrich Prinz, Gilles Quispel, Alfredo Mordechai Rabello, Tessa Rajak, Brian Rapske, Stefan Rebenich, Eric Rebillard, David Rensberger, Pierre Riché, R. Riesner, Gregory J. Riley, John Rist, Charlotte Roueché, Christopher Rowland, Rosemary Radford Ruether, David Runia, Michele Salzman, Ross Saunders, Clemens Scholten, Daniel N. Schowalter, Heinz Schreckenberg (with Kurt Schubert), Alan B. Scott, Brent Shaw, Gregory Shaw, Teresa Shaw, Richard N. Slater, Michael Slusser, Dorothy Sly, E. Mary Smallwood, Christopher Stead, Columba Stewart, Gedaliahu G. Stroumsa, Basil Studer, Gerd Theissen, Françoise Thélamon, Carsten Peter Thiede (with Matthew D'Ancona), Carlo Tiblietti, Janet Timbie, Annewies van den Hoek, Armand Veilleux, Luc Verheijen, Arthur Vööbus, François Vouga, C.C. Walters, Carolinne White, Lionel Wickham, Daniel H. Williams, Antoinette Clark Wire, M.R. Wright, Edward Yarnold and Irving M. Zeitlin.

INDEX

Acts, Apocryphal, 107, 132–136, 147, 162
Acts of the Apostles, 3, 7, chapter 2 (23–45) *passim*, 55, 61, 68, 72, 89, 92, 97, 105, 114, 124, 127, 156, 161, 191, 316
Acts of the Martyrs, 159–167
  see also martyrdom
Acts of the Scillitan Martyrs, 69, 86
Alexandria
  its importance as a Christian centre, 27, 68, 87, 112–114, 130, 181, 190, 252, 276, 303
  its exegetical and theological traditions, 114, 139, 145, 147–148, 170, 227, 251
  see also Athanasius, Clement, Cyril, monophysite, Origen, Theophilus (of Alexandria)
allegory, 111, 129, 136, 138–139, 142
Ambrose, bishop of Milan (*c.* 339–397), 148, 190, 199, 219, 229, 231–232, 239, 242, 244–246, 249, 253, 266, 270, 282, 299
Ammianus Marcellinus, 189, 191, 197, 285, 287
Anastasius (emperor 491–518), 285–286, 301
Anicetus, bishop of Rome (d. *c.* 166), 176
Antioch
  its importance as a Christian centre, 25, 44, 68, 89, 110, 190–192, 230–231, 274–275, 305
  its exegetical and theological traditions, 114, 251, 273, 301, 303–304
  see also Ammianus Marcellinus, Eustathius, Ignatius, John Chrysostom, Julian, Libanius, Lucian, Nestorius, Paul (of Samosata), Severus, Syria, Theodore, Theophilus (of Antioch)
Antony of Egypt, 190, 197, 256–257, 289
Apocalypse
  see Revelation, Book of
Apocalypse of Peter, 65, 71, 116
apocalyptic literature, 32, 74, 106–107, 118–120, 156, 170
  see also eschatology
Apollinarius, bishop of Laodicea (*c.* 310–390), 273–274
Apollos, possible rival of Paul, 27–28, 43, 64, 68
apologists, 167–172
  see also Aristides, Athenagoras, Justin, Melito, Miltiades, Quadratus, Tatian, Tertullian, Theophilus
apostle, authority and qualifications of, 27–28, 42–45
  see also Acts, Apocryphal
Apostolic Constitutions, 178, 203
Apostolic Fathers
  see Clement (of Rome), Hermas, Ignatius, Papias, Polycarp, *Barnabas* (*Letter of*), *Clement* (*Second Letter of*), *Didachē*, *Diognetus* (*Letter to*)
Apostolic Tradition, 177, 203
Arcadius (emperor 395–408), 241–242, 253, 282, 285, 297
Aristides, apologist, 67, 168
Arius, Arianism, 79, 149, 190–192, 197, 224–231, 242, 245, 247, 272–274
  Arianism of the barbarians, 226, 240, 264, 288, 295–296, 305

· 323 ·

Index

Arnobius (d. *c.* 330), 148, 194
art and architecture, 41, 129, 142, 159, 190, 202–205, 28, 284, 286, 299–300
ascetics, asceticism, 10, 16, 100, 103, 106–108, 110, 118–119, 129, 131, 133, 144, 148–149, 164, 166–167, 173–174, 193, 202, 223, 229, 248, 250, 252, 254–261, 265, 269, 281, 286, 290–292, 296, 298–299, 305, 318
  see also biography, body, miracles, monasticism, virginity
Athanasius, bishop of Alexandria (d. 373), 67, 164, 190, 223–227, 229, 247, 253
Athenagoras, apologist, 67, 168
Augustine, bishop of Hippo (d. 430), 148–149, 190, 192, 199, 201, 222, 231–232, 239, 245–246, 249, 252, 253–255, 265–270, 289, 295, 299, 314
  City of God, 17, 163, 207, 212, 244, 265, 268–270, 291, 308
  Confessions, 198, 247, 267–268, 293–294

baptism, 35–37, 41, 43, 63, 75, 79, 90–92, 98–99, 126, 147, 166, 177–178, 182, 198, 203, 228, 254–255, 260, 266, 281, 317
  see also worship
barbarians, 10, 19, 149, 220–221, 233, 237–238, 240–243, 261–265, 270, 280–283, 286–298
  see also Franks, Huns, Lombards, Ostrogoths, Vandals, Visigoths
Barnabas, Letter of, 87, 91, 95, 99–100, 104, 117
Basil, bishop of Caesarea (d. 379), 227–232, 245–246, 248–249, 256, 289
Basileides (late 1st, early 2nd cent.), 112–113
Bauer, Walter, 11, 88

Benedict of Nursia (*c.* 480–550), 256, 267, 292, 306, 308
biography, Christian, 49–50, 127, 161–162, 248, 256–257, 260, 288–294, 298–299
bishops
  challenges to their authority, 9, 16, 105, 129, 135, 137, 179, 292–295, 318
  see also teachers
  developing office of, 16, 18, 44–45, 88–92, 96, 109–110, 116, 120, 126, 177, 181, 212
  after the accession of Constantine, 188–189, 194, 204–205, 216–217, 240, 245–247, 260–261, 265, 281, 309, 315
body, attitudes to the, 12, 14–15, 102, 106–108, 120, 144, 201–202, 254–255
  see also asceticism, spirit, virginity
Boethius (*c.* 480–*c.* 524), 267, 306

Caesarius, bishop of Arles (*c.* 470–542), 294, 299
Callistus I, bishop of Rome (d. 222), 111, 174, 176–177, 179–180
canon of the New Testament, formation of the, 56–57, 64–70, 85, 106, 127–128
  see also gospels
'Cappadocian Fathers', 148, 244, 249, 254, 267, 299
  see also Basil of Caesarea
Caracalla (emperor 198–217), 183
Carthage, church in
  see Cyprian, Donatists, Perpetua, Tertullian
Cassian, John (*c.* 360–435), 99, 144, 249, 257, 290–291, 306
Cassiodorus, 295, 306
Celestine I, bishop of Rome (d. 432), 274
Celsus (d. late 2nd cent.), 16, 130, 159, 179, 194–195

Index

Chalcedon, council of (451), 222, 267, 272, 275–276, 292
  aftermath of, 300–305
Christology
  see Jesus of Nazareth
Chrysaphius, 259, 271, 275, 282
Chrysostom
  see John Chrysostom
churches (Christian communities), characteristic components of
  see cities, households, paganism (boundaries, common ground, integration), unity, social structure
cities and towns, as characteristic centres of church life, 16, 18, 36–38, 43–44, 61–62, 132–136, 154, 164–167, 171–173, 181, 188–194, 202–205, 207, 217, 230, 240, 243, 256–257, 261, 265, 284–285, 289–290, 296, 298–299
  see also households, rural society
classical culture
  see paganism
Clement, bishop (probably) of Rome, 'apostolic father' (*fl.* 90s), 53, 65–66, 69, 85–90, 93, 99–100, 103–104, 181, 213
Clement of Alexandria (d. *c.* 215), 67–68, 70, 79, 113–116, 125–126, 131, 133, 135–141, 145–148, 171–174, 178, 181–182, 184, 226, 228
Clement, Second Letter of, 66
Clementine literature, 177
collegia, as paradigms of churches, 16, 60, 153
  see also social structure
Colossians, Paul's *Letter to the*, chapter 2 (23–45) *passim*, 107
Constantine I (emperor 306–337), 3, 19, 149, 179, 182–185, 187–188, 194–195, 214–220, 238, 246, 255, 263, 272
  later image of, 189, 281, 283–285, 296, 317–318

Constantinople, 189–190, 217, 221, 230, 238, 252, 257–258, 276, 284
Constantinople, council of (381), 226, 232, 245
Constantinople, council of (553), 303–304
Constantius II (emperor 337–361), 197, 219–221, 226, 229, 238, 242, 246–247, 253, 255, 285
Coptic (Christian Egyptian) culture, 68, 190, 193, 305
  see also Alexandria
Corinthians, Paul's *Letters to the*, chapter 2 (23–45) *passim*, 87, 105, 117, 157
Cornelius, bishop of Rome (d. 253), 175
councils and synods as instruments of church government, development of, 10, 164, 181, 192, 204, 281, 286, 293
Cyprian, bishop of Carthage (d. 258), 86, 130, 148, 161–163, 166, 180, 190, 224
Cyril, bishop of Alexandria (d. 444), 190, 274–275
Cyril of Scythopolis (d. later 6th cent.), 298

Damasus I, bishop of Rome (d. 384), 175, 189, 229, 254
deacons, 44–45, 89, 97
death and the afterlife, Christian attitudes towards, 1–2, 55–56, 155–159
  see also resurrection
Decius (emperor 249–251), 154, 161–162, 166, 175, 180, 184, 196, 224
Diatessaron
  see Tatian
Didachē, 66, 87, 90–92, 96, 99–102, 133, 203
Didascalia apostolorum, 178
Diocletian (emperor 284–305; d. 312), 163–164, 184, 187, 189, 197, 201, 208, 211, 215, 221, 231, 238–239, 248

Index

Diognetus, Letter to, 135, 207
Dionysius, bishop of Alexandria (d. c. 264), 130, 180
Dionysius, bishop of Rome (d. 268), 180
Dioscorus, bishop of Alexandria (d. 454), 275
docetism, 75–77, 106, 117–118, 132, 145, 165
Donatism, 222–223
   see also Augustine
Dorotheus of Gaza (d. later 6th cent.), 298–299
Dura-Europos, Christian church at, 130, 134, 205

east and west, increasing division between, 238–241, 266, 270, 272, 280–281, 284–286, 295–305, 310, 317–318
Easter, controversy over the dating of, 175–177
Edessa, 179, 193, 300–301
   see also Ephraem, Ibas, Jacob, Syria
Enoch, Similitudes of, 74, 94
Ephesians, Paul's *Letter to the*, 17, chapter 2 (23–45) *passim*, 173
Ephesus, council of (431), 243, 259, 272–275, 303
Ephraem, 193, 202, 239, 247–248
Epiphanius, bishop of Salamis (c. 315–403), 250, 252
eschatology, 31–32, 39, 54, 58–59, 93–97, 106–108, 111, 157, 175, 206, 210, 244, 308, 313–314
eucharist, 37, 41–42, 53, 59, 94, 126, 170, 177, 205, 228, 281, 317
   see also worship
Eudocia, wife of Theodosius II, 257–259, 271
Eudoxius, bishop of Antioch and Constantinople (300–370), 231
Eugenius (usurper 392–394), 199, 219–220
Eunapius of Sardis, 196–197, 263
Eunomius, 231

Eusebius, bishop of Caesarea and author of an *Ecclesiastical History* (d. c. 340), 18, 67–68, 110, 135, 148, 161, 163, 168, 175, 179–181, 184, 196, 211–215, 217–218, 242, 247, 263, 287
Eusebius, bishop of Nicomedia (d. c. 342), 224, 226
Eustathius, bishop of Antioch (d. 330), 226, 231
Eutyches, 259, 275, 301–302
Evagrius of Pontus (d. 399), 99, 144, 249, 255
exegesis, exegete, 10, 14, 16, 26, 54, 65, 78, 111–112, 114, 129, 139–140, 142, 144, 145, 149, 153, 156, 168, 170, 192, 194, 206, 211, 228–229, 232, 249–251, 255, 266, 273, 297
   see also Jewish scriptures

Fabian, bishop of Rome (d. 250), 180, 188
faith, 2, 3–5, 11, 33–34, 38, 40–41, 47, 55–57, 59–60, 67, 87, 89, 98–103, 125, 128, 131, 138, 140, 145
Franks, 240, 262, 264, 281, 283, 286–288, 296, 307, 309

Galatians, Paul's *Letter to the*, chapter 2 (23–45) *passim*, 105, 116
Galla Placidia, 240, 262
Gelasius I, bishop of Rome (d. 496), 189, 307
gender, 16, 104, 107
gnostics, 11–15, 30, 78, 103–107, 110, 125–128, 131, 133, 139–140, 147, 165, 169, 171–172, 176, 228
'gnostic' gospels, 68, 70–73, 116–117, 124–125
   see also Thomas, Gospel of
other gnostic texts, 71, 73, 108, 110, 113, 116, 126
   see also Nag Hammadi

Index

gospels, chapter 3 (47–81) *passim*, 156–158
  see also canon of the New Testament, formation of the; John, Luke, Mark, Matthew; gnostics
Gratian (emperor 375–383), 219, 221, 241, 245, 247, 253
Gregory I, bishop of Rome (d. 604), 149, 189, 244, 267, 291–295, 304, 306–310, 313
Gregory, bishop of Tours (*c.* 540–594), 283, 287, 291, 296

hagiography
  see biography
Harnack, Adolph, 11, 17
Hebrews, Letter to the, 53, 74, 87, 94, 156, 158, 168
heresy
  see Arius, monophysite, Pelagius, unity
Hermas, 'apostolic father' (2nd cent.), 65–66, 76–77, 87–88, 90–91, 93, 95–96, 99–103
Hermogenes, 111
Hilary, bishop of Poitiers (d. 367), 148, 227, 229, 246, 249
Hippolytus (d. after 222), 13, 109, 111–112, 117, 125, 136, 142, 172–181, 188, 211, 227
history, a sense of: its central importance in Christian thought, 2, 9, 15, 28–30, 34, 80, 89, 93–97, 103–106, 112, 114–115, 117–118, 128, 137, 149–150, 170, 206–214, 230, 251, 314
  see also Jesus of Nazareth, humanity and historicity of
homily, 10, 134, 149, 194, 204, 232, 260–261, 264–265, 292–295, 299
Honorius (emperor 395–423), 217, 241, 255, 270, 282
households: as settings for Christian commitment and paradigms of churches, 16, 18, 37–38, 43–45, 96–97, 134, 177, 179, 200, 260
  see also cities, social structure
Huns, 238–239, 243, 270–272, 275, 282

Iamblichus, 196–197
Ibas, bishop of Edessa (d. 457), 275, 301, 303
  see also 'Three Chapters'
Ignatius, bishop of Antioch, 'apostolic father' (d. *c.* 107), 66, 77, 85, 87–88, 90–91, 93, 100–101, 106, 119, 127, 144, 158, 161, 165–167, 169, 181, 191
'image and likeness of God' (*homoiōsis*), humans created in the, 29–30, 80–81, 104, 140, 143–144, 182, 254–255, 267, 272, 317
incarnation
  see Jesus of Nazareth, humanity and historicity of
Irenaeus, bishop of Lyon (d. *c.* 200), 12, 63, 67, 78–81, 86, 92, 108–111, 115–116, 118, 125, 129–130, 133, 135–136, 156, 171–172, 175–176
Isidore, bishop of Seville (*c.* 560–636), 287, 294
Islam, 149, 192, 238–239, 305, 310, 313, 318–319

Jacob Baradaeus, bishop (from 542) of Edessa (*c.* 500–578), 301–303
James, brother of Jesus
  see Jerusalem, early Christian community in
Jerome (d. 420), 69, 102, 145, 148, 199, 208, 227, 232, 239, 244, 246, 249–255, 257–258, 266, 289
Jerusalem
  early Christian community in, 7, 25, 64, 177
  after Constantine, 190–191, 252, 274, 284

Index

Jesus of Nazareth
  divinity of, chapter 3 (47–81) *passim*,
    but especially 73–81; 271–276,
    282, 315
  humanity and historicity of, 29–30,
    chapter 3 (47–81) *passim*, 84, 101,
    106, 125, 140, 150, 169, 182,
    226–227, 250, 252, 271–276
  Logos, 78–81, 111–112, 125–126, 136,
    140, 142, 169, 175–176, 182,
    227–228
    see also Trinity
  relation of believer with, 1–2, 8, 29–31,
    34, 37, chapter 3 (47–81) *passim*,
    104–105, 114, 118, 124–126, 140,
    147, 165, 169, 182, 205, 211, 213,
    228, 250, 252, 254, 272, 317
    see also faith
Jewish revolts, 52, 60, 94–95, 154
Jewish scriptures
  Christian rejection of, 65, 137
    see also Marcion
  Christian appropriation of, 69, 127,
    140–142, 167–168, 281, 314
    see also gnostics
  Christian notion of 'fulfilment', 69–70,
    149–150, 168–169, 182, 206,
    213–214
    see also allegory, canon, exegesis,
    Origen, prophecy
Jewish society and tradition, 9, 14, 95,
    104, 154–155, 167–168, 170
  early Christianity as part of, 7–10,
    24–26, 32–35, 40, 69, 106, 130,
    316
  acknowledgement and assertion of
    Christian continuity with, 106,
    109, 120, 127, 138, 170–172
  Christian claims over the history of, 10,
    142, 167–169
    see also Jewish scriptures
Jews, Christian antagonism towards, 10,
    35, 58–64, 69–71, 171, 316
John (gospel writer), 4, chapter 3 (47–81)
    passim, but especially 62–63
  subsequent influence of the
    'Johannine' tradition, 4, 63, 67,
    72–73, 78–79, 102, 107, 110, 119,
    175
John Chrysostom, bishop of
  Constantinople (d. 407), 190–191,
    228–229, 231, 244, 246, 250,
    252–253, 257–258, 299
John Moschus (d. 619), 298
John of Ephesus (d. 586), 298, 302–303
Jovinianus, 254
Judaism
  see Jewish, Jews
Julian the 'Apostate' (emperor 361–363),
    191–192, 197–198, 200, 204, 217,
    219–221, 226, 231–232, 238, 242,
    247, 250–251
Julius Africanus, 172, 174, 179
Julius, bishop of Rome (d. 352), 229
Justin Martyr, apologist (d. *c.* 165), 13, 63,
    66–67, 78–79, 86, 91–92, 109,
    111–112, 125–126, 128, 130–131,
    133–134, 136, 138, 140–141, 144,
    146–147, 156, 160, 165, 167–172,
    175, 181, 195, 207
Justinian I (emperor 527–565), 192, 216,
    238, 241, 264, 271, 281–285, 288,
    295–297, 302–304, 307–308

kingdom
  as a basic Christian concept, 37, 42,
    51–52, 59–60, 72, 95, 157, 160,
    169–170, 217, 234, 264
  as a concept freshly amenable in the
    period of barbarian settlement,
    264, 280, 296–297

Lactantius (*c.* 240–320), 148, 184, 190,
    194, 208–211, 222–223, 287
laity, gathering influence of, 200, 241,
    246, 253, 255, 258, 260, 284, 294,
    298, 305
lapsi, 164, 180, 223–224
law, Christian legislation, 10, 90, 117, 170,
    202, 204, 209, 211, 215–220, 241,

Index

247–248, 265, 268–269, 276, 281, 283–285, 293, 297
  see also councils
leadership within the Christian communities, 15–17, 66–67, 88–92, 107, 128, 179
  see also bishops, presbyters, teachers
Leo I, bishop of Rome (d. 461), 189, 222, 267, 275–276, 301–302, 304
Leontius, bishop of Antioch (344–357), 231
Lérins, 290, 294
Libanius, 191, 197, 231, 252
Liber pontificalis, 180–181
Liberius, bishop of Rome (d. 366), 229
liturgy
  see worship
lives of the saints
  see biography
Logos
  see Jesus of Nazareth
Lombards, 262, 288, 308–309
  see also Gregory I
Lucian of Antioch (d. 312), 224, 227, 231
Luke (gospel writer), chapter 3 (47–81) *passim*, but especially 61–62; 118
  see also Acts of the Apostles

Maccabees, 8, 154, 168
Manichees, Manichaeism, 128, 200–202, 232, 250, 316
Marcellus, bishop of Ancyra (d. *c.* 374), 226–227
Marcian (emperor 450–457), 271, 275, 282
Marcion, 67, 69, 109, 113, 118, 128, 135, 144–145, 147, 165, 169
Marius Victorinus, 196, 198
Mark (gospel writer), chapter 3 (47–81) *passim*, but especially 58–60; 74
marriage, 12, 107, 115, 131–133, 254, 284
  see also asceticism, body, gender, virginity, women
Martin, bishop of Tours (d. 397), 285, 289–290

martyrdom and persecution, 95, 102, 144, 153–174, 179, 181–182, 184, 195, 218, 231–233
  see also Acts of the Martyrs
martyrs, cult of (after Constantine), 203–204, 223, 232–233
Matthew (gospel writer), chapter 3 (47–81) *passim*, but especially 60–61
Maximin Daia (emperor 308–313), 163–164, 218
Melania the Younger, 257–258, 266–267
Melitians, 223–224
Melito, bishop of Sardis, apologist (d. *c.* 190), 169, 207
Methodius of Olympus, bishop (d. *c.* 311), 107, 196
Miltiades, apologist (2nd cent.), 168
Miltiades, bishop of Rome (d. 314), 224
miracles, 44, 52–53, 57, 59, 203, 233, 286, 288, 290–292
mission, 11, 17, 26–28, 58, 93, 128
monasticism (as a specific institution), 164, 256, 276, 306
  see also asceticism
monophysites, 274, 300–305
  see also Jesus of Nazareth, humanity and historicity of
Montanus (late 2nd cent.), Montanism, 66–67, 110, 118–120, 144, 146, 165, 192, 227
Muratorian Fragment, 65, 67

Nag Hammadi, 13–14, 71, 73, 104, 108, 110, 112
Nestorius, bishop of Constantinople (d. *c.* 451), Nestorianism, 191, 227, 259, 274–275, 300–305
Nicaea, council of (325), 225, 230, 247, 272–273
  see also Arius
Novatian, 69, 175, 180, 224

'Old Testament'
  see Jewish scriptures

· 329 ·

Index

Origen (d. *c.* 254), 67, 100, 114, 117, 125–127, 130–131, 133, 135–145, 147–149, 156, 163, 166, 170–172, 178–182, 184, 194–195, 206, 213, 226–227, 232, 267, 299, 303
   'Origenist controversy', 249–254, 257, 272
orthodoxy
   see unity
Ossius, bishop of Cordova (d. 357), 187–188
Ostrogoths, 240, 262, 264, 270, 283, 286, 288, 297, 303–304, 306–307

Pachomius, 256–257
paganism
   inadequacy of the term, 10, 195, 219, 241
   early boundaries between Christians and non-Christians, 40, 111, 131, 172–173
   common ground with, 4, 6–9, 101, 316
   integration of Christians in the wider society, 14, 35, Chapter 6 (153–185) *passim*
   after Constantine, changed relations with, 194–200, 282, 284
   Christian attacks on, 218–220, 241, 257, 289
      see also law
   Christian inheritance of philosophical traditions, 78, 102, 109, 131, 136–138, 154–155, 170–171, 177, 183, 195–196, 200, 306
   Christian misgivings about traditional argument and eloquence, 102–103, 111, 255, 289
   see also apologists, asceticism, cities, Clement, martyrdom, Origen, Plotinus, Porphyry, social structure, teachers, Tertullian
Palladius, bishop of Helenopolis and author of the *Lausiac History* (*c.* 365–425), 258, 267, 298

Pamphilus (d. 309), 161–162
papacy
   see Rome, bishop of
Papias, bishop of Hieropolis, 'apostolic father' (d. *c.* 130), 66, 79
Paul, bishop of Samosata (260–268), 227, 274
Paul of Tarsus, 14, chapter 2 (23–45) *passim*, 73, 75, 84, 93, 102, 105–106, 111, 114–118, 124, 126–128, 133, 136–137, 142, 144, 157–158, 179, 181, 183, 200, 217, 316
   Letters of, or attributed to: *see Colossians, Corinthians, Ephesians, Galatians, Philippians, Romans, Thessalonians, Timothy, Titus*
Paulinus, bishop of Nola (353–431), 246, 285
Pelagius (late 4th, early 5th cent.), Pelagianism, 246, 253–255, 258, 266, 272, 274, 295
Perpetua, 119, 147, 161–162, 165–167
persecution
   of Christians by non-Christians
      see martyrdom
   of Christians by Christians, 241, 248–249, 255, 316
Persia, 5, 183–184, 191, 201–202, 214, 222, 231, 238–239, 263, 280, 297, 301, 305, 313
Peter, disciple of Jesus, 7, 58, 64, 72–73, 105, 109, 177
Peter, Letters of, 65, 87, 90, 93, 100, 106, 169, 206–207
   see also Apocalypse of Peter
Pharisees, 9, 41, 49, 60
Philippians, Paul's *Letter to the*, chapter 2 (23–45) *passim*, 73, 157
Philo, 138–139, 170–171
Philostratus, 183, 211
Philoxenus, bishop of Mabbug (d. 523), 68, 302–303
pilgrimage, 190–191, 202, 252, 257, 260, 266, 274–275, 286

Index

Plotinus, neoplatonist philosopher (d. 270), 120, 183, 195–196, 225
Polycarp, bishop of Smyrna, 'apostolic father' (d. c. 155), 66, 77, 79, 81, 87–88, 90, 96, 101, 110, 135, 160, 162, 165, 176, 181
Pontian, bishop of Rome (d. 235), 174
poor, the: an important constituency for bishops, 194, 202, 230, 260–261, 272, 293
Porphyry, neoplatonist philosopher, 102, 183, 195–196
Praxeas, 176, 179, 227
prayer
see worship
presbyters, 89–91, 96–97
Procopius, historian, 282–283
prophecy, as both an enduring and a contested gift, 9–10, 40, 42, 44, 51–53, 59, 63, 77, 89, 90, 92, 96, 100–101, 103, 105–106, 108, 116, 129, 158, 202, 211, 296, 318
see also Jewish scriptures, Montanus
Prudentius, 175
Ptolemy, gnostic and writer of *Letter to Flora*, 131
Pulcheria, sister of Theodosius II, 258–259, 271, 274–275, 282

Quadratus, apologist (2nd cent.), 168
Quartodecimans
see Easter
Qumran, 13, 53, 93–94

redemption
see Jesus of Nazareth, relation of believer with
relics, 204, 233, 286
see also martyrs, cult of
repentance, 59, 96, 98–101, 103, 136, 164, 203, 223–224, 248
resurrection, 1–2, 31–33, 43, 50, 53, 55, 71–72, 77, 89, 93, 98, 106, 119, 132, 144, 155–157, 159, 250
see also body

Revelation, Book of, 4, 74, 87, 94–96, 107–108, 118–119, 127, 155–156, 158, 206
Romans, Paul's *Letter to*, chapter 2 (23–45) *passim*, 95, 105, 117, 181, 255
Rome, bishop of, 92, 110, 176, 179–181, 189, 255, 276, 285, 301, 304, 307
see also Anicetus, Celestine I, Clement (I, of Rome), Cornelius, Damasus I, Dionysius, Fabian, Gregory I, Leo I, Miltiades, Pontian, Sixtus II, Stephen I, Victor I, Vigilius,
Rome, church in, 86–87, 131, 160, 174, 176, 180–181, 188–190
Rome, sack of (410), 219, 239, 242, 244, 265, 270
Rufinus of Aquileia (c. 345–410), 100, 212, 249, 251–252, 254, 257
rural society, Christianity's gradual impact upon, 192–194, 205, 289–290, 292–294, 296, 298–299

Sabas, 257
Sabellius, Sabellianism, 176, 179–180, 226–227, 273
sacrament
see worship
salvation
see Jesus of Nazareth, relation of believer with
Salvian of Marseille, 243, 263, 287
school, as paradigm of church
see teachers
scripture
see allegory, canon, exegesis, gospels, Jewish scriptures
sermon
see homily
Severus, bishop of Antioch (c. 465–538), 257, 301–303
Sextus, Sentences of, 100–104
Shenoute of Atripe (d. c. 450), 193
Shepherd
see Hermas.

· 331 ·

Index

Sidonius Apollinaris, bishop of Clermont (*c.* 423–480), 263, 288
Silvanus, Teachings of, 104–105, 126
Simon Magus, 105, 109–110, 117
Sixtus II, bishop of Rome (late 260s), 101
slavery, 36–39, 216, 284
social structure of early Christianity, 6–7, 15–17, 35–40, 93–94, 97–103, 115, 124–136, 181–182, 206–208
Socrates of Constantinople, historian, 212, 220, 242–244, 259
Sozomen, historian, 243, 259
spirit, emphasis on, 30–31, 113, 116, 119, 125, 127, 137, 140, 142–143, 146, 149, 166, 179, 182, 226, 250–251, 254–255, 267
  see also body
Stephen, the 'first martyr', 158
Stephen I, bishop of Rome (d. 257), 180
Sulpicius Severus, 285
synods
  see councils
Syria, church in, 66, 68, 87, 112, 118, 132, 191–193, 202, 239, 298–301, 305
  see also Antioch, Edessa, Ephraem, Theodoret

Tatian, apologist (later 2nd cent.), 68, 131, 135, 168, 192
teachers, their authority within the churches, 9–10, 17, 54, 104–105, 115, 124–136, 154, 160, 164–169, 174, 176–177, 179, 181, 188, 260–261
Tertullian, apologist (d. *c.* 225), 13, 67, 69, 86, 108, 110–111, 114–115, 118–120, 130, 134, 136, 145–149, 156, 161, 165–166, 168, 170–171, 173, 177–180, 182–184, 192, 206–207, 223, 227
Thecla, 133–134
Theodora, wife of Justinian I, 282–283, 302, 304

Theodore, bishop of Mopsuestia (*c.* 350–428), 273–275, 301, 303
Theodoret, bishop of Cyrrhus (*c.* 393–466), 257, 275, 298, 301, 303
  see also 'Three Chapters'
Theodosius I (emperor 379–395), 199, 202, 219–222, 226, 232, 239–245, 252, 255, 262, 282
Theodosius II (emperor 408–450), 212, 220, 242, 258–259, 270, 274, 282, 285
Theodotus (2nd cent.), 70, 113
Theophilus, bishop of Alexandria (d. 412), 190, 250–252, 257
Theophilus, bishop of Antioch, apologist (late 2nd cent.), 168–169, 191
Thessalonians, Paul's *Letters to the*, chapter 2 (23–45) *passim*, 74, 88
Thomas, bishop of Heraclea (late 5th, early 6th cent.), 68
Thomas, Gospel of, 58, 68, 72, 108, 131
'Three Chapters' controversy, 222, 303–304, 306–307
Timothy, Letters to, 89, 92, 96–97, 106–107, 128–129, 136
Titus, Letter to, 96
Trinity, theology of the, 79, 169, 176, 180–182, 267, 273, 295
  see also Arius, Jesus of Nazareth

unity of belief and practice
  gradual achievement of, 2, 11–15, 23, 37, 50, 56, 64–67, 75, 85–88, 99, 120, 127, 128, 178–184, 189, 192, 205, 243, 316
  as an instrument of Christian imperial government, 182–183, 188, 197, 215, 217–218, 228

Valens (emperor 364–378), 219, 221–222, 226, 238, 241–242, 245, 264, 288
Valentinian I (emperor 364–375), 217, 219, 221, 226, 239–241

Index

Valentinian II (emperor 375–392), 199, 221, 241, 245
Valentinian III (emperor 423–455), 240, 242–243, 271
Valentinus (2nd cent.), 71–2, 109, 111, 113–117, 131, 135, 181
Vandals, 192, 222, 239, 243, 262, 265, 271, 287–288, 296–297, 305
Victor I, bishop of Rome (d. 198), 176–177, 180
Victricius, bishop of Rouen (*c*. 330–407), 285
Vigilius, bishop of Rome (d. 555), 303–304, 306–307
virginity, 1, 102, 107, 115, 144, 173, 178, 216, 254, 281–282
see also asceticism, body, gender, marriage, women
Visigoths, 219, 222, 226, 232, 241–242, 261–262, 264–265, 270, 283, 286–288, 296–297

widows, 39, 96–97, 103, 107, 133–134, 200, 281
women, 38–40, 73, 96–97, 106–108, 119, 132–135, 173, 178, 199–200, 253, 263, 284
see also gender, marriage, virginity, widows
Word, Jesus as the
see Jesus of Nazareth (*Logos*)
worship, 15, 40–42, 89–92, 104, 113, 115, 120, 128, 134, 143, 177–179, 182, 198, 202–205, 218, 260–261, 281, 284–285, 293–294, 299, 315, 317
see also baptism, eucharist

Zeno (emperor 474–491), 270, 297, 301